HVAC/R Termi~~nology~~
A Quick Refere~~nce~~

HVAC/R Terminology: A Quick Reference Guide

Richard Wirtz
Columbus State Community College

Prentice Hall
Upper Saddle River, New Jersey   Columbus, Ohio

Library of Congress Cataloging-in-Publication Data
Wirtz, Richard.
    HVAC/R terminology: a quick reference guide / by Richard Wirtz.
      p. cm.
    ISBN 0-13-592973-3
    1. Heating—Dictionaries. 2. Ventilation—Dictionaries. 3. Air conditioning—Dictionaries. 4. Refrigeration and refrigerating machinery—Dictionaries.   I. Title.
TH7007.W57   1998
697—dc21

97-7726
CIP

Cover photo: © Photodisc
Editor: Ed Francis
Production Editor: Linda Hillis Bayma
Design Coordinator: Julia Zonneveld Van Hook
Text Designer: Pagination
Cover Designer: Rod Harris
Production Manager: Pamela D. Bennett
Electronic Text Management: Marilyn Wilson Phelps, Matthew Williams, Karen L. Bretz, Tracey B. Ward
Marketing Manager: Danny Hoyt

This book was set in Century Schoolbook by Prentice Hall and was printed and bound by R.R. Donnelley & Sons Company. The cover was printed by Phoenix Color Corp.

© 1998 by Prentice-Hall, Inc.
Simon & Schuster/A Viacom Company
Upper Saddle River, New Jersey 07458

Printed in the United States of America

10 9 8 7 6 5 4 3 2 1

ISBN: 0-13-592973-3

Prentice-Hall International (UK) Limited, *London*
Prentice-Hall of Australia Pty. Limited, *Sydney*
Prentice-Hall of Canada, Inc., *Toronto*
Prentice-Hall Hispanoamericana, S. A., *Mexico*
Prentice-Hall of India Private Limited, *New Delhi*
Prentice-Hall of Japan, Inc., *Tokyo*
Simon & Schuster Asia Pte. Ltd., *Singapore*
Editora Prentice-Hall do Brasil, Ltda., *Rio de Janeiro*

This book is dedicated to my
wife Margaret. She is someone
special who puts up with all of
my difficult ways. Thanks for
being there.

Contents

Preface

I started writing this book out of a need for a comprehensive technical reference for first-year students starting in the Heating and Air Conditioning Technology program at Columbus State Community College. While teaching classes such as Principles of Refrigeration or Air Conditioning Systems, I realized that these students are continually exposed to new words and phrases that cross over into other disciplines such as electricity, piping, airflow, and psychrometrics. The glossaries in these individual books are very limited (or missing altogether) and often do not include words and terms that are found inside the text. I am sure that many other teaching institutes have found themselves in the same situation.

Since I have not found (or there is none) technical reference manual or book in the marketplace that incorporates all of these technical terms in one place, I have tried to offer a solution for this problem. I believe this technical reference guide will be an excellent resource or reference for your students or educational institute. I hope it will be a great asset to those people who are either going into or are already in this great industry we know as HVAC/R. It is my way of giving something back to the industry.

This book will never be completely done. It will always be in a state of flux. New words, terms, and phrases are always coming out. As the industry evolves, so will this book. I believe this is a great start.

ACKNOWLEDGMENTS

It is not possible to write a document of this size and magnitude without the helpful assistance of other people and organizations. As with any book of this type, it is a team effort. They have helped me gather vital information that was critical to the successful completion of this book:

Honeywell Inc.
Honeywell Plaza
Minneapolis, MN 55408

Bud Healy
NHRAW
1389 Dublin Rd.
Columbus, OH 43216

Reznor Division
FL Industries
McKinley Ave.
Mercer, PA 16137

Royal Electric
95 Grand Ave.
Pawtucket, RI 02862

I would also like to thank those who have reviewed the manuscript: Bennie Barnes, Live Oaks; Alan B. Clay, Vatterott College; John Griffith, TSTC; Ray Havrella, Long Beach City College; Richard Jazwin, Universal Technical Institute; Marvin Maziarz, Niagara County Community College; William E. Whitman, Triton College; and Joseph Zagrobski, Massasoit Community College.

The Dictionary

A

A symbol used for the measurement of current flow.

AABC Associated Air Balance Council.

ABC Associated Builders and Contractors.

ABMA American Boiler Manufacturers Association.

ABS Acrylonitrile-Butadiene-Styrene.

AC alternating current.

acb air circuit breaker.

ACCA Air Conditioning Contractors of America.

ACEC American Consulting Engineers Council.

ACEEE American Council for an Energy Efficient Economy.

ACGIH American Conference of Governmental Industrial Hygienists.

ACH air changes per hour.

acr air-conditioning and refrigeration.

ADC Air Diffusion Council.

ADDA American Design Drafting Association.

ADI Air Distribution Institute.

aec annual energy cost.

AEE Association of Energy Engineers.

AEV automatic expansion valve.

AFFI American Frozen Food Institute.

AFUE annual fuel utilization efficiency.

AGA American Gas Association.

AGAL American Gas Association Lab.

AGC Associated General Contractors of America.

AGMA American Gear Manufacturers Association.

AHAM Association of Home Appliance Manufacturers.

AIA American Institute of Architects.

AIEE American Institute of Electrical Engineers.

AIHA American Industrial Hygienists Association.

ail amber indicator light.

AIPE American Institute of Plant Engineers.

am ammeter.

amb ambient.

AMCA Air Movement and Control Association.

amp ampere.

ann annunciator.

ANSI American National Standards Institute.

API American Petroleum Institute.

ARI Air Conditioning and Refrigeration Institute.

ARL Applied Research Laboratories.

arm armature.

ARW Air Conditioning and Refrigeration Wholesalers.

as ammeter switch.

ASA Acoustical Society of America, American Standards Association, American Subcontractors Association, or American Supply Association.

ASCII   American Standard Code for Information Interchange.

ASES   American Solar Energy Society.

ASHRAE   American Society of Heating, Refrigerating, and Air Conditioning Engineers.

ASI   American Standards Institute.

ASME   American Society of Mechanical Engineers.

ASPE   American Society of Plumbing Engineers or American Society of Professional Estimators.

ASSE   American Society of Sanitary Engineers or American Society of Safety Engineers.

ASTM   American Society for Testing and Materials.

atm   atmosphere.

auto   automatic.

aux   auxiliary.

AWG   American wire gauge.

AWS   American Welding Society.

AXV   automatic expansion valve.

abort   premature termination of a program during execution.

abrasion   a scrape or other damage on an object's surface.

abrasion resistance   the ability of a material or cable to resist surface wear.

ABS pipe   Acrylonitrile-Butadiene-Styrene plastic pipe that is used for water, drains, waste, and venting.

absolute humidity   the total amount of moisture that is present in one cubic foot of air, as indicated by grains per cubic foot.

absolute pressure   the common gauge expresses a pressure in pounds per square inch called gauge pressure. When the gauge is open to the atmosphere, it reads zero. Absolute pressure is defined as the sum of gauge pressure (psig) plus atmospheric pressure (14.696 lb per square inch). Atmospheric pressure is 14.7 psi at sea level. It varies with location and atmospheric conditions. It is accurately indicated by a barometer. Absolute pressure can be zero only in a perfect vacuum.

absolute temperature   the measurement of temperature from absolute zero (–459.7°F). The temperature as read on the Fahrenheit scale plus 460 degrees.

absolute zero temperature   the temperature at which molecular motion theoretically stops. This temperature is considered to be –459.7°F and –273°C. At absolute zero there is theoretically a complete absence of heat.

absorb   to soak up.

absorbent   substance that has the ability to pick up, take up, or hold some other substance.

absorber   the component, in an absorption cycle, where the heated refrigerant vapor is re-absorbed into the solution.

absorber plate   the section of the solar collector responsible for gathering the solar radiation from the sun.

absorption   a process whereby a material extracts one or more substances present in an atmosphere or mixtures of gases or liquids. It is accompanied by physical change, chemical change, or both, of the material.

absorption refrigerator   a system in which the refrigerant, as it is absorbed in another liquid, maintains the pressure difference needed for successful operation of the system.

absorption system   one of the most common types of cooling systems associated with solar radiation.

absorptivity   the ratio of radiant energy from an actual surface at a given temperature to the energy absorbed by a black body at the same temperature.

accelerate   (1) to add to the speed or velocity of a moving object; (2) to hasten the progress of development.

accelerated aging   a test performed on materials that simulates or duplicates long time environmental conditions in a relatively short period of time.

acceleration time   when a motor is used to accelerate a rotating load, acceleration time is the response time of the motor to bring the load from zero to normal running speed.

accelerator   a chemical additive which hastens a chemical reaction under specific conditions.

acceptable air quality   air in which there are no known contaminants at harmful concentrations and with which a substantial majority (usually 80%) of the people exposed do not express dissatisfaction.

access door   a door, cover, or lid that can be moved or opened for inspection or servicing of internal components.

access fitting   a valve or fitting that provides or creates an opening into a closed system.

access time   the time it takes a computer to produce a bit of information from its memory section (read time) or the time it takes a computer to store information in its memory section (write time).

accessible   easily approached, removed, or exposed. Not permanently concealed.

accessible hermetic   the assembly of the motor and compressor inside a single bolted housing. Also referred to as a semihermetic compressor.

accessible, readily   having direct access without the need of removing any panel, door, or similar covering of the item described.

accessories   those items that add to the effectiveness or convenience of a system, but are not essential to its operation.

accrual accounting   this is the form of accounting legally required of most small businesses. In this form of accounting, both cash and credit transactions are recorded as they occur.

accumulator (electronics)   the register within a computer where the results of all arithmetic and logical operations are placed.

accumulator (refrigeration)   a storage tank which receives liquid refrigerant from the evaporator and prevents it from flowing into the suction line. It allows small amounts of liquid refrigerant to boil away before entering the compressor. It is sometimes used to store excess refrigerant in heat pump systems during the heating cycle.

accuracy   the precision of a reading in relation to the actual measurement.

acetone   a liquid solvent used in acetylene storage tanks.

acetylene   a fuel gas used for soldering, brazing, or cutting.

acid   either an inorganic or organic compound that (1) reacts with metals to yield hydrogen; (2) reacts with a base to form a salt; (3) dissociates in water to yield hydrogen or hydronium ions; (4) has a pH of less than 7.0; (5) neutralizes bases or alkaline media. All acids contain hydrogen and turn litmus paper red. They are corrosive to human tissue and are to be handled with care.

acid condition   condition in which refrigerant or oil in a refrigeration system is mixed with acidic fluids.

acid test   a test that provides a positive indication of whether the concentration of acid level in the oil being tested is safe or unsafe.

acidity   acidity (or alkalinity) of a substance is known as the hydrogen-ion concentration and is called the pH value. A pH value of 7.0 indicates neutral; a value less than 7.0, acidity; and a value greater than 7.0, alkalinity.

Water, for example, is a chemical combination of hydrogen (H) and oxygen (O) that is represented by the formula H_2O. It may also be treated as a chemical combination of hydrogen ions (H^+) and hydroxyl ions (OH^-). If there is a greater number of hydrogen ions than hydroxyl ions as a result of the chemical action of impurities or solutes, the solution is acid. A greater number of hydroxyl ions results in an alkaline solution.

A-coil   component on the low-pressure side of the refrigeration system where liquid evaporates and absorbs heat into the evaporator. Its physical shape resembles an "A."

acoustical   pertaining to sound.

acoustical duct lining   a duct lining designed to control or absorb sound and to prevent transmission of sound from one room to another.

ACR tubing   air-conditioning/refrigeration grade tubing. This tubing is a type "L" copper that is very clean and dry with both ends sealed to prevent contaminants from entering.

across the line   a method of motor starting that connects the motor directly to the supply line on starting or running. It is also known as full voltage starting.

activated alumina   a chemical (aluminum oxide) that is found as a desiccant in filter driers. Operates by adsorption of water molecules.

activated carbon   a specially processed carbon that is used in filter driers or used to filter and/or clean air.

activator   a chemical additive used to initiate a chemical reaction in a specific chemical mixture.

active region   an area of transistor operation between cut-off and saturation.

active solar system   solar system that uses the forced movement of a fluid to transfer heat from the collector to the heated space.

System that uses electrical and/or mechanical devices to help collect, store, and distribute the sun's energy.

actual air delivery in scfm   The standard cubic feet per minute of compressed air actually delivered at the air compressor's discharge port.

actual body rating   see *valve body rating*.

actual torque   the torque required to drive a machine. It is the torque measured at the input shaft of a machine being driven.

actuator   a controlled motor, relay, or solenoid in which the electrical energy is converted into a rotary, linear, or switching action. An actuator can effect a change in the controlled variable by operating the final control elements a number of times. Valves and dampers are examples of mechanisms which can be controlled by actuators. Also see *proportional, spring return,* and *two-position actuators*.

acute angle   an angle less than 90 degrees.

adapter   a special fitting used to quickly and easily connect different parts for different applications.

address   a numeric code which precedes a controller's command to the controlled device. The controlled device will respond only to commands preceded by its assigned address code number.

address bus   a unidirectional bus over which digital information appears to identify either a particular memory location or a particular I/O device.

address selector   switches on a controlled device which are used to assign it to an address code number.

adhesion filter   this type of filter is used by most window air conditioners. It removes up to 90% of the dirt until it gets full. Adhesion filters can be of the permanent or throwaway type.

adiabatic   describes a system or process in which virtually no gain or loss of heat is allowed to occur with (to or from) the surroundings.

adiabatic compression   the ability to compress a gas without removing or adding heat.

adiabatic expansion   when gas is expanded in such a manner that there is no heat flow into or away from the gas and all the heat energy lost by the gas is converted into work, the process is called "adiabatic expansion." For example, steam expanding behind the piston of a steam engine after the point of cut-off approaches adiabatic expansion.

adiabatic process   a process in which there is neither a loss nor a gain in the total heat content.

adjacent conductor   any conductor next to another conductor either in the same multiconductor cable layer or in adjacent layers.

adjustable   capable of being brought to a more satisfactory state or of being regulated.

adjustable autotransformer   a transformer in which parts of one winding are common to both the primary and the secondary circuits. The output voltage is adjustable from zero to line voltage.

adjustable differential   a means of changing the difference between the control cut-in and cut-out points.

adjustable wrench   an adjustable wrench has a sliding jaw that moves by an adjusting screw. This wrench should not be used in place of an open end wrench. It is used when an odd size nut or bolt needs to be worked on.

adjustment   the procedure required to produce the exact setting, response, or effect desired.

adsorb   to collect substances on a surface in a condensed layer.

adsorbent   a substance which has the property to hold in suspension molecules of fluids without causing a chemical or physical change. Certain solid materials such as silica gel, activated carbon, and activated alumina have this property.

adsorption   the action, associated with surface adherence, of a material in extracting one or more substances present in an atmosphere or mixture of gases and liquids, unaccompanied by physical or chemical change.

advertising   is the act of attracting public attention to a product or business. Advertising is usually understood to mean public attention you have paid to attract.

aeration   the exposure of a substance to air circulation.

aerosol   an assemblage of small particles, solid or liquid, suspended in air. The diameters of the particles may vary from 100 microns down to 0.01 micron or less. Examples would be dust, fog, and smoke.

affinity   an attractive force between two substances or particles that causes them to enter into and remain in chemical combination. Refrigeration oil has an affinity for moisture.

agitator   a device that is used to cause motion in a confined fluid.

air   the elastic, invisible mixture of gases that surrounds the earth. It is composed of 78% nitrogen, 21% oxygen, and 1% rare gases including carbon dioxide, krypton, neon, argon, ozone, helium, and ammonia. Also called atmosphere. One Btu will raise the temperature of 55 cubic feet of air 1°F. Also see *ambient, atomizing, combustion, compressed, excess, induced, preheated, primary, seal, secondary,* and *ventilation air.*

air acetylene   a mixture of air and acetylene gas that is used for soldering, brazing, and other applications.

air, ambient   the surrounding air.

air-atomizing oil burner   see *atomizing oil burner.*

air balancing meter an instrument that reads directly from exhaust or supply grilles in ceilings, floors, or walls. It reads out in cubic feet per minute.

air blast forced air circulation.

air bound a condition in which a bubble or other pocket of air is present in a pipeline or item of equipment and, by its presence, prevents or reduces the desired flow or movement of the liquid or gas in the pipeline or equipment.

air break an inverted opening placed in the chimney of a gas furnace to prevent back pressure from outside wind from reaching the furnace flame or pilot.

air change(s) the number of times in an hour the air in a room is changed either by mechanical means or by the infiltration of outside air into the room through cracks around the windows or doors.

air, circulating air for cooling, heating, or ventilation distributed to habitable spaces.

air circulation natural or imparted circulation of air.

air cleaner a device designed for the purpose of removing airborne impurities, such as dust, gas, vapor, fumes, and smoke. Air cleaners include air washers, air filters, electrostatic precipitators, and charcoal filters.

air coil a coil used with some types of heat pumps which may be used as either an evaporator or a condenser.

air compressor a device used to compress air. Also used to activate pneumatic controls.

air conditioner any device or equipment that is used to control the temperature, humidity, cleanliness, and the movement of air in a conditioned space.

air conditioner (room) encased assembly designed as a unit for mounting in a window, through a wall, or as a console. It is designed for free delivery of conditioned air to an enclosed space without ducts.

air conditioner (unitary) an evaporator, compressor, and condenser combination where one or more assemblies are designed to be assembled together to form one system.

air conditioner (window) self-contained room conditioner arranged to be supported in, or connected with, a window opening, circulating outside air over the high-side coil (condenser) and room air over the low-side coil (evaporator).

air-conditioning the simultaneous control of all, or at least the first three of the following factors affecting the physical and chemical conditions of the atmosphere within a structure: temperature, humidity, motion, distribution, dust, bacteria, odors, toxic gases, and ionization—most of which affect human health or comfort.

air-conditioning, comfort the process of treating air so as to control simultaneously its temperature, humidity, cleanliness, and distribution to meet the comfort requirements of the occupants of the conditioned space.

air-conditioning, industrial air-conditioning for uses other than comfort.

air-conditioning, summer comfort air-conditioning carried out primarily when outside temperature and humidity are above those to be maintained in the conditioned space.

air-conditioning unit a device designed for the treatment of air. It consists of a means for ventilation, air circulation, air cleaning, and heat transfer with a control to maintain the temperature within the prescribed limits.

air-conditioning, winter heating, humidification, air distribution, and air cleaning, where outside temperatures are below the inside or room temperature.

air-cooled condenser a piece of equipment by which the heat of compression is transferred from condensing coils to the surrounding air. This transferring process may be either by natural convection currents or by a fan or blower.

air cooler   a device or mechanism designed to lower the temperature of the air passing through it. It may or may not remove latent heat.

air cooler, dry   removes sensible heat from dehydrated air whenever it leaves the dehydrator at an elevated temperature.

air core inductor   a coil wound on a hollow insulated core which does not have a metal center.

air core solenoid   solenoid which has a hollow core instead of a solid core.

air cushion tank   a closed tank, generally located above a boiler and connected to a hydronic system in such a manner that when the system is initially filled with water, air is trapped within the tank. When the water in the system is heated it expands and compresses the air trapped within the air cushion tank, thus providing space for the extra volume of water without creating excessive pressure. Also called an expansion tank.

air cycle air conditioner   any system that removes heat from the air and transfers this heat to the air.

air diffuser   a circular, square, or rectangular air distribution outlet, generally located in the ceiling and composed of deflecting members discharging supply air in various directions and planes. It is arranged to promote mixing of primary air with secondary air.

air, dry   air without water vapor.

air duct   the network of pipes and fittings that are used to control airflow to and from the conditioned space.

air exchange rate   the number of times the volume of air in a space is exchanged with outdoor air in a given period of time (usually expressed as air changes per hour or ACH).

air film   interior and exterior air surface film coefficients for winter design conditions.

air/fuel ratio   the ratio of air supply flow rate to the fuel supply flow rate, measured in the same units under the same conditions. The optimum air/fuel ratio is the minimum ratio that will provide complete combustion of the fuel with enough excess air to maintain a stable flame. Also see *stoichiometric air/fuel ratio*.

air gap   the space between the magnetic poles or between rotating and stationary assemblies in a motor or generator.

air/gas ratio   the ratio of combustion air supply flow rate to the fuel gas supply flow rate.

air handler   the fan blower, heat transfer coil, filter, and housing parts of the system. Does not have provisions for heating or combustion.

air heat exchanger   a device used to exchange heat between air and another medium at different temperature levels, such as air-to-air, air-to-water, or air-to-refrigerant.

air heater   an indirect-fired appliance intended to supply heated air for space heating and other purposes, but not intended for permanent installations.

air infiltration   the leakage of air into structures through cracks, crevices, windows, doors, and other openings. It is caused by wind pressure and/or temperature difference.

air infiltration retarder   fabric or film material or system designed and installed primarily to reduce the movement of air through a wall or into the thermal insulation.

air inlet valve   a door or opening that lets either outside or inside air enter the plenum assembly.

air lateral   pipe which supplies the air to the ice cans contained in a freezing tank.

air main   pipe which carries air to the air laterals supplying ice cans contained in freezing tanks.

air mixing valve   A valve that opens ducts to blend hot and cold air to get desired output temperature. It is sometimes called the blend door.

air movement, active   the movement of air by means of a mechanical device such as a fan or blower.

Air Movement and Control Association (AMCA)   a nationally recognized association which establishes standards, and tests and certifies the performance of air-moving devices.

air movement, passive   the movement of air by the difference in the weight of the air due to the temperature difference of the air.

air, outdoor   air taken from outdoors and not previously circulated through the system.

air outlet valve   a door that directs either through the heater core or through the evaporator.

air, outside   external air. Atmosphere exterior to the refrigerated or heated space. Ambient air.

air-over   describes motors that are intended for fans or blower service. These motors must be located in the airstream to provide motor cooling.

air pressure control   a switch used to detect air pressure drop across the coil in an outdoor heat pump unit due to ice buildup.

air, primary   the air necessary for combustion that is mixed with the gas in a burner before ignition takes place.

air, recirculated   return air passed through the conditioning unit before being supplied again to the conditioned space.

air register   a burner mounting which may admit secondary air to the combustion chamber.

air, reheated   the final step in treatment in an air-conditioning system, in the event the air's temperature is too low.

air, return   the air that is returned from the conditioned or refrigerated space.

air-rich   describes an air/fuel ratio supplied to a furnace that provides more air than the optimum ratio.

air, saturated   the mixture of dry air and saturated water vapor all at the same dry bulb temperature.

air, secondary   the air surrounding a flame that is necessary to complete combustion.

air sensing thermostat   a thermostat in which the sensing element is located in a conditioned space or outside ambient air.

air sensor   a device that registers changes in air conditions such as pressure, velocity, temperature, or moisture content.

air shutter   an adjustable device for varying the size of the inlet or inlets regulating primary and/or secondary air. An air shutter may be automatically or manually operated.

air, specific heat   the quantity of heat absorbed by a unit weight of air per unit temperature rise. The specific heat of air is .24.

air spillover   the refrigerating effect produced by the cold air from the freezing compartment in the refrigerator spilling over, or flowing, into the normal storage area of the refrigerator.

air, standard   air having a temperature of 70°F, a relative humidity of 36%, an atmospheric pressure of 14.696 psi, a specific volume of 13.33 ft^3, and a specific density of 0.075 lb/ft^3.

air standard conditions   conditions at which Btu/h ratings for summer air conditioning equipment are rated. These are defined as 95°F dry bulb and 75°F wet bulb at the condenser inlet, and 80°F dry bulb and 67°F wet bulb at the evaporator inlet.

air tunnel a refrigerated tunnel with rapid air circulation through which the product is to be frozen or passed.

air-type collector a solar collector that uses the air as a transfer fluid.

air vent a valve, either manual or automatic, used to remove air from the highest point of a coil or piping assembly.

air vent riser a vertical length of pipe at the highest point in the system used to gather and retain air in the system as the liquid flows past the riser. The air vent is located at the top of the riser.

air, ventilation the quantity of supply air drawn from outdoors needed to maintain the desired amount of oxygen and the quality of air within a designated space.

air washer a device used to clean air, which may increase or decrease the relative humidity.

airflow switch any controller that is used to prove proper air movement by measuring pressure or air velocity. Also known as a sail switch. Also see *lockout* and *running interlocks*.

alarm an audible or visible signal indicating a nonstandard or abnormal condition.

alarm circuit an electrical circuit that includes a bell, horn, or similar device to signal desired conditions.

alcohol brine a solution of water and alcohol which remains a liquid at or below 32°F.

aldehyde a class of highly reactive organic compounds, which can be produced during incomplete combustion of a fuel gas. They have a pungent distinct odor.

algae a low form of plant life, found floating free in water.

alignment the process of being brought into a straight line.

alkali broadly, any compound having highly basic properties, i.e., one that readily ionizes in aqueous solution to yield OH^- ions, has a pH above 7, and turns litmus paper blue. Alkalies are hydroxides of an alkali metal and belong to group Ia of the periodic table (Li, Na, K, Rb, Cs, Fr). Ammonium salts may also be alkalies. Alkalies are caustic. Their high concentrations of OH^- ions in solution destroy tissue by abstracting fluids or by corrosive deoxidation. Alkali burns are to be treated by quickly washing the afflicted area with copious amounts of water. Common commercial alkalies are sodium carbonate (soda ash), lye, potash, caustic soda, water glass, and bicarbonate of soda.

alkylbenzene an organic lubricant that is made from the raw chemicals propylene, a colorless hydrocarbon gas, and benzene, a colorless liquid hydrocarbon. Used often when incorporating HCFC-based refrigerant blends. Some HCFC-based blends are soluble in a mixture of mineral oil and alkylbenzene up to 20% concentration of mineral oil.

Allen head screw a screw which has a recessed head designed to be turned with a hexagon-shaped wrench.

Allen wrench a hexagonal (6-sided) tip tool used to fit socket headed screws or set screws. Can be straight, 90°, T-handled, folding, or socket.

allergen any substance or vapor which causes a person to react with skin eruptions or eye and nose irritations.

allergic rhinitis inflammation of the mucous membranes in the nose.

allowance minimum clearance between mating parts.

alloy a combination of two or more metals forming a new or different metal.

alnico an alloy of aluminum, nickel, iron, and cobalt used to make permanent magnets.

alpha particle a positively charged atomic particle that is ejected in certain radioactive transformations.

alphanumeric a numbering system containing numbers and letters.

alternating current (AC) a flow of electricity which reaches maximum in one direction, decreases to zero, then reverses itself and reaches maximum in the opposite direction. This cycle is repeated continuously and can be single-phase, two-phase, three-phase, or polyphase. The number of such cycles per second is the frequency in hertz (Hz). The average value of voltage during any cycle is zero. In a 60-cycle current, the direction of flow reverses every 120th of a second. Its advantage over direct or unidirectional current is that its voltage can be stepped up by transformers to the high values which reduce transmission costs.

alternating current resistance the resistance offered by any circuit to the flow of alternating current.

alternation one half of a sine wave. There is a positive and a negative alternation for each alternating current sine wave.

alternator an alternating current generator which changes mechanical energy into electrical energy.

altitude correction the change in atmospheric pressure at higher altitudes has the same effect on a vapor pressure bellows as does a barometric change. The effects of altitudes are greater and of a permanent nature so that adjustments may be made in the control settings to correct for the effect of altitude.

aluminum a lightweight but relatively strong metal. Often alloyed with copper to increase hardness and strength.

ambient surrounding.

ambient air generally, the dry bulb air temperature surrounding or in the vicinity of an object or person.

ambient compensated describes a unit designed so that varying temperatures of air at the control do not affect the control setting.

ambient conditions surrounding conditions; conditions on all sides.

ambient sensor a sensor that measures the temperature of the outside air temperature.

ambient switch an open-on-temperature fall switch that keeps the compressor from coming on if the ambient temperature is below a preset value.

ambient temperature the temperature of the air or other medium immediately surrounding an object or device.

American Gear Manufacturers Association (AGMA) an association of member companies who manufacture speed reducers, enclosed gear drives, open gearing, and gear-type shaft couplings. It establishes standards for the design and application of gear products. The combined experience of company members and technical members assures gear users that products will perform satisfactorily when built, selected, and tested in accordance with AGMA standards.

American national standard thread a group of three main series of threads, consisting of national fine, national coarse, and national pipe.

American National Standards Institute (ANSI) an organization which sets building and manufacturing standards.

American Standard Code for Information Interchange (ASCII) a standard, eight-level code developed by an ANSI subcommittee, having seven code bits for data and an eighth bit for parity. Developed to simplify and standardize the intercommunication links among computers, communication circuits, and digital output equipment, such as a printer or video.

American standard pipe thread type of screw thread commonly used on pipe and fittings to assure a tight seal.

American wire gauge (AWG) a standard used in the determination of the physical size of a conductor determined by its circular mil area. It is usually expressed as AWG. As the diameter gets smaller, the number gets bigger, e.g., AWG #14 = 0.0641 in. while AWG #12 = 0.0808 in. (previously referred to as the Brown and Sharpe gauge).

ammeter   an electric meter calibrated and used to measure the amperes that are present in a circuit. Ammeter styles are either in-line or clamp-on.

ammonia   a chemical combination of nitrogen and hydrogen (NH_3). Identified as R-717. Boiling point at atmospheric pressure is –28°F. Color code is black.

amp   ampere.

ampacity   total amperes expected at maximum load times 1.25. Current carrying capacity expressed in amperes.

amperage   the electron or current flow in coulombs per second past a given point in a circuit.

amperage interrupting capacity   the point beyond which a circuit protection device can no longer interrupt current flow.

ampere   the standard unit of electrical current. Equivalent to 6.28 quintillion electrons flowing through one ohm of resistance pushed by one volt of electrical energy in one second. Symbol is "I" for intensity of current.

ampere fuse rating   the current capacity of a fuse. When a fuse is subjected to a current above its ampere rating, it will open the circuit after a predetermined period of time.

ampere-hour   a capacity rating of storage batteries that refers to the maximum current that can flow from the battery during a specified time frame.

ampere squared seconds   the measure of heat energy developed within a circuit during the fuse's clearing. It can be expressed as "melting I^2T" or as "clearing I^2T." "I" stands for effective let-through current

(rms), which is squared, and "T" stands for the time of opening, in seconds.

ampere-turns   the unit used to measure magnetic force. Represents product of amperes times number of turns in coil of electromagnet. Base unit of magnetomotive force.

amplification   the increasing in value of an input signal by an amplifying device. The types of amplification are voltage, current, and power amplification.

amplifier   a device used to increase the magnitude of a small input signal to proportions sufficient to perform some desirable function. Also see *flame signal amplifier*.

amplifier saturation   the point at which an increased input signal no longer increases the amplifier output.

amplitude   the maximum deviation from a baseline of a varying sine wave.

amplitude modulation (AM)   a method of transmitter modulation achieved by varying the strength of the RF carrier at an audio signal rate.

amps   a measurement of the electrical current flowing in an electrical circuit.

analgesia   loss of sensitivity to pain.

analog   a descriptive term meaning continuous or having a continuous range of values.

analog inputs and outputs   an input or output of variable value which is provided to a control system. Usually a variable voltage, current, or pressure.

analog meter   a meter that uses a mechanical magnetized needle movement to indicate the measured value.

analogy   an explanation of an idea or object by comparing it with something else that is usually more familiar than the idea or object being explained.

analyze   to separate into parts so as to find out their nature, purpose, and use. To examine the parts of a whole carefully and in detail.

analyzer   a device in the high side of an absorption system for increasing the concentration of refrigerant in the vapor entering the rectifier or condenser.

analyzer (electronics)   a device used to check the condition of electrical components.

anemometer   an instrument for measuring the rate or speed (velocity) of flowing air.

anesthesia   loss of sensation or feeling.

angle   the figure formed when two lines come together at some point.

angle iron   a structural shape whose section is a right angle.

angle of lead or lag   the angle between the applied voltage (EMF) and current flow (I) in an AC circuit in degrees. In an inductive (L) circuit, voltage (E) leads current (I); in a capacitive (C) circuit, current (I) leads voltage (E).

angle valve   a type of globe valve design, having pipe openings at right angles to each other. Usually, one opening is on the horizontal plane and one is on the vertical plane.

angstrom unit (Å)   a unit of measurement of a wavelength of light and other electromagnetic radiation, equal to one ten-thousandth (1/10,000) of a micron.

anhydrous   without water. Describes a substance in which no water is present in the form of a hydrate or as water of crystallization.

anhydrous ammonia   ammonia that is free of water, especially water of crystallization.

anhydrous calcium sulfate   a dry chemical made of calcium, sulfur, and oxygen ($CaSo_4$).

anion   a negative ion. An ion which moves toward the anode in electrolysis.

anneal   to subject to high heat with subsequent cooling. Relative to copper, the act of heating to just below its melting point and then allowing it to cool slowly. This usually lowers the tensile strength while improving the flex life and its flexibility characteristics.

annealed tubing   annealed copper tubing is also simply called soft copper tubing. It has been heat treated to make it soft, easy to bend, and easy to flare. Over time, or as a result of pounding, rough handling, or bending, the tubing also tends to harden. Because annealed tubing is so flexible, it needs support from clamps or brackets. Soft copper tubing is used in home refrigeration and air-conditioning and in some commercial installations. It is available in 25-, 50-, and 100-foot rolls. It can be flared, soft soldered, or brazed.

annual fuel utilization efficiency (AFUE)   ratio of annual output energy to annual input energy, which includes any non-heating season pilot input loss, and for gas or oil fired furnaces or boilers, does not include electrical energy.

annunciator light   a light which is illuminated at the time a point exceeds a preset alarm limit. An individual annunciator light can be provided for each input variable being alarm scanned, or a common alarm annunciator light can be utilized to indicate trouble somewhere in the system. It can also be used to indicate a status.

annunciator panel   a device which indicates an off-standard or abnormal condition by visual and/or audible signals.

anode   the positive terminal or electrode of an electronic device such as a solid state diode. The P region of a P-N junction diode.

anticipating control   a control which is artificially forced to cut in or out before it would otherwise, therefore starting cooling before needed or stopping the heating before the control point is reached. This tends to reduce the temperature fluctuation or override of the control.

anticipation   a method of reducing the operating differential of a system by adding a small resistive heater inside the thermostat to raise the internal temperature of the thermostat faster than the surrounding room temperature. This causes the thermostat to shut off the heating equipment and start the cooling equipment sooner than it would if it were affected only by the room temperature.

anticipator   a small heater placed inside the thermostat housing used to adjust or "anticipate" the thermostat operation to produce a closer temperature differential than the mechanical capability of the control. A heating thermostat anticipator is wired in series with the thermostat contacts while a cooling thermostat anticipator is wired in parallel with the thermostat contacts.

antidote   a remedy to relieve, prevent, or counteract the effects of a poison. Eliminating the poison, neutralizing it, or absorbing it are effective.

anti-flooding device   a primary control which causes the flow of fuel to be shut off upon a rise in fuel level or upon receiving excess fuel, and which operates before the hazardous discharge of fuel can occur.

antifreeze   materials such as salt, alcohol, or glycol products that are added to water to lower the freezing point.

antioxidant   a substance which slows down decomposition caused by oxygen.

antiozonant   a substance which slows down material degradation due to ozone reaction.

anti-short-cycling device   a control that prevents a load from stopping and starting in rapid succession. This device is used mainly to prevent compressors from being restarted within a certain time after they have been stopped.

aperture   a service connection used to make access into a sealed refrigeration system. Two common types are the clamp-on piercing valve and the schrader valve.

aperture disc   a thin, flat, circular plate of any material with an opening or hole (orifice) of predetermined diameter to restrict the area viewed through it.

apparatus dew point   the dew point temperature of the air leaving the air-conditioning (evaporator) coil.

apparent power   the product of the measured voltage and current in a circuit containing reactance. A circuit in which voltage and current reach their peak values at different times in a cycle.

appliance   (1) a current-consuming device that utilizes energy or raw materials to produce light, sound, heat, power, refrigeration, or air-conditioning. (2) Any device which contains and uses a Class I or Class II substance as a refrigerant and which is used for household or commercial purposes, including any air conditioner, refrigerator, chiller, or freezer.

applied voltage   the amount of voltage connected to a circuit or device.

apprentice   a beginner in a trade, usually serving several years as a helper to a journeyman.

approach temperature   the difference in temperature between the refrigerant and the leaving water in a chilled water system. In an evaporative cooling device, the difference between the average temperature of the circulating water leaving the device and the average wet bulb temperature of the entering air.

approved   acceptable to an authority or regulatory agency having jurisdiction.

aquadag tube   an electron tube sensitive to ultraviolet radiation. When saturated with ultraviolet radiation, this tube delivers less than one microwatt to the flame signal amplifier.

aquastat   a switching device that is sensitive to heat, located on a hot water line, coil, tank, or boiler. It controls the heating or temperature of the water, turning the fuel burning equipment on or shutting it off when it reaches a preset or given temperature.

aqueous   describes a water-based solution or suspension. Frequently describes a gaseous compound dissolved in water.

arc   a portion of a circle.

arc (electrical)   an electrical discharge between two poles of opposite charge.

arc gap protector   a device which conducts at high voltage levels to bypass an electronic network, thus protecting the network against damage from the voltage interference.

arc weld   to weld by electric arc. The work is usually the positive terminal.

architectural drawings   drawings that show walls, roofs, partitions, floor plans, mechanical equipment, elevations, and sections. From these drawings you should have a good idea of what the structure will look like when it is completed.

arcing   the forming of an electric arc across two physically separated contacts.

arcing time   the amount of time from the instant the fuse link has melted until the overcurrent is interrupted or cleared.

area   square measure found by multiplying length times width, or (for a circle) the pi value of 3.141 by the radius squared.

area, core   the total plane area of the portion of a grille, face, or register, bounded by a line tangent to the outer edges of the outer openings through which air can pass.

area, free   the total minimum area of the openings in an air inlet or outlet through which air can pass.

armature   the moving element in an electromechanical device, such as the movable iron core in a solenoid, the rotating part of the generator or motor, the movable part of a relay, or the spring-mounted iron portion of a bell or buzzer.

armature reaction   the effect in direct current generators and motors in which current flow through the armature conductors reacts with the main magnetic field and increases sparking between the brushes and commutator.

armor   a covering or wrapping of metal that is used to protect interior conductors.

armor clamp   a fitting used to attach armored cable to a junction box or other device.

armored cable   a flexible metal protective covering enclosing electrical conductors. See *Bx cable*.

arrestor (lightning rod)   a device used to protect buildings, including electrical devices, from damage by lightning.

artificial fuels   man-made fuels, including all manufactured and by-product fuels.

artist cap   a fabricated hood, usually of sheet metal, placed on top of a stack to prevent down drafts or erratic drafts because of the directional wind effects.

asbestos   a fire-resistant, heat-resistant mineral (a silicate of calcium and magnesium) used in fireproofing and insulation.

ash   the noncombustible matter that remains after a fuel is burned.

ASME boiler code   standard specifications issued by the American Society of Mechanical Engineers for the construction of boilers.

aspect ratio   in air distribution outlets, the ratio of the length of the core opening of a grille, face, or register to the width. In rectangular ducts, the ratio of the width to the depth. In buildings, the ratio of the length to the width.

asphyxia   lack of oxygen and thus interference with the oxygenation of the blood. Can lead to unconsciousness.

asphyxiant   a vapor or gas that can cause unconsciousness or death by suffocation (lack of oxygen). Most simple asphyxiants are harmful to the body only when they become so concentrated that they reduce the available oxygen in the air (normally about 21%) to dangerous levels (18% or lower). Some are chemical asphyxiants like carbon monoxide (CO) or cyanide, which reduce the blood's ability to carry oxygen. Other examples are CO_2, N_2, H_2, methane, and hydrocarbon gases.

asphyxiation   a condition that causes asphyxia or suffocation. Asphyxiation is one of the principal potential hazards of working in confined spaces.

aspirating burner   a power burner which uses venturi action to pull the gas into the airstream. Also see *venturi* and *zero governor burner.*

aspirating psychrometer   an instrument which draws a sample of air for humidity measurement purposes.

aspiration   the movement produced in a fluid by suction or the induction of room air into the airstream.

aspirator hole   a small hole drilled inside of the accumulator dip tube. It permits small quantities of oil to enter the outlet tube and be drawn back to the compressor.

aspirator mixer   a gas/air proportioning device that causes the flow of combustion air to induce the proper amount of gas into the airstream. It is used with low-pressure air and zero gas pressure. Also called a suction-type mixer. Also see *zero governor burner.*

assembly   portion of an envelope component represented by an arrangement and connection of building construction materials with a specific thermal transmittance or thermal conductance.

ASTM standards   standards issued by the American Society of Testing Materials.

atmosphere   (1) the invisible mixture of gases (air) surrounding the earth. (2) A unit of pres-

sure defined as the pressure of 760 millimeters of mercury at sea level and at 0°C (32°F), which is equal to 14.696 pounds per square inch (psi), or 29.921 inches of mercury.

atmospheric burner   a gas burner relying on atmospheric pressure to bring in combustion air. It simply permits the air required for combustion to enter the combustion chamber, or it draws air into the combustion chamber from the air surrounding the burner. Two methods are used to draw air into the combustion space:

1. natural draft burner - the natural draft produced by the products of combustion moving up through the chimney, or stack, draws air in at the bottom of the burner.
2. inspirating burner - the fuel gas is allowed to escape at high velocity into the throat of a venturi tube, creating a lower static pressure which draws in the air. Also called an injection or venturi mixing burner.

A typical atmospheric burner draws in part of the combustion air by venturi action and the rest by a natural draft.

atmospheric dust spot efficiency   measurement of a device's ability to remove atmospheric air from test air.

atmospheric pressure   the pressure exerted on the earth's surface by the weight of the air and moisture above it. A unit of pressure equal to about 14.696 psi, or 29.92 inches Hg mercury, at 32°F at sea level. Also called barometric pressure. Pressure is measured in pounds per square inch.

atmospheric regulator   see *zero governor.*

atom   the smallest particle of an element that can exist alone or in combination. Every atom is made up of a positively charged nucleus and a set of negatively charged electrons that revolve around the nucleus. The nucleus is made up of positively charged protons and neutrons that have no charge. Atoms link together to form molecules.

atomic excitation   the application of some form of external energy to an atom.

atomic number   the number of electrons or protons in the center or nucleus of an atom.

atomic weight   the weight of an atom, approximately equal to the number of protons and neutrons in its nucleus.

atomization   the process of making a liquid into a mist-like spray.

atomize   to reduce a liquid into a multitude of tiny droplets or a fine spray.

atomizer   a device which breaks liquid fuel into tiny droplets. It may require the assistance of an atomizing medium such as steam or air. Also see *mechanical atomizer*.

atomizing air   the air supplied to an air-atomizing oil burner (usually about 10%) which is used to break the oil stream into tiny droplets. The atomizing air is also used later for combustion.

atomizing medium   a supplementary fluid, such as steam or air, which assists in breaking oil into a finely divided state.

atomizing oil burner   an oil burner which delivers fuel oil to the combustion zone in the form of tiny droplets. It uses some form of nozzle or orifice to spray the oil into the combustion chamber. An atomizing oil burner is classified by the medium used to break up the oil into fine particles.

1. Air-atomizing oil burner - compressed air.
2. Steam-atomizing oil burner - steam at pressures greater than 25 pounds per square inch (psig).
3. Mechanical-atomizing oil burner-no medium - the oil is pumped at high pressures (50 to 300 psig) through a suitable burner nozzle orifice which breaks it into a fine mist. Synonymous with pressure-atomizing oil burner. Also see *pressure-atomizing gun-type burner*.

Air- and steam-atomizing oil burners can be further classified by the location at which the atomization takes place.

a. External mix oil burner - the high-velocity air or steam strikes the oil after it has left the nozzle.
b. Internal mix oil burner - the high-velocity air or steam strikes jets of incoming oil in a mixing chamber, and the oil is discharged from the nozzle in a completely atomized form.

attachment plug   a device which is inserted into a receptacle and establishes the connection between the conductors of the attached flexible cord and the conductors attached permanently to the receptacle.

attenuation   the sound reduction process in which sound energy is absorbed or diminished in intensity as the result of energy conversion from sound to motion or heat.

attenuator   a device that decreases the amount of signal voltage or current.

attic   that part of a structure immediately below the roof. Many times HVAC equipment is located here and must be accessed for proper service.

attic fan   an exhaust fan used to discharge air near the top of a building while cooler air is forced (drawn) in at a lower level.

audio frequency   pertaining to that band of frequency which is audible to the human ear. Usually 20–20,000 cycles per second.

auger   the screw-like center part of an ice flaker that scrapes ice from a cylindrical evaporator.

authority   the percentage of influence of each of two or more control sensing devices teamed together.

auto   short for automatic.

automatic   self-regulating or self-acting; capable of responding to certain predetermined conditions.

automatic burner   a burner that starts and stops automatically.

automatic changeover thermostat   a thermostat that selects either heating or cooling, depending on room temperature and the heating and cooling set points.

automatic combination gas valve   a valve for gas furnaces that incorporates a manual shutoff control, an internal 100% safety pilot shutoff, gas valve, and pressure regulator.

automatic control   a system that reacts to a change or imbalance in one of its variables by adjusting the other variables to restore the system to the desired balance. For example, a system for control of air/fuel ratio can be set up so that a change in the setting of the combustion air valve results in a corresponding change in the fuel input.

automatic control valve   an electrically operated valve which contains a valve body and a valve actuator or motor. A signal from some remote point can energize the actuator or motor to open or close the valve, or to proportion the rate of flow through the valve. Also see *constant-level, firing rate, modulating, motorized,* and *safety shutoff valves.*

automatic defrost   a system that removes ice or frost from evaporators automatically.

automatic expansion valve (AEV or AXV)   pressure controlled valve which reduces high-pressure liquid refrigerant to a low-pressure liquid/vapor mixture refrigerant.

automatic feed water valve   a valve that controls the high and low water levels in the boiler, opening and closing automatically.

automatic fire check   a device for stopping the progress of a flame front in burner mixture lines (flashback) and for automatically shutting off the fuel/air mixture.

automatic flue damper   a device used between the vent system and the draft diverter on a heating furnace to prevent heat from escaping through the vent system during the "off" cycle.

automatic gas pilot device   a gas pilot incorporating a device which acts to automatically shut off the gas supply to the appliance burner if the pilot flame is extinguished.

automatic gas shutoff device   a device constructed so that a water temperature in a hot water supply system in excess of some predetermined limit causes the gas to the system to be shut off.

automatic ice cube maker   refrigerating mechanism designed to produce ice cubes in quantity automatically.

automatic ignition   a system in which a burner is ignited directly without manual intervention by an automatically supervised ignition spark or pilot.

automatic pilot   a device that is designed to shut off the gas supply automatically to the burner(s) in the event the source of ignition fails. This device may interrupt gas flow to the main burner, the pilot, or both.

automatic refrigerating system   one which regulates itself to maintain a definite set of conditions by means of automatic controls and values usually responsive to temperature or pressure.

automatic reset   a compensating feature incorporated into certain control instruments. It automatically resets the instrument control point when the controlled medium (air or water, etc., under the instrument's control) deviates from the instrument set point. This shift in control point returns the controlled medium to the set point condition. The reset function is continuous during the time period the deviation exists.

automatic safety shutoff valve   see *safety shutoff valve.*

automatic system   a system which regulates itself and requires no manual operations. A system in which the burner is cycled completely automatically under control of an automatic temperature or pressure controller.

automatically ignited burner   a burner in which fuel to the main burner is automatically turned on and ignited.

autotransformer   a transformer in which both the primary and secondary coils have turns in common. Step-up or step-down of voltage is accomplished by taps on the common windings. Output of the secondary depends on whether all or part of the split coil (primary or secondary) is connected to the load.

auxiliary contacts   extra switches added to magnetic contactors or starters that operate simultaneously with the load contacts. Such switches are used to energize secondary circuits.

auxiliary drain pan   a complete drain pan that is larger than the outside dimensions of the unit that contains the evaporator coil. Used to prevent water damage to surfaces under the unit in the event of blockage of the condensate drain.

auxiliary drive   belt, chain, or gear drive used with a gear motor or speed reducer to provide additional speed reduction and/or torque multiplication.

auxiliary heat (heat pump)   heating provided by equipment other than the heat pump when the heat loss exceeds the balance point of the structure. When this auxiliary heat is electric, auxiliary heaters may be called strip heaters. These strip heaters may be staged by outdoor thermostats.

auxiliary heat (solar)   a backup heating system that is used when there is not enough solar radiation to operate the primary solar system. These backup systems can be gas, oil, or electric.

auxiliary potentiometer   a potentiometer, mounted in or on a modulating motor, which is used to control an external device in response to movements of the motor.

auxiliary switch   a device which may be added to a damper or valve motor to provide electric switching action at a predetermined point in the motor travel. It is sometimes called an end switch because of its customary location on the motor.

available head   the difference in pressure which can be used to circulate water in a system. The difference which may be used to overcome friction within the system.

available heat   the quantity of heat released in a combustion chamber that is available for useful purposes. It is the total quantity of heat released minus both the dry flue gas loss (sensible heat) and the moisture loss (latent heat).

avalanche   the breakdown of a diode resulting when the reverse voltage reaches a value sufficient to ruin the diode.

average voltage   an AC voltage or current value based on the average of all instantaneous values for one alternation. Found from this formula: $E_{avg} = E_{peak} \times 0.636$.

averaging control   control achieved when two or more control sensing elements are paired together to give one signal in response to the average condition sensed by the two. Such elements are often used to avoid excessive control due to sudden changes at any single location.

averaging thermostat element   a thermostat sensing element that responds to the average temperature sensed at many different points in a duct or process medium.

aviation snips   hand tools used to cut sheet metal straight or in a circle.

Avogadro's law   equal volumes of gases at the same temperature and pressure contain the same number of particles.

A-weighted   a term which refers to the single number logarithmic summation of the 8 octave bands which have been adjusted to account for response of the human ear to sound pressure level.

awl a pointed instrument used for making or piercing small holes.

axial fan term used to describe propeller-type fan blades.

axial thrust load the external loading or force acting lengthwise along a shaft.

axis the centerline of a geometric figure.

azeotrope a refrigerant having constant maximum and minimum boiling points.

azeotropic mixture a constant boiling point mixture of two liquids that boils at constant composition, i.e., the vapor's composition is the same as the liquid's. When the mixture boils, the vapor at first has a higher proportion of one component than is present in the liquid, so this proportion in the liquid falls over time. Eventually, maximum and minimum points are reached, at which the two liquids distill together with no change in composition. An azeotrope composition depends on pressure. An example of an azeotropic mixture would be R-502 where the mixture consists of 48.8% R-22 and 51.2% R-115. The refrigerants do not combine chemically, yet an azeotropic mixture provides the refrigerant characteristics desired.

azimuth the angular distance between true south and the point on the horizon which is directly below the sun.

B

bat battery.

bat chg battery charger.

bc back connected.

bei biological exposure indexes.

BHCC Better Heating-Cooling Council.

bhp brake horsepower.

bi backward-inclined.

bkr breaker.

BOCA Building Officials and Code Administrators.

BOMA Building Owners and Managers Association.

bpcdh74 break point cooling degree-hours base 74°F.

bphdd65 break point heating degree-days base 65°F.

BSI British Standards Institute.

Btu British thermal unit.

Btu/h one Btu per hour; one million Btu/h is equivalent to seven gallons of oil per hour, 800 pounds of steam per hour, or a boiler input of 20 boiler horsepower (BoHP).

bv back view.

babbitt a soft alloy for bearings, mostly of tin with small amounts of copper and antimony.

back draft a common result from down-draft. When poor draft is unable to carry hot gases from the heating appliance, the result is that gases force themselves back into the boiler room through dampers and fire doors. In extreme cases, back draft can result in considerable damage.

back EMF the amount of voltage produced across the start and common terminals or connections of a single-phase motor. Also referred to as counterelectromotive force.

back pressure pressure against which a fluid is flowing, resulting from friction in lines, restrictions in pipes, valves, pressure in vessel to which fluid is flowing, hydrostatic head, or any other impediment that causes resistance to fluid flow.

back pressure (refrigeration) the pressure in the low side of a refrigerating system. Also called suction or low-side pressure.

back pressure regulator an automatic valve in the suction line that prevents the suction pressure from dropping below the desired set point.

back seat port a port entering the valve body behind the back seat. Since no pressure can reach this port when the valve is back-seated, the port can be used for attaching test gauges or making other connections to the system while it is under pressure.

back-seated term describing the turning of the stem counterclockwise until it stops at the wide-open position. It is in this position that the valve usually closes off the gauge connection fitting or port. For normal operation, the valve is always in a back-seated position.

backfire a condition that causes the brazing torch flame to go out with a loud cracking sound. Also referred to as extinction pop.

backward-inclined fan a fan on which the tips of the blades are inclined away from the direction of rotation. Used in commercial/industrial heating and cooling systems which require heavy-duty construction, nonoverloading characteristics, and stable air delivery. These blowers operate at higher efficiencies than forward-curved blowers. They are not as quiet as forward-curved blowers because they operate at higher speeds. Can be used in systems up to 3″ static pressure. Smaller-diameter wheels are supplied with flat blades; larger-diameter wheels are supplied with airfoil blades to improve efficiency.

baffle a metal or refractory surface used to direct the flow of air or flue gases or to minimize the effects of flame, heat, or flue gases.

bag assembly closely related filter media parts grouped together in a single package to remove dust particles from the airstream.

bag filter house see *bag assembly.*

balance fitting a pipe fitting or valve designed so that its resistance to flow may be varied. It is used to balance the pressure drop in parallel circuits.

balance point the outdoor temperature at which the output of the heat pump in a specific application is equal to the heat requirements of the structure.

balance point, initial the outdoor ambient temperature at which the heating capacity of the heat pump only balances the heat loss of the conditioned space.

balance point, second the outdoor temperature at which the heating capacity of the heat pump plus the auxiliary heat capacity balances the heat loss of the conditioned space.

balance pressure ventilating system a system where the mechanical fresh air supply is balanced against the mechanical exhaust to maintain a constant air pressure in the conditioned space.

balanced port TXV a thermostatic expansion valve that will meter refrigerant at the same rate as when the condenser's head pressure is low.

balanced valve a valve designed so that the fluid pressure exerted on the valve discs is equalized, or balanced, thereby reducing the force required by the operator to open and close the valve.

balancing relay a relay with an armature pivoted between two electromagnetic coils. The armature controls the position of the wiper on a feedback potentiometer in the electrical circuit. If the currents through the two coils differ, the armature moves toward the coil with the most current (strongest electromagnetic force). As the armature moves, the potentiometer wiper changes the resistance in series with both coils until the currents are equal. The armature stops when the circuit is balanced. Besides the electromechanical type, there is also a solid state type which performs the same functions electronically. A balancing relay is used in a Honeywell modutrol motor to position it. Also called a mouse trap.

ball bearing   an antifriction device that is used to allow free turning and support of the rotating member of the device. It consists of an outer and inner ring with races and has steel balls sandwiched between the rings. Used where higher load capacity is required or periodic lubrication is impractical.

ball check valve   a device consisting of a ball and orifice. Pressure on one side of the device will seat the ball across the orifice and stop flow. Pressure in the opposite direction will shift the ball from the seated position permitting flow. It has a large pressure drop across it.

ball peen hammer   a 12- or 16-ounce hammer used for hammering and for rounding rivets and metal. Also known as a machinist's hammer.

ball valve   a straight-through valve that creates very little pressure drop or resistance to flow.

ballast   a special type of resistor whose resistance increases rapidly with an increase in current through it. It then limits the current flow through it and a load (such as a fluorescent lamp) connected to it.

balloon-type gasket   a flexible refrigerator door gasket having a large cross section.

bar   a unit of pressure. One bar equals .98690 atmospheres.

bar chart   a representation of the operating sequence of a control or controller using shaded bars to show the times when various circuits are energized.

bar magnet   a magnet with poles at both ends of a straight metal bar.

barometer   an instrument used to measure atmospheric pressure. It may be calibrated in pounds per square inch or inches of mercury.

barometric draft regulator   a balanced damper device attached to a chimney, vent connector, breeching, or flue gas manifold to protect combustion equipment by controlling chimney draft. A double-acting barometric draft regulator is one whose balancing damper is free to move in either direction to protect combustion equipment from both excessive draft and back draft.

barometric pressure   see *atmospheric pressure.*

base   the main supporting frame or structure of an assembly, excluding the legs.

base, chemical   a substance that (1) liberates OH$^-$ ions when dissolved in water; (2) liberates negative ions in a solvent; (3) receives a hydrogenation from a strong acid to form a weaker acid; (4) gives up two electrons to an acid. Bases have a pH value less than 7 and turn litmus paper blue.

base, electronic   the semiconductor region between the collector and emitter of a transistor. The base controls the current flow through the collector-emitter circuit.

base metal   the metal which you are going to weld, braze, or cut.

base, thermostat   the portion of the thermostat that contains the internal wiring. This is the portion of the thermostat that contains the sensing device and contacts for activating the heating and/or cooling system.

baseboard   a terminal unit resembling the room base trim of a house. These units are the most popular terminal unit for residential systems.

baseboard system   an electric or hot water system that is used for whole house, spot, or individual room heating. They are economical to install and can be controlled by individual room thermostats. The units are thin and mounted on an outside wall just above the carpet or flooring. The heaters are natural draft and as the air enters near the bottom it passes over the heating element, is heated, and rises in the room. Since there is a difference in the density of the air, the cool air falls and sets up the nat-ural-draft convection air current.

basement   that part of the building that is wholly or partly below ground level.

basic refrigeration control   device that starts, stops, regulates, and/or protects the refrigeration system and its components.

basic refrigeration cycle   a process in which a circulating refrigerant absorbs heat from a place where it is not wanted and transfers it to a place where it is unobjectionable.

batch-type furnace   a furnace that is shut down periodically to remove the old charge and add new charge (as distinguished from a continuous furnace).

bath   a liquid solution used for cleaning, plat-ing, or maintaining a specified temperature.

battery   electricity-producing cells, con-nected in series, which use interaction of metals and chemicals to create direct cur-rent electrical flow.

battery capacity   the ability of a battery to produce a given current over a period of time measured in ampere hours. A rated 100 ampere-hour battery will theoretically produce one ampere for 100 hours or two amperes for 50 hours, etc.

battery resistance   the internal resistance between plates and electrolyte in a cell or battery.

Baudelot cooler   a heat exchanger in which water flows by gravity over the outside of tubes or plates.

bead   a narrow layer or layers of metal deposited on the base metal as the electrode melts.

beam   a term used to describe joists, rafters, and girders.

beam compass   a compass used to draw or make large circles and arcs.

bearing   a low-friction device for supporting and aligning a moving part. Basic types are sleeve, ball, and unit.

becquerel   the SI unit for the rate of radioactive decay in a sample of material. One becquerel (Bq) equals one disintegra-tion per second. Also see *curie*.

bel   a measurement unit of gain that is equivalent to a 10:1 ratio of power levels. Symbol is "B."

bell transformer   a small transformer used to change the line voltage to a lower and safer voltage for operation of doorbells and chimes.

bellows   a metallic accordion-like box which can be compressed mechanically or with a fluid pressure (like a spring), and which will return to its normal shape when the pres-sure is released.

bellows seal   a method of sealing the valve stem. The ends of the sealing material are fas-tened to the bonnet and to the stem. The seal then expands and contracts the stem level.

belt   a continuous loop of rubber-like mater-ial placed around two or more pulleys to transfer rotary motion from the drive pul-ley to the driven pulley.

belt-driven   describes a driver-and-driven arrangement, such as motor and a compres-sor, equipped with suitable sheaves or pul-leys and connected by one or more belts to operate at a speed ratio established by the relative diameters of the pulleys.

bench grinder   a rotating machine that takes off unwanted material by running an abrasive wheel against the work. It may also be used to redress chisels and sharpen tools.

bending spring   a coil spring which is mounted on the inside or outside of a tube to keep it from collapsing while bending.

bent tube boiler   see *water-tube boiler*.

bentonite   a clay material used in well drilling to seal the walls of the bore hole to reduce the loss of drilling mud into the earth.

Bernoulli's theorem   in a stream of liquid, the sum of elevation head, pressure head, and velocity remains constant along any line of flow, provided no work is done by or upon the liquid in the course of its flow, and it decreases in proportion to energy lost in flow.

bevel   an angle that is formed by a line or a surface that is not at a right angle to another line or surface.

bezel   a sloping or slanting surface, such as the cutting edge of a chisel.

bias   a DC voltage applied to the base of a transistor to preset its operating point.

bidirectional data bus   a data bus in which digital information can be transferred in either direction. With reference to a microcomputer, the bidirectional data path by which data is transferred among the CPU, memory, and input-output devices.

billing charges, utility   a charge for the use of a unit of electricity. See *demand charge* and *energy charge*.

billing unit   unit of electricity for which a charge is assessed. See *watt, kilowatt,* and *kilowatt-hour.*

bimetal element   an element with two metals each having different rates of expansion for each change in temperature. For a typical room thermostat the materials are brass and invar, with brass having the greatest coefficient of expansion. Other materials could be steel and copper. These two metals are fused together in such a manner as to form one piece. When they are heated or cooled, one will expand at a faster rate than the other, which causes a bending of the two metals. This action can be used to open or close electrical contacts or other suitable movement.

bimetal overload   a simple thermal overload that breaks the power supplying a small motor directly. When it reaches a high enough temperature, the bimetal opens by warping. When the overload cools, the bimetal will warp back and close the circuit.

bimetal relay   an overload device that opens a set of contacts by a temperature that corresponds to the current draw of a load.

bimetal strip   an element which is welded together from two dissimilar metals with unequal expansion rates. The two metals have different coefficients of expansion and bend with changes in temperature, thereby opening or closing the contact points. This type of element is used commonly in room thermostats but can be used in insertion controllers as well.

bimetallic   in a bimetallic device, two dissimilar metals are fastened together. They respond differently to temperature changes. These different responses cause the assembly to distort and move.

bimetallic strip   see *bimetal strip.*

bin, ice storage   a container in which ice can be stored.

bin weather data   tables published by the Air Conditioning Contractors Association showing the number of hours per year the local ambient temperatures will be. Shown in 5-degree increments.

binary   having two elements, parts, or divisions.

binary code   a code having only two conditions or values, usually opposed pairs like "on" and "off," "minimum" and "maximum," or "open" and "closed." These states are usually given the symbols 0 and 1.

binary counter   an interconnection of flip-flops having a single input arranged so as to permit binary counting. Each time a pulse appears at the input the counter changes state and tabulates the number of input pulses for readout in binary form. It has 2^n possible counts, where n is the number of flip-flops.

binder   usually a spirally serrated tape or thread used for holding assembled cable components in place awaiting further manufacturing operations.

binding post   a threaded terminal for connecting wire to electric equipment. Also known as a stud.

biological exposure indexes a system to determine the amount of a material absorbed into the human body by measuring it or its metabolic products in tissue, fluid, or exhaled air.

biologicals biological contaminants. Agents derived from living organisms or that are living organisms such as bacteria, fungi, and viruses.

bit abbreviation for *bi*nary digi*t*. A unit of information equal to one binary decision, or the designation of one of two possible and equally likely values or states (such as 0 or 1) of anything used to store or convey information.

black oxides contaminants that form by the combination of oxygen and copper during the brazing process.

blade screwdriver a tool used to tighten or loosen slotted head fasteners.

blast freezer a low-temperature evaporator which uses a fan to force air rapidly over the evaporator surface.

blast furnace gas a gas of low Btu content recovered from a blast furnace as a by-product and used as a fuel.

bleed a process of slowly reducing the pressure of liquid or gas from a system or cylinder by slightly opening a valve.

bleed-off the continuous or intermittent wasting of a small fraction of the circulating water to a cooling tower to prevent the buildup and concentration of scale-forming chemicals in the water.

bleed port valve located on the oil pump (fuel oil unit) for bleeding air from the system. Bleeding of the air from the lines is only needed on a one-pipe application.

bleed resistor a fixed resistor that is installed to permit built-up electrons to slowly and safely flow from one side of a capacitor to the other side of the capacitor until the two sides are equal in charge.

bleed valve a valve with a small opening inside of it which permits a minimum fluid flow when the valve is closed.

bleeder an intentional leak, usually used to reduce pressure.

bleeding intentional leakage (usually of gas). Leakage that might occur during shut-down in a safety shutoff valve "block-and-bleed" arrangement. Gas bleeds off to the atmosphere through a normally open vent valve. When the safety shutoff valve(s) is open, the vent or bleed valve closes and bleeding stops. Also see *double-block-and-bleed*.

blind hole one that does not penetrate completely through a component.

blind rivet a permanent metal fastener used to join two pieces of sheet metal with a strong connection that will not loosen with vibration.

block-and-bleed see *double-block-and-bleed*.

block diagram a diagram used to show how the parts of a system fit together.

blocked suction a method of cylinder unloading. The suction line passage to a cylinder in a reciprocating compressor is blocked, thus causing that cylinder to stop pumping.

blow, throw the distance an airstream travels from an outlet to a position at which air motion along the axis is reduced to a velocity of 50 feet per minute.

blow down a system in a cooling tower whereby some of the circulating water is bled off and replaced with fresh water to dilute the sediment in the sump.

blow through a term applied to central fan systems which are arranged so that coils, sprays, and other air-treating elements are on the discharge side of the fan.

blower motor-driven, forward-curved, centrifugal-type fan which delivers air to the desired space under pressure. May be either belt- or direct-drive.

blower relay   an electromagnetic device that energizes the blower motor during the cooling cycle and continuous fan operation mode.

blower section   the motor and centrifugal-type fan that circulate air through the furnace or fan coil unit for treatment of heating, cooling, or ventilation.

blueprint   a photographic print in white on a bright blue ground, used especially for copying maps, mechanical drawings, and architectural drawings or plans.

body rating   see *valve body rating*.

boil   to heat to a point where bubbles of vapor rise and break at the surface. To evaporate.

boiler   a closed vessel in which a liquid is heated or vaporized. Used to supply hot water or steam for heating, processing, or power purposes. If steam is generated, it is a steam boiler. If the temperature of the water is raised without boiling, it is classified as a hot water boiler. Also see *cast iron sectional, dryback, firebox, fire-tube, high-pressure, high-temperature, low-pressure, packaged, scotch, water-tube,* and *wetback boilers*.

boiler heating surface   the area of the heat-transmitting surfaces in contact with the water (or steam) in the boiler on one side and the fire or hot gases on the other.

boiler, high-pressure   a boiler furnishing steam at pressures of 15 pounds per square inch gauge or higher (205kPa).

boiler horsepower   the equivalent of the heat required to evaporate 34.5 pounds of water per hour from a temperature of 212°F (100°C) into dry, saturated steam at the same temperature. Equivalent to 33,472 Btu/h, 9.803 kilowatts, or 40 pounds of steam per hour.

boiler, hot water   a boiler furnishing hot water at pressures not more than 30 pounds per square inch gauge.

boiler, low-pressure   a boiler furnishing steam at pressures that are not more than 15 pounds per square inch gauge.

boiling   see *boil*.

boiling point   the temperature at which the vapor pressure of a liquid is equal to the surrounding atmospheric pressure so that the liquid becomes a vapor, i.e., the temperature at which the upward pressure of the molecules escaping from the surface equals the downward pressure of the atmosphere. Flammable materials with low boiling points generally present special fire hazards.

boiling temperature   temperature at which a fluid changes from a liquid to a gas.

boil-out   the evaporation of water which occurs when the storage water is heated to the boiling point and solar heating continues.

bolt   a fastener that is used with a nut and normally used for fastening heavy metal parts together.

bolt circle   a circular center line on a drawing, containing the centers of holes about a common center.

bolt extractor   a threaded tool used to remove a broken bolt or screw.

bond   the continuity of an electric connection across a joint or otherwise separated conductors.

bonding   a safety practice. The interconnecting of two objects (tanks, cylinders, etc.) with bonding clamps and bare wire. This will equalize the electrical potential between the objects and help prevent static sparks or discharge that could ignite flammable materials.

bonding jumper   a conductor between metal parts which establishes electrical continuity.

bonnet   the part of the furnace casing which forms a plenum chamber from where supply ducts receive conditioned air. Also called supply plenum.

booster   common term applied to the use of a compressor when used as the first stage in a cascade refrigerating system.

booster heater a heater used to raise the temperature of oil from that required for pumping to that required for atomization.

bore, cylinder the inside diameter of a cylindrical hole.

bore, machine to enlarge a hole with a boring bar or tool in a lathe, drill press, or boring mill.

borehole hole made with a rotary drill rig and bit without a well casing. Boreholes are used for vertical ground loop systems.

bottled gas liquefied petroleum (LP) gas, predominantly propane.

bottoming tap is used first to cut threads to the bottom of a hole. A bottoming tap is used when threads must be cut to the bottom of a blind hole. For most threading cases, the thread is started with the tapered tap, then cut with the plug tap, and finally with a bottoming tap.

Bourdon tube a tube that responds to pressure changes. The tube, with an elliptical cross section, is shaped into an arc or spiral with one end attached to an indicating, recording, or controlling device. A pressure within the tube makes it less elliptical and more nearly circular, thus actuating the attached device.

Bowden cable a tube containing a wire that is used to regulate a valve or control from a remote point.

box an enclosed panel for connecting conductors or mounting devices.

box header boiler see *water-tube boiler*.

box wrench generally used where nuts and bolts cannot be reached by a socket wrench. Box wrenches are generally 6 or 12 point and give the technician a strong and safe grip. These wrenches come in straight, offset, or double-offset types. Almost all box wrenches are double-ended. Both ends may have the same size with one end offset or may be the same pattern and different sizes.

Boyle's law a law of physics which states that the volume of a gas varies as the pressure varies, if the temperature remains the same. If pressure is doubled on quantity of gas, volume becomes one half. If the volume is doubled, the gas has its pressure reduced by one half. $P_1V_1 = P_2V_2$

bracket another term for the end shield or end bell of a motor.

braid a fibrous or metallic group of filaments interwoven in cylindrical form to form a covering over one or more wires.

brake winding the winding in an electric motor which holds the armature against a brake shoe to hold the motor in its open position after the motor limit switch opens. When both the motor winding and the brake winding are energized, the strength of the motor winding overcomes the brake winding.

brake wire wire used in mobile home, travel, and truck trailers to supply current to the electrical braking system.

branch circuit, electrical a secondary circuit leading from the main electrical circuit to a load or a group of loads.

branch circuit, general that portion of a piping system which connects a terminal unit to the circuit.

branch circuit, oil a secondary circuit leading from a main oil circulating loop to a burner or group of burners.

branch circuit (pneumatic) air lines, used in a pneumatic control system, which transmit the varying air pressure, produced by a pneumatic controller. This changing air pressure positions actuators, such as damper motors, control valves, or similar devices.

branch circuit center a central supply from which the branch circuits extend.

branch connection a pipeline that runs away from the main or run of a pipeline.

branch current   the current through a parallel branch.

branch line   see *branch circuit.*

branch resistance   the total resistance of a parallel branch.

branch voltage   the voltage across a parallel branch.

brass   an alloy of copper and zinc.

braze welding   a weld produced by heat and a filler metal without the help of capillary action.

brazing   a method of joining metals with nonferrous filler (without iron) using heat between 800°F and the melting point of the base metal.

brazing filler metal   a metal or alloy used to fill the space between the two parts being joined.

brazing sheet   brazing filler material in sheet form.

brazing temperature   the temperature to which the base metal is heated for brazing.

break   electrical discontinuity in a circuit generally resulting from the operation of a switch or circuit breaker.

break lines   used on blueprints when you cannot see the whole object. They are also used to show that, to save space, the full length of the object has not been shown. When the break on the drawing is long, long break lines are used. Short breaks are used when the break is short, such as across a beam.

breakdown torque   the maximum torque that a motor will develop under increasing load conditions without an abrupt drop in speed and power.

breakdown voltage   that voltage at which an insulator or dielectric conducts current.

breaker   a device usually used in a breaker panel that is capable of being used as a disconnect switch and an overload for the circuit it is supplying power to. Can be either thermal or current-activated.

breaker panel   an electric panel that houses breakers used to distribute power to circuits in the structure.

breaker points   metal contacts that open and close a circuit at timed intervals.

breaker strip   a strip of wood or plastic used to cover the joint between the outside case and the inside liner of a refrigerator.

breakout   a term used to define a wire or group of wires in a multiconductor configuration which terminates somewhere other than at the end of the configuration.

breeching   a passageway to conduct flue gases from the furnace or boiler to the chimney. Also called flue pipe or vent connector.

bridge circuit   an electrical network arranged so that the voltage at a given point in the circuit can be zeroed by adjusting the electrical parameters (resistance, inductance, and capacitance) in the branches until the currents balance.

bridge rectifier   a device constructed with four diodes that converts both positive and negative cycles of AC voltage into DC voltage. The bridge rectifier is one type of full wave rectifier.

brine   a solution of water and salt to prevent the freezing of water below 32°F.

bring-up time   the time required to raise a cold furnace to operating temperature.

British thermal unit (Btu)   the means to define and measure heat energy. One Btu will raise the temperature of one pound (approximately one pint) of water 1°F from 62° to 63°. One Btu will also raise the temperature of approximately 55 cubic feet of air from 70° to 71°F. This is equivalent to the heat content of a standard kitchen match completely burned. The rate of heat transfer, whether heating or cooling, is expressed in

Btu per hour (Btu/h). Heating and cooling equipment capacity is rated on this basis. Also defined as 778.169 foot-pounds.

bronze   an alloy of eight or nine parts of copper and one part of tin.

Brown and Sharpe   the former name of the American Wire Gauge system of designation of wire sizes.

brown-out   low line voltage which can cause misoperation of and possible damage to equipment.

brush   (1) sliding contact made of carbon and graphite that makes connections to a rotating armature in a generator or motor. (2) An instrument used to apply paste soldering flux to items to be soldered.

Btu meter   a device that indicates to an operator how many Btu are being generated by a unit.

bucket brigade   a colloquial term for the electronic self-checking circuitry in the flame signal amplifier of some flame safeguard controls. The term refers to the periodic discharging (dumping) of one capacitor in the circuit into another. If this dumping stops due to a failure in the flame detection system, the control shuts down the burner.

bucket trap, inverted   a float trap with an open float. The float or bucket is open at the bottom. When the air or steam in the bucket has been replaced by condensation, the bucket loses its buoyancy, sinks, and opens a valve to permit the condensate to be pushed into the return.

bucket trap, open   the bucket (float) is open at the top. Water surrounding the bucket keeps it floating and the pin is pressed against the seat. Condensate from the system drains into the bucket. When enough condensate has drained into it so that the bucket loses its buoyancy, it sinks and pulls the pin off its seat and steam pressure forces the condensate out of the trap.

buff   to finish or polish on a buffing wheel composed of fabric with abrasive powders.

buffer   a digital circuit element that may be used to handle a large fan-out or to invert input and output values.

building   a separate and distinct structure.

building automation system   a centralized control system which organizes the many tasks of operating a building into manageable segments. These segments include gathering data, analyzing data, and taking corrective action. Also referred to as a facilities management system.

building envelope   the exterior surfaces of a building—specifically, walls, roof, and floor (if over unheated basement, slab, or crawlspace).

building-related illness   a term that refers to a discrete, identifiable disease or illness which can be traced to a specific pollutant or source within a building.

building wire   wire used for light and power in permanent installations utilizing 600 volts or less. Usually in an enclosure which will not be exposed to outdoor environments.

bulb, sensing   that part of a sealed fluid device which reacts to the temperature to be measured or which will control a mechanism.

bull dog snips   hand-operated tin snips used to cut 24- to 16-gauge metal. They can be used to cut either straight or medium-sized outside circles and curves.

bull head tee   the installation of a pipe tee in such a way that water enters (or leaves) the tee at both ends of the run (the straight-through section of the tee) and leaves (or enters) through the side connection only.

bunch strand   any number of conductor strands twisted together in one direction with the same lay length.

bunker   in commercial installations, the space in which ice or a cooling element is installed.

bunker "C"   a term for heavy oil.

Bunsen-type burner   a gas burner in which combustion air is injected into the burner by the gas jet emerging from the gas orifice; the air is premixed with the gas supply within the burner body before the gas burns on the burner port.

buried cable   cable which lies below the grade surface. Also called direct burial cable.

burner   a device which introduces fuel and air properly mixed and in the correct proportions into a combustion chamber where the mixture is burned and the products of combustion removed. Burner types are injection, atmospheric, power, and yellow flame. Also see *atmospheric, atomizing oil, automatic, automatically ignited, combination, inshot, long flame, main, manually ignited, multiport, nozzle mixing, partial-premix, power, premix, raw gas, rotary oil, semiautomatic, upshot,* and *warm-up burners.*

burner controller   an automatic temperature- or pressure-sensing device connected in the input circuit of a flame safeguard control. It indirectly acts to turn a burner on or off in order to maintain pressure, air temperature, water temperature, or liquid level within the desired limits.

burner, fan   centrifugal-type fan, located inside the burner assembly, that supplies primary air for mixing with the fuel.

burner flexibility   the degree at which a burner can operate with reasonable characteristics with a variety of fuel gases and/or variation in input rate (gas pressure).

burner head   that end of a burner beyond the nozzle or ports.

burner input control valve   see *firing rate valve.*

burner motor   the motor which drives the blower or fan that delivers air at proper velocity into the combustion chamber. With an oil burner assembly the burner motor also operates the fuel pump unit.

burner refractory   see *refractory.*

burning speed   the speed that the flame travels through the gas/air mixture.

burning velocity   see *flame propagation rate.*

burnish   to finish or polish by pressure upon a smooth rolling or sliding tool.

burnout   accidental passage of high voltage which causes damage through an electrical circuit or device.

burr   a fine feathered or jagged edge on the inside surface of materials resulting from punching or cutting.

bus   a path over which digital information is transferred, from any of several sources to any of several destinations. Only one transfer of information can take place at any one time. While such transfer of information is taking place, all other sources that are being used and are tied to the bus must be disabled.

bus bar   a primary power distribution source which is connected to a main power source. Usually a heavy, rigid metallic bar or strap which carries a large current and makes a common connection between several circuits. Bus bars are usually uninsulated and located where the service enters the building.

bus, bidirectional   a twisted pair of wires over which two-way communications are transmitted between the controller and controlled devices.

bushing   a usually removable lining or sleeve of metal or other material that is inserted or screwed into an opening to limit its size, resist wear or erosion, serve as a guide, or protect wires from abrasion and possible short circuit. An internally and externally threaded plug for connecting a pipe or fitting it with another of a different size.

butane   a gaseous hydrocarbon fuel; also, a mixture of easily liquefiable hydrocarbon gases, principally butane. Butane is one of the components of raw natural gas and is also refined from petroleum refining processes. Its chemical formula is C_4H_{10}, maximum burning speed is 33 inches per second, ignition temperature is 800°F, and specific gravity is 2.0.

butterfly damper   a single-blade damper, pivoted about its center. The blade somewhat resembles the opened wings of a butterfly.

butterfly valve   a throttling valve for a pipe, consisting of a rotating hinged plate that somewhat resembles the open wings of a butterfly. It is often used as a firing rate valve. This type of valve does not close tightly, so a separate safety shutoff valve must be used with it for final close-off.

Bx cable   a flexible armored electric cable.

bypass   a pipe or duct, usually controlled by a valve or damper, for conveying a fluid around an element of a system.

bypass, hot-gas   a connection from the discharge directly to the suction side of the compressor. Sometimes used as a means of capacity control.

bypass line   tubing that permits refrigerant flow to bypass the expansion valve when the coil is operating as a condenser in a heat pump installation.

bypass, relief   a connection from the discharge directly to the suction side of the compressor, made either internally or externally. A port which opens at a set point and relieves abnormally high discharge pressure to the suction side of the compressor.

bypass, switch   a function of a timing device whereby the circuit across a control mechanism is de-energized until a desired state has been achieved, e.g., until a desired temperature or pressure has been reached.

byte   a group of eight contiguous bits that occupy a single memory location in a microcomputer or computer.

C

C   (1) thermal conductance; (2) centigrade.

CAA   Clean Air Act.

CABO   Council of American Building Officials.

CAGI   Compressed Air and Gas Institute.

cap   (1) capacity; (2) capacitor.

cat   catalog.

CBAC   Commercial Building Air Conditioning Center.

cc   closing coil.

ccw   counterclockwise.

CDA   Copper Development Association.

cdh74   cooling-degree hours base 74°F.

CEC   California Energy Commission.

cemf   counterelectromotive force.

CERI   Clean Energy Research Institute.

cf   cubic feet. Standard measurement for natural gas.

cfh   cubic feet per hour.

cfm   cubic feet per minute. A measurement of volume flow. Metric equivalent is m^3/h, cubic meters per hour.

CFR   Code of Federal Regulations.

CGA   Canadian Gas Association.

CI   Combustion Institute.

ckt   circuit.

Cl   chlorine.

clf   cooling load factor.

cond   (1) conductor; (2) condition.

conn   connection.

COP   coefficient of performance.

cp   centipoise.

CPSC   Consumer Products Safety Commission.

CPU   central processing unit.

CPVC   chlorinated polyvinyl chloride.

CRMA   Commercial Refrigerator Manufacturers Association.

CSA Canadian Standards Association, or Cryogenic Society of America Inc.

CSI Construction Specifications Institute.

csr acronym for capacitor-start, capacitor-run motor.

CTI Cooling Tower Institute.

CV capacity index.

cw clockwise.

cw/ccw reversible.

CWA Clean Water Act.

C factor the amount of heat, in Btu, conducted through one square foot of a material of a specified thickness, per hour, per degree of temperature difference.

cabinet an enclosure used to house branch circuit connections and protective devices.

cable an arrangement of conductors in a protective covering. It is arranged so that the conductors can be used separately or in groups. Small cable is called stranded wire or cord.

cable joint a connection of two or more lengths of cable. Often called a splice.

CAD cell see *cadmium sulfide cell.*

CADD computer aided drafting and design. Sometimes referred to as CAD.

cadmium alloys brazing alloys containing cadmium, which is a toxic metal when molten, emitting highly poisonous cadmium oxide fumes that can cause illness or death.

cadmium plated describes parts that have a thin corrosion-resistant covering of cadmium metal.

cadmium sulfide cell (cad cell) a photoconductive device that responds to visible light. In the presence of visible light, the electrical resistance of the cadmium sulfide becomes very low and the cell conducts current. The cad cell is used in flame detectors for oil burner systems.

cage valve a single-seated valve containing a flame or box (cage) inside of which the plug slides, opening the ports.

calcium a soft, silver-white metallic element found in chemical compounds in limestone, chalk, marble, etc. An element that is often dissolved in water, causing hardness.

calcium chloride $CaCl_2$, a chemical used to absorb moisture from refrigerants.

calcium sulfate a chemical compound ($CaSO_4$) which is used as a drying agent or desiccant in liquid line driers.

calibrate to reposition indicators as required to obtain accurate measurements.

calibration the systematic adjustment of graduations so that the actual output matches the desired output.

calipers instrument for measuring both inside and outside diameters.

call for heat a condition where the controlled temperature or pressure drops below the operating set point, and the burner controller contacts initiate burner operation.

callback a return trip to a piece of equipment that was not properly serviced the first time.

calorie two different calorie units are used by scientists. (1) The calorie used by medical science. It is a small heat unit. It equals the quantity of heat required to raise the temperature of one gram of water from 4°C to 5°C. (2) The calorie used by engineering science. It is a large heat unit. It is equal to the amount of heat required to raise the temperature of one kilogram of water 1°C. In the SI system it is recommended that the joule unit of energy be used in place of the calorie.

calorimeter a device used to measure quantities of heat or to determine specific heats.

cam a mechanical component which is oblong, giving a reciprocating motion when rotated.

Canadian Standards Association (CSA) an organization in Canada that sets safety standards for motors and electrical equipment.

candle a unit of luminous intensity or brightness.

candling (candlelighting) the deterioration of the pilot to an unsatisfactory condition, characterized by a lazy, yellow flame. It is usually caused by a high ambient temperature or an excessively large pilot burner orifice.

cap a fitting which seals off the end of a pipe or tubing.

capacitance property of a nonconductor (condenser or capacitor) that permits the storage of electrical energy in an electrostatic field. The inherent property of an electric circuit that opposes a change in voltage.

capacitive circuit a circuit that contains at least one capacitor.

capacitive coupling electrical interaction between two conductors caused by the capacitance between them.

capacitive load a leading load; a load that is predominantly capacitive, so that the alternating current leads the alternating voltage, i.e., the voltage does not change direction until after the corresponding current does.

capacitive reactance the opposition or resistance to an alternating current as a result of capacitance; expressed in ohms.

capacitor an electrical storage device that consists of two conductive metal plates with a dielectric insulator between the plates. It is used to boost voltage for a single-phase wound motor. The two types of capacitors are starting (electrolytic) and running (oil filled). Capacitors are rated in microfarads. Also, an electrical condenser used for power factor correction.

capacitor analyzer an instrument that determines whether a capacitor is open or shorted and whether it is within its micro-farad ratings and operating at the correct power factor percentage.

capacitor-start motor a modified version of the split-phase motor, employing a capacitor in series with its starting winding to produce a phase displacement for starting.

capacitor-start, induction-run motor type of motor commonly used in situations where the motor must start under a heavy load, but once started can operate with just the run winding.

capacitor-start, capacitor-run motor a motor with a high starting torque and good running efficiency. It utilizes a start capacitor to increase starting torque and a run capacitor to increase running efficiency. This type of motor must be used in single-phase refrigeration systems that use a thermostatic expansion valve as the metering device.

capacity (1) a measure of the ability of air-conditioning equipment to remove or add heat. Usually given in terms of Btu/h or watts (metric). (2) The ability to hold, contain, or absorb.

capacity charge see *demand charge*.

capacity, condensing unit the refrigerating effect in Btu/h produced by the difference in total enthalpy between refrigerant liquid leaving the unit and the total enthalpy of the refrigerant vapor entering the unit. Generally measured in tons or Btu/h.

capacity control term used for various methods of control intended to prevent the compressor from cycling on and off.

capacity control actuator a device which responds to variations in the suction pressure and proportions a fluid pressure to a mechanism on the cylinder liner which loads or unloads the compressor cylinders.

capacity, cooler refrigerating, net the rate of heat removal from a fluid flowing through a cooler (air, water, brine, etc.). At stated conditions, it is the difference in specific enthalpies of the cooling fluid entering and leaving the cooler; the latent heat of fusion and the subcooling heat of the ice (frost) must be added in determining the net cooler refrigerating capacity.

capacity, expansion valve   the refrigerating effect in Btu/h, or tons, each of 12,000 Btu/h produced by the evaporation of refrigerant passed by the valve under specified conditions.

capacity, heat   the amount of heat necessary to raise the temperature of a given mass one degree. Numerically, the mass multiplied by the specific heat.

capacity, ice-making   actual productive ability of a system making ice. This is less than the rated (ice making) capacity since some refrigeration is used in cooling the water to freezing point, cooling the ice below the freezing point, and overcoming heat leakage.

capacity, ice-melting   refrigeration equal to the latent heat of fusion of a stated weight of ice at 144 Btu/h.

capacity, ice-melting equivalent   the amount of heat absorbed by one pound of ice at 32°F in liquefying to water at 32°F, or 144 Btu.

capacity index (CV)   the quantity of water, in gallons per minute at 60°F, that flows through a given valve with a pressure drop of one psi. The flow of any fluid through the same valve can be calculated from the CV. Also called flow coefficient.

capacity modulation   a method of varying the capacity of a compressor.

capacity modulation, compressor   a mechanism to control the capacity of a compressor by rendering one or more cylinders ineffective.

capacity modulation, cylinder   the method used for modulating the capacity of a compressor cylinder by interrupting the normal action of the suction valve. Usually activated by a device controlled by electricity or oil pressure.

capacity modulation, multistep compressor   a compressor capacity modulation system arranged to reduce capacity in two or more consecutive steps.

capacity modulation, single-step compressor   a compressor capacity modulation system arranged to reduce capacity in one step. Usually reduces capacity to one-half of full capacity.

capacity, peak   output of a machine or system for a short time under an extreme load.

capacity reducer   in a compressor, a device such as a clearance pocket, movable cylinder head, or suction bypass by which compressor capacity can be adjusted without otherwise changing the operating conditions.

capacity, refrigerating   (1) the ability of a refrigeration system, or part thereof, to remove heat expressed as a rate of heat removal, usually measured in Btu/h or tons/24 hr. (2) The rate of heat removed from a medium or space to be cooled, at stated conditions. The term refrigerating effect is used to denote heat transfer to or from the refrigerant itself in a refrigerating system, whereas the term refrigerating capacity is used to denote the rate of heat removal from a medium or space to be cooled.

capacity, refrigerating, gross   the total rate of heat removal from all sources by the evaporator of a refrigerating system at stated conditions. It is numerically equal to the system refrigerating effect.

capacity, refrigerating, net   the remaining rate of heat removal from all sources by the evaporator of a refrigerating system, at stated conditions, after deducting internal and external heat transfers to the evaporator that occur before distribution of the refrigerating medium and after its return.

capacity, refrigerating, useful   the refrigerating capacity available for the specific ultimate cooling function for which the system was designed.

capacity, refrigerating, volumetric   the refrigerating capacity of a system per unit volume of refrigerant circulated at the compressor suction.

capacity, useful latent (dehumidifying)   the available refrigerating capacity of an air conditioner for removing latent heat from the space to be conditioned.

capacity, useful sensible   the available refrigerating capacity of an air conditioner for removing sensible heat from the space to be conditioned.

capillary action   the phenomenon of liquid rising in a small interstice due to surface tension.

capillary tube   a type of refrigerant metering device. Usually consists of several feet of tubing having a small inside diameter. Selection criteria are based on length and inside diameter. Friction of liquid refrigerant and bubbles of vaporized refrigerant within the tube serve to restrict flow so that correct high- and low-side pressures are maintained while the compressor is operating. A capillary tube refrigerant control allows high- and low-side pressures to balance during the off cycle. Also a small-diameter tubing used to connect temperature control bulbs to control mechanisms.

capillary tube cleaner   a service tool used to apply up to 15,000 psi of pressure to force and clear any obstruction out of the interior of the tube.

capital investment   an expenditure for an investment whose returns are expected to extend beyond one year.

carbon   one of the elements used in refrigeration.

carbon dioxide (CO$_2$)   a heavy (1.5 times as heavy as air), colorless gas produced by the combustion and decomposition of organic substances and as a by-product of many chemical processes. CO$_2$ will not burn and is relatively nontoxic and unreactive. High concentrations, especially in confined spaces, can create hazardous oxygen-deficient environments that can cause asphyxiation. It is useful as a fire extinguishing agent because it blocks the oxygen and smothers the fire. It is also used as a refrigerant. Its refrigerant number is R-744.

carbon filter   an air filter using activated carbon as an air-cleansing agent.

carbon monoxide (CO)   a colorless, odorless, flammable, and very toxic gas produced by the incomplete combustion of carbon compounds and as a by-product of many chemical processes. A chemical asphyxiant, it reduces the blood's ability to carry oxygen. Hemoglobin absorbs CO two hundred times more readily than it does oxygen.

carbon monoxide indicator   a test instrument used to check flue gas samples of fossil fuel units to determine percent of carbon monoxide present.

carbon steel   by common custom, steel is considered to be carbon steel when no minimum content is specified or required for aluminum, boron, chromium, cobalt, columbium, molybdenum, nickel, titanium, tungsten, vanadium, zirconium, or any other element added to obtain a desired alloying effect; when the specified minimum for copper does not exceed 0.40 percent; or when the maximum content specified for any of the following elements does not exceed the percentages noted: manganese, 1.65; silicon, 0.60; copper, 0.60.

carbon tetrachloride   a colorless, nonflammable, and very toxic liquid used as a solvent. It should never be allowed to touch skin, and its fumes must not be inhaled.

carbonization   formation of carbonaceous deposits which may be produced by decomposition of lubricating oil or other organic materials.

carburize   to heat a low-carbon steel to approximately 2000°F in contact with material which adds carbon to the surface of the steel, and to cool it slowly in preparation for heat treatment.

carburizing flame   the flame (also called a reducing flame) that results from supplying excess acetylene.

carcinogen   a chemical that has been demonstrated to cause cancer in animals and, therefore, is considered capable of causing cancer in humans. Findings are based on the feeding of abnormally large quantities of a chemical to test animals or by the application of concentrated solutions to the animal's skin. A chemical is considered to be a carcinogen if (1) it has been evaluated by the International Agency for Research on Cancer and found to be a carcinogen or potential carcinogen; (2) it is listed as a carcinogen in the annual report on carcinogens published by the National Toxicology Program; (3) it is regulated by OSHA as a carcinogen; (4) if one positive study has been published.

cargo, chilled   cargo maintained at an assigned temperature above its freezing point.

cargo, refrigerated   cargo maintained at an assigned temperature by means of mechanical refrigeration.

Carnot cycle   a sequence of operations forming the reversible working cycle of an ideal heat engine of maximum thermal efficiency. It consists of isothermal expansion, adiabatic expansion, isothermal compression, and adiabatic compression to the initial state.

carrene   a chemical combination of carbon, chlorine, and fluorine. A refrigerant in Group 1. It is referred to as R-11.

carrying capacity   the ability of a conductor to carry a current, expressed in amperes.

carryover   (1) the spillage of water, from a boiler, into steam lines. (2) The crossover of flame from one burner to another.

cartridge fuse   a large-ampere-capacity fuse consisting of a current-responsive element inside a fuse tube with terminals on both ends that fit into special holders.

CAS number   an assigned number used to identify a material. CAS stands for Chemical Abstracts Service, a Columbus, Ohio based organization that indexes information published in chemical abstracts by the American Chemical Society and provides index guides by which information about particular substances may be located in the abstracts when needed. CAS numbers identify specific chemicals and are assigned sequentially. The number is useful because it is a concise, unique means of material identification.

cascade system   an arrangement in which two or more refrigerating systems are used in series. It uses the cooling coil of one machine to cool the condenser of another machine. This type of system produces ultra-low temperatures.

case   in a commercial installation, an individual cooling system. A grocery store will typically have a number of cases operating at different temperatures.

case-hardening   heat-treating ferrous metals (iron) to make the surface layer harder than the interior or core.

casement window   a window that is attached by vertical hinges and swings out to open.

casing   an enclosure forming the outside of an appliance, no parts of which are likely to be subjected to intense heat.

casing loss   heat loss through the walls of a heater or furnace to the space surrounding the appliance.

cast brass   brass that is cast in sand molds and is used for water valve housings and boat propellers.

cast iron   iron melted and poured into molds that usually has a rough texture.

Cast iron has a gray, grainy appearance. It is a ferrous metal and can be brazed or fusion welded with an oxyacetylene torch.

cast iron sectional boiler   a boiler composed of a number of separate sections fastened together, resulting in a large heat transfer area. It can be fired by an upshot or inshot gas burner or by a pressure-atomizing oil burner.

casting   making an object by pouring molten metal into a mold.

catalytic combustion stove   a stove that contains a cell-like structure consisting of a substance, washcoat, and catalyst producing a chemical reaction which causes pollutants to be burned at a much lower temperature.

categories   classes or divisions in a system of classification.

cathode   the negative terminal of an electrical device, for example, the N region of a P-N junction diode. Electrons leave the device at this terminal.

cathode ray tube (CRT)   a large vacuum tube in which electrons emitted from a cathode are formed into a narrow beam and accelerated so that upon striking a phosphorescent screen a visible pattern of light energy is produced.

cation   a positively charged ion, which is attracted to the cathode during electrolysis.

caulk   to fill cracks and seams with caulking compound.

caustic embrittlement   this refers to the cracking of boiler steel occurring while the boiler is in service but not subjected to excessive pressure or temperature. Such failures are attributed to the boiler water's being too caustic, that is, too alkaline.

cauterizing flame   a flame that results from too much acetylene.

cavitation   localized gaseous condition that is found within a liquid stream.

cds cell   acronym for photoresistant cell made of cadmium sulfide. This solid-state device changes its electrical resistance when exposed to light. Used on oil burners as a safety burner shutdown device.

ceiling outlet   a round, square, rectangular, or linear air diffuser located in the ceiling which provides a horizontal distribution pattern of primary and secondary air over the occupied zone and induces low-velocity secondary air motion through the occupied zone.

cell   a single unit that produces voltage or current by converting chemical or radiant energy into electrical energy. Also see *cadmium sulfide* and *lead sulfide cells*.

Celsius   German word for centigrade. It refers to the metric system temperature scale originated by Andrew Celsius, in which 0° equals the freezing point of water and 100° equals the boiling point.

center distance   when applied to speed reducers, the distance between the center lines of the input (high speed) shaft and the output (low speed) shaft. Shaft center lines may be parallel or at right angles to each other. Center distance is often used to designate a single reduction worm gear speed reducer, such as 1.33″, 1.75″.

center drill   a special drill to produce bearing holes in the ends of a work piece to be mounted between centers. Also called a combined drill and countersink.

center lines   center lines on blueprints showing the centers of the objects in the building which can be divided into two equal halves. They are not used for the entire building but are used to show the centers of columns, equipment, and fixtures. This line is light in weight and is shown as alternate long and short dashes.

center punch   a tool that has a 60° to 90° point and is generally used for starting detailed drilling work.

center tap a connection at the electrical center of a winding, or midway between the electrical ends of a resistor or other portion of a circuit. Commonly used in the secondary of a transformer with 240 volts on the primary to provide two 120-volt branch circuits from the secondary.

centigrade a temperature scale that is divided into 100° increments, on which water boils at 100° and freezes at 0°. Its abbreviation is "C." See also *Celsius*.

centimeter metric unit of linear measurement which equals 0.3937 inches. One hundredth part of a meter.

centipoise the metric measure of viscosity of a liquid.

central control a system whereby all data analysis and control actions are performed at a single point.

central fan system a mechanical indirect system of heating, ventilating, or air-conditioning consisting of a central plant where air is heated and/or conditioned and then circulated by fans or blowers through a system of distributing ducts.

central furnace a self-contained, indirect fired furnace designed to supply heated air through ducts to spaces remote from or adjacent to the furnace location.

central heater a stationary, indirect fired, vented appliance in one of three classes: boilers; central furnaces, floor furnaces, and recessed furnaces; and floor-mounted unit heaters connected to a duct system.

central processing unit (CPU) that section of a computer that controls all information transfers and arithmetic operations in the computer. In most computers, it also controls the sequence of operations and initiates the proper commands to the computer circuits after decoding an instruction.

central station central location of a condensing unit with either a wet- or an air-cooled condenser. The evaporator is located as needed and connected to the central condensing unit.

centralized computerized controller energy control device, centrally located, which makes control decisions based on operating data, programmed information, and stored data. Can be used to optimize energy consumption of many devices throughout a building.

centrifugal moving or tending to move away from the center.

centrifugal atomizing oil burner see *rotary oil burner*.

centrifugal blowers air-moving devices in which the airflow is perpendicular to the shaft on which the wheel is mounted. The wheel is mounted in a scroll-type housing which is necessary to develop the rated pressures. The four classes of centrifugal blowers are determined by wheel blade position with respect to the direction of rotation.

centrifugal compressor compressor which compresses gaseous refrigerants by centrifugal force. It is not positive displacement but it is similar to a blower. A compressor used for large refrigeration systems.

centrifugal fan a fan rotor or wheel within a scroll-type housing which includes driving mechanism supports for either belt or direct drive.

centrifugal force the force that an object moving along a circular path exerts on the body constraining the object and that acts outwardly away from the center of rotation.

centrifugal pump a fan-shaped impeller rotating in a circular housing, pushing liquid towards a discharge opening. Usually used where large flow of liquid at relatively low pressure (head or lift) is desired.

centrifugal switch a switch that is wired in series with the start capacitor and/or start winding. When the motor reaches approximately 75% of its total rpm, the device opens and disconnects either the start capacitor or start winding from the circuit. The switch then closes when the motor slows to approximately 50% of total rpm.

ceramic   pertaining to a product made from inorganic, nonmetallic materials fused or fired at high temperatures. Used as an insulation in cables when extremely high temperatures are to be encountered.

ceramic ignitor   electric ignition system used to create ignition of the gas/air mixture in the combustion chamber.

ceramic radiants   clay insulators which act as heat radiators when they themselves are heated.

certified refrigerant recycling or recovery equipment   equipment certified by an approved equipment testing organization as meeting EPA standards.

chain tongs   used in place of a pipe wrench when installing very large pipe. A chain takes the place of the upper hook jaw used in the common pipe wrench, making it easier to handle.

chain wrench   this wrench is a type of pipe wrench. It is adjustable and can work more easily in confined areas and on round, square, or irregularly-shaped objects.

chamfer   a narrow inclined surface along the intersection of two surfaces.

change of air   introduction of new air to a conditioned space, measured by the number of complete enclosed space changes per unit time (usually per hour).

change of state   the process that a substance (either a compound or element) goes through when changing from one physical state to another. An example of this would be when water becomes ice or water becomes steam.

change plate   holds the post in place and allows the dies to recede to make the taper on the thread. The change plate must be between the two standard marks when starting a thread.

changeover   the process of switching an air-conditioning system from heating to cooling, or vice versa.

channel   a conductive path through a semiconductor between the source and the drain.

characterized guide   a valve guide with notches or Vs cut into it to determine the valve flow characteristic. It is also known as a skirted guide.

charge   a load; the maximum or necessary quantity that a container or apparatus is built to accommodate, e.g., fuel in a furnace. (1) In electricity, it is the electrical energy stored in a capacitor or battery or held on an insulated object. (2) In refrigeration, it is the amount of refrigerant in a system or the putting of refrigerant into a system.

charge, basic   amount of refrigerant placed in a refrigerating unit.

charge, holding   evaporators and replacement compressors are shipped with a holding charge to prevent the entrance of air and moisture. This charge may be either nitrogen or refrigerant.

charge, operating   the total amount of refrigerant required by a system for correct operation.

charge, test   an amount of gas forced into a refrigerating system for leak testing purposes.

charging board   a specially designed panel or cabinet fitted with gauges, valves, and refrigerant cylinders used for charging refrigerant and oil into the refrigeration system.

charging cylinder   a calibrated container by which a predetermined weight of refrigerant may be charged or dispensed into a refrigeration system. Commonly used on small systems.

charging, electrical   the storing of electrical energy.

charging hose   a flexible plastic or rubber hose, capable of withstanding high system pressures and used to transfer refrigerant from one component to another. Charging hoses are designed for a working pressure of 500 psi and an average breaking or bursting pressure of 2000 psi.

charging manifold   a device specifically designed for technicians to charge, evacuate, and recover refrigerant into and out of refrigerating and air-conditioning units.

charging, refrigerant   the procedure of adding refrigerant to the system.

charging station   a piece of equipment used to charge a unit, an appliance, or an automobile's air-conditioning unit. The station includes a vacuum pump, a charging cylinder, manifold gauges, and other useful charging instruments.

Charles' law   a gas law that explains the relationship between pressure and volume. It states: "At a constant pressure, the volume of a confined gas varies directly as the absolute temperature; at a constant volume, the pressure varies directly as the absolute temperature."

chase   (1) to cut threads with an external cutting tool. (2) An opening for piping, ductwork, and wiring in a multistory construction.

chaser dies   steel tools for cutting or finishing screw threads.

chassis   a sheet-metal box, frame, or single plate on which the components of a device are mounted; the assembled frame and parts.

chatter   the rapid opening and closing of a relay or solenoid due to a malfunction. Also see *relay chatter.*

cheater   pipe extension used to increase leverage of a wrench. Not recommended for safety reasons.

check valve   a flow control device which permits fluid flow in only one direction.

checking relay   a relay in the self-checking circuit of some flame safeguard controls which makes and breaks periodically (checking or pecking action) when the flame signal is strong enough. While checking, it transfers energy to hold in the flame relay. It stops checking if the flame signal becomes too weak or disappears.

cheek   the side of a hammer head.

chemical cell   a source of DC electricity which converts chemical energy into electrical energy.

chemical instability   the tendency of substances to break down into other, possibly corrosive substances.

chemical sensitivity   the development in humans of health problems characterized by effects such as dizziness, eye and throat irritation, chest tightness, and nasal congestion that appear whenever they are exposed to certain chemicals. People may react to even trace amounts of chemicals to which they have become sensitized.

chill   to harden the outer surface of cast iron by quick cooling, as in a metal mold.

chill factor   calculated number based on temperature and wind velocity.

chilled water system   a closed, circulating cooling system in which a mechanical refrigerating system at a central location cools water which is then piped to various parts of the building.

chiller   an air-conditioning system which circulates chilled water to various cooling coils in an installation.

chiller, dry-expansion   a device designed to utilize the evaporation of refrigerant within a tube bundle, the refrigerant being metered to the inside of the tubes by means of one or more thermostatic expansion valves. The liquid to be chilled passes through the chiller between the shell and tubes.

chiller, flooded   a device designed to utilize the evaporation of refrigerant on the outside surface of a tube bundle with the refrigerant level being maintained by a float valve. The liquid to be chilled passes through the tubes of the chiller.

chiller purge unit a system that removes air and noncondensables from a low-pressure chiller.

chilling (cooling) the lowering of the temperature of a substance by the removal of heat in the temperature range above freezing.

chilling room room where products are cooled prior to cold storage.

chimney a vertical shaft enclosing one or more flues for conveying flue gases to the outside atmosphere. Can be one of the following types:
1. factory-built chimney - a chimney composed of listed factory-built components assembled in accordance with the terms of listing to form the completed chimney.
2. masonry chimney - a field-constructed chimney of solid masonry units, bricks, stones, listed masonry chimney units, or reinforced portland cement concrete, lined with suitable chimney flue liners.
3. metal chimney - a field-constructed chimney of metal.

chimney connector the pipe which connects a fuel-burning appliance to the chimney. It is also called a smoke pipe.

chimney effect the tendency of air or gas in a duct or other vertical passage to rise when heated due to its lower density compared with that of the surrounding air or gas. In buildings, the tendency toward displacement (caused by the difference in temperature) of internal heated air by unheated outside air due to the difference in density of outside and inside air.

chimney flue flue gas passageway in a chimney.

chip to cut away metal with a cold chisel.

chips excess pieces broken off; fragments.

chisel a hand tool with a cutting edge at one end and used to cut when struck on the blunt end with a hammer.

chlorinated polyvinyl chloride (CPVC) type of plastic pipe and fittings made from chlorinated polyvinyl chloride that can be used at temperatures up to 180°F at 100 psig.

chlorine monoxide a chemical compound with a molecule made of one oxygen atom and one chlorine atom. It is found in the stratosphere when ozone depletion is taking place. By measuring chlorine monoxide, scientists can determine the degree of ozone depletion.

chlorofluorocarbon (CFC) any of several compounds made up of carbon, chlorine, and fluorine. CFCs were used as aerosol propellants and refrigerants until they were found to be harmful to the earth's protective ozone layer.

choke an inductor designed to present an impedance to AC current, or to be the current filter of a DC power supply.

choke coil an inductor coil used to block the flow of AC current and pass DC current.

choke tube a throttling device used to maintain correct pressure difference between the high and low sides of the refrigeration system. Capillary tubes are sometimes called choke tubes.

chronic health effect an adverse effect on a human or animal body with symptoms that develop slowly over a long period of time or that recur frequently.

chronic toxicity adverse or chronic effects resulting from repeated doses of, or exposures to, a substance over a relatively prolonged period of time. Ordinarily used to denote effects noted in experimental animals.

chuck a mechanism for holding a rotating tool or workpiece.

circuit a tubing, piping, or electrical wire installation which permits flow from the energy source back to the energy source.

circuit breaker   a safety device designed to open and close a circuit by nonautomatic means, and to open the circuit automatically on a predetermined overload of current, without injury to itself when properly applied within its rating. There are thermal and magnetic types.

circuit, electrical   an electron path that completes a loop. A circuit generally consists of a power source, conductors, a load, and a switch to control the current flow.

circuit main   the portion of the main in a multiple circuit system that carries only a part of the total capacity of the system.

circuit, parallel   an arrangement of electrical devices in which all positive terminals are joined to one conductor and all negative terminals to the other conductor. It is considered to be a current divider circuit when the voltage is the same across all load circuits.

circuit, pilot   secondary circuit used to control a main circuit or a device in the main circuit.

circuit protection devices   fuses and circuit breakers.

circuit, refrigerating   the assembly of refrigerant containing parts and their connections used in a refrigerating cycle.

circuit, series   electrical path in which electricity must pass through all loads and then back to the energy source. It is considered to be a voltage divider circuit when the current is the same through all parts of the circuit.

circuit switching   an on-off control function. Conduction occurs during the on time with no conduction during the off time.

circular mil   the area of a circle .001 inch in diameter. It is a unit of measurement used to express wire cross-sectional area.

circulating loop   the main loop in which oil is circulated from the storage tanks to the branch circuits and then back to the storage tanks.

circulation   the free flow of fluids.

circulator   a motor-driven device used to mechanically circulate water in a system. Also called a pump.

circumference   the perimeter of a circle.

circumscribe   to draw a line around.

clamp-on ammeter   a current-measuring device with jaws that are placed around a single current-carrying conductor. The clamp-on ammeter measures current by sensing the strength of the magnetic field around the conductor.

clamshells   sections of the heat exchanger. Burners fit into special openings in the bottom of the clamshells.

Class I atmospheres

Group A; acetylene.

Group B; butadiene, ethylene oxide, hydrogen, propylene oxide, manufactured gases containing more than 30% hydrogen by volume.

Group C; acetaldehyde, cyclopropane, diethyl ether, ethylene.

Group D; acetone, acrylonitrile, ammonia, benzene, butane, ethanol, ethylene, dichloride, gasoline, hexane, isoprene, methane (natural gas), methanol, naphtha, propane, propylene, styrene, toluene, vinyl acetate, vinyl chloride, and xylene.

Class II atmospheres

Group E; aluminum, magnesium, and other metal dusts with similar characteristics.

Group F; carbon black, coke, or coal dust.

Group G; flour, starch, or grain dust.

Class III atmospheres   easily ignitable fibers, such as rayon, cotton, sisal, hemp, cocoa fiber, oakum, excelsior, and other materials of similar nature.

Class 10 or 20   refers to time needed for a bimetallic overload relay to trip (disconnect) the motor from the load. Class 10 takes 10 seconds at 6 times the rated trip current. Class 20 takes 20 seconds at 6 times the rated trip current.

Class CC fuses   660-volt, 200,000-ampere interrupting rating, branch circuit fuses with overall dimensions of $13/32''$ × $1.5''$. Their design incorporates a rejection feature that allows them to be inserted into rejection fuse holders and fuse blocks that reject all lower-voltage, lower-interrupting rating $13/32''$ × $1.5''$ fuses. They are available from $1/10$ amp through 30 amps.

Class G fuses   300-volt, 100,000-ampere interrupting rating branch circuit fuses that are size-rejecting to eliminate overfusing. The fuse diameter is $13/32''$ while the length varies from $15/16''$ to $2 1/4''$. These are available in ratings from 1 amp through 60 amps.

Class H fuses   250-volt and 600-volt, 10,000-ampere interrupting rating branch circuit fuses that may be renewable or non-renewable. These are available in ampere ratings of 1 amp through 600 amps.

Class J fuses   these fuses are rated to interrupt 200,000 amperes AC. They are labeled "current-limiting," are rated for 600 volts AC, and are not interchangeable with other classes.

Class K fuses   these are fuses listed as K-1, K-5, or K-9 fuses. Each subclass has designated I^2T and IP maximums. These are dimensionally the same as Class H fuses, and they can have interrupting ratings of 50,000, 100,000, or 200,000 amps. These fuses are current-limiting; however, they are not marked "current-limiting" on their label since they do not have a rejection feature.

Class L fuses   these fuses are rated for 601 through 6,000 amperes, and are rated to interrupt 200,000 amperes AC. They are labelled "current-limiting" and are rated for 600 volts AC. They are intended to be bolted into their mountings and are not normally used in clips. Some Class L fuses have built-in time-delay features for all-purpose use.

Class R fuses   these are high-performance fuses rated from $1/10$ to 600 amps in 250-volt and 600-volt ratings. All are marked "current-limiting" on their labels and all have a 200,000-amp interrupting rating. They have identical outline dimensions with the Class H fuses but have a rejection feature which prevents the user from mounting a fuse of lesser capabilities (lower interrupting capacity) when used with special Class R fuses; will fit into either rejection or nonrejection clips.

Class T fuses   a UL classification of fuses in 300-volt and 600-volt ratings from 1 amp through 1,200 amps. They are physically very small and can be applied where space is at a premium. They are fast-acting fuses, with an interrupting rating of 200,000 amps RMS.

classes of fuses   the industry has developed basic physical specifications and electrical performance requirements for fuses with voltage ratings of 600 volts or less. These are known as standards. If a type of fuse meets the requirements of a standard, it can fall into that class. Typical classes are K, RK1, RK5, G, L, H, T, CC, and J.

classes of refrigerating systems   ASHRAE Standard 34—Number Designation and Safety Classification of Refrigerants— provides an alphanumeric classification system whereby all refrigerants are placed in one of six categories based on flammability and toxicity. An "A" designation indicates low toxicity; "B" higher. Numbers 1, 2, and 3 indicate increasing flammability. Thus A1 is no-flame-propagation, low-toxicity refrigerant; B3 indicates higher-flammability, higher-toxicity refrigerant. This system is used in the ASHRAE Standard 15—Safety Code for Mechanical Refrigeration.

clean room   a specially designed, conditioned space where air cleanliness is critical to the room's function.

clearance   the distance by which one part clears another part.

clearance pocket   a small space in the compressor cylinder from which compressed gas is not completely expelled. This space is called the compressor clearance space or pocket. For effective operation, compressors are designed to have as small a clearance space as possible.

clearance space   the space in the cylinder area not occupied by the piston at the end of the compression stroke, or the volume of gas remaining in cylinder at the same point. Measured in percentage of piston displacement.

clearance volume   the volume at the top of the stroke in a compressor cylinder between the top of the piston and the valve plate.

clearing time   the total time between the beginning of the overcurrent and the final opening of the circuit at rated voltage by an overcurrent protective device. Clearing time is the total of the melting time and the arcing time.

climate   the sum total of weather which takes place over a period of years.

climate control   a space in which an ideal climate is maintained by some devices.

clock   a pulse generator that controls the timing of clocked logic devices and regulates the speed at which such devices operate. It serves to synchronize all operations in a digital system.

clock input   that terminal on a flip-flop whose condition or change of condition controls the admission of data into the flip-flop through the synchronous inputs, thereby controlling the output state of the flip-flop. The clock signal performs two functions: (1) it permits data signals to enter the flip-flop and (2) after entry it directs the flip-flop to change state accordingly.

clock thermostat   a thermostat with a built-in clock which automatically readjusts the control point at a predetermined time at night and restores the daytime setting at another predetermined time in the morning.

clock timer   a time-delay device that uses an electric clock to measure the time delay.

clockwise   from left to right in a circular motion. The direction in which the hands on a clock move.

close nipple   a short section of pipe threaded along its entire length.

closed circuit, electrical   an electrical circuit which forms a complete path so that electrical current can flow through it.

closed-circuit oil system   a system in which oil may be pumped completely through the circulating loop and back into the oil storage tank.

closed container   container sealed by means of a lid or other device so that neither liquid nor vapor will escape from it at ordinary temperatures.

closed cycle   any cycle in which the refrigerant is used over and over again.

closed delta   a four-wire connection that uses three transformers to provide 120-volt single-phase, 240-volt three-phase, and 208-volt (wild leg) power.

closed impeller   see *impeller.*

closed loop   an automatic control system that reflects the results of the controller back to the controller, so that it can again take corrective action if the set point is not being maintained.

close-off   the maximum allowable pressure difference to which a valve may be subjected while fully closed.

close-off rating   the maximum allowable pressure drop to which a valve may be subjected while fully closed. It is a function of the power available from the valve actuator for holding the valve closed and is independent of the valve body rating.

clutch, armature   the part of the automotive compressor magnetic clutch which is attracted by the magnetic field and causes the compressor to be turned on by the belt drive when the magnetic field is energized.

clutch, field   the coils of wire through which the current flows to create the magnetic force which engages the magnetic clutch.

clutch head   a screwdriver used with screws for sheet metal and trim where appearance is important. The tip of the screwdriver is very strong and stays in the screw opening with only a small amount of effort.

clutch, magnetic   a clutch built into an automobile compressor flywheel, operated magnetically, which allows the pulley to revolve without driving compressor when refrigerating effect is not required.

clutch rotor   that part of the clutch that is driven by the belt whether the clutch is engaged or not.

CO₂ indicator   an instrument used to indicate the percentage of carbon dioxide in flue gases.

coal gas   fuel gas produced by the distillation of coal.

coaxial   describes a cable configuration having two cylindrical conductors with coincidental axes, such as a conductor with a tubular shield surrounding the conductor and insulated from it.

cock   a manually operated faucet or valve for shutting off or throttling down the flow of a liquid or gas, usually by means of a tapered plug.

code   the local, state, or national rules that govern safe installation and service of systems and equipment for the purpose of the safety of the public and trade personnel.

code conversion   the changing of the bit grouping for a character in one code into the corresponding bit grouping in another code.

code installation   a refrigeration or air-conditioning installation which conforms to the local or national code for safe and efficient installations.

coefficient of conductivity   the measure of the relative rate at which different materials conduct heat. Copper is a good conductor of heat and, therefore, has a high coefficient of conductivity.

coefficient of coupling (K)   a decimal value that indicates the amount of magnetic coupling between coils.

coefficient of discharge   for an air diffuser, the ratio of net area or effective area to the free area of the opening at vena contracta of an orificed airstream.

coefficient of expansion   increase in unit length, area, or volume for one degree rise in temperature.

coefficient of heat transmission, overall   the amount of heat (Btu) transmitted from air to air in 1 hr/ft^2 of the wall, floor, roof, or ceiling for a difference in temperature of 1° between the air on the inside and outside of the wall, floor, roof, or ceiling. Its symbol is U.

coefficient of performance (COP)   a term used to measure the efficiency of a heating system. It is defined as the heat output of a heat pump or electric elements divided by the heating value of power consumed in watts at standard test conditions of 17° and 47°F.

cogeneration   a process in which a primary source of energy is used to produce a secondary source of energy. An example would be the use of waste heat from an electrical energy generation system to heat a building.

coil   (1) any heating or cooling element made of pipe or tubing connected in series. (2) Wire arranged in a helical or spiral shape which creates a magnetic field when current passes through it.

coil deck insulated horizontal partition between refrigerated space and bunker.

coil, direct-expansion evaporator coil that allows or permits liquid refrigerant to evaporate inside of it.

coil, expansion an evaporator constructed of pipe or tubing.

coil, holding that part of a magnetic starter or relay that causes the device to operate when energized.

coil, refrigerant an evaporator or condenser made up of tubing either with or without extended surfaces such as fins.

coil, solenoid an electrical winding having an open core. Used for operating relays, contactors, valves, and motor starters.

cold the relative absence of heat.

cold anticipator a device that anticipates a need for cooling and starts the cooling system early enough for it to reach capacity when it is needed.

cold deck the cooling section of a mixed air zone system.

cold joint a soldered joint made with insufficient heat.

cold junction that part of a thermoelectric element which is attached to a load, through which electricity generated by the thermocouple is conducted to the load. The electricity generated by a thermocouple increases as the temperature difference between the hot and cold junctions increases.

cold-plate evaporator with this evaporator, the tubing is attached to a metal plate. The metal plate is wrapped around the freezer compartment. This type is often used in systems that do not have forced-air evaporators.

cold-rolled steel open hearth or Bessemer steel containing 0.12% to 0.20% carbon that has been rolled while cold to produce a smooth, quite accurate stock.

cold storage a trade or process of preserving perishables on a large scale by refrigeration.

cold-wall describes a refrigerator construction which has the inner lining of the refrigerator serving as the cooling surface.

collapse the phenomenon that occurs when a magnetic field suddenly changes from its maximum value to a zero value.

collar a round flange or ring fitted on a shaft to prevent sliding.

collector base junction the P-N junction formed by the collector and base regions.

collector efficiency the ratio of the weight of dust collected to the total weight of dust entering the dust collector.

collector, electrical semiconductor section of a transistor, connected to the same polarity as the base.

collector rings metal rings mounted on a rotating part of an electric machine (such as a generator) so that stationary brushes, riding on the rings, can conduct electrical current in or out of the rotating part.

collector, solar a panel-like item used to collect and absorb solar energy.

color code a color system for circuit identification by use of solid colors, tracers, braids, surface printing, etc.

colorimetric detection device a device for detecting the presence of a particular substance, such as carbon monoxide, which will cause a color change in a material in the detector.

combination burner a burner by which more than one fuel can be burned, either separately or simultaneously. Also called a multifuel burner. A dual-fuel burner uses one prime fuel, but can switch to a standby fuel under peak load conditions. A gas/oil burner is capable of burning either gas or oil; some types can burn both at the same time.

combination circuit a circuit that has one portion connected in series and another part connected in parallel with the voltage source. Sometimes referred to as a complex circuit.

combination fan and limit control a temperature-operated control that regulates the operation of the blower assembly and provides safety protection against overheating of the furnace heat exchanger.

combination heating-cooling thermostat a temperature-activated control that is installed when adding an air-conditioning system to an forced-air furnace system.

combination pliers pliers designed to permit jaws to be opened for gripping larger diameters and also to cut wires and cotter pins by use of a side-cutting jaw.

combination snips sheet-metal snips used for straight cutting of metal, ranging from 30 to 26 gauge. They can cut medium-sized outside curves or circles. They are the most common sheet-metal snips used in the HVAC industry.

combustible a term used by the NFPA, DOT, and others to classify certain liquids that will burn at certain flash points. Both NFPA and DOT generally define combustible liquids as having a flash point of 100°F (38°C) or higher. Nonliquid substances such as wood and paper are classified as ordinary combustibles by the NFPA. OSHA defines combustible liquid within the hazard communication law as any liquid having a flash point at or above 100°F (38°C), but below 200°F (93.3°C). Also, any mixture having components with flash points of 200°F (93.3°C) or higher, the total volumes of which make up 99% or more of the total volume of the mixture, is classified as combustible.

combustible constituent that part of a fuel which will burn and release energy.

combustible liquids liquids having a flash point at or above 140°F (60°F). These are known as Class 3 liquids.

combustible material a material that will ignite and burn. As pertaining to materials adjacent to or in contact with heat-producing appliances, chimney connectors, steam and hot water pipes, and warm air ducts, it is material made of or surfaced with wood, compressed paper, plant fibers, or other material that will ignite and burn. Such material shall be considered as combustible even though flame-proofed, fire-retardant treated, or plastered.

combustion the act or process of burning; the rapid oxidation of fuel accompanied by the production of heat and light. Complete combustion requires an adequate supply of oxygen. Also see *complete, incomplete,* and *perfect combustion.*

combustion air the air required for complete and satisfactory combustion of the fuel; does not include the air used for atomization. Also called main air or secondary air. The actual amount of air supplied is usually expressed as a percentage of the theoretical amount required for complete combustion.

combustion air switch see *airflow switch.*

combustion analysis the measurement of the efficiency of a given flame, based on such factors as air/fuel ratio, stack temperature, CO_2, and O_2.

combustion appliance a fuel-burning (oil, gas, coal, or wood) device such as a range, furnace, or water heater.

combustion chamber the portion of the heating or process equipment where fuel is burned. Also called the fire box.

combustion control see *firing rate controller.*

combustion control valve see *firing rate valve.*

combustion detector see *flame detector.*

combustion, perfect the complete burning of a fuel, with ash or smoke resulting. Not practical to achieve.

combustion products   constituents in the exhaust stream resulting from the combustion of flue gas in air, including the inert gases (like nitrogen and argon), water vapor, and ash, but excluding excess oxygen.

combustion rate   see *firing rate.*

combustion safeguard   see *flame safeguard control.*

combustion tests   a group of checks made on a furnace or boiler to determine that efficient combustion is taking place. Sample tests are smoke, draft, stack temperature, CO_2, and O_2.

comfort air-conditioning   the process of treating air to simultaneously control its temperature, humidity content, cleanliness, and distribution to the conditioned space. A temperature level of 70° to 74°F with 40% to 60% relative humidity is generally accepted as being ideal. Nature provides very few hours when temperature and humidity are simultaneously within these ranges. In the winter it is normally necessary to heat the air and add humidity to achieve comfort. Normal summer operation is to lower the temperature and humidity levels.

comfort chart   chart used in air-conditioning to show the dry bulb temperature and humidity for human comfort conditions.

comfort cooler   a system used to reduce the temperature in the living space in homes. This system is not a complete air conditioner since it does not provide complete control of heating, humidifying, dehumidification, and air circulation.

comfort cooling   refrigeration for comfort as opposed to refrigeration for storage or manufacture.

comfort line   a line on the comfort chart showing a relationship between the effective temperature and the percentage of adults feeling comfortable.

comfort zone   the area on a psychrometric chart which shows conditions of temperature, humidity, and sometimes air movement, in which 50% or more adults feel comfortable.

commercial buildings   such buildings as stores, shops, restaurants, motels, and large apartment buildings.

commercial refrigeration system   a reach-in or service refrigerator of commercial size with or without the means of cooling.

common   a terminal, connection, lead wire, circuit, or other part of an electrical network which is shared by other parts of the network.

common name   a designation for a material other than its chemical name, such as its code name, code number, trade name, brand name, or generic name.

common terminal   terminal on a motor that is connected to both the start and the run windings and/or a junction terminal.

commutation   the process of applying direct current of the proper polarity at the proper time to the rotor windings of a DC motor through split rings and brushes.

commutator   that part of the armature of an electric motor to which the coils of the motor are attached. It consists of segmented sections, electrically insulated from the rotor and from each other. Brushes ride on the commutator, thereby connecting the armature coils to the power source.

comparator   a linear circuit used for comparing two input signals and providing a digital output in accordance to the input signals.

compartment   an enclosed subdivision within a ship. Also refers to a room.

compartment, freezer   the freezer compartment in a household refrigerator is the compartment designed for short-term storage of food temperature below 32°F (0°C). In a household combination refrigerator-freezer, it is that compartment(s) designed for storage of foods at a temperature of 8°F (−13.3°C); in a household freezer, it is that compartment, or compartments, designed for extended storage of frozen foods at a recommended rating temperature of 0°F (–17.8°C) and having inherent capacity for the freezing of food.

compensated control   a method of control in which the setting of one controller is automatically changed when the conditions at another control point change. The change is made in accordance with a definite schedule. The term more commonly used is reset. For example, in a system using hot water for heating, the water temperature may be reset from 100°F up to 180°F as the outside air temperature ranges from 60°F down to 0°F.

compensation   a correction to keep a controller from drifting from its control point with changes in load or to help the controller shift its response with special changes.

complete combustion   burning with stoichiometric proportions of air and fuel plus a moderate amount of excess air to ensure that all of the fuel is burned.

complex circuit   another term for a combination circuit.

compliant scroll compressor   term used to describe the yielding mating scrolls inside a scroll compressor. They will give or separate from each other in the presence of liquid refrigerant.

comply   to act in accord with a rule, standard, or law.

component   one (or more) of the parts of a whole.

component arrangement diagram   the portion of a label diagram that illustrates the physical location of the electrical components in the unit.

composition disc   a washer made from fiber, leather, neoprene, or some other material which will withstand change in pressure or temperature.

compound   the chemical combination of two or more elements to make an entirely different material.

compound gauge   instrument for measuring pressures both above and below atmospheric pressure.

compound motor   a motor with a shunt field coil and a series field coil to the armature. It has characteristics of both a series and a shunt motor.

compound refrigerating system   a system which has several compressors or compressor cylinders in series. The system is used to pump low pressure vapors to condensing pressures.

compound retard gauge   a special compound gauge that allows an accurate reading, within a certain range, between 0 and 100 psig.

compressed air   air at a pressure of five or more pounds per square inch above atmospheric pressure.

compressed-air atomizing oil burner   see *atomizing oil burner.*

compressed gas   a gas or mixture of gases in a closed container having an absolute pressure exceeding 40 psi at 70°F (21.2°C) or an absolute pressure exceeding 104 psi at 130°F (54.4°C) regardless of the pressure at 70°F (21.2°C). Also a liquid having a vapor pressure exceeding 40 psi at 100°F (38°C) as determined by ASTM D-323-72.

compressible flow   flow of high-pressure gas or air which undergoes a pressure drop sufficient to result in a significant reduction of its density.

compression   the term used to denote increase of pressure on a fluid by using mechanical energy.

compression, compound   compression by stages in two or more cylinders.

compression, dual   split suction valving arrangement on a compressor for carrying two suction pressures.

compression, efficiency the ratio of work required to compress, adiabatically and reversibly, all the vapor delivered by a compressor (per stage) to the actual work delivered to the vapor by the piston or blades of the compressor.

compression fitting pipe and tubing fitting used for applications that involve relatively low pressure.

compression gauge instrument used to measure positive pressures (pressures above atmospheric pressures) only. These gauges are usually calibrated from 0 to 300 pounds per square inch of gauge (psig).

compression, multistage compression in more than one step. Usually the discharge of one compressor goes into the suction of another compressor.

compression ratio ratio of the volume of the clearance space to the total volume of the cylinder. In refrigeration it is also the ratio of the absolute low-side pressure to the absolute high-side pressure.

compression, single-stage compression in one stage.

compression system a refrigerating system in which the pressure-imposing element is mechanically operated. Distinguished from an absorption system that uses no compressor.

compression tank a closed tank containing air that can be compressed to provide additional room for expanding water.

compression, wet a system of refrigeration in which some liquid refrigerant is mixed with vapor entering the compressor so as to cause the discharge vapors from the compressor to be saturated rather than superheated.

compressor the pump of a refrigerating mechanism which draws a vacuum or low pressure on the cooling side of the refrigerant cycle and squeezes or compresses the gas into the high-pressure or condensing side of the cycle. Three main types of compressors are reciprocating, centrifugal, and rotary.

compressor, booster a compressor used to raise very low pressures, usually discharging into the suction line of another compressor.

compressor, centrifugal a nonpositive displacement compressor which depends, at least in part, on centrifugal force for pressure rise.

compressor, compound a compressor having two or more cylinders in which the discharge of one cylinder is fed to another cylinder for greater compression.

compressor crankshaft seals seals that prevent air from entering, and oil and refrigerant from escaping, the compressor.

compressor displacement volume, in cubic inches, represented by the area of the compressor piston head or heads multiplied by the length of the stroke.

compressor, double-acting one which has two compression strokes per revolution of the crankshaft per cylinder, i.e., both of the faces of the piston are working faces.

compressor, double-suction split suction; a compressor with a valving arrangement for carrying two suction pressures.

compressor, external-drive see *compressor, open-type.*

compressor, hermetic a mechanical compressor combination consisting of a compressor and a driving motor, both of which are enclosed in the same housing, with no external shaft seals. The motor operates in the refrigerant atmosphere.

compressor, horizontal a compressor with a horizontal cylinder, or, in small sizes, with a horizontal crankshaft.

compressor, multistage a compressor having two or more compressive stages. Discharge from each stage is the intake pressure of the next in series.

compressor, open-type a compressor in which the crankshaft extends through the crankcase and is driven by an external motor.

compressor, positive-displacement a refrigerant compressor in which an increase of refrigerant gas or vapor pressure is attained by changing the internal volume of the compression chamber.

compressor, reciprocating a compressor which uses a piston and cylinder mechanism to provide pumping action. A positive displacement-type compressor.

compressor, reciprocating hermetic a sealed, reciprocating compressor and motor combination with no external coupling.

compressor, reciprocating open a reciprocating compressor coupled externally to an open motor or drive source.

compressor, refrigerant that component of a refrigerating system which increases the pressure of a compressible refrigerant fluid, and simultaneously reduces its volume, while moving the fluid through the device.

compressor, rotary a positive displacement compressor in which a rotating cylinder revolves on an axis that is offset from the cylinder centerline. This system uses vanes, eccentric mechanisms, or other rotating devices to provide pumping action.

compressor, screw the spiral flutes of one screw act as a cylindrical pathway for the refrigerant to be moved and compressed by the mating screw as the screws are rotated at high speed.

compressor, semihermetic a hermetic refrigerant compressor whose housing is sealed by one or more gasketed joints and is provided with means of access for servicing internal parts in the field.

compressor shaft seal a leakproof seal between the crankshaft and compressor body.

compressor, single-stage a compressor having only one compression step between the high- and the low-side pressure.

compressor unit a condensing unit without the condenser and liquid receiver.

compressor valve a reed-type normally closed valve found inside the compressor. It lets the low-pressure gas coolant enter the compressor and discharges the high-pressure gas from the compressor.

compressor, vertical compressor with a vertical cylinder, or, in small sizes, with a vertical crankshaft.

computer a series of electrical components which accepts input from an operator and controls output.

concave describes a curved depression in an object.

concealed rendered inaccessible by the structure or finish of the building. Wires in concealed raceways are considered to be concealed, even though they may become accessible by withdrawing them.

concentrating collector a device that uses reflective surfaces to concentrate the sun's rays onto a smaller area, where they are absorbed and converted to heat energy.

concentration the quantity of one constituent dispersed in a defined amount of another; for example, the amount of gas or gases present in a space. Usually expressed in percent of total volume, parts per million (ppm), or percent of the lower explosive limit (LEL).

concentrator that part of an absorption chiller where the dilute salt solution is boiled to release the water.

concentric having a common center.

concrete a mixture of portland cement, sand, gravel, and water.

condensable describes a gas which can be easily converted to liquid form, usually by lowering the temperature and/or increasing pressure.

condensate the liquid which separates from a gas (including flue gases) due to a reduction in temperature. In a steam heating system, it is the water formed by cooling steam as in a radiator. The capacity of traps, pumps, etc., is sometimes expressed in pounds of condensate that can be handled per hour.

condensate pan container located under the evaporator coil to catch the condensate or defrost water and having provisions for a drain tube.

condensate pump a device used to remove fluid condensate that collects beneath an evaporator coil.

condensate water drain a U-shaped channel or pan placed underneath an evaporator coil to catch the condensed water vapor as it drops from the coil. Provisions are made in this pan to connect a condensate drain fitting.

condensation liquid or droplets which form when a gas or vapor is cooled below its dew point.

condense to change a gas or vapor to a liquid.

condenser (1) a heat exchanger where the heat absorbed by the refrigerant in the evaporator is rejected. It is where latent heat of condensation takes place. Heat flows from the refrigerant to the air passing across the condenser, causing the gas to change back to a liquid without a change in temperature or pressure. Condensing temperature must be higher than that of the ambient air. (2) In electronics, an electrical device which stores an electrical charge.

condenser, air-cooled a heat exchanger which transfers heat to the surrounding air.

condenser, atmospheric a condenser cooled with water which is exposed to the atmosphere.

condenser coil in mechanical refrigeration, a section of coiled tubing where gas refrigerant is cooled below its boiling point.

condenser comb a comb-like device, metal or plastic, which is used to straighten the metal fins on condensers or evaporators.

condenser, double-pipe a condenser with two concentric tubes in which the vapor in the outer tube is condensed by water flowing through the inner tube.

condenser, evaporative a condenser in which part of the heat rejection may be accomplished by raising the temperature of an airstream passing over a heat exchange surface and the remainder by evaporation of water sprayed or otherwise distributed over the heat exchange surface.

condenser fan forced-air device used to move air through an air-cooled condenser.

condenser flooding a method of maintaining a correct head pressure by adding liquid refrigerant to the condenser from a receiver to increase the head pressure.

condenser, open shell-and-tube a condenser in which the water passes in a film over the inner surfaces of the tubes, which are open to the atmosphere.

condenser, shell-and-coil a condensing coil enclosed in a cylinder filled with cooling water.

condenser temperature split condensing temperature of the refrigerant vapor less the dry bulb temperature of the air flowing over the condenser coil.

condenser, water-cooled heat exchanger which is designed to transfer heat from hot gaseous refrigerant to water.

condenser, water pump a forced water-moving device used to move water through a condenser.

condensing furnace a high-efficiency (usually 85% and above) gas or oil forced-air appliance that allows the condensation of the products of combustion thereby extracting the latent heat of vaporization. This condensate then gets drained away to a convenient drain.

Combustion air intake and exhaust vent pipes are usually PVC Schedule 40 plastic pipe.

condensing medium   a substance, such as air or water, that is used to remove heat from the condensing coil to change the refrigerant vapor to a liquid.

condensing pressure   the pressure inside a condenser at which refrigerant vapor gives up its latent heat of vaporization and becomes a liquid. This varies with the condensing temperature.

condensing temperature   the temperature inside a condenser at which refrigerant vapor gives up its latent heat of vaporization and becomes a liquid. This varies with the pressure.

condensing unit   that part of a refrigerating mechanism which draws vaporized refrigerant from the evaporator, compresses it, liquefies it in the condenser, and returns the liquid refrigerant to the refrigerant control.

condensing unit service valves   shutoff hand valves mounted on the condensing unit to enable the service person to install and/or service unit.

conditioned space   cooled, heated, or indirectly conditioned space.

conductance, electrical   the ability of an object to permit the flow of electrons. The opposite of resistance. Conductance is the ratio of the current flow to the potential difference causing the current flow.

conductance, surface film   the time rate of heat flow per unit area between a surface and the ambient fluid under steady conditions for a unit of temperature difference between the surface and the fluid. In English units its value is usually expressed in Btu per (hour) (square foot) (Fahrenheit degree temperature difference between surface and fluid).

conductance, thermal   the amount of heat (Btu) transmitted from surface to surface in one hour through 1 ft^2 of a material or construction for the thickness of material or type of construction under consideration for a difference in temperature of 1°F between the two surfaces. Its symbol is C.

conduction   the transfer of heat from particle to particle without movement of the object.

conduction band   the outermost energy level of an atom.

conduction level   the point at which an amount of voltage or current will cause a device to conduct.

conduction, thermal   the process of heat transfer through a material medium in which kinetic energy is transmitted by particles of the material from particle to particle without movement of the material.

conductive losses   heat lost from a building by contact with outside air or heat lost by leakage and by infiltration.

conductivity, electrical   a term used in describing the capability of a material to carry an electrical charge. Usually expressed as a percentage of copper conductivity, copper being one hundred percent (100%). Conductivity is expressed for a standard configuration of conductor.

conductivity, thermal   the amount of heat (Btu) transmitted in one hour through 1 ft^2 of a homogeneous material 1 in. thick for a difference in temperature of 1°F between the two surfaces of the material. Its symbol is K. Materials are considered homogeneous when the value of K is not affected by variation in thickness or in size of sample within the range normally used in construction.

conductivity circuit   a flame proving circuit which operates on an alternating current flame signal and utilizes the electrical conduction of a flame, as distinguished from flame rectification. Also see *conductivity flame rod system* and *flame conductivity*.

conductivity flame rod system   a flame rod detection system based on the ability of the flame to conduct a current. It conducts the same amount of current in either direction, as distinguished from flame rectification.

conductivity values   indication of the Btu per square foot of area for each Fahrenheit degree of temperature difference per hour for each inch of thickness of the material.

conductor   a substance or body that is capable of transmitting electricity or heat. A substance which allows electrons or heat to flow freely through it. An object that has good conductance.

conductor, thermal   a material which readily transmits heat by means of conduction.

conduit   a tube or trough for carrying and protecting electrical wires. Can be either rigid or flexible, metallic or nonmetallic.

conduit body   a separate and accessible portion of a conduit system.

conduit fittings   connectors used to connect a conduit system of electrical wiring.

conduit run   a continuous electrical duct between two points or devices.

confined space   an equipment room that contains less than 50 cubic feet per 1000 Btu/h of heater input capacity.

congeal   to come together and lose viscosity.

conical   shaped like a cone.

connected load   the electrical power that would be needed if every load connected to the system were drawing power at the same time.

connected load, boiler   the total load in Btu/h attached to the boiler. It is the sum of the outputs of all terminal units and all heat to be supplied by the boiler for process applications.

connecting rod   that part of a compressor mechanism which connects the pistons to the crankshaft, transmitting the back-and-forth motion of the crankshaft levers to the pistons, causing the pistons to move back and forth. One end of the connecting rod is connected to a wrist pin which is connected to the piston. The other end of the connecting rod is connected to the crankshaft.

connection   joining of two or more parts; a union.

connection diagram   a circuit diagram which shows the connections of an installation or its component parts. It may cover internal or external connections. Referred to as a pictorial wiring diagram.

Conradson test   a test which indicates the percentage of carbon residue resulting from the burning of a given fuel oil. Also known as a carbon residue test.

conservation of energy   the principle which assumes that energy can be neither created nor destroyed.

console   a total unit or system of controls located in one area and enclosed. A window air conditioner is a console air conditioner.

constant-level valve   an automatic control valve for maintaining, within a reservoir, a constant level of fuel for delivery to the burner.

constant pilot   see *continuous pilot*.

constant-pressure valve   an automatic expansion valve that holds the pressure at a constant level regardless of the load.

constant-speed motor   a motor whose speed is constant, or substantially constant, over the normal range of loads.

constant-temperature valve   a control valve that maintains a set, desired fluid pressure.

constantan   a copper and nickel alloy used in a J-type thermocouple.

constrictor   a tube or orifice used to restrict flow of a gas or a liquid.

consumed   used up; wasted; destroyed, as by a fire.

consumption   the maximum amount of gas per unit of time, usually expressed in cubic feet per hour, or Btu per hour, required for the operation of the appliance or appliances supplied.

contact, auxiliary   a pilot or auxiliary contact that is operated whenever the main contact or contacts are closed, such as the holding circuit contact in a magnetic starter. Also called an interlock contact.

contact bounce   when mechanical switches close, then open and close several times before finally settling together. This situation can be eliminated by using controls that employ some method of detent action such as over center, mercury, bimetal, or magnetic.

contact chatter   see *contact bounce.*

contact points   two movable points or areas that complete a circuit when pressed together. These points are usually made of tungsten, platinum, or silver.

contactor   an electrical device for making or breaking load-carrying contacts by a pilot circuit through a magnetic coil.

contacts   conducting devices which may open or close to interrupt or complete a circuit.

contaminant   dirt, moisture, or other substance foreign to the refrigerant or oil in a system. These foreign materials can cause unwanted chemical reactions or component failure.

continuity   an unbroken, continuous path or line through which electricity may flow.

continuity check   a test to see if a circuit is an open or closed path.

continuity equation   an equation expressing the conservation of mass in a steady-flow system.

continuity testing   using an ohmmeter to check for open circuits.

continuous-check relay   see *dynamic self-check.*

continuous component check   see *dynamic self-check.*

continuous-cycle absorption system   a system which has a continuous flow of energy input.

continuous duty   the operation of a circuit or device under a constant load without exceeding certain temperature limits for an indefinite period of time.

continuous furnace   a furnace operated on an uninterrupted cycle, in which the charge is being constantly added to, moved through, and removed from the furnace. It is to be distinguished from a batch furnace.

continuous ignition   ignition by an energy source which is continuously maintained throughout the time the burner is in service, whether the main burner is firing or not.

continuous pilot   a pilot that burns without turndown throughout the entire time the burner assembly is in service, whether the main burner is firing or not. The pilot ignites fuel which may leak into the combustion chamber when the burner is off, thus preventing a hazardous condition at start-up. "Continuous pilot" is the Underwriters Laboratories Inc. term for the old term "standing pilot."

contour   the outline or shape of an object.

contraction   shrinkage resulting from cold temperatures.

contrahelical   a term meaning the application of two or more layers of spirally twisted, served, or wrapped materials where each successive layer is wrapped in the direction opposite to the preceding layer.

control   a device which directly operates a system to regulate the fuel, air, water, or electrical supply to the controlled equipment. It may be automatic, semiautomatic, or manual.

control agent   the medium which is manipulated by the control system to cause a change in the controlled medium. For example, suppose a heating coil through which steam is flowing is used to heat a room. The room thermostat is placed so that it measures temperature (controlled variable) in the room air (controlled medium), and operates a valve which regulates the flow (manipulated variable) of the steam (control agent) through the heating coil. Heat from the coil is thus furnished to the room.

control, anticipating one which, by artificial means, is activated sooner than it would be without such means to produce a smaller differential of the controlled property.

control bus a set of signals that regulate the operation of a microcomputer system, including I/O devices and memory. They function much like traffic signals or commands. They may also originate in the I/O devices, generally to transfer signals to, or receive signals from the CPU.

control cable a multiconductor cable made for operation in control or signal circuits. It is usually flexible, relatively small in size, and with a relatively small current rating.

control circuit a circuit that controls some load in the entire control system, whether it be a relay, contactor coil, or a major load.

control, compressor see *motor control*.

control, defrosting a device to automatically defrost the evaporator. It may operate by means of a clock, door cycling mechanism, or the "off" portion of the refrigerating cycle.

control, high-pressure a pressure responsive device (usually an electric switch) actuated directly by the refrigerant pressure on the high side of the refrigeration system.

control hunt a condition of extreme instability, in which the controlled condition changes rhythmically from a value much larger than that desired to one much smaller, as the controller alternately overcorrects in each direction.

control, low-pressure a pressure responsive device (usually an electric switch) actuated directly by the refrigerant pressure on the low side of the refrigeration system.

control module contains the printed circuit card, relays, and switches to receive input signals, interpret the values, and make correcting changes.

control, motor a temperature or pressure operated device used to control the running of the motor.

control piping all piping, valves, and fittings used to interconnect pneumatic, compressed gases, or hydraulically operated control apparatus, or instrument transmitters and receivers.

control point the actual value of the controlled variable (temperature, pressure, or humidity) being maintained by a controller at any given time. It is not necessarily the same as the control set point.

control, pressure motor a high- or low-pressure controller which is connected into the electrical circuit and used to start and stop the motor when there is a need for refrigeration or for safety.

control range the difference between the maximum and minimum points of an adjustable control.

control, refrigerant a device used to regulate the flow of liquid refrigerant into the evaporator such as a capillary tube, expansion valves, or high- and low-side float valves.

control relay a switch or switches (contacts) together with a magnetic coil that controls the switch operation.

control system the entire system, including the controlled system and the automatic control equipment. See *controlled system*.

control, temperature a thermostatic device which automatically stops and starts the motor, the operation of which is based on temperature changes.

control valve valve which regulates the flow or pressure of a medium which affects a controlled process. Control valves are operated by remote signals from independent devices using any of a number of control media such as pneumatic, electric, or electrohydraulic.

control voltage the voltage used in an electrical circuit that contains low-current devices such as thermostats.

control zone the section of a furnace in which temperature is controlled by the throttling action of a single valve. Also see *valve zone*.

controlled device a device in a control system that responds to the signals sent by a controller to start, stop, or otherwise vary the operation of conditioning equipment.

controlled evaporator pressure a controlled system which maintains a definite pressure or range of pressures in the evaporator.

controlled medium the substance (usually air, water, or steam) whose characteristics (such as temperature, pressure, flow rate, volume, level, or concentration) are being controlled.

controlled space the volume of the controlled medium. For example, the area of a room in which the air temperature is being controlled.

controlled system a system made up of all equipment in which the controlled variable exists, but which does not include the automatic control equipment.

controlled variable that quantity or condition of a controlled medium which is measured and controlled. For example, temperature, pressure, flow rate, volume, level, or concentration.

controller a device which senses and measures changes in temperature, pressure, or moisture content and indirectly acts to maintain the controlled variable within preset limits. A system of switches, relays, and instrumentation used to regulate voltage, current, speed, and other predetermined actions of an electrical machine or group of machines.

controller, dual-pressure a controller consisting of two pressure bellows which operate a switch within a single enclosed case. When applied to a compressor control, one bellows functions on a change in suction pressure, the other bellows on a change in discharge pressure.

controller feedback the change in the controller's output in response to a measured change in the controlled variable transmitted back to the controller input for evaluation.

controller, humidity a controller sensitive to changes in humidity.

controller, pressure an automatic control device that is actuated and responsive to pressure.

controller, temperature a controller sensitive to changes in temperature.

controls devices designed to regulate the gas, air, water, or electrical supply to a gas appliance. These may be either manual or automatic.

convection the transfer of heat energy in liquids and gases from one location to another by the motion of molecules which carry heat. Convection is natural when the movement of the liquid or gas is due to the difference in the weight of hot and cold liquid or gas. Convection is forced when fans, jets, or pumps are used to move the liquid or gas.

convection, forced the transfer of heat resulting from the forced movement of liquid or gas by means of a fan, jet, or pump.

convection loss heat loss through the walls and roof of a building caused by movement of heated air.

convection, natural the circulation of a gas or liquid due to the difference in density resulting from temperature differences.

convector a concealed radiator. An enclosed heating unit located (with enclosures) within, adjacent to, or exterior to the room or space to be heated, but transferring heat to the room or space mainly by the process of convection. A shielded heating unit is also termed a convector. If the heating unit is located exterior to the room or space to be heated, the heat is transferred through one or more ducts or pipes.

convenience outlet, gas a permanently mounted, hand-operated device providing a means for connecting and disconnecting an appliance or an appliance connector to the gas supply piping. The device includes an integral, manually operated gas valve with a nondisplaceable valve member so that disconnection can be accomplished only when the manually operated gas valve is in the closed position.

conventional current flow current flow that is assumed to be in one direction from positive charge concentration (+) to negative charge concentration (–).

conversion burner a unit consisting of a burner and its controls utilizing gaseous fuel for installation in an appliance originally utilizing another fuel.

conversion factors force and power may be expressed in more than one way. A horsepower is equivalent to 33,000 foot-pounds of work per minute, 746 watts, or 2,546 Btu/h. These values can be used for changing horsepower into foot-pounds, Btu, watts, etc.

converter a heat exchange unit designed to transfer heat from one distributing system to another. This may be either a steam-to-water or a water-to-water unit. It is usually of the shell-and-tube design.

convex describes an outwardly rounded surface on an object.

cooled space enclosed space within a building that is cooled by a cooling system whose sensible capacity exceeds 5 Btu/h (ft^2) or is capable of maintaining a space temperature of 90°F or less at design cooling conditions.

cooler a heat exchanger which removes heat from a substance.

cooling anticipator a nonadjustable heating resistor that is placed in parallel with the cooling circuit inside the thermostat. It produces a false heat in the thermostat during the equipment off cycle to cause a shorter off cycle and to maintain a more even temperature inside the space.

cooling coil any section of coiled tubing (usually an evaporator coil) used to lower the temperature of the surrounding area. Also see *evaporator coil*.

cooling degree hours a unit, based upon temperature difference and time, used in estimating cooling loads of residences in summer. For any hour when the dry bulb temperature is greater than a reference temperature (base 74°F for this standard) there are as many cooling degree hours as degrees Fahrenheit difference in temperature between the average hourly temperature and the reference temperature.

cooling leg a length of uninsulated pipe through which the condensate flows to a trap and which has sufficient surface to permit the condensate to dissipate enough heat to prevent flashing when the trap opens. In the case of a thermostatic trap, a cooling leg may be necessary to permit the condensate to drop a sufficient amount in temperature to permit the trap to open.

cooling mode the operating phase of a system that removes heat and/or moisture from a conditioned space.

cooling run factor the percent of time that the unit is expected to operate to handle the cooling load during the warmest month of the year.

cooling system, direct-expansion   a cooling and dehumidification device which cools air or other fluids by the evaporation of mechanically compressed gas in an evaporator coil. A condensing coil then removes this transferred heat to a different space.

cooling system, evaporative   a system housed in a cabinet containing a pump, distribution tubes, water pads, and a blower. The pump supplies water to the distribution tubes which carry the water to pads on three sides of the cabinet. The blower draws outdoor air through the moist water pads. Some of the water in the pads absorbs heat from the air and evaporates. The air cannot be recirculated. This system works most effectively in relatively dry climates.

cooling system, multiple-stage   a cooling system that increases its capacity by stages in response to cooling demand.

cooling tower   a device which cools water by water evaporation in air. Water is cooled to the wet bulb temperature of air.

cooling tower, forced-draft   a cooling tower in which the flow of air is created by one or more fans discharging air into the tower.

cooling tower, induced-draft   a cooling tower in which the flow of air is created by one or more fans drawing the saturated air out of the tower.

cooling tower, natural-draft   a cooling tower in which the flow of air depends upon natural air currents or a breeze. Generally applied where the spray water is relatively hot and will cause some convection currents.

cooling water   water used for condensation of refrigerant; condenser water.

coordinates   the position or location of a point on the X, Y, and Z planes.

copper   a metal which conducts electricity and which is also widely used in piping systems. It is recognizable by its brownish-red color. Its symbol is Cu.

copper losses   the heat losses in electrical machines due to the resistance of the copper wire used for windings; also called I^2R losses.

copper plating   a film of copper deposited by electrical, immersion, or other means on the surface of another material such as iron or steel; in refrigeration it is usually placed on compressor walls, pistons, discharge valves, and shaft seals.

copper tubing   copper tubing is the most widely used tubing type in the HVAC/R industry. It has a high thermal conductivity. Copper is also easy to solder, braze, bend, and flare, and it has a high resistance to corrosion. It takes a coolant that is caustic as ammonia to corrode copper. Copper cannot be used in systems where ammonia is the coolant. Copper tubing is classified in terms of wall thickness, temper, and type.

core, air   a coil of wire not having a metal core.

core area   the total plane area of the portion of the grille, face, or register, bounded by a line tangent to the outer edges of the outer openings, through which air can pass.

core, cables   a term used to denote a component or assembly of components over which other materials are applied such as additional components, shield, or armor.

core loss   refers to the conversion of electrical energy to heat energy in the core material of a magnetic device.

core, magnetic   iron or steel used to make laminated internal sections of electromagnets. The magnetic center of a magnetic field.

core saturation   when the atoms of a metal core material are aligned in the same pattern so that no more magnetic lines of force can be developed.

core solder   this is a solder wire or bar with flux as the core.

corona   a discharge due to ionization of a gas (usually air) caused by a potential gradient exceeding a certain critical value.

corrective action   the built-in action of a controller to correct drift. The action taken by a controller to keep the control point as close as possible to the set point.

corrosion   the process or result of a material being eaten or worn away, usually by chemical reaction.

corrosive   a chemical that causes visible destruction of, or irreversible alterations in, living tissue by chemical action at the site of contact; or in the case of leakage from its packaging, a liquid that has a severe corrosion rate on steel. A solid or liquid waste that exhibits a "characteristic of corrosivity," as defined by the Resources Conservation and Recovery Act (RCRA), may be regulated by EPA as a hazardous waste.

cotter pin   a split pin used as a fastener, usually to prevent a nut from unscrewing.

coulomb   the quantity of electricity transferred by an electric current of one ampere in one second. This unit of measurement equals 6.25×10^{18} electrons.

counter   a device capable of changing states in a specified sequence upon receiving appropriate input signals. The output of the counter indicates the number of pulses which have been applied. A counter is made from flip-flops and some gates. The output of all flip-flops is accessible to indicate the exact count at all times.

counterbore   to enlarge a hole a given amount.

counterclockwise   from right to left in a circular motion.

counterelectromotive force   generator action which takes place in motors when voltage (EMF) is induced in the rotor conductors which opposes the source voltage (EMF). The voltage produced by self-inductance. Also see *back EMF*.

counterflow   flow in the opposite direction.

counterflow condenser   a water-cooled condenser in which the cooling water first contacts the condenser near its coolest point (outlet) and is tapped off near its warmest point (inlet).

counterflow furnace   same as a downflow furnace.

countersink   to bevel a hole to receive a flat or fillister head fastener.

counterweight   a dead weight added to a compressor crankshaft to balance the crankshaft.

coupling   a sleeve used to join the ends of two lengths of pipe or tubing.

coupling, electrical   the amount of mutual inductance between coils.

covalent bond   atoms joined together to form a stable molecule by sharing electrons.

cover   the cover protects the internal wiring of a thermostat base from dust, lint, and other harmful substances. It also contains the temperature setting lever, system switching levers, and the temperature indicator.

cover plate   a sheet of glass or transparent plastic that sits above the absorber in a flat plate collector.

crackage   joint in a structure which permits movement of a gas or vapor through it, even under a small pressure difference.

cracked   state in which a valve is opened slightly by turning the stem about one or two turns.

cracking   the process of breaking down hydrocarbons by heat and pressure into lighter hydrocarbons of lower molecular weight. For example, the breaking down of petroleum into gasoline.

cracking a valve   opening of a valve a very small amount.

crankcase   the housing for the compressor crankshaft and a sump for the compressor oil.

crankcase heater   a heating device fastened to the crankcase or lower portion of the compressor housing intended to keep the oil in the compressor crankcase at a higher temperature than the rest of the system. This reduces the migration of the refrigerant to the coldest part of the refrigeration system.

crankcase pressure regulator   an automatic valve installed in the suction line that prevents the pressure in the crankcase from exceeding the set point.

crankshaft   the shaft in a compressor that is driven by a motor and rotates to provide movement to the pistons.

crankshaft seal   a leakproof joint between the crankshaft and the compressor body.

crankshaft throw   the distance between the center line of the main bearing journal and the center line of the crank pin or eccentric.

creosote   a mixture of unburned organic materials found in the smoke from a wood-burning appliance.

crest   the top edge of two adjoining threads.

crimp   to squeeze or contract. Also a collapse or kink in a section of tubing at a bend in the tubing.

crimp termination   a wire termination that is applied by physical pressure of terminal to wire.

crisper   a drawer or compartment in a refrigerator designed to provide high humidity along with low temperature to keep vegetables, especially leafy vegetables, cold and crisp.

criteria, pollutant   standards set forth by the EPA for the following pollutants in outdoor air: nitrogen dioxide, sulfur dioxide, ozone, lead, carbon monoxide, and total suspended particles.

critical charge   describes a refrigeration system in which the amount of refrigerant contained within must be exact.

critical point   the state point of a substance at which liquid and vapor have identical properties.

critical pressure   the condition of refrigerant at which liquid and gas have the same properties.

critical pressure drop   see *pressure drop*.

critical pressure ratio   the ratio of the pressure at the minimum area in a converging-diverging nozzle to the inlet pressure. The velocity at this section of the nozzle is sonic under certain conditions.

critical temperature   the highest temperature at which vapor and liquid can have a transition and still be condensable by the application of pressure.

critical temperature, electronics   the temperature at which a doped semiconductor will lose its intrinsic properties.

critical time override   an electromechanical device which bypasses the normal operation of a load management system during times that are extremely busy for building operation.

critical time programmer   a clock that programs loads to bypass their normal cycling schedule during critical times.

critical velocity   the velocity above which fluid flow is turbulent.

critical vibration   vibration which is noticeable and harmful to structure or machinery.

crocus cloth   used as a sandpaper with a smooth surface.

cross   a four-way connector fitting for pipe or tubing.

cross-charged   describes a sealed container containing two fluids which together create a desired pressure-temperature curve.

cross-connected   describes two pipes or systems of flow connected to each other, usually to provide an equalization or interplay of pressures.

cross-drum boiler   see *water-tube boiler*.

cross hairs   the crossed vertical and horizontal lines on a CAD graphic display unit that represent the cursor position, or the vertical and horizontal lines of an input device like a digitizing puck.

cross-liquid charge bulb   a type of charge in the sensing bulb of the TXV that has different characteristics from the system refrigerant. This is designed to help prevent liquid refrigerant from flooding to the compressor at start-up.

crossover igniter   a slotted length of metal that acts as a bridge between burners.

cross-reference   a book which lists the mechanical or electrical twin of a part made by the same or a different manufacturer.

cross-sectional area   the area of the cut surface of an object cut at right angles to the length of the object.

cross talk   electrical interference between two adjacent insulated conductors whereby a signal in one of the conductors will be picked up by the adjacent conductor.

cross-vapor charge bulb   similar to the vapor charge bulb but contains a fluid different from the system refrigerant. This is a special type of charge that produces a different pressure/temperature relationship under different conditions.

crown   the raised contour, as on the surface of a pulley.

crude oil   unrefined oil in its natural state as it comes from the ground. Also called petroleum or crude.

cryogenic fluid   a substance which exists as a liquid or gas at temperatures of –250°F or lower.

cryogenics   the science of refrigeration which deals with producing temperatures of –250°F or lower.

crystal   (1) a body that is formed by the solidification of a chemical element, a compound, or a mixture and has a regularly repeating internal arrangement of its atoms and often external plane faces. (2) A crystalline material used in electronics as a frequency-determining element or a rectifying device.

crystallization   when a chemical solution (e.g., salt in water) becomes too concentrated and part of the solution turns to a crystalline solid.

cuber analyzer   a device used for checking the control module and probes in an ice-making machine. Thermistor probe signals are substituted by operating switches in the analyzer, which send all combinations of signals to the card. Thus a defective component can be identified by the process of elimination. This can also be used to dry cycle an electronic cuber for demonstration or schools.

cubic feet per minute (cfm)   the volume of air passing through a piece of equipment. The movement is expressed as cubic feet per minute.

cubic foot of gas   the amount of gas that would occupy one cubic foot when at a temperature of 60°F (16°C), saturated with water vapor, and under a pressure equivalent to that of 29.92 inches mercury column.

cubic measurement   the measure of volume, found by multiplying height, width, and length.

cumulative compound motor   a compound motor in which the magnetic field of the series coils aids the magnetic field of the shunt coil.

curie   a unit used to describe the rate of radioactive decay in a sample of material. One curie (Ci) equals 37 billion disintegrations per second.

current   transfer of electrical energy in a conductor by means of electrons changing position. It is usually expressed in amperes. Symbol is "I" for intensity of current.

current-carrying capacity   the current a conductor of a given size is capable of carrying safely without exceeding its own insulation and jacket temperature limitations.

current limitation   a fuse operation relating to short circuits only. When a fuse operates in its current-limiting range, it will clear a short circuit in less than half a cycle. Also, it will limit the instantaneous peak let through current to a value substantially less than that obtainable in the same circuit if that fuse were replaced with a solid conductor of equal impedance.

current overload   an overload that opens a set of contacts on high current draw and allows them to close when the current draw has decreased. It usually is a pilot duty device.

current penetration   the depth a current of a given frequency will penetrate into the surface of a conductor carrying the current.

current relay   a relay that is opened or closed by the starting current of an electric motor. The relay allows the start capacitor and start windings to drop in or out of the starting circuit.

current transformer   a transformer used to extend the range of an AC ammeter.

curtain-type damper   a damper composed of flexible material, which moves in a vertical plane as it is rolled.

curved line   a line of which no part is straight.

curved-tooth file   a file that is used on aluminum and steel sheets. Most are designed to cut on the forward stroke.

cushion, hydraulic   a deceleration device sometimes built into the ends of a cylinder to restrict the flow of fluid at the outlet port.

customer relations   the ability to gain customer confidence and trust by effectively and promptly serving their wants and needs.

cutaway   an illustration of a component in which the outer walls or housing are partially removed to permit viewing of internal parts.

cut-in   the temperature or pressure value which closes a control circuit.

cutoff   immediate shutdown of a system after loss of the main burner flame, with no attempt to recycle or to relight the burner.

cutout   temperature or pressure value which opens a control circuit.

cut-through resistance   the ability of a material to withstand mechanical pressure, usually a sharp edge or prescribed radius, without separation.

cutting attachment   this is a separate cutting attachment attached to the cutting torch.

cutting oxygen lever   a lever-actuated valve on an oxyacetylene cutting attachment, used to supply the stream of oxygen needed for cutting.

cutting tip   this is the part of the oxygen cutting torch from which the oxyacetylene gas is released.

cyanosis   a dark purplish coloration of the skin and the mucous membrane due to deficient oxygenation of the blood.

cycle, control   a sequence of operations under automatic control intended to maintain the desired conditions at all times.

cycle, electric   the voltage generated by the rotation of a conductor through a magnetic field from a zero reference, in a positive direction, back to zero, then in a negative direction and back to zero. One complete cycle equals 360° of rotation.

cycle, system   series of events or operations which have a tendency to repeat in the same order.

cycles per second   the number of complete alternating current waves in one second of current flow.

cycling   (1) continuous oscillation occurring without periodic stimuli. (2) A situation in a closed-loop system where the controller's response (sensitivity) to an input change causes instability.

cycling rate the number of complete cycles that the system goes through in one hour. One complete cycle includes both "on" and "off" times.

cylinder (1) a device that converts fluid power into linear mechanical force and motion. This usually consists of movable elements such as a piston and piston rod, plunger, or ram, operating within a cylindrical bore. (2) A closed container for fluids.

cylinder head that part which encloses the compression end of the compression cylinder.

cylinder, hydraulic a part of the valving mechanism which is used in a capacity control actuator system.

cylinder, refrigerant cylinder in which refrigerant is purchased and dispensed. Color code painted on the cylinder or a color band indicates the type of refrigerant that the cylinder contains.

cylinder spring the spring located between the cylinder head and discharge valve assembly of a reciprocating compressor to ensure protection against damage from slugs of liquid refrigerant or oil. The entire discharge valve assembly will "lift" against the spring and pass the slug, then return to its normal operation.

cylinder unloading a method of providing capacity control by causing a cylinder in a reciprocating compressor to stop pumping.

cylindrical commutator a commutator with contact surfaces that are parallel to the rotor shaft.

D

db decibel.

Dba sound level reading on the a-weighted scale of a sound meter. This a-weighted scale adjusts response of the meter to approximate that of the human ear.

DC direct current.

DDC direct digital control.

dia diameter.

diag diagram.

diff differential.

disc disconnect.

dm demand meter.

DMM digital multimeter.

DMS Drill Manufacturer's Standard.

DOE Department of Energy.

DOT Department of Transportation.

dpc differential pressure control.

DPDT double-pole, double-throw.

DPST double-pole, single-throw.

ds disconnecting switch.

dsv discharge service valve.

dwg drawing.

dx direct expansion.

daily range the range of outdoor ambient temperatures encountered in an area over a 24-hour period. The temperatures are taken at the design high and low temperature for the area.

daily range, high a range of both high and low outdoor ambient design temperatures that exceeds 25°F. A low-humidity area.

daily range, low a range of both high and low outdoor ambient design temperatures that is less than 15°F. A high-humidity area.

daily range, medium a range of both high and low outdoor ambient design temperatures that is in the 15° and 25°F range. A medium-humidity area.

Dalton's law the vapor pressure exerted on a container by a mixture of gases is equal to the sum of the individual vapor pressures of the gases contained in mixture.

damper a device for introducing a variable resistance for regulating the volumetric flow of gas or air. Also see *butterfly, curtain-type, flap-type, louver-type, slide-type, opposed-* and *parallel-blade dampers.*

damper, fire   a damper placed in a duct or at an outlet to prevent or retard the emission of smoke and/or heat into a room or space during a fire. Such devices are also designed to prevent or retard the spread of fire throughout the structure, thus confining it to a specific area.

damper motor   a motor which, through mechanical linkage, opens or closes a damper. Also see *firing rate motor.*

D'arsonval meter   the internal portion of a meter which has a stationary permanent magnet, an electromagnetic coil, and a pointer that moves in direct proportion to the current flow through the coil.

data byte   the eight-bit binary number that the microprocessor chip will use in an arithmetic or logical operation or store in memory.

data plate   an equipment identification label, usually including such items as brand name, model, serial, voltage, and amperage.

daughters (progeny)   the new radionuclides formed by the radioactive decay of a parent radionuclide.

DC generator   a rotating machine that produces a form of direct-current (DC) voltage.

DC power supply   an element of an electronic system consisting of three components: a full wave rectifier, a filter, and a voltage regulator.

dead   describes a portion of an electrical system having no voltage or charge.

dead air space   a sealed layer of dry, motionless air having an insulating value.

dead band   a temperature band between the on and off of an output in the on-off control action. No heating or cooling takes place. Band occurs between the times when the heat is turned off upon rising temperature and turned on upon falling temperature.

dead end line/system   the end of a pipeline which does not lead back to an oil storage tank, so the oil in that end of the line cannot be recirculated. A system which does not contain a return line to an oil storage tank, so the oil cannot be recirculated in a closed circuit.

dead front   the part of a heating or cooling appliance that has no exposed operating parts.

dead leg   a grounded phase of a three-phase delta transformer.

dead short   a connection that permits an unrestricted flow of electrons.

dead space   the short distance between a burner port and the base of the flame.

dead time   any time period of delay between the action of the controller and the resulting action of the actuator.

deaeration   the act of removing air from substances like a boiler's water supply.

debug   the process of removing a problem or trouble from a system or piece of equipment.

decibel (db)   unit used for measuring the relative loudness of sounds. One decibel is equal to approximate difference of loudness ordinarily detectable by the human ear, the range of which is about 130 decibels on a scale beginning with one for the faintest audible sound.

decimal equivalent   a fraction converted to the number of tenths or hundredths that the fraction is equal to.

deck (coil deck)   insulated horizontal partition between refrigerated space and the evaporator space.

declination of sun   the angle above or below the equatorial plane. It is plus if north of the plane, and minus if below. Celestial objects are located by declination.

decomposition   the breaking up of structures by a process of chemical change; spoilage.

dedendum   distance from pitch circle to bottom of tooth space.

dedicated   set apart or committed to a definite use. Addressed to a specific task, job, or circuit.

dedicated circuit (electrical)   an electrical circuit that supplies power to one appliance only. Fused for that one circuit only.

dedicated geothermal well   a system where water is drawn from the top of the well and is returned to the bottom of the well. The well is dedicated to supply water for the use of the heat pump only.

de-energize   to stop the electron flow to an electric device.

deep vacuum   a vacuum reading approaching 30 in. of mercury.

deep well submersible pump   a centrifugal pump in which a number of impeller assemblies, in a housing, are mounted on a shaft directly coupled to a submersible motor. The entire assembly is located at the bottom of the well. Power is brought to the motor by a waterproof cable.

default value   a value which will automatically be selected by the controller if a specific value is not manually chosen.

deficiency of air   a supply of air which is inadequate for complete combustion of a fuel. This is the same as excess of fuel. Also see *fuel-rich*.

definite-purpose contactor   similar in construction to a general-purpose contactor. However, it is lighter duty and often considered to be a throwaway product when compared to an equivalent NEMA or IEC contactor. Used in HVAC, data acquisition, and food processing equipment.

definite-purpose motor   a motor designed for use on a particular application, with operating characteristics and mechanical construction required by the application. Examples are a sump pump motor or an oil burner motor.

deflect   to swerve; to bend or turn to one side.

deflection   the departure of an indicator or pointer from the zero reading on the scale of an instrument.

defrost   to melt or do away with frost and ice.

defrost, automatic   an automatic defrost system is one in which the defrost cycle is automatically initiated and terminated, with automatic resumption of normal refrigeration at the conclusion of the defrost action. The defrost water is disposed of automatically.

defrost control   a device that senses the accumulation of frost on an evaporator and/or initiates and terminates the defrost cycle. This control causes the system to reverse the refrigerant flow to remove the frost and/or ice from the coil.

defrost cycle   refrigerating cycle in which the evaporator frost and ice accumulation is melted.

defrost, manual   one in which defrosting of the refrigerated surface is accomplished by natural or manual means with manual initiation and manual termination of the overall defrost operation.

defrost mode   the portion of the operation of the system in which the frost and/or ice on the evaporator is removed.

defrost termination thermostat   a temperature-sensing device that initiates and terminates the defrost cycle at preset temperatures.

defrost thermostat   a temperature-sensing device that initiates and terminates the defrost cycle at predetermined temperatures.

defrost timer   a device connected into an electrical circuit which shuts unit off long enough to permit ice and frost accumulation on the evaporator to melt.

defrosting   the process of removing frost accumulation from evaporators.

defrosting, hot-gas   the use of high-pressure refrigerant gas to defrost the low side of the refrigerant system. May be started by time, temperature, or a combination of the two.

defrosting-type evaporator   an evaporator operating at such temperatures that ice and frost on the surface melts during the off portion of the operating cycle.

degreasing solvent   a solution or solvent that is used to remove oil or grease from parts.

degree day   a unit that represents 1° of difference from a given point in average outdoor temperature of one day and is often used in estimating fuel requirements for a building. Degree days are based on average temperature over a 24-hour period. As an example, if an average temperature for a day is 50°F, the number of degree days for that day would be equal to 65°F minus 50°F or 15 degree days. Degree days are useful when calculating requirements for heating purposes.

degree, electrical   the 360th part of the angle subtended at the axis of the machine by two consecutive field poles of like polarity. One mechanical degree is thus equal to as many electrical degrees as there are pairs of poles in the machine.

degree, physics   a unit of temperature measurement.

degree of superheat   the difference between the boiling point of the refrigerant and its actual temperature above the boiling point.

dehumidification   the condensation of water vapor from air by cooling below the dew point or removal of water vapor from air by chemical or physical methods.

dehumidifier   a device used to remove moisture from air in an enclosed space. Can either be an air cooler or washer used for lowering the moisture content of the air passing through it or an absorption or adsorption device for removing moisture from the air.

dehumidifier, surface   an air-conditioning unit, designed primarily for cooling and dehumidifying air through the action of passing the air over wet cooling coils.

dehumidify   to remove water vapor from the atmosphere. To remove water or liquid from stored goods.

dehumidifying effect   the difference between the moisture contents, in pounds per hour, of the entering and leaving air, multiplied by 1.060.

dehydrate   to remove water or water vapor; to become dry; to lose water. Liquid water, hygroscopic water, and water of crystallization or water of hydration are included.

dehydrated oil   a lubricant which has most of the water removed.

dehydration   the removal of water vapor from air by the use of absorbing or adsorbing materials or the removal of water from stored goods.

dehydrator   a refrigeration accessory that removes water from liquid refrigerant. Most commonly called a drier or filter drier.

dehydrator/receiver   a small tank which both serves as a liquid refrigerant reservoir and contains a desiccant to remove moisture. Used on most automobile air-conditioning installations.

de-ice control   a device used to operate a refrigerating system in such a way as to provide melting of the accumulated ice or frost.

delay   the period of time before an event, or the period of time of an event.

delay-on-break   a function of a timing device whereby delay is initiated when the switch is opened or the circuit is de-energized. When the set time has elapsed, load may energize immediately on normal demand. If abnormal conditions are sensed, load will de-energize and delay is initiated.

delay-on-make a function of a timing device whereby delay is initiated when the switch is closed or when the circuit is energized.

delayed mixing a process in which the fuel and air leave the burner nozzle unmixed and, thereafter, mix relatively slowly, largely through diffusion. This results in a long, luminous flame, called diffusion flame, long flame, luminous flame, or yellow flame. Also see *long flame burner*.

delta transformer a three-phase electrical transformer which has the start end of one winding connected to the finished end of the second. Power input lines come into the junctions of the windings. The circuit configuration resembles the Greek letter delta (Δ).

delta winding a winding layout of some three-phase motors, where the beginning of the windings is connected to the ending of the windings.

de minimis minimum. According to Section 608 of the Clean Air Act of 1990, the smallest quantity of refrigerant released in the course of making good faith attempts to recapture and recycle or safely dispose of refrigerant.

demand (1) the amount of power that a power company must supply at any given time or period. (2) The instantaneous consumption requirements of a device on an electrical power circuit.

demand billing the demand upon which billing of a customer is based, as specified in a rate schedule or contract. The billing demand need not coincide with the actual measured demand of the billing period.

demand charge the specified charge to be billed on the basis of the billing demand, under an applicable rate schedule or contract.

demand load the amount of power which would probably be needed at any given time.

Generally, the minimum demand load is considered to be about 35% of the connected load.

demand meter a device which indicates or records the demand or maximum demand. Since demand involves both an electrical factor and a time factor, mechanisms responsive to each of these factors are required as well as an indicating or recording mechanism. These mechanisms may be either separate from or structurally combined with one another. Demand meters may be classified as follows: Class 1—curve-drawing meters, Class 2—integrated-demand meters, Class 3—lagged-demand meters.

density weight per unit volume of a substance.

deodorizer a device which absorbs various odors, usually by the principle of absorption. Activated charcoal is the substance commonly used in these devices.

depletion mode the operation of a field effect transistor in response to an increase in the gate-to-source voltage in an effort to reduce the drain current.

depletion region an area that is depleted of carriers on either side of a P-N junction that contains impurity ions.

depression the difference between the wet and dry bulb temperatures.

depressor fork a device which, when energized, moves to hold open the cylinder suction valves in certain compressor capacity modulation systems.

derating factor a factor used to reduce a current-carrying capacity of a wire when used in environments other than the environment for which the value was established.

desiccant a substance used to collect and hold moisture in a refrigerating system. A drying agent. Common desiccants are activated alumina or silica gel.

design cooling conditions summer outdoor design conditions listed for selected locations.

design heat loss   the heat loss of a building or room at design indoor/outdoor temperature difference.

design heating conditions   winter outdoor design conditions listed for selected locations.

design load   the design heat loss plus all other heating requirements to be provided by the heating appliance.

design pressure   highest or most severe pressure expected during operation. Sometimes used as the calculated operating pressure plus an allowance for safety.

design temperature difference   the difference between the design indoor and outdoor temperatures.

design temperature, indoor   the temperature to be maintained within the conditioned space.

design temperature, outdoor   the outdoor temperature arbitrarily established as the maximum against which the system must be able to maintain the desired indoor conditions; used when figuring heat loss and heat gain calculations.

design value   the amount of heating or cooling a system is designed to produce at maximum conditions.

design water temperature   the average of the temperatures of the water entering and leaving the boiler when the system is operating at design conditions.

design water temperature difference   the difference between the temperatures of the water leaving the unit and entering the unit when the system is operating at design conditions.

design water temperature drop   the difference between the temperatures of the water leaving the boiler and returning to the boiler when the system is operating at design conditions. In large systems employing subcircuits the design temperature drop is usually taken as the difference in the temperatures of the water entering and leaving each subcircuit.

design working pressure   the maximum allowable working pressure that a given component will withstand.

desuperheater   an accessory that lowers the temperature of superheated steam to saturation conditions.

detail drawings   drawings that show enlarged views of different parts of the structure. They show parts that are unusual or have a special design, such as an arch or duct design.

detector   a device that produces an electrical output that is a measure of the radiation incident on the device. Also see *flame detector, smoke detector,* and *sensor.*

detector, leak   a device used to detect and locate refrigerant leaks.

detent   as in a rotary switch, the means by which the switch is snapped into a given position and held there. Different types of detent actions are magnetic, bimetal, over-center, and mercury.

detergent   a cleaning agent, like soap, but made synthetically, not from fats and lye.

deterioration   becoming or being made worse; depreciation.

deviation   the difference between the set point and the value of the controlled variable at any instant.

device   a component that primarily carries, but does not utilize, electrical energy. Examples are an electrical switch or receptacle.

dew   condensed atmospheric moisture deposited in small drops on cool surfaces.

dew point, apparatus   that temperature which would result if the psychrometric process occurring in a dehumidifier, humidifier, or surface cooler were carried to the saturation condition of the leaving air while maintaining the same ratio of sensible to total heat load in the process.

dew point rise   increase in moisture content (specific humidity) of air expressed in terms of rise in dew point temperature.

dew point temperature   the temperature at which water vapor (at 100% humidity) begins to condense and deposit as free water.

diac   a semiconductor often used as a voltage-sensitive switching device.

diagnosis   deciding the nature of trouble or difficulty by careful observation and examination.

diagonal   a line running from opposite corners.

diagonal cutter   a hand tool made for pulling cotter pins, spreading cotter pins, and cutting small-gauge wire.

diagram, electrical   a drawing which indicates the parts and layout of an electrical circuit.

dial stem thermometer   a type of thermometer that can be operated by a bimetallic strip or a bellows charged with a volatile fluid. Some dial stems have a sensing bulb connected to the bellows by a capillary tube. The temperature range is from -40°F to 250°F.

diameter   the length of a straight line running through the middle of the circle. The distance across the widest part of a circle.

diametral pitch   number of gear teeth per inch of pitch diameter.

diaphragm   a flexible membrane usually made of thin metal, rubber, or plastic that separates two pressure differences.

diaphragm valve   a solenoid-operated gas valve in which a membrane or partition separates the inlet and outlet. When the solenoid is de-energized, the main gas supply applies pressure to the top of the diaphragm to help hold the valve closed. When the solenoid is energized, a plunger opens a bleed port in the top side of the valve. As the gas bleeds off the top of the diaphragm, main gas pressure on the underside of the

diaphragm opens the valve. These valves are generally used on atmospheric-type gas burners for smooth lightoff. They feature variable, slow-opening, and fast-closing action. Also see *solenoid*.

dichlorofluoromethane   refrigerant commonly known as R-12. Chemical formula is CCl_2F_2. Cylinder color code is white. Boiling point at atmospheric pressure is –21.62°F.

dictates   controls; regulates.

die   any of various devices used for cutting out, forming, or stamping material; any of several component pieces that are fitted into a die stock to cut external threads on screws or bolts.

die cast   a process of molding low-temperature metals in accurately shaped metal molds.

die stock   a tool used to hold dies with external threads.

dielectric   the insulating material separating the conducting surfaces of a capacitor. Materials could be air, mica, plastic, wax-impregnated paper, or ceramic.

dielectric constant   a number (K value) that represents the ability of a dielectric to develop an electrostatic field compared to air, which has a value of 1.0. The higher the K value, the better the dielectric material.

dielectric fluid   a fluid with a high electrical resistance.

dielectric strength   a term used to describe the limit, without damage to an insulating material, of an applied voltage potential.

dies, thread   tools used to cut external threads.

difference in potential   the voltage across two points of a circuit.

differential   the smallest range through which the controller variable must pass in order to move the final control element from one to the other of its two possible positions, such as on to off or cut-in to cut-out.

differential control   a control that monitors the difference between two factors.

differential gap   this term applies to two-position controllers. It is the smallest range through which the temperature, pressure, or relative humidity must pass to make the controller move from one to the other of its fixed positions.

differential pressure control   a controller which measures and controls the difference between two separate pressures.

differential thermostat   a device which provides the control functions for solar heating and domestic hot water systems by measuring the leaving water temperature at the collector outlet and comparing it with the temperature of the water in the storage tank.

diffuse radiation   this is scattered sunlight from the entire sky vault that forms air molecules, dust, and water vapor.

diffuser   a grille over an air supply duct having vanes to distribute the discharging air in a specific pattern or direction.

diffusion brazing   a brazing process which bonds metals by heating filler metal by either capillary attraction or diffusion of the filler metal.

diffusion flame burner   see *long flame burner.*

diffusity   the ability of earth material to take on or give off heat energy depending on its density and moisture content.

digital   describes information in discrete quantities; usually referring to a display that uses discrete numbers.

digital code   a system of symbols that represent data values and make up a special language that a computer or a digital circuit can understand and use.

digital device   a device that has only two states of operation, on or off.

digital input/output   input or output information translated into binary numbers (on-off signals) which can be processed by a digital computer.

digital logic   circuit elements connected in such a manner as to solve problems using components that have only two states of operation.

digital meter   a meter that uses electronic circuitry to provide a direct numerical read-out of a measured value.

digital signal   discrete or discontinuous signals whose various states are discrete intervals apart.

digital voltmeter   a voltmeter that uses direct current reading numerical display as opposed to a meter movement.

dilemma   a situation requiring a choice between equally undesirable results.

dilution air   air which enters a draft hood and mixes with the flue gases.

dimension and extension lines   thin lines that show the extent and direction of dimensions on blueprints or plotted prints. These lines tell you the length of an object and in which direction it is going. Direction lines usually end against extension lines with arrowheads or tick marks.

dimensions, overall   the projected dimensions of a device, usually on horizontal and vertical planes, that can be used to determine whether the device will fit in an assigned space or can be moved through a designed passageway.

diode   a solid state device composed of both P-type and N-type material. When connected to a circuit one way, current will flow. When the diode is reversed, current will not flow. It serves as a rectifier.

dioxin   a family of chemicals involving chlorine, hydrogen, and carbon atoms. It is formed during combustion when chlorine is present, but also as a by-product in some manufacturing processes, such as paper manufacturing. There are 75 forms with 2,3,7,8-TCDD, the most toxic. Diesel-fueled vehicles and hospital waste incinerators are significant sources.

dip soldering a soldering process in which the heat comes from a molten metal bath.

dip tube tube that extends to about one-half inch from the bottom of the receiver to assure that only liquid enters the liquid line at the receiver outlet.

direct acting controller a controller that increases the air pressure on a pneumatic control system with an increase in the temperature, pressure, etc., of the controlled variable.

direct-connected describes a driver-and-driven system, such as a motor and compressor, positively connected in-line to operate at the same speed.

direct current (DC) a normally constant-value current that flows in only one direction in a circuit. Varying current in one direction is a pulsating direct current, which may be derived from rectified alternating current.

direct current motor an electric motor that requires direct current supply and is primarily used for adjustable speed drive applications or motor vehicles.

direct current resistance the resistance offered by any circuit to the flow of direct current.

direct digital control (DDC) the use of a digital computer to perform required automatic control operations in a total energy management system.

direct drive a mechanical linkage where the shaft of the prime mover, or motor, is directly connected to the driven shaft or blower wheel, with both operating at the same speed.

direct expansion evaporator an evaporator coil using an automatic expansion valve (AXV), a thermostatic expansion valve (TXV), or a capillary or fixed-orifice plate-type refrigerant control to supply liquid refrigerant at the correct pressure and boiling point to obtain the desired rate and heat absorption into the liquid refrigerant.

direct-fired external heater any oven heating system in which the products of combustion from the burners are discharged into the oven chamber by a circulating fan or blower, and in which the burners are in a combustion chamber effectively separated from the oven chamber. There are two types:

1. nonrecirculating - products of combustion are discharged into the oven chamber and are not returned to the combustion chamber.
2. recirculating - oven chamber atmosphere is circulated to the combustion chamber and is in contact with the burner flame.

direct-fired heater a heater in which the products of combustion (flue gases) are mixed with the medium being heated (e.g., air). Also see *direct-fired external* and *direct-fired internal heaters.*

direct-fired internal heater heating system in which the burners are within the oven chamber, and the products of combustion are in contact with the oven atmosphere.

direct-fired make-up heater a heater in which all the products of combustion generated by the fuel-gas-burning device are released into the outside airstream being heated.

direct method refers to a way of taking advantage of solar heating through sunlight that enters windows of a house or structure.

direct return system, hot water a two-pipe hot water system in which the water, after it has passed through a heating unit, is returned to the boiler along a direct path so that the total distance traveled by the water from each radiator is the shortest feasible. There is, therefore, a considerable difference in the lengths of the several circuits composing the system.

direct spark ignition   use of an ignition spark, generated by a high-voltage transformer, to light the main burner; applies to burners not using a pilot, usually small oil burners. Also see *proved spark ignition.*

direct vent appliances   appliances that are constructed and installed so that all air for combustion is derived directly from the outside atmosphere and all flue gases are discharged to the outside atmosphere.

directly proportional   when one quantity increases or decreases, causing another quantity to do the same. For example, with a 120-volt to 24-volt rated step-down transformer that has a voltage of 60 volts placed on the primary, the output would be directly proportional to the input and deliver an output voltage of 12 volts.

dirt   refers to scale, sludges, flux, and metallic particles. These contaminants must be removed to protect the operation of the solenoid, compressor, expansion valves, or capillary tube and the refrigeration system as a whole.

discharge   output of a pump, fan, or compressor.

discharge bypass valve   a modulating valve that controls the hot-gas bypass to automatically maintain a desired minimum evaporator pressure.

discharge coefficient   the ratio of the actual flow rate of a gas from an orifice or port to the theoretical, calculated flow rate. It is always less than one.

discharge line   the refrigeration line that runs from the outlet of the compressor to the inlet of the condenser coil. Also called the hot-gas line.

discharge muffler   this device made up of a shell (with or without baffles) smooths out and quiets the compressor discharge pulsations on reciprocating compressors. Location can either be internal or external to the compressor.

discharge port   hole through the valve plate of the compressor where hot gas is discharged.

discharge pressure   pressure at the outlet of a fluid-moving device.

discharge shutoff valve   a manual valve installed on the compressor discharge line designed to isolate the compressor from the rest of the refrigeration system.

discharge valve   a valve in the compressor valve plate that controls the flow of hot high-pressure gas to the discharge line.

disconnect switch   an electrical switch that is used to disconnect electrical power to the load device. Can be single-pole, double-pole and/or triple-pole, single-throw arrangements. Also see *master switch.*

discus compressor   a reciprocating compressor distinguished by its disc-type valve system.

discus valve   a reciprocating compressor valve design with a low clearance volume and large bore.

disk   a circular plate with magnetic material on both sides, continuously rotated for reading or writing data by means of one or more read/write heads mounted on movable or fixed arms. Disks may be permanently mounted on a shaft, or they may be removable as a package and others placed on the shaft.

diskette   a magnetic data recording medium which functions like a disk, except that it is flexible and is similar to a 45-rpm record. Used only in floppy disk drives.

dismantle   to take apart, to strip of covering.

disperse   to break up and scatter in all directions.

displacement, actual the actual volume of gas or vapor, at compressor inlet conditions, moved by a compressor per revolution or per unit of time.

displacement, piston the volume obtained by multiplying the area of the cylinder bore by the length of the piston stroke.

displacement, theoretical the total volume displaced by the working strokes of all the pistons of a compressor per revolution or per unit of time.

display hold when a digital meter continues to display the last reading even after the probes have been removed from the test circuit.

disposable cylinder a one-trip refrigerant cylinder, not to be refilled.

disposal any process leading to and including the discharge, deposit, dumping, or placing of any discarded appliance or component parts into or on any land or water.

dissipation factor the ratio of the conductance of a capacitor, in which the material is the dielectric, to its susceptence; the ratio of its parallel reactance to its parallel resistance; or the ratio of the power loss to the circulating KVA. Used to indicate relative energy loss in a capacitor.

dissociation the breaking up of combustion products into combustibles and oxygen, accompanied by an absorption of heat. This usually occurs at high temperatures, and it is one of the factors limiting the maximum temperature of the flame.

distill the process of separating constituents of a liquid by boiling it and condensing the vapor that is produced. Distillation can be used to purify water and other substances, or to remove one component from a mixture, as when gasoline is distilled from crude oil.

distillate oil the oil separated from crude oil by fractional distillation.

distillation removal of gaseous substances from solids or liquids by applying heat.

distilling apparatus the fluid reclaiming device used to reclaim used refrigerants. Reclaiming is usually done by vaporizing and then recondensing the refrigerant.

distortion in welding, refers to the warping of a piece of metal.

distributed control network a group of independently functioning controllers under the supervision of a central controller (supervisory computer), yet having the capability of data analysis and control action at each controller.

distribution center an electric panel used to distribute electric supply to several places in a large structure. It can be a fused or circuit breaker design.

distribution controls systems which help to evenly and efficiently transfer the heating or cooling medium to the area where it is needed.

distributor a fluid delivery manifold, particularly the one that distributes liquid refrigerant from the metering device to the different passes of an evaporator coil.

distributor tester also known as a field analyzer, this tester will test individual components, the control module, status indicator, and all four probes individually without being mounted on the cuber. This tester is designed as a bench tester for a shop, or a countertop tester for large dealers and distributors handling many spare parts.

district heating and cooling the use of a central utility system designed to provide heating and cooling to large residential and industrial areas.

disturbed earth effect denotes the heat content change that affects the earth temperature by the addition to, or removal from the heat energy by the heat pump system.

diversity factor   ratio of the maximum probable demand to the maximum possible demand.

divert   to turn in a different direction.

diverter, draft   a fitting installed in the vent or flue of a heating appliance that will (1) provide a draft if there is none in the flue, (2) prevent a downdraft from entering the appliance, or (3) neutralize the chimney effect in the flue.

diverting switch   a pneumatic switch for connecting a common air line to either of two branches. Multiposition switches provide for several different air connections, usually including a vent connection for exhausting air from one air line.

diverting valve   a three-way valve with one inlet and two outlets. A fluid entering the inlet port is diverted to either of the two outlet ports in any proportion desired by moving the valve stem. A diverting valve is double-seated with a disc for each seat, so it can generally be used in mixing applications also.

dolly   a cart or rack with wheels, used to move heavy components or appliances.

domain theory   a theory of magnetism which assumes that groups of atoms produced by the movement of electrons align themselves in groups called domains in magnetic materials.

dome hat   the sealed metal container for the motor compressor of a refrigerating unit.

domestic equipment   air-conditioning or refrigeration equipment normally operated by the consumer.

domestic hot water   the heated water used for domestic or household purposes such as laundry, dishes, bathing, etc.

domestic refrigeration   any cooling unit that is used in the home. It includes air conditioners, refrigerators, and freezers.

door switch   a normally open single-pole switch used in appliances that operates by the opening and closing of the doors or panels.

doping   adding an impurity to a semiconductor to produce a desired charge.

dosimeter   a device that records the amount of something that a person is exposed to and then reads it back at the end of a day. It usually measures sound or radiation.

DOT identification numbers   four-digit numbers, preceded by UN or NA, that are used to identify particular substances for regulation of their transportation.

double-block and bleed   a valve arrangement in which a normally open vent valve just downstream from an automatic safety shutoff valve (SSOV) allows any gas that leaks past the SSOV during shutdown to escape to the outside atmosphere. A second SSOV just downstream from the vent valve blocks any gas which is not vented. When the SSOVs are open, the vent valve is closed. Also see *bleeding*.

double-cut file   a hand file that has two sets of cuts which cross one another on the face. Double-cut files are used for taking off material quickly.

double-duty case   a commercial refrigerator of which part is used for refrigerated storage and part is equipped with glass windows for display purposes.

double flare   a connection used on copper, aluminum, or steel tubing that folds the tubing wall to a double thickness.

double heat transfer   the transfer of heat from the plant to the heated medium (usually liquid) and from the liquid to the air in the conditioned space.

double-hung window   a window having two vertically sliding sashes, each covering one half of the opening.

double-pole breaker switch   a circuit breaker switch that is used to disconnect both hot wires with a single switch-off function.

double-pole, double-throw switch   a switch that has two poles and two contacts for each pole, so two contacts are always closed and two contacts are always open. This switch makes it possible to control a variety of loads from one location.

double-pole, single-throw switch an electrical switch arranged so that both switches are simultaneously opened or closed.

double-reduction describes a multiple reduction unit containing two stages of gear reduction housed in a single enclosure. The overall speed reduction (ratio) is the product of the gear ratios provided by the individual stages.

double-riser system a system in which two vertical hot gas discharge risers are used when a single vertical hot gas discharge riser sized for 1500 fpm at a minimum load would have an excessive pressure drop at maximum load. The smaller riser is sized for 1500 fpm gas velocity at minimum load while the larger is sized so the velocity through both risers will not be less than 1500 fpm at maximum load conditions.

double-seated valve a valve with two seats and discs arranged so that in the closed position there is very little fluid pressure forcing the stem toward the open or closed position; requires less power to operate than a single-seated valve of the same size; often has a larger port area for a given pipe size; does not have a tight shutoff.

double-thickness flare copper, aluminum, or steel tubing which has been formed into a two-wall thickness. This flare is usually at a 37° or 45°angle.

double-throw describes a contact arrangement in which each contact form included is a break make. Where one contact opens its connection to another contact and then closes its connection to a third contact.

dowel pin an accurately dimensioned pin pressed into one assembly part and slipped into another assembly part to ensure accurate alignment.

downdraft excessively high air pressure existing at the outlet of a chimney or stack which tends to make gases flow downward in the stack.

down-feed one-pipe riser, steam a pipe that carries steam downward to the heating units and into which the condensate from the heating unit drains.

down-feed system, steam a steam heating system in which the supply mains are above the level of the heating units which they serve.

downflow furnace a forced-air, central furnace with essentially vertical airflow, which discharges air at or near the bottom of the furnace (as distinguished from an upflow furnace).

downstream a point further from the source of fluid flow than another point.

draft the movement of air into and through a combustion chamber; breeching, stack, and chimney. Draft may be natural, resulting from the difference in density of the heated air rising through the stack and the cooler displacing air. Artificial draft may be provided by mechanical means. This could be either induced draft or forced draft. Draft is affected by chimney height, temperature difference, cross section, wind, make-up air opening in the furnace room, and weather conditions. Also see *forced, induced, mechanical, natural,* and *overfire draft.*

draft diverter a fitting on the furnace between the heat exchanger and the venting system which is designed to (1) assure the ready escape of the products of combustion in the event of no draft, backdraft, or stoppage beyond the draft diverter; (2) prevent a backdraft from entering the appliance; and (3) neutralize the effect of stack action of a chimney or gas vent upon the operation of the appliance.

draft gauge a gauge used to measure very small pressures (above and below atmospheric) and compare them to the atmosphere's pressure. Used to determine the flow of flue gas in a chimney or vent.

draft hood   see *draft diverter.*

draft indicator   an instrument used to indicate or measure stack draft or combustion gas movement. Draft is measured in units of 0.01 inch of water column.

draft loss   the reduction of draft intensity caused by resistance to flow of flue gases through the boiler, breeching, and chimney, plus any resistance to flow of air through the burner.

draft regulator   a device which acts to maintain a desired draft by automatically controlling the chimney draft intensity at the desired value.

drain   to make or become gradually dry or empty.

drain cock   a valve installed in the lowest point of a boiler, or at low points of a heating system, to provide for complete drainage of water from the system.

drain, electronics   a collector of the majority carriers.

drain pan   pan-shaped panel or trough used to collect condensate from the evaporator.

drain pipe   a pipe for the removal of condensate, excess water, or fluids.

drain wire   in a cable, an uninsulated wire laid over the component or components and used as a ground connection.

drawdown   the difference between the static water level and the pumping water level in a water well.

drawdown, pressure tank   the amount of liquid the tank will deliver per minute within a specified pressure range before the pump starts.

drier   a device containing a drying agent or substance placed in the refrigerant circuit to keep the moisture level in a system at a

safe level. Its purpose is to collect and hold excess water from the system.

drift, controls   the tendency of a controller to have a deviation between the control point and the set point.

drift punch   a hand tool used to drive out keyways and to line up holes in matching material.

drift, water tower   entrained unevaporated water carried from a cooling tower by air movement through it.

drill   a tool for drilling and boring, and for installing all types of screws. Drill sizes can be fractional, number, or letter.

drill bit   drill bits are used to do the actual drilling or boring of a hole. They are used for installation and repair work. Drill bits are available for working in metal, wood, plastic, and masonry. Most have a straight shank.

Drill Manufacturer's Standard (DMS) equivalent to standard twist drill or steel wire gauge numbers.

drill rod   an accurately ground and polished steel rod.

drilled port burner   a burner in which the ports have been formed by drilled holes in a thick section in the burner head or by a manufacturing method which results in holes similar in size, shape, and depth.

drilled supply well   small-diameter hole bored into the earth by a screw-type shaft attached to a drilling rig, using a stream of water or drilling mud to flush out the material loosened by the drill. The hole is bored to find water up to 500 feet if necessary.

drilling   cutting round holes in material by use of a cutting tool called a drill.

drinking water cooler   an assembly which either employs or is used in conjunction with a mechanical condensing unit for the purpose of cooling drinking water.

drinking water cooler capacity the quantity of water a water cooler will cool in a given ambient temperature with a given incoming water temperature and a given outgoing water temperature, under steady-state conditions.

drip leg a dead-end section of pipe at the lowest point in a gas supply line that accumulates any foreign matter that may have gotten into the gas or piping system. It is this pocket that keeps this material from entering the gas controls.

drip pan a pan shaped to collect moisture condensing on an evaporator coil in an air-conditioning or refrigeration system.

drip-proof motor a motor that has the ventilation openings in the end shields and shell placed so that drops of liquid falling within an angle of 15° from vertical will not affect performance. Usually employed for indoor usage in fairly clean locations.

drive method refers to the method used to drive or power a reciprocal compressor, such as a motor.

drive pulley a pulley attached to the shaft of the prime mover and from which power is transmitted.

driven describes a component that does not have its own power, but derives it from a separate engine or motor.

driver a digital circuit element coupled to the output stage of a circuit to increase the power or current-handling capability, or fan-out, of the stage.

droop lowering of the operating temperature of a thermostat below the set point, due to artificial heating of the bimetal by the heat anticipator or other heating source.

drop the vertical distance that a projected airstream falls between the grille and the end of its throw.

drop, service the overhead service conductors between the utility company's last pole and the customer's first point of attachment.

drop, voltage the electromotive force needed to cause the current to flow through a load.

dropout voltage or amperage at which the magnetic field around the coil of a control is no longer strong enough to attract the armature or contacts.

dry to separate or remove a liquid or vapor from another substance. The liquid may be water, but the term is also used for the removal of liquid or vapor forms of other substances.

dry air air which contains no moisture vapor.

dry air cooler removes sensible heat from the dehydrated air whenever it leaves the dehydrator at an elevated temperature.

dry bulb an instrument with a sensitive element which measures sensible ambient air temperature.

dry bulb temperature the air temperature as indicated by an ordinary thermometer.

dry bulb thermometer instrument which measures air temperature, independent of humidity.

dry capacitor condenser an electrolytic electrical device (start capacitor) that is used to store electrons, made of dry metal and dry insulation.

dry cell battery an electrical device used to provide a direct current potential difference. This device has no liquid in the cells.

dry compression the compression of a vapor in a vapor/liquid compression refrigeration system.

dry contacts contacts isolated from any source of power.

dry expansion a process of heat removal by a refrigerant in an evaporator fed by a flow control, responsive to temperature or pressure or both at some point in the evaporator, or to the difference between the high- and low-side pressures, but not to the liquid level in the evaporator; all entering refrigerant is evaporated before being recirculated.

dry gas   a gas having a moisture and hydrocarbon dew point below any normal temperature to which the gas piping is exposed.

dry ice   a refrigerating substance made of solid carbon dioxide which changes directly from a solid to a gas (sublimates). It sublimates at a temperature of –109°F.

dry media filter   a filter that traps and holds dust without being coated with a sticky material.

dry return   a return pipe in a steam heating system that carries both air and water from condensate.

dry steam   superheated water vapor containing no more than 0.5% moisture.

dry system   a refrigerating system which has the evaporator liquid refrigerant mainly in the atomized or droplet condition.

dry-type evaporator   an evaporator in which all the liquid refrigerant boils off while flowing through the coil, before reaching the suction line.

dryback boiler   a scotch, fire-tube boiler with a ceramic baffle at the back of the furnace to direct the products of combustion from the combustion chamber to the second pass. The baffle is separate from the pressure vessel and is constructed of heat-resistant material (generally refractory brick and insulation). Also see *fire-tube* and *scotch boilers*.

D-type flip-flop   D stands for data. A flip-flop whose output is a function of the input that appeared one clock pulse earlier. For example, if a logic 1 appeared at the input, the output after the next clock pulse will be a logic 1.

dual-element fuse   a device that interrupts an electrical circuit after excessive current over an extended time period (time-delay element) or after excessive momentary current.

dual-fuel burner   a burner using one prime fuel, but capable of using a standby fuel

under peak load conditions. Changeover from one fuel to the other can be made automatically using an electric temperature controller or by use of a manual switch. Also see *combination burner*.

dual-pressure control   a control that senses, and is actuated by, both high- and low-side refrigeration system pressure.

dual-purpose condenser   a water-cooled condenser that can be used on either city water or cooling tower water.

dual-run capacitor   an electrical storage device that has two run capacitors, one for the fan and one for the compressor, built into one case.

dual-voltage motors   motors manufactured to operate on either of two specified supplied voltages.

duct   a tube, channel, or canal through which a fluid moves; a protective pipe through which wires or cables are run.

duct coil   a heat-exchanging coil mounted inside an air delivery supply duct.

duct fan   see *tubeaxial fan*.

duct furnace   a central furnace designed for installation in a duct of an air distribution system to supply warm air for heating. For air circulation, it depends on a blower not furnished as part of the furnace.

duct heat gain   a situation where, after leaving a unit, air is warmed on its way to the registers, so the air is warmer at the end of the air-conditioning path than at the beginning.

duct heater   an electric resistance heater mounted inside an air delivery duct that provides supplementary heat to the delivered air.

duct loss   heat loss through the walls of ductwork to the space surrounding the ducts.

ductility   the ability of a metal to be formed or shaped.

Dulong's formula   an equation for estimating the heat content of a pound of coal based on its content of carbon, hydrogen, oxygen, and sulfur.

dummy terminals   terminals that have no effect on the operation of the relay or equipment, but provide connection points for wires. Dummy terminals could also be located on terminal strips.

duplex receptacle   a double-outlet receptacle used in house wiring. It provides outlets to connect lamps and appliances. The duplex receptacle is mounted in a electrical box in the wall section.

dust   an air suspension (aerosol) of particles of any solid material, usually produced from crushing, grinding, abrading, or blasting, with particle size less than 100 micrometers.

duty   a requirement of service which defines the degree of regularity of the load.

duty cycle   the relationship between operating and rest time. When applied to motors, duty cycle is usually referred to as continuous- or intermittent-duty.

Dx coil   an evaporator coil where the expansion of refrigerant inside the coil happens directly. A dry-type evaporator.

dynamic ampli-check   a Honeywell trademark; a feature in some infrared flame signal amplifiers. The circuitry tests only the flame signal amplifier during burner operation and shuts down the burner if the amplifier fails (including a flame-simulating failure).

dynamic braking   using a DC motor as a generator to produce countertorque and thereby produce a braking action. Applying direct current to the stator winding of an AC induction motor to cause a magnetic braking action.

dynamic self-check   a Honeywell trademark; a feature in the rectification-type flame signal amplifiers of some flame safeguard controls. The circuitry tests all electronic components in the flame detection system (amplifier and detector) 60 to 240 times a minute during burner operation and shuts down the burner

if the detection system fails (including a flame-simulating failure).

dynamometer   a device that measures the power input and/or the power output of a mechanism.

Dytel   trade name for a refrigerant that has a red dye added to it to aid in the visual detection of leaks.

E

E   a symbol for voltage (electromotive force).

E_c efficiency, combustion.

EASA   Electrical Apparatus Service Association.

ECI   Evaporative Cooling Institute.

eco   energy cut off.

EEA   Earth Energy Association.

EEI   Edison Electric Institute.

EER   energy efficiency ratio.

EEREC   Energy Efficiency and Renewable Energy Clearinghouse.

eff_{ss} efficiency, steady state.

EIA   Environmental Information Association.

EIC   Environmental Industry Council.

EJMA   Expansion Joint Manufacturers Association.

ela   effective leakage area.

elem   elementary.

ELI   a term used to help remember that voltage (E) in an inductive (L) circuit leads current (I).

EMA   Environmental Management Association.

EMF   electromotive force.

emi   electromagnetic interference.

emt   electrical metallic tubing. Another name for thinwall conduit.

encl   enclosure.

EPA   Environmental Protection Agency.

epr   evaporator pressure regulator.

EPRI Electric Power Research Institute.

equip equipment.

etr evaporator temperature regulator.

early spark termination a feature of some programming controls which allows ignition cutoff before the main fuel valve(s) opens, resulting in a period during which only the pilot is on.

earth terminology for zero reference ground.

earth aquifer the water quantity below the surface of the earth.

earth temperature, maximum (T_{max}) the highest temperature the earth will reach in the summer season. This will depend on location and weather conditions.

earth temperature, minimum (T_{min}) the lowest temperature the earth will reach in the winter season. This will vary with location and weather conditions.

earth tester an instrument used to measure the electrical resistance of a ground rod, steel tower, or actual earth resistance.

ebullator a pointed or sharp-edged solid substance inserted in a flooded-type evaporator used to improve the evaporation of the refrigerant in the coil.

eccentric a circle or disk mounted off center. Eccentrics are used to adjust controls and connect compressor drive shafts to the connecting rods.

eccentric reducer a pipe fitting designed to change from one pipe size to another and to keep one edge of both pipes in line. These fittings should be installed so that the "in-line" section of pipe is at the top.

ecological having to do with the study of the environment of the human species.

ecology the science of the interaction of life forms on earth.

economic balance point the lowest outdoor temperature at which the heat pump is more economical to operate than the furnace.

economizer a system of controls and dampers on an air-conditioning system that mixes varying volumes of outdoor air with air in the conditioned space by using the lower mixed-air temperature to achieve "free cooling."

economizer control a system of ventilation control in which outdoor and return air dampers are controlled to maintain proper mixed-air temperatures for the most economical operation.

economizer cycle a method of operating an air-conditioning system to introduce extra outside air when the temperature and relative humidity are in the correct proportion.

eddy current induced current flowing in a magnetic core that is created by a varying magnetic field.

eddy current tests a test that uses induced currents flowing in a magnetic core to find potential failure faults in different types of tubing.

Edison base fuses 15-, 20-, and 30-amp fuses that have the same base configuration as a regular-base incandescent bulb.

effect, chimney the tendency of air or gas in a duct or other vertical passage to rise when heated due to its lower density compared to that of the surrounding air or gas. In buildings, it is the tendency toward displacement (caused by the difference in temperature) of internal heated air by unheated outside air due to the difference in density of outside and inside air.

effect, refrigerating the rate of heat removed by a refrigerant in a refrigerating system; this is equal to the product of the mass rate of refrigerant flow in the system and the difference in specific enthalpies of the refrigerant at two designated points in the system or two designated thermodynamic states of the refrigerant.

effect, total cooling the difference between the total enthalpy of the dry air and water vapor mixture entering a unit per hour and the total enthalpy of the dry air and water vapor (and water) mixture leaving a unit per hour, expressed in Btu per hour.

effective area   the actual flow area of an air inlet or outlet. The gross area minus area of vanes or grille bars. Net free area. It is equal to the free area of the device times the coefficient of discharge.

effective heat allowance   an allowance added to the test output of certain designs of radiation to compensate for a better distribution of heat within the heated space. Some agencies do not permit the use of effective heat allowance.

effective temperature   the overall apparent temperature sensed by a person in the conditioned space. An index that is a combination of temperature, humidity, and air movement.

effective temperature difference   the difference between the room temperature and the supply air temperature at the outlet to the room.

effective value   the root mean square value of alternating current or voltage.

effective voltage   a value of an AC sine wave voltage which has the same heating effect as an equal value of DC voltage; $E_{eff} = E_{peak} \times 0.707$.

efficiency   the ratio of output power to input power, usually expressed as a percentage. A measure of how well the electrical energy input to a motor is converted into mechanical energy at the output shaft. The higher the efficiency, the better the conversion process and the lower the operating costs.

efficiency, overall   the ratio obtained by dividing the theoretical power required by the actual power required.

efficiency, volumetric   term used to express the relationship between the actual performance of a compressor or a vacuum pump and the calculated performance of the compressor or pump based on its displacement.

ejector   a device such as a venturi, which uses high fluid velocity, to create low pressure or vacuum at its throat to draw in fluid from another source.

elastomer   any elastic, rubber-like substance such as natural or synthetic rubber.

elbow   a fitting with two openings at a 90° angle to each other.

electric circuit   a path for electrons to follow. The circuit may be open or closed depending on the position of its switches.

electric current   the movement of electrical charges through a conductive material.

electric defrosting   the use of electric resistance heating coils to melt ice and frost off evaporators during defrosting.

electric energy   energy that is produced by a movement of electrons. The energy can be produced by chemical, light, thermal, or mechanical means.

electric field   a magnetic region in space which has force and direction.

electric filament lamp   a light source consisting of a glass bulb containing a filament electrically maintained at incandescence. A lighting unit, consisting of an electric filament lamp with shade, reflector, enclosing globe, housing, or other accessories, is also commonly called a lamp. In such cases, in order to distinguish between the assembled lighting unit and the light source within it, the latter is often called a bulb.

electric furnace   a device constructed of high-resistance wire or other material which produces heat when a current is passed through it.

electric heating   a house heating system which uses heat from electrical resistance units to heat rooms.

electric heating element   a unit assembly consisting of a resistor, insulated supports, and terminals for connecting the resistor to the electric power.

electric ignition   ignition of a pilot or main burner by an electric spark generated by a transformer, which is either automatically or manually energized. Also see *direct spark ignition.*

electric meter   a device used to measure some electrical characteristic of a circuit such as the voltage, amperage, resistance, or wattage.

electric motor   a machine which transforms electrical energy into mechanical energy.

electric-pneumatic relay   a small electrically operated diverting valve, specially designed or suitable for diverting air from one control line to another. See also *electropneumatic relays.*

electric potential   the potential for electron flow between a positive and a negative pole. Electrical potential is measured in volts.

electric power   the rate at which electricity is being used, measured in watts.

electric precipitator   a device for removing dust from the air by means of electrostatic charges induced on the dust particles.

electric pressure   another term used to refer to electromotive force, potential difference, and voltage.

electric switch   a device that opens or closes to control some load in an electric circuit. It can be opened or closed by temperature, pressure, humidity, flow, or manual means.

electric valve   a solenoid-type (electrically operated) valve used to operate the final end use.

electrical angle   the method specifying the exact instant in an alternating current cycle. Each cycle is 360°; therefore 180° would indicate one-half of a cycle, 45° one-eighth of a cycle, etc.

electrical charge   there are two types of electrical charges—negative and positive. Like charges repel and unlike charges attract.

electrical circuit   an electrical path between two or more points; the interconnection of a number of devices in one or more closed paths to perform a desired electrical or electronic function. Also see *dynamic amplicheck* and *dynamic self-check;* and *alarm, bridge, conductivity, firing rate switching circuit, flip-flop, high-voltage, isolated limited secondary, line-voltage, low-voltage, open, short,* and *tuned circuits.*

electrical control circuit   a wiring diagram showing how the various pieces of the control circuit are to be connected for proper operation.

electrical degree   one 360th of an alternating current or voltage cycle.

electrical drawing   an electrical drawing shows the electrical layout. Plan views show the location of switches, receptacles, lights, and other related electrical equipment.

electrical impulse   the electrical current fed from one control instrument to another to indicate that a position change is required.

electrical interlock   when the contacts of one device or circuit prevent the operation of some other device or circuit.

electrical load   that part of the electrical system which actually uses the energy or does the work required.

electrical plan   a schematic of the electrical location of the meter, distribution panel, switches, convenience outlets, and special outlets such as door bells, telephones, and gfics.

electrical power   power is measured in watts. One watt is equal to one ampere flowing with a potential of one volt. Watts = volts × amps. ($P = E \times I$)

electrical shock   an electrical current that travels through a human body.

electrical symbols   standardized simple drawings used for ease of communication in schematic diagrams.

electrically reversible motor   one which can be reversed by changing the external connections.

electricity   energy that is capable of producing a flow of electrons. An unbalanced condition that results when electrons can be easily moved from atom to atom.

electrode   a conductor by means of which a current passes into or out of a gas; often one terminal of a lead. Examples: ignition electrodes, flame rods, or electron tube elements.

electrode, welding   a thin metal rod coated with a special substance and used as a filler to join the metal to be welded.

electrolysis   the production of chemical changes by passage of current through an electrolyte.

electrolyte   a nonmetallic substance, used in dry and wet cells, that conducts an electrical current in solution by movement of ions rather than electrons.

electrolytic capacitor   a plate or surface capable of storing small electrical charges. Common electrolytic capacitors are formed by rolling thin sheets of foil between insulating materials. Capacitor capacity is expressed in microfarads.

electromagnet   a magnet made by winding a coil of wire around a soft iron core. When an electric current is run through the wire, the coil becomes magnetic.

electromagnetic energy   energy which has both electrical and magnetic characteristics. Solar energy, for example, is electromagnetic.

electromagnetic field   the space around an inductor that changes due to current flow through a coil. The field expands and collapses with applied AC.

electromagnetic interference   stray electrical or magnetic fields that may induce damaging current or interference in other electrical equipment.

electromagnetic spectrum   a chart or graph showing the relationship among all known electromagnetic waveforms classified by wavelengths.

electromagnetic wave   the radiant energy produced by oscillation of an electric charge. Included are radio waves; infrared, visible, and ultraviolet light waves; and X, gamma, and cosmic rays.

electromagnetism   the phenomenon of a magnetic field generated around a conductor by electrical current flowing through it.

electromechanical   a term used to describe controls which contain both electrical and mechanical components.

electromotive force (EMF)   electrical force (voltage) which causes current to flow or move in an electrical circuit. Its unit of measure is the volt. It can be either AC (alternating current) or DC (direct current).

electron   the elementary particle or portion of an atom which carries a negative charge. Electrons surround the positively charged nucleus of the atom. Electrons are the means by which the transfer of electrical energy can take place.

electron current flow   current flow that is assumed to be in the direction of electron movement from a negative (–) potential to a positive (+) potential.

electron-hole pair   the free electron and its hole that are produced by thermal excitation of a valence electron.

electronic   of or pertaining to devices, circuits, or systems utilizing the motion or emission of currents of free electrons, especially in vacuum, gas, or phototubes, and special conductors or semiconductors.

electronic air cleaner   a device that produces a powerful electric field to ionize dirt and dust particles in the air. The particles are then collected on electrically charged plates.

electronic charging scale   an electronically operated scale used to accurately charge refrigeration systems by weight.

electronic combustion analyzer   an electronic combustion analyzer is used to measure various items related to the combustion process. They can measure % of CO_2, % of O_2, stack temperature, ppm of CO, and overall combustion efficiency.

electronic control   a control or system using electronic amplifiers to build up control signals for system operations.

electronic control diagnostics   trouble codes which may be referenced on an automatic climate control system to diagnose problems.

electronic expansion valve   a metering valve that uses a thermistor as a temperature-sensing element which varies the voltage to control the flow of refrigerant to the evaporator.

electronic ignition   a system that saves fuel by eliminating a continuously burning pilot light. The pilot flame is ignited by an electric spark and the pilot burns only upon a call for heat.

electronic leak detector   an electronic instrument which measures electronic flow across a gas gap. Electronic flow changes indicate the presence of refrigerant gas molecules.

electronic relay   an electronic switch, such as a triac, which controls a power-consuming device.

electronic sight glass   a device that sends an audible signal when the refrigerant system is low in refrigerant.

electronic sound tracer   an instrument used to detect leaks by locating the source of high-frequency sound caused by the leak.

electronic thermistor   electrical device that senses temperature changes to control an output source. Also see *thermistor*.

electronic thermostat   thermostat that uses electronic components to accomplish various sensing, switching, timing, staging, and display functions.

electronics   the field of science that deals with electronic devices and their uses.

electroplate   the term used to indicate the application of a metallic coating on a surface by means of electrolytic action.

electropneumatic relays   small electrically operated air valves used in the operation of pneumatic controls.

electrostatic   a term referring to electricity at rest.

electrostatic charge   the electrical energy located on the surface of insulating material or in a capacitor because of an excess or deficiency of electrons.

electrostatic field   the space around a charged material in which the influence of the electrical charge is experienced.

electrostatic filter   that type of filter which gives a particle of dust an electrical charge. This causes particles to be attracted to plates so that they can be removed from the airstream or atmosphere.

electrostatics   the science or study of electricity at rest.

element, bimetallic   one formed of two metals having different coefficients of thermal expansion such as are used in temperature indicating and controlling devices.

element (control)   usually refers to the measuring part of a controller which senses a change in temperature, pressure, or humidity. It produces a corresponding effect of force, pressure, or electrical impulse to cause the actuator to function.

element (electric heating)   a unit assembly consisting of a resistor, insulated supports, and terminals for connecting the resistor to electric power.

elements   the basic materials that make up all other materials; they exist by themselves (such as copper, hydrogen, carbon) or in chemical combination with other elements (water is a combination of the elements hydrogen and oxygen).

elevation drawing   these drawings show the view of the building from the outside. Usually four drawings are needed. These display the front, rear, right and left sides of the building.

eliminate   to get rid of or to do away with.

eliminator   stationary vanes or louvers in a duct or plenum that remove any liquid from the gas passing through it.

ellipse   a closed curve in the form of a symmetrical oval.

ells   prebent tubing, factory-designed as soldered or flared fittings that let refrigerant lines be routed between components. Also refers to sheet metal fittings.

emergency heat switch   control on a heat-pump-type subbase used to energize auxiliary heat for a heat pump system.

emission rate   amount of a contaminant released into the air by a source in a specified amount of time.

emissivity   the capacity of a material to emit radiant energy. Emittance is the ratio of the total radiant flux emitted by a body to that emitted by an ideal black body at the same temperature.

emitter   the lead of a transistor shown using an arrow with a head on it.

emitter-base junction   the P-N junction formed by the emitter and the base regions.

emitter N-region   that region of an NPN transistor that emits a relatively large number of electrons in response to a relatively small number of electrons coming from the P region.

employee   is a worker whose services are hired by an employer, and from whose pay state and federal taxes are deducted.

enclosure   open drip-proof motors are for use in areas that are dry, clean, and well ventilated. If installed outside, a motor of this type must be protected with a cover that does not restrict airflow. Damp or dirty conditions require totally enclosed construction. Hazardous conditions, no matter how slight, require an explosion-proof (hazardous-location) motor. A hazardous-location machine is a totally enclosed motor whose enclosure is designed and constructed to withstand an explosion of a specified gas or vapor which may occur within it and to prevent the ignition of the specified gas or vapor which may occur within the motor casing.

enclosures of motors   induction type according to NEMA.

1. Open type (OT) - an open motor is self-ventilated, having no restriction to ventilation or to the enclosure other than that necessitated by mechanical construction.
2. Drip-proof (DP) - constructed with ventilation openings so that falling liquid at an angle of 15° from vertical will not enter the motor.
3. Totally enclosed (TE) - constructed with no openings in brackets or frame. Includes totally enclosed non-vented (TENV), totally enclosed fan-cooled (TEFC), and totally enclosed air-over (TEAO) explosion-proof (XP).

encode   to use a code, frequently one composed of binary numbers, to represent individual characters or groups of characters in a message. Also to change from one digital code to another. If the codes are greatly different, the process is called code conversion.

encrustation   the buildup of slimy orange-brown deposits on the water side of pipes caused by iron bacteria in the water.

end bell   the shield at the end of the motor which supports the bearings. Also called end plates or end shields.

end play   the slight movement of the shaft along the center line.

end wrench   the same as a pipe wrench except that the movable jaw is offset to get into tighter or closer positions.

endothermal describes a chemical reaction in which heat is absorbed.

energize to supply or put power to an electrical load.

energy the ability or capacity to do work. Mechanical energy is expressed in foot-pounds or horsepower-hours; electric energy, in kilowatt hours; and heat energy, in British thermal units.

energy audit process of accurately determining the current energy consumption for a given area.

energy bands the grouping of energy levels that occurs when atoms are bonded together in solid materials.

energy charge that part of an electric bill based on kWh consumption. Expressed in cents per kWh. Energy charge covers the cost of utility fuel, general operating costs, and part of the amortization of the utility's equipment.

energy conservation the process, upon reviewing the calculations for determining heat loads, of instituting changes that will result in energy savings.

energy cutoff a protective device placed in series with the thermocouple in a control system which opens the thermocouple circuit, thereby shutting down the burner operation in case of abnormally high temperatures.

energy efficiency ratio (EER) the ratio of the rated cooling capacity in Btu per hour divided by the amount of electrical power used in watts.

energy levels the energy states of electrons in an atom.

energy management control system controllers used in a system which optimize total energy usage in a building or residence.

energy utilization index (EUI) a number which is used to compare energy usages for different areas. It is calculated by dividing the energy consumption (in Btu) by the square footage of the conditioned space area.

engine a prime mover; a device for transforming fuel or heat energy into mechanical energy.

enhancement mode the operation of a field effect transistor that occurs with an increase in the gate-to-source voltage in an effort to increase the drain current.

enthalpy the total amount of heat (both latent and sensible) in one pound of a substance that is calculated from an accepted base of 32°F. For refrigeration the accepted base is –40°F. Expressed in Btu/lb.

enthalpy switch-over automatic switching or regulation of outside air and return air dampers. Total heat content of inside and outside air is compared before selecting either inside or outside air, or a mixture of the two, for ventilation, which will require the least amount of refrigeration, humidification, or dehumidification.

entrained describes a liquid which is absorbed and held, but not dissolved, in a medium, as in air.

entrainment the induced flow of room air by the primary air from an outlet, creating a mixed air path (commonly called secondary air motion).

entrance cap a weatherproof, insulated cap for terminating the power line connections to a building; service head.

entrance ell a metal box to complete a 90° angle with a conduit. The cover allows the electrician to pull wires through a conduit in either direction.

entrance, service the part of the electrical installation from the service drop to the main service panel.

entropy the ratio of the heat added to a substance to the absolute temperature at which it is added. A mathematical factor used in engineering calculations. The amount of energy in a system.

envelope component   major section of the entire envelope, such as the opaque walls above-grade, ceilings, slabs, floors, glazings, doors, or walls below-grade.

environment   surroundings; conditions and influences surrounding and affecting development and behavior.

environmental control system   the means of controlling the environment by heating, cooling, humidifying, dehumidifying, or cleaning the air.

enzyme   a complex organic substance originating from living cells that speeds up the chemical breakdown of food. Enzyme action is slowed by cooling.

epidemiology   a science that deals with the incidence, distribution, and control of diseases in a population.

epoxy   a synthetic plastic adhesive.

equal percentage characteristic   a valve flow characteristic which causes like movements of the valve stem at any point of the flow range to change existing flow an equal percentage, regardless of the existing flow quantity.

equalizer   a piping arrangement to maintain a common liquid level or pressure between two or more chambers.

equalizer, crankcase double-pipe   a system in which both the gas pressure and the oil level in all compressors connected in multiple are equalized.

equalizer, crankcase single-pipe   a pipe or tube connection between the crankcases of the compressors of a multiple compressor system, the function of the pipe or tube being to equalize the pressures between the crankcases.

equalizer, external   in a thermostatic expansion valve, a tube connection from a selected control point in the low-side refrigeration circuit to the pressure-sensing side of the control element such that the control-point pressure is transmitted to the actuating element (diaphragm or bellows). This connection provides a means for compensating for the pressure drop through accessories and the evaporator coil.

equalizer, internal   in a thermostatic expansion valve, an integral internal part or passage which provides exposure of the actuating element (diaphragm or bellows) to pressure leaving the valve.

equalizer line   a line that equalizes the gas or oil pressure in two or more pieces of equipment.

equalizer tube   a device that is used to maintain equal pressure or equal liquid levels between two containers.

equalizer valve   a device that regulates the flow of gases or liquids. It is used to balance pressures on both sides of some recovery machines.

equalizers   connections used with thermostatic expansion valves when the superheat setting of the expansion valve cannot control the amount of refrigerant which flows through the coil.

equalizing   the balancing of refrigerant system pressures.

equation of state   a thermodynamic relation giving the functional dependence of the properties of the substances with each other.

equilateral   describes a figure that has equal length sides.

equilibrium   conditions that exist at saturation or balance.

equipment (service)   all the necessary equipment which constitutes the main control and cut off of the electrical supply to the premises.

equivalent direct radiation (EDR)   a unit of heat delivery of 240 Btu per hr.

equivalent evaporation   the amount of water a boiler would evaporate, in pounds per hour, if it received feed water at 212° F. and vaporized it at the same temperature and corresponding atmospheric pressure.

equivalent length of pipe   a term used to describe the pressure drop caused by a given component in terms of the pressure drop caused by an equivalent length of pipe.

equivalent resistance   a resistance value that would be the same value in a circuit as two or more parallel resistances in a circuit.

erratic   having no fixed course. Irregular, wandering.

error   the difference between the correct value and the reading taken.

escutcheon   a decorative, protective plate covering the body or wiring of a component.

ester-based synthetic oil   an oil that is wax free, has a low floc point, and is used with hydrofluorocarbon (HFC) refrigerants. Any of a class of organic compounds corresponding to the inorganic salts formed from an acid by the replacement of hydrogen by an alkyl radical.

estimate   a prediction of the expected cost for equipment or repair work.

estimated tax   a tax payment made four times a year by a self-employed person to the Internal Revenue Service based on what he or she expects to earn that year.

ethane   a refrigerant (R-170) sometimes added to other refrigerants to improve oil circulation.

ethylene glycol   a liquid chemical used as a water antifreeze.

eutectic alloy   a metal with a low and sharp melting point used in thermal overload relays.

eutectic mixture (solution)   that certain mixture of two substances providing the lowest melting temperature of all the various mixes of the two substances.

eutectic point   freezing temperature for eutectic solutions.

eutectic salts   a special salt that melts at low temperatures by absorbing large quantities of heat. The most common eutectic salt is glaubers salt. These salts are used as a heat storage medium for solar systems.

eutectic solution   a mixture that melts and freezes at the lowest possible temperature for mixtures of the included substances.

evacuate   to withdraw from; to make empty; to remove the contents from. To remove, through the use of a vacuum pump, all non-condensables and moisture from a system.

evacuation   removal of air (gas) and moisture from a refrigeration or air-conditioning system.

evaporate   to change a state of matter from a liquid to a vaporous state.

evaporating temperature   the temperature at which a liquid will vaporize at a given pressure.

evaporation   the physical process of changing a liquid to a vapor through the addition of heat energy.

evaporative condenser   a device which uses open spray or spill water to cool a condenser. Evaporation of some of the water cools the condenser water and reduces water consumption.

evaporative cooling   a system in which the absorption of latent heat by evaporating water cools the air it contacts. This system is used where the % of RH in the air is low. This system will add humidity to the air.

evaporative cooling tower   a device that dissipates heat energy by the evaporation of water. The water is recirculated to cool refrigeration condensers.

evaporative equilibrium (of a wet bulb thermometer)   the condition attained when the wetted wick has reached a stable and constant temperature (when the instrument is exposed to air at velocities over 900 fpm, this temperature may be considered to approach the true wet bulb temperature).

evaporator that part of a refrigeration system in which the refrigerant absorbs heat and evaporates. Considered to be on the low side of the refrigeration system. Design evaporating temperature must be lower than the air passing over or through the coil.

evaporator coil a device made of a coil of tubing which functions as a refrigerant evaporator.

evaporator, direct expansion an evaporator designed to cool a medium in direct contact with the evaporator.

evaporator, dry-type an evaporator in which refrigerant is fed from a pressure-reducing valve. Little or no liquid refrigerant collects in the evaporator.

evaporator fan a fan that moves air over heat exchange surfaces of evaporator coil so heat can be absorbed from the airstream.

evaporator, flooded an evaporator containing liquid refrigerant at all times.

evaporator pressure regulator a valve located at the outlet of the evaporator that will close if the evaporator pressure falls below a given point. The control which maintains a predetermined refrigerant pressure, and therefore temperature, in a cooling coil.

evaporator pressure regulator valve operates by bellows; refrigerant pressure on the diaphragm of the bellows compresses the spring and holds the valve open.

evaporator superheat the actual temperature of the refrigerant vapor at the evaporator outlet as compared to the saturated vapor temperature indicated by the suction pressure.

excess air air which passes through the combustion chamber and flues in excess of the quantity which is theoretically required for complete combustion. Usually stated as

a percentage of the air required for complete combustion.

excise tax an internal tax such as the tax levied on those who produce chlorofluorocarbons (CFCs).

exfiltration slow flow of air from the building to the outdoors.

exhaust a vent or opening for unwanted or used air.

exhaust air that air which is removed from the conditioned space by the ventilation system and discharged outdoors.

exhaust fan a fan which provides a suction to remove the air, gases, and products of combustion from the furnace or oven. In some systems, it also brings in combustion air. Also called a ventilator.

exhaust opening any opening through which air is removed from a space which is being heated, cooled, humidified, dehumidified, or ventilated.

exhaust port that opening which carries the fluid to the downstream pressure of a fluid system.

exhaust valve a movable port which provides an outlet for the cylinder exhaust gases in a compressor or engine.

exhauster a fan used to withdraw air under suction.

exothermal describes a chemical reaction in which heat is released.

expandable partitions these are heavyweight vinyl folding parts located on the sides of a window unit installation. They expand so the same unit can fit windows that differ in width and also insulate the room from the outside.

expanding pilot a pilot that burns throughout the entire time the burner assembly is in service, whether the main burner is firing or not. Upon a call for heat, the pilot flame is automatically increased in size so as to reliably ignite the main burner. This pilot may be turned down automatically at the end of the main burner flame-establishing period.

expansion increase in volume due to increased temperature or decreased pressure.

expansion, dry where all of the refrigerant entering the evaporator is vaporized, as contrasted with a flooded evaporator.

expansion joint device in piping designed to allow movement of the pipe caused by the pipe's expansion and contraction.

expansion loop a coil or U-shaped bend in a length of tubing that provides flexibility for expansion or contraction of the tubing.

expansion point in a mechanical refrigeration system, a restriction or orifice which regulates the flow of refrigerant into the evaporator coil. May be in the form of a thermal expansion valve or a capillary tube.

expansion ratio the ratio of the total volume at the end of the expansion process of a cycle to the volume in the cylinder at the beginning of the process.

expansion tank an overflow space in a hydronic system that provides for the increased volume of water as it is heated. Also see *air cushion tank*.

expansion tank, bladder-type a tank having a rubber bladder that separates the air from the liquid in the tank. No absorption of the air into the liquid is possible. This is the only expansion tank that should be used in closed-loop or supply-type heat source/sink systems.

expansion valve a device in a refrigeration system which maintains a pressure difference between the high side and the low side and is operated by pressure.

expansion valve, automatic an expansion valve designed to maintain a constant pressure in the evaporator regardless of super-

heat. Seldom used in air-conditioning where loads generally fluctuate. Cannot be used on systems with multiple valve installations.

expansion valve capacity the refrigerating effect in Btu per hour, or tons, each to 12,000 Btu per hour, produced by the evaporation of refrigerant passed by the valve under specified conditions.

expansion valve, float a valve designed to maintain a constant liquid level in a flooded evaporator.

expansion valve superheat the difference between the temperature of the thermal sensing bulb and the temperature corresponding to the pressure at the outlet, or at the equalizer connection, when provided, of a thermostatic expansion valve.

expansion valve superheat change the change in superheat of a thermostatic expansion valve required to open the valve a predetermined amount.

expansion valve, thermostatic an expansion valve designed to meter the flow of liquid to a dry expansion evaporator at a rate sufficient to maintain a constant superheat in gas leaving the evaporator.

expendable refrigerant system a refrigerating system in which the refrigerant is sprayed directly into the area to be cooled and must be replenished when consumed. No longer valid after July 1, 1992.

expense the amortizing or writing off of an investment in one year. A purchase.

exploded view a diagram intended to depict the order of assembly and placement of parts in a mechanism.

exploring tube a small flexible tube attached to a halide torch in such a manner that air is continually drawn through the tube to the torch flame. When the free end of the searching tube is placed near a refrigerant leak, some of the refrigerant is carried to the flame where its presence is indicated by a change in the color of the flame.

explosimeter   an instrument which indicates the combustibility of air in an enclosed space.

explosion   combustion occurring within a confined environment at such a rapid rate as to cause detonation, called a fireside explosion. Also the rupturing of a vessel due to the build-up of pressure of water or steam, called a waterside explosion.

explosion heads   a protective device for relieving excessive pressure in a premix system by the bursting of a rupturable disc.

explosion-proof   describes a type of construction designed to contain an explosion and prevent its propagation to the outside atmosphere; usually implies the use of a heavy metal enclosure.

explosion-proof motor   a totally enclosed motor whose enclosure is designed and constructed to withstand an explosion of a specified gas or vapor which may occur within the motor and to prevent the ignition of this gas or vapor surrounding the motor.

explosive limits   see *flammability limits.*

explosive mixture   a flammable mixture in a confined space.

exposed area   the area of any wall, window, ceiling, floor, or partition separating a heated room from the outdoors or from an unheated space.

extended plenum   an air delivery system in which a main duct is run from the plenum, and branch ducts run from the main duct to the various zones.

extended surface   heat transfer surface, one or both sides of which are increased in area by the addition of fins, discs, or other means.

extended-surface filter   a filter in which the filtering medium is increased by pleating or baffling it.

extended-surface heating unit   a heating unit having a relatively large amount of extended surface that may be integral with the core containing the heating medium or assembled over such a core by both pressure and soldering. An extended-surface heating unit is usually placed within an enclosure and therefore functions as a convector.

extension rod   an extension rod is used to connect a socket to the drive handle of a ratchet to give the socket longer reach to gain access to recessed areas.

external-drive   term used to describe a compressor driven directly from the shaft or by a belt using an external motor. Compressor and motor are serviceable separately.

external equalized valve   a valve that resembles the internally equalized type, but evaporator pressure on the underside of the diaphragm is supplied from the evaporator outlet rather than the inlet.

external equalizer tube   a tube connected to the low side of an expansion valve diaphragm and to the exit of the evaporator. Used on evaporator coils that have an excessive pressure drop.

external heat gain   (1) the heat that both infiltrates and is conducted into a cooled space; (2) the heat that escapes, both by air leakage and conduction, from a heated space or building.

external heater   a heater in which the burners and combustion chamber are effectively separated from the oven chamber or the medium being heated. Also see *direct-fired external* and *indirect-fired external heaters.*

external-mix oil burner   see *atomizing oil burner.*

extinction pop   an undesirable flame characteristic in which burner flames strike back into a burner to burn there and create a popping sound after the gas supply has been turned off.

extinguishing media   the types of fire extinguisher or extinguishing methods appropriate for use on a specific chemical. Some chemicals react violently in the presence of water, so other suggested methods, such as foam or CO_2, should be followed.

extrinsic semiconductor   a semiconductor that has been doped.

extruded   a term meaning pushed out through a die. Bars of ice as well as metal rods, shapes, and tubes are all made by this method.

F

F   abbreviation for farad, frequency, fluorine, or Fahrenheit.

FAA ap   Federal Aviation Administration (airport).

FDA   the (United States) Food and Drug Administration.

FEMA   Federal Emergency Management Agency.

fid   flame ionization detector.

fig   figure.

fla   full load amps.

FM   Factory Mutual or frequency meter.

FOB   free on board.

fpm   feet per minute.

fs   full scale.

FSEC   Florida Solar Energy Center.

ft   foot or feet.

ft/lb   foot-pound.

fu   fuse.

face and bypass   a heating system in which the mixed airflow is divided into two duct sections, one through the coil (face) and the other around the coil (bypass). Dampers work in opposition (face damper closes while bypass damper opens, and vice versa) to regulate the amount of air that is heated. Used with either a steam or hot water coil system. Demonstrates on-off control of coil and modulating control of airflow across coil.

face velocity   the velocity (or speed) of the air passing through an air outlet or an air return. Measured in feet per minute (fpm).

facilities management system   see *building automation system*.

factor of evaporation   if 970.3 Btu is added to 1 pound of liquid water which is at atmospheric pressure and 212°F, the water will be converted into steam and the steam will be at atmospheric pressure and 212°F. This is termed "evaporation from and at 212°F," or, briefly, "from and at." The heat added to a pound of water by the heating vessel (from the time at which it enters until it leaves as steam) divided by 970.3 is the factor of evaporation.

factor of safety (in pressure vessels)   the ratio of ultimate stress to design working stress.

factory-installed wiring   the wiring installed in a piece of equipment at the factory. This wiring is usually the connections between the components in the control panel and the system components in the unit itself.

Factory Mutual   the identification of the Factory Mutual system and the Factory Mutual Engineering Corporation, an established United States approval agency for gas detection instrumentation.

factual diagram   a wiring diagram that is a combination of the pictorial and schematic diagrams.

Fahrenheit scale   a thermometric scale in which, under standard atmospheric pressure of 14.696 psi at sea level, the boiling point of water is 212°F and its freezing point is 32°F above zero. Its abbreviation is F.

fail-safe control   a device which opens a circuit when the sensing element fails to operate.

false defrost   a situation in which the system goes into the defrost mode even if the outdoor has no frost and/or ice build-up.

fan   any device or machine used to set up artificial currents of air. An air-moving device comprising a wheel or blade, and housing or orifice plate. Also see *blower* and *burner motor;* and *exhaust, forced-draft,* and *induced-draft fans.*

fan and limit control   usually a combination control and safety device that turns a heater fan or blower on and off according to preset temperatures; it shuts off the main burner gas if a malfunction causes combustion or chamber temperature to rise above a preset limit value.

fan, centrifugal   a fan rotor or wheel within a scroll type of housing which includes driving mechanism supports for either belt or direct connection.

fan coil   a complete unit located in the room being conditioned consisting of a coil through which hot or cold water is circulated, a fan that circulates room air through the coil, a filter to remove lint and dust, a cabinet, a grille, and a control system. The boiler or chiller supplying the water is located centrally within the building.

fan cycle control   device used to control the condenser fan(s). When head pressure drops below acceptable limits, the fans are turned off.

fan cycling   the use of a pressure controller to turn a condenser fan(s) on and off to maintain the correct pressure within the system.

fan economizer   a device which prevents the operation of the fan motor as a cold diffuser during the shutdown period after the coil has been defrosted.

fan laws of air-moving equipment   the performance of all fans and blowers is governed by certain rules of physics known as fan laws. Cubic feet per minute (cfm), revolutions per minute (rpm), static pressure (sp), and horsepower (hp) are all related to each other in a known manner and when one changes, all the others change. For example, when cfm is changed, rpm, sp, and hp will also change. Cfm is the variable most commonly changed in an air-moving system. Therefore the following example of fan law application is based on a change from an existing cfm to a new cfm.

1. To determine performance at a new cfm, first calculate the ratio of the new cfm to existing cfm (new cfm divided by the existing cfm):

$$\text{Ratio} = \frac{\text{new cfm}}{\text{existing cfm}}$$

2. To determine the new rpm, multiply ratio in step #1 times existing rpm:

$$\text{new rpm} = \frac{\text{new cfm}}{\text{existing cfm}} \times \text{existing rpm}$$

3. To determine new sp, multiply ratio of step #1 times itself, times existing sp:

$$\text{new sp} = \left(\frac{\text{new cfm}}{\text{existing cfm}}\right)^2 \times \text{existing sp}$$

4. To determine new hp required, multiply ratio in step #1 times itself twice, and then times existing hp:

$$\text{new hp} = \left(\frac{\text{new cfm}}{\text{existing cfm}}\right)^3 \times \text{existing hp}$$

Sample calculations: Existing conditions are 5000 cfm, 1000 rpm, 0.5″ sp, 0.5 hp motor. New cfm desired is 6000.

1. $\text{Ratio} = \dfrac{6000}{5000} = 1.2$

2. Calculate new rpm: 6000/5000 = 1.2 × 1000 = 1200 rpm.
3. Calculate new sp: 6000/5000 = $(1.2)^2$ = 1.44 × 0.5 = 0.72″ sp.

4. Calculate new hp: $6000/5000 = (1.2)^3 = 1.73 \times 0.5 = .86$ hp.

New conditions show that the cfm increased 20%, rpm increased 20%, sp increased 44%, and the hp increased 86%.

fan-mix burner   a mechanical-draft burner which uses the energy of high-pressure gas (10 to 50 psi) to completely premix the air and gas. Gas is permitted to escape through a row of small orifices on the edge of propeller-like blades mounted on a free-spinning shaft. Reaction of the escaping gas rotates the blades, which are mechanically coupled to a fan that draws in the primary air. The speed of the fan varies with the gas pressure, thereby automatically adjusting the air volume to maintain optimum combustion. Also see *mechanical-draft* and *premix burners*.

fan mixer   an air blower in which gas is admitted to the inlet to be mixed with air.

fan performance curves   charts that illustrate and relate the various factors affecting fan operation and efficiency.

fan (propeller)   a propeller or disc-type wheel within a mounting ring or plate and including driving mechanism supports for either belt drive or direct connection.

fan relay   electromechanical control used to operate the furnace blower motor.

fan relay coil   a magnetic coil that controls the starting and stopping of a fan through opening and closing of the fan relay contacts.

fan switch   a plenum-mounted, warm-air furnace thermostat that energizes the fan on temperature rise and stops it when the temperature falls to the off setting of the control.

fan (tubeaxial)   a propeller or disc-type wheel within a cylinder which includes driving mechanism supports for either belt drive or direct connection.

fan (vaneaxial)   a disc-type wheel within a cylinder with a set of air guide vanes located either before or after the wheel and including driving mechanism supports for either belt drive or direct connection.

farad   a unit of electrical capacity. The capacity of a device (either a capacitor or a condenser) which, when charged with one coulomb of electricity, gives a difference of one volt of potential.

farad experiment   silver chloride absorbs ammonia when cooled and releases ammonia when heated. This is the basis on which some absorption refrigeration systems operate.

fast-acting fuse   a fuse which opens on overloads and short circuits very quickly. This type of fuse is not designed to withstand temporary overload currents associated with inductive and capacitive loads.

fast-food freezing   method that uses liquid nitrogen or carbon dioxide to turn fresh food into long-lasting frozen food. It is often referred to as cryogenic food freezing and/or freeze drying.

fatigue resistance   the ability of a metal to bend over and over again without going beyond its elastic limit or breaking.

fault directory   a look-up table or equipment label used to translate numeric or alphanumeric fault codes into text messages.

feed water treatment   feeding a chemical mixture into a boiler to prevent internal scaling or corrosion on the shell and tubes.

feedback   in a control system, feedback is the signal (or signals) fed back from a controlled process to denote its response to the command signal. Feedback is derived by comparing actual response to desired response, and any variation is fed as an error signal into the original control signal to help enforce proper system operation. Systems employing feedback are called closed-loop systems, with feedback closing the loop.

feedback control system   control system that is constantly correcting the condition. Also called a closed-loop system.

feedback potentiometer the potentiometer in a modulating motor which forms part of a bridge circuit along with the controller potentiometer and balancing relay in the motor. When the wiper on the controller potentiometer moves due to a change in the controlled variable, the motor runs and drives the wiper on the feedback potentiometer in the proper direction to rebalance the bridge circuit. When the circuit is balanced, the motor stops.

feeder screw a threaded screw with a handle at one end to apply tension on an object being held in place, as in a yoke vise, or on other objects to be cut.

feeders a conductor or group of conductors between the service equipment and the final branch circuit overcurrent device.

feet of head the term used to designate the flow resistance the pump must overcome to deliver the required amount of liquid. 2.307 feet of head = 1 psig.

feet per minute (fpm) a velocity measurement of a moving airstream. Usually expressed as fpm.

female thread the internal thread on fittings, valves, machine bodies, and the like.

fenestration all light-transmitting envelope component assemblies in a building wall or ceiling used for light transmittance, ventilation, entry, or exit where such component assemblies enclose conditioned space.

ferromagnetic a highly magnetic material such as iron, nickel, steel, etc.

ferrous metal metal that contains iron.

ferrule-type cartridge fuse a special fuse with round metal caps on a cylinder case.

festoon lighting an outdoor string of lights suspended between points more than 15 ft. apart.

fibrosis the formation of fibrous tissue, as in a reparative or reactive process to particulates, in excess of amounts normally present in the lung tissue walls. This reduces the oxygen and CO_2 exchange efficiency.

field an area of force, usually electrical or magnetic.

field coil a coil of insulated wire wrapped around an iron core. A magnetic field is produced by current flowing in the coil. Used in devices such as motors.

field effect the application of a perpendicular electric field to cause a varying effect on the conductivity of the current path.

field effect transistor a transistor controlled by voltage rather than current. The flow of current through the transistor is controlled by the effect of an electric field that is exerted by an electric charge in a region located close to the channel called the gate. Sometimes known as a unipolar transistor. May have either a P channel or an N channel in its construction.

field of force the area around a magnet that is affected by the strength of the magnet.

field pole that part of the stator of a motor which concentrates magnetic field of field winding.

field wiring wiring that must be done at the installation site (in addition to factory wiring) in order to complete an installation.

figure of merit for a thermoelectric material used in a thermoelectric device whose operation is based on the Seebeck effect or the Peltier effect, the quotient of the square of the absolute Seebeck coefficient divided by the product of the electrical resistivity and the thermal conductivity.

file a metal hand tool used to scrape rough surfaces smooth.

file card a tool used to clean material out of metal files.

fill valve a device that allows water to enter a machine, generally operated by a pressure switch.

fillet   (1) the curved line connecting two lines that form an angle. (2) A bead of solder at the point where the joined pieces meet.

film factor   the relationship between the medium giving up heat and the heat exchange surface (evaporator). This relates to the velocity of the medium passing over the evaporator. When the velocity is too low, the film between the air and the evaporator becomes greater and becomes an insulator, which slows the heat exchange.

filter, air   a device to remove solid material from a fluid (liquid or gas). In furnace filters, a porous material (fiberglass or foam plastic) which is installed in the air circulation system of a furnace or fan coil unit to remove dust particles and pollen. Some are disposable, whereas others may be cleaned and reused.

filter drier   device to absorb remaining moisture and catch any foreign particles circulating with the refrigerant after evacuation.

filter, electronics   in electronics, a selective network of resistors, inductors, or capacitors which offers comparatively little opposition to certain frequencies or to direct current, while blocking or attenuating other frequencies.

filter, electrostatic   an electrical filtering device for the removal from air of smoke and other particles too small for the usual mechanical-type, throwaway filter. The very small particles are forced to adhere to collector plates because of the electric charges imparted by the power pack.

filtration   this is the method used to remove dust from air during the conditioning process. Air filtration is one of the items needed for a total comfort system.

fin   an extended surface used to increase the heat transfer area, such as metal sheets attached to tubes.

fin comb   a hand tool used to straighten out bent coil fins.

final control element   the last component in a control chain. That portion of the controlled device that regulates the final control agent like a valve or damper.

fines   finely crushed or powdered material or fibers, especially those smaller than the average in a mix of various sizes.

finned tube   a heat exchange device consisting of a metal tube through which water, steam, or refrigerant may be circulated. Metal plates or fins are attached to the outside of the tube to increase the heat transfer surface. Finned tube, or fin tube, may consist of one, two, or three tiers and is designed for installation bare, or with open-type grilles, covers, or enclosures having top, front, or inclined outlets. Usually finned-tube units are for use in other than residential buildings.

fire brick   ceramic brick used to line combustion chambers.

fire damper   a temperature-actuated damper in a duct that closes during a fire. Prevents the spread of flames by the air system.

fire-efficiency finder/stack-loss slide rule   a slide rule that uses the CO_2 percentage and temperature of a vapor to determine the efficiency of a fossil fuel heating system.

fire extinguisher   typically a small hand-held device which is used to put out small fires. There are four types of fire extinguishers: A, B, C, and D.

fire point   the minimum temperature at which a liquid will produce sufficient vapors to flash near its surface and continue to burn. Usually 10 to 30°C higher than the flash point.

fire safety switch   if the ignition bracket assembly overheats or if there is an external fire that affects the assembly, this switch will turn off the ignition sequence. Also referred to as a flame roll-out switch.

fire-tube boiler   a boiler in which the products of combustion pass through straight tubes surrounded by water and steam. The tubes may run horizontally or vertically.

The horizontal-return tube (HRT) type has a horizontal shell containing the tubes. The products of combustion pass from the external combustion chamber underneath the bottom of the shell to the end of the boiler, and return through the tubes. If the products of combustion are passed through the shell more than once, it is called a multipass boiler.

The vertical type has a vertical, cylindrical shell containing the tubes. The products of combustion pass from the internal combustion chamber below the shell up through the tubes. In a submerged vertical type, the water level extends higher than the top ends of the tubes. Also see *firebox, multipass,* and *scotch boilers.*

firebox   see *combustion chamber.*

firebox boiler   a horizontal, fire-tube boiler with a small, internal combustion chamber of cubical design. The short, first-pass bank of tubes is connected between the rear of the combustion chamber and the rear of the boiler. The remaining banks of tubes extend the full length of the boiler above the combustion chamber and the first-pass bank. The combustion chamber may be steel, refractory, or water-cooled refractory. Also see *fire-tube, multipass,* and *water-leg boilers.*

fireplace   a fire chamber and hearth constructed of noncombustible material for use with solid fuels and provided with a chimney. May be one of the following types:

1. masonry fireplace - a hearth and fire chamber of solid masonry units such as bricks, stones, listed masonry units, or reinforced concrete provided with a suitable chimney.
2. factory-built fireplace - a fireplace composed of listed factory-built components

assembled in accordance with the terms of listing to form the completed fireplace.

fireside explosion   see *explosion.*

firestat   a thermostat that senses temperature in a return air duct and shuts down the fans in the event of a fire.

firing device   a burner, oil, gas, or coal.

firing rate   combustion rate; the rate at which fuel or an air/fuel mixture is supplied to a burner or furnace, expressed in volume, weight, or heat units supplied per unit time. Also see *high fire, low fire,* and *modulating fire.*

firing rate controller   a controller which positions the firing rate motor to automatically regulate the burner firing rate at a predetermined air/fuel ratio in accordance with load demand. It may position the air and fuel supplies for low fire or for high fire, or it may be a proportioning (modulating) type which gradually varies the air and fuel supplies within limits to meet the load demand. Also see *firing rate motor.*

firing rate motor   a modulating or a two-position (open-closed) motor which switches external devices at predetermined times to control the firing rate of the burner.

firing rate switching circuit   a circuit in a programming control which switches external devices at predetermined times to control the firing rate of the burner.

firing rate valve   an automatic control valve for regulating the input of fuel to a burner in response to load demand. Also called a burner-input control valve, combustion control valve, metering valve, or throttling valve. Also see *butterfly, modulating,* and *motorized valves.*

first impression   the feeling someone forms about you when you are first introduced.

first out indication   a device (usually a lamp) for each burner in a multiburner system. The device indicates the first burner having flame failure.

first stage oil valve   in oil burners with more than one firing rate level (stage), the automatic safety shutoff valve which opens first to admit the fuel required for the lowest rate of combustion. In direct spark ignition systems, the first stage may take the place of a gas pilot.

fish tape   a flexible wire that can be pushed through conduit and around bends. Used to pull wire through conduit.

fishing   a means of pulling wires through an enclosed wall section or conduit by means of a single wire or rope.

fit   degree of tightness or looseness between two mating parts.

fitting   mechanical accessory, like a bushing or locknut, of a wiring system.

fitting brushes   brushes used to clean out the insides of tubes that are about to be soldered or brazed. These brushes should only be turned clockwise.

fixed   describes a control or part that cannot be adjusted.

fixed-bore orifice   an expansion device with a fixed diameter that does not adjust to varying load conditions.

fixed resistor   a nonadjustable resistor. The resistance cannot be changed.

fixture   a receptacle attached to a plumbing system in which water or other waste may be collected for ultimate discharge into the plumbing system.

fixture branch   the part of a drain from the fixture trap to the junction of the drain with a vent.

fixture drain   a unit flow rate from a fixture. The unit flow rate is determined to be one cubic foot per minute (or 7.5 gpm). A design factor to determine the drainpipe size for a fixture.

fixture stud   a special fitting used to connect a light fixture to an outlet box.

flame   the visible or other physical evidence of the chemical process of rapidly converting fuel and air into products of combustion.

flame arrestor   a nonvalve device for use in a gas/air mixture line containing a means for temporarily stopping the progress of a flame front (flashback).

flame blow-off   the phenomenon which occurs when a flame moves away from a burner, often resulting in the flame being extinguished. A flame blows off when the air/fuel mixture leaves the burner at a velocity greater than the velocity with which the flame front progresses through the mixture.

flame conductivity   the ability of the ionized gases of a flame to conduct an electric current.

flame current   see *flame signal*.

flame detection system   the flame detector, flame signal amplifier, and flame relay (in a flame safeguard control) which together determine whether a sufficient flame is present to continue the operation of a burner.

flame detector   the components of a flame detection system which detect the presence or absence of a flame. Also see *detector* and *flame rod;* and *infrared, optical, rectification-type, rectifying photocell,* and *ultraviolet flame detectors*.

flame detector relay   a control consisting of a flame detection electronic network and a switching relay which pulls in when a flame is detected. This control is not a primary control because it does not sequence burner operation, nor does it provide a safe start check or safety shutdown. Do not confuse it with flame relay.

flame envelope   the confines (not necessarily visible) of the combustion process (converting fuel and air into products of combustion).

flame failure device   a combustion safeguard to shut off the supply fuel if ignition does not occur within a predetermined time.

flame failure response time   the time interval between the loss of flame and the dropping out of the flame relay in a flame safeguard control, which then de-energizes the automatic fuel valve(s).

flame front   the plane along which combustion starts, or the base of the flame.

flame propagation rate   the rate at which a flame front travels through a combustible mixture of fuel and air. It is a function of air/fuel ratio, mixture temperature, and the ambient pressure. Also called burning velocity, flame speed, and flame velocity.

flame rectification   the phenomenon which causes a flame to conduct more current in one direction than in the other. It is due to the ionization of air in and around the flame and to the difference in area of the electrodes in the flame envelope. (The ground area is at least four times the area of the flame rod.)

flame rectifier pilot   see *pilot burner assembly*.

flame relay   the relay in a flame safeguard control which pulls in when a flame, or a condition simulating a flame, is detected. It drops out on loss of flame signal, causing the flame safeguard control to shut down the burner. Do not confuse it with flame detector relay.

flame retention device   a device added to a burner which aids in holding the flame base close to the burner ports.

flame retention nozzle   a burner nozzle surrounded with small ports which act as pilots to relight the main burner flame if it blows off. The velocity through the small ports is less, so the flame almost never blows off them. Also called a stick-tight nozzle.

flame rod   a metal or ceramic rod projected into the flame envelope to function as an electrode in a flame detection circuit. Also

see *conductivity flame rod system* and *rectifying flame rod*.

flame rollout   a condition where flame rolls out of a combustion chamber when the burner is turned on.

flame safeguard control   a safety control which provides a means for starting the burner in the proper sequence, proving that the pilot or burner flame is established, and supervising the flame during burner operation. Safety shutdown occurs if the pilot or burner flame is not established, or if the flame goes out. Also see *cutoff; ignition return;* and *modulating, nonrecycling, on-off, primary, programming,* and *recycling controls*.

flame safeguard system   the set of equipment used to provide safe control of burner operation. This usually includes the flame safeguard control, the flame detection system, all controllers, all limits, interlocks, all fuel valves, the ignition system, the firing rate control system, and any other auxiliary equipment.

flame sensing element   see *flame detector* and *sensor*.

flame signal   the current measured at the meter jack of a flame signal amplifier in a flame safeguard control. The current is produced by the flame detector when it senses a flame.

flame signal amplifier   the part of the flame detection system which increases the flame signal to a magnitude sufficient to pull in the flame relay in the flame safeguard control. The amplifier may be a permanent part of the flame safeguard control, or it may be a replaceable, plug-in unit.

flame simulator   a device used to substitute for the presence of flame in a flame detection circuit. It is used during troubleshooting to check the performance of the flame detection system. Flame simulators are available for use with rectification or ultraviolet amplifiers. In infrared systems, the flame signal can be simulated with a wire.

flame speed see *flame propagation rate*.

flame test for leaks (halide leak detector) a tool which is principally a propane torch; when an air/refrigerant mixture is fed into the flame, this flame will change from a blue color to a green color in the presence of a heated copper element.

flame velocity the speed at which a flame moves through a fuel/air mixture.

flammability limits the maximum and minimum percentages of fuel in an air/fuel mixture that will ignite easily and burn rapidly.

flammable capable of being ignited and burned; commonly used as a synonym for combustible.

flammable aerosol an aerosol that yields a flame projection of eighteen inches at the full valve opening or a flashback at any degree of valve opening when tested.

flammable gas a gas that at ambient temperature and pressure forms a flammable mixture with air at a concentration of 13% by volume or less; or a gas that at ambient temperature and pressure forms a range of flammable mixtures with air greater than 12% by volume, regardless of the lower limit.

flammable liquid a liquid having a flash point below 100°F (38°C), except that this term does not include any liquid mixture having one or more components with a flash point at or above 100°F that make up 99% or more of the total volume of the mixture.

flammable solid a solid that will ignite readily and continue to burn or that is liable to cause fires under ordinary conditions or transportation (through friction or retained heat from manufacturing or processing) and that burns so vigorously and persistently as to create a serious transportation hazard.

flange union a method for joining pipe wherein flanges are screwed onto the ends of the pipe and the flanges are bolted together.

flap-type damper a damper consisting of one or more blades, each pivoted about one edge, and all linked together for simultaneous operation. Also see *opposed-* and *parallel-blade dampers*.

flapper valve the type of valve used in refrigeration compressors which allows gaseous refrigerants to flow in only one direction. Also referred to as a reed valve.

flare copper tubing is often connected to parts of a refrigerating system by use of flared fittings. These fittings require that the end of the tube be expanded at a 45° angle. This flare is firmly gripped by fittings to make a strong leakproof seal.

flare bonnet copper insert used to convert an ordinary flare nut into a cap nut.

flare cap nut female nut that is used to seal off a male-threaded fitting.

flare elbow a fitting used to connect two flare nuts of the same size while providing an accurate bend of either 45° or 90°.

flare fitting a type of soft tubing connector that requires that the tube be flared to make a mechanical seal.

flare nut a fitting used to clamp a tubing flare against another fitting.

flare nut wrench a special box-end wrench used to help connect tubing using flare nut couplings. The flare nut wrench is like a box end wrench but the ends are cut out. The openings allow the box end to fit over the tubing and onto the flare nut.

flare plug fitting used to seal a flare nut or similar female-threaded opening.

flare tee fitting that makes it possible to connect a branch onto an existing line.

flare union a fitting that is used to connect two flare nuts of the same size.

flaring block   special tool used to hold tubing for the flaring process or for enlarging in the swaging process.

flaring single-thickness connection   a process of expanding or spreading tubing so that the tube end is formed into either a 37.5° or 45° angle.

flaring tool   usually, a two-piece tool consisting of a block and a yoke, with which tubing is flared.

flash   the rapid passing into steam of water at a high temperature when the pressure that the water is under is reduced so that its temperature is above that of its boiling point for the reduced pressure.

flash boiler   a boiler with very limited water capacity. Usually about one gallon of water per 1000 Btu/h net rating.

flash chamber   the space between the expansion valve and evaporator from which the flash gas that normally occurs at the evaporator inlet is drawn off and bypassed around the evaporator.

flash gas   the instantaneous evaporation of some of the liquid refrigerant in the evaporator which in turn cools the remaining liquid refrigerant to its desired evaporation temperature. Subcooling prevents flash gas.

flash point   the minimum temperature at which sufficient vapor collects above a liquid oil for it to catch fire if exposed to open flame.

flash tank   a tank in which water continuously flashes into steam.

flash weld   a resistance-type weld in which the mating parts are brought together under considerable pressure, and a heavy electrical current is passed through the joint to be welded.

flashback   the phenomenon which occurs when a flame front moves back through a burner nozzle (and possibly back to the air/fuel mixing point). Flashback occurs because the flame propagation rate exceeds the velocity with which the air/fuel mixture flows through the burner nozzle.

flashback arrestor   a metal gauze, grid, or any other portion of a burner assembly used to avert flashback.

flashtube   an ignition device, commonly used for ignition gas on range top burners. An air/gas mixture from the burner body is injected into the end of a short tube. The mixture moves along the tube and is ignited by a standing pilot flame at the other open end of the tube. The flame travels back through the mixture in the flashtube to ignite the gas at the burner ports.

flat rate schedule   a listing of the amount of time allotted to do various repair jobs for the purpose of estimating the labor charge on a job.

flex life   the ability of a conductor, wire, or cable to withstand repeated bending.

flexible connector   a fitting which permits some movement of the lines it connects. Examples would be either a duct connector or a pipe connector.

flexible coupling   a rubber sleeve used to extend and connect shafts.

flexible duct   a duct that can be routed around obstacles by bending it gradually.

flip-flop circuit   a circuit which provides automatic alternation between two possible circuit paths.

float and thermostatic trap   a float trap with a thermostatic element for permitting the escape of air into the return line.

float trap   a steam trap operated by a float. When enough condensate has drained (by gravity) into the trap body, the float is lifted which in turn lifts the pin off its seat and permits the condensate to flow into the return until the float has been sufficiently lowered to close the port. Temperature does not affect the operation of a float trap.

float valve   type of valve which is operated by a sphere or pan which floats on the liquid surface and controls the level of the liquid.

floating action   movement of the controlled device toward either its open or its closed position until the controller is satisfied, until the controlled device reaches the end of its travel or until a corrective movement in the opposite direction is required. Generally there is a neutral zone in which no motion of the controller device is required by the controller.

floating control   a type of control in which two contacts are used, in the controller, with a neutral zone between them. The actuator (valve or damper operator) may assume any position from minimum to maximum to maintain the conditions within the neutral zone of the controller.

floating flames   an undesirable burner operating condition, usually indicating incomplete combustion, in which flames leave the burner ports or heat exchanger to "reach" for combustion air.

floc point   the temperature at which wax separates out (precipitates) from a mixture of 10% oil and 90% refrigerant (R-12). The floc point is a measure of an oil's relative tendency to separate wax when mixed with an oil-soluble refrigerant.

flood   to fill with an abundance or an excess.

floodback   liquid in the suction line, resulting from too much liquid being metered into the evaporator.

flooded evaporator   one that is full of a liquid refrigerant at all times. Additional liquid is permitted to enter only to replace that which boils away.

flooded suction   a situation where the liquid source is higher than the pump, and liquid flows to the pump by gravity. Preferable for centrifugal pump installations.

flooded system   a type of refrigerating system in which liquid refrigerant fills the evaporator.

flooded system, high-side float   refrigeration system which has a critical charge and is operated by the float level of the high-side liquid refrigerant.

flooded system, low-side float   refrigerating system which has a low-side float refrigerant control.

flooding   term applied to a refrigeration system when the liquid refrigerant reaches the compressor.

floor furnace   a completely self-contained furnace installed in the floor of a space being heated and covered with a grille.

floor plan   this plan provides the largest amount of information about a structure. From this plan you can see the basic layout of the structure. Individual rooms, partition walls, cabinets, and mechanical and electrical layouts can be viewed using floor plans.

floppy disk   a type of disk drive, in a computer, which uses a storage medium which is of a flexible nature. Sometimes called a flexible disk. Also see *diskette*.

flow   the measure of the fluid volume capacity of a pump. Given in gallons per hour (gph) or gallons per minute (gpm). To convert gph to gpm, divide by 60.

flow characteristics   see *valve flow characteristic*.

flow check piston   piston assembly, with an orifice in the center, which can operate as a metering device.

flow coefficient   see *capacity index*.

flow control valve   a specially designed check valve, usually installed in the supply pipe, to prevent gravity circulation of hot water within the heating system when the pump is not in operation.

flow diagram   a block diagram that outlines the operation of a heating and air-conditioning unit.

flow, laminar fluid flow in which each fluid particle moves in a smooth path substantially parallel to the paths followed by all other particles.

flow meter instrument used to measure velocity or volume of fluid movement.

flow rate the amount of fluid passing a given point per unit time. Also, the fuel input to a burner measured in suitable units, e.g., cubic centimeters per minute, gallons per hour, pounds per hour. It is referred to as the firing rate.

flow, turbulent fluid flow in which the fluid moves transversely as well as in the direction of the tube or pipe axis, as opposed to streamline or viscous flow.

flow work the product of the pressure and specific volume of a fluid in a given state in a flow process.

flowchart a diagram showing all the logical steps of a program or the sequence of operation of a component or piece of equipment. A program is made by writing down the successive instructions that will cause the piece of equipment to operate as it does.

flue gas or air passage which usually depends on natural convection to cause the products of combustion (flue gases) to flow through it and exit to the outside atmosphere.

flue, appliance the passage(s) within an appliance through which combustion products pass from the combustion chamber of the appliance to the draft hood inlet opening (on an appliance equipped with a draft hood) or to the outlet of the appliance (on an appliance not equipped with a draft hood).

flue, chimney the passage(s) in a chimney for conveying the flue or vent gases to the outside atmosphere.

flue collar the portion of an appliance designed for attachment of the chimney to the flue pipe. Also see *flue pipe*.

flue gas gaseous by-products of combustion and excess air in an appliance's flues or heat exchangers before the draft hood.

flue gas analyzer instrument used to analyze the operation of fossil-fuel-burning equipment, such as oil and gas furnaces, by analyzing the flue gases for CO_2, stack temperature, and O_2.

flue gas loss the sensible heat carried away by the dry flue gas, and the sensible and latent heat carried away by the water vapor in the flue gas. Also referred to as stack loss.

flue outlet the opening provided in an appliance for the escape of flue gases.

flue pipe the duct connecting an appliance with the vertical flue of a chimney; also called breeching or vent connector. (A flue collar is the part of the appliance for attaching the flue pipe.)

fluid any substance that can flow, i.e., move and change shape without separating when under pressure; can be liquid or gas.

fluid coupling device which transmits drive energy to an energy absorber through a fluid.

fluid flow the movement of a fluid by a pressure difference created by mechanical means or difference in density created by the addition or removal of heat energy.

fluid, heat transfer any gas, vapor, or liquid used to absorb heat from a source at a high temperature and reject that heat into a source at a lower temperature.

fluid power a Honeywell trademark for the actuators used with V5055 industrial gas valves to provide a family of automatic safety shutoff valves. It is driven by a fluid (usually oil) pumped by an electric motor.

fluid, primary the refrigerant, as distinguished from a secondary fluid or brine.

fluid, refrigerating any fluid used to transfer heat between cold refrigerant and the substance or bodies to be cooled by circulation of the fluid without change of state, or by an evaporation-condensation process at essentially equal pressures.

fluid, secondary   fluid cooled by the refrigerant in the indirect method of refrigeration.

fluorescent lamp   a lamp consisting of a vapor-filled tube with electrodes at both ends. When a given potential is imposed across the electrodes, the release of free electrons from the electrodes causes a current flow to take place through the vapor. The vapor emits invisible ultraviolet light which in turn causes a fluorescent material coating on the inside of the tube to emit visible white light.

fluorocarbon   a chemical compound with molecules that contain fluorine and carbon atoms.

flush   (1) an operation to remove any material or fluids from refrigeration system parts by purging them to a waste collection tank using refrigerant or other fluids. (2) A term describing objects arranged with adjacent sides, surfaces, or edges close together; even with.

flute   groove, as on twist drills, reamers, and taps.

flux (brazing and soldering)   substance applied to surfaces to be joined by brazing or soldering to free them from oxides and facilitate a good joint.

flux density   the number of lines of force per unit area of a magnetic material or circuit.

flux, magnetic   the magnetic lines of force of a magnet that connect the north and south poles of the magnet.

flux meter   a device used to measure the strength of magnetic fields.

fly ash   suspended ash particles carried in the flue gas.

flywheel   a pulley (sometimes weighted) that is attached to the external crankshaft of a motor.

foam   a type of fire-fighting material (medium) consisting of small bubbles of air, water, and concentrating agents. Chemically, the air in the bubbles is suspended in the fluid. It clings to vertical and horizontal surfaces and flows freely over burning materials. Foam will put out a fire by blanketing it, excluding air and preventing the escape of volatile vapors. Its flowing properties will resist mechanical interruption and reseal the burning material.

foam leak detector   a system of soap bubbles or special foaming liquids brushed over joints and connections to locate leaks.

foaming   the formation of foam or froth in an oil-refrigerant mixture due to rapid evaporation of refrigerant dissolved in the oil when the pressure is suddenly reduced. This occurs when the compressor starts operating and, if large quantities of refrigerant have been dissolved, large quantities of oil may boil out and be carried through the refrigerant lines.

fog   liquid droplets suspended in a gas generated by condensation from the gaseous to the liquid state, or by breaking up a liquid into a dispersed state, such as by splashing, foaming, and atomizing.

Food and Drug Administration   the FDA is the federal agency that establishes requirements for the labeling of food and drugs to protect consumers.

foot-candle   a unit of measurement of light; the light produced on a surface from a source of one candle at a distance of one foot.

foot of water   the pressure created by a column of water one foot in height. Equivalent to 0.433 lb/per square inch.

foot-pound   a unit of work. A foot-pound is the amount of work done in lifting one pound through a distance of one foot.

forbidden energy band   the band of energies that is located between the valence and conduction bands and contains nonpermissible energy levels.

force that which produces, or tends to produce, motion. It is the accumulated pressure and is expressed in pounds. If the pressure is 10 psi on a plate of 10 sq in. area, the force is 100 lbs.

force-feed oiling a lubrication system which uses a pump to force oil to surfaces of the moving parts.

force of adhesion the result of attraction between the molecules of solder and the metal part being soldered.

forced-air furnace a central furnace equipped with a fan or blower to provide the primary means for circulation of air.

forced convection the movement of fluid by mechanical force such as fans or pumps.

forced draft mechanically produced airflow into and through the combustion chamber, blown in by a fan or blower located at the inlet air passage to the furnace. This air movement minimizes problems resulting from insufficient stack, wind, weather, and other conditions.

forced-draft burner a gas burner in which combustion air is blown in by a motor-driven fan. Commonly called a power burner. Examples are aspirating, gun-type, mechanical-premix, and zero governor burners. Also see *mechanical-draft burner.*

forced-draft cooling tower a device that cools water by mechanically forcing air through a tower.

forced-draft fan a fan or blower that blows air into a combustion chamber.

forced hot water hot water heating systems in which a pump is used to create the necessary flow of water.

forced ventilation mechanically produced airflow through a room or an area.

forecooler in an ice plant, a device for cooling the water for ice making before it enters the cans.

foreign object an object which does not belong where it is found.

formaldehyde (HCHO) a colorless, gaseous compound, used in the manufacture of resins and dyes and as a preservative and disinfectant. Present in many synthetic materials.

forward bias voltage applied to a P-N junction diode so that the potential barrier is neutralized (a positive voltage on a P region or a negative voltage on an N region).

forward breakover voltage the value of the anode-to-cathode voltage required for the silicon-controlled rectifier to turn on.

forward current the current flow across a P-N junction when it is forward biased.

forward-curved blower a blower where the tips of the fan blades are inclined in the direction of rotation; the most common type of centrifugal blower. Normally used in residential heating and air-conditioning systems and light-duty exhaust systems where maximum air delivery and low noise levels are required. Capable of pressures up to approximately 1.5″ static pressure.

forward switching voltage that value of anode-to-cathode voltage at which a four-layered diode switches.

forward voltage as measured in a diode, it is the amount of excess voltage on the anode as compared to the voltage on the cathode.

fossil fuels minerals or gases that are burned to produce heat. Fossil fuels include natural gas, butane, propane, fuel oil, coal, and wood.

fouling blocking by dirt, soot, scale, algae, or any other foreign matter.

fouling factor factor that determines loss of heat transfer due to deposits of foreign material in the water side of tubing in refrigeration condensers or chillers.

foundation plans foundation and basement plans are found on the same site plan when a basement is part of the structure.

Foundation plans are a key part of any working drawings and show a great deal of structural information. The plan includes the foundation walls, footings, piers, fireplaces, stairways, and other built-ins.

four-way switch   a switch used in conjunction with a three-way switch when control is desired at three or more places.

four-way valve   a type of reversing valve used to automatically divert the refrigerant in a heat pump to the proper indoor or outdoor coils.

fractional horsepower   a horsepower value less than one.

fractionation   when one or more refrigerants of a blend leak at a faster rate than the other refrigerants in the blend, changing the composition of the blend. Fractionation is possible only when liquid and vapor exist at the same rate.

frame (motor)   usually refers to the NEMA system of standardized motor mounting dimensions. The supporting structure for the stator parts.

frame size   usually refers to the NEMA system of standardized physical dimensions of motors. These dimensions consist of shaft length, shaft diameter, shaft height, and location of base mounting holes.

framing plans   these plans are required for complex structures, but may be left out on smaller ones. They contain the framing for the roof, floors, and various wall sections. They will also show the size and shape of the material used on the roof and walls.

frangible disk   a circular (round and dished) device used on some refrigeration equipment to provide pressure release for safety purposes. The frangible disk suddenly breaks when a certain excessive pressure is reached.

free air delivery   a situation where there are no effective restrictions to airflow (no static pressure) at the inlet or outlet of an air-moving device.

free area   the amount of unobstructed air space through a grille or diffuser.

free electrons   electrons located in the outer orbit of an atom which are easily removed and result in electrical current flow.

free enthalpy   a thermodynamic property which serves as a measure of the available energy of a system with respect to surroundings at the same temperature and same pressure as that of the system. No process involving an increase in available energy can occur spontaneously.

free on board   a shipping term meaning that the parts or materials ordered are free of shipping charges to the point specified. Beyond that point, the purchaser must pay for shipping.

free-wheeling   continued rotation of the magnetic clutch on an automotive compressor when the clutch is disengaged.

freeze   to be formed into a solid state (e.g., liquid water into ice); to be hardened or solidified by removing heat.

freeze up   the formation of ice in the refrigerant control device which may stop the flow of refrigerant into the evaporator. Frost on a coil may stop the airflow through the coil.

freezer   any box used to store and maintain products at subfreezing temperatures.

freezer alarm   device used in many freezers which sounds an alarm (bell or buzzer) when the freezer temperature rises above safe limits.

freezer burn   a condition which applies to food which has not been properly wrapped and that has become hard, dry, and discolored.

freezing   change of state from liquid to a solid.

freezing point   the temperature at which a liquid will solidify upon removal of heat.

The freezing temperature for water is 32°F at atmospheric pressure.

freezing point depression   temperature at which ice will form in a solution of water and salt relative to the freezing temperature of pure water.

freezing time   time for any complete freezing process to take place.

Freon   trade name for a family of synthetic chemical refrigerants manufactured by Dupont de Nemours Inc.

frequency   the number of recurrences of a periodic phenomenon in a unit of time. Expressed in hertz (Hz). The number of cycles that an AC electric current completes in one second.

fresh air intake   source of outside air feeding the return air plenum of an air distribution system.

friction   resistance to relative motion set up between particles of two surfaces in contact with each other.

friction head   in a hydronic system, the friction head is the loss in pressure resulting from the flow of water in the piping system.

front-seated   describes the position of a service valve when the compressor and gauge ports are open and the line port is closed.

frost   frozen water vapor.

frost back   a condition in which liquid refrigerant flows from an evaporator into the suction line as indicated by frost formation on the suction line.

frost control, automatic   a control which automatically cycles the refrigerating system based on frost formation on the evaporator.

frost control, manual   a manual control used to change the refrigerating system to produce defrosting conditions.

frost control, semiautomatic   a control which starts the defrost part of a cycle manually and then returns the system to normal operation automatically.

frost-free refrigerator   a refrigerated cabinet which operates with an automatic defrost during each cycle.

frostbite   the injury that results when skin freezes.

frosting-type evaporator   a refrigerating system which maintains the evaporator at frosting temperatures during all phases of the cycle.

frozen   a term that describes either water in a solid form or machine parts seized due to lack of lubrication.

frozen storage   the storage of an already frozen product at a constant temperature, usually 0°F (–18°C) or lower.

frustrum   a figure formed by cutting off a portion of a cone or pyramid parallel to its base.

fuel   any material which is burned to supply heat or power.

fuel/air ratio   see *air/fuel ratio*.

fuel gas   any substance in a gaseous form used for combustion.

fuel oil   kerosene or any hydrocarbon oil as specified by U.S. Department of Commerce commercial standard CS12 or ASTM D396-1969, or the Canadian government specification board, 3-GP-28, and having a flash point of not less than 100°F.

fuel oil burner, pressure-atomizing or gun-type   a burner designed to atomize the oil for combustion under an oil supply pressure of 100 psig.

fuel oil burner, rotary-type   a burner employing a thrower ring that mixes the oil and the air.

fuel oil burner, vaporizing or pot-type   this burner uses the heat of combustion to vaporize the oil in a pool beneath the vaporizing ring, and this vapor rising through the ring ignites and maintains combustion in the burner.

fuel-rich   describes a ratio of air to fuel supplied to a furnace which provides more fuel than the optimum air/fuel ratio.

full-floating   describes a mechanism construction in which a shaft is free to turn in all the parts in which it has been inserted.

full load   the nominal speed at which an induction motor operates under rated horsepower conditions. This will always be less than the synchronous speed and will vary depending on the rating and characteristics of the particular motor. For example, a four-pole 60 hertz fractional horsepower motor has a synchronous speed of 1800 rpm, a nominal full-load speed (as shown on the nameplate) of 1725 rpm, and an actual full-load speed ranging from 1715 to 1745 rpm.

full-load amps   line current (amperage) drawn by a motor when operating at rated load, voltage, and frequency. Important for proper wire size selection and motor starter heater selection.

full-load torque   the amount of torque produced by a motor when it is running at full-load speed at rated horsepower.

fully halogenated CFC   a chemical compound in which all the hydrogen atoms in a hydrocarbon molecule are replaced with chlorine or fluorine atoms.

fume   smoke; aromatic smoke; odor emitted, as of flowers; a smoky or vaporous exhalation, usually odorous, as that from concentrated nitric acid. The word fume is so broad and inclusive that its usefulness as a technical term is very limited. Its principal definitive characteristic is that it implies an odor. The terms vapor, smoke, fog, etc., which can be more strictly defined, should be used whenever possible. It is also defined as solid particles generated by condensation from the gaseous state, generally, after volatilization from molten metals, etc., and often accompa-

nied by a chemical reaction such as oxidation. Fumes flocculate and sometimes coalesce.

function switch   on a multifunction machine or instrument, the switch that selects the desired application.

fungi   a group of parasitic lower plants that lack chlorophyll, including molds and mildews.

furnace   an enclosed chamber or structure, including a burner and combustion chamber, which is provided for the combustion of fuel. The heat produced is used for heating a building or for processing materials. Also see *batch-type, central, continuous, downflow, duct, forced-air, horizontal, industrial,* and *upflow furnaces.*

furnace, central   a self-contained appliance designed to supply heated air through ducts to spaces remote from or adjacent to the appliance location. May be one of the following types:

1. forced-air furnace - a furnace equipped with a fan or blower that provides the primary means for circulation of air:
   a. downflow (counterflow) - a furnace designed with airflow discharge vertically downward at or near the bottom of the furnace.
   b. horizontal furnace - a furnace designed for low headroom installation with airflow across the heating element essentially in a horizontal path.
   c. upflow furnace - a furnace designed with airflow discharge vertically upward at or near the top of the furnace. This classification includes "highboy" furnaces, with the blower mounted below the heating element, and "lowboy" furnaces, with the blower mounted beside the heating element.
2. gravity furnace - a furnace depending primarily on circulation of air by gravity.

furnace, direct-vent central   a system consisting of (1) a central furnace for indoor installation, (2) combustion air connections between the central furnace and the outdoor atmosphere, (3) flue gas connections between the central furnace and the vent cap, and (4) a vent cap for installation outdoors, supplied by the manufacturer and constructed so that all air for combustion is obtained from the outdoor atmosphere and all flue gases are discharged to the outdoor atmosphere.

furnace, enclosed   a specific heating, or heating and ventilating, furnace incorporating an integral total enclosure and using only outside air for combustion.

furnace pressure   the gauge pressure in a furnace combustion chamber. The furnace pressure is said to be positive if greater than atmospheric pressure, negative if less than atmospheric pressure, and neutral if equal to atmospheric pressure.

fuse   an electrical safety device consisting of a strip of fusible metal placed in series in a circuit which melts when subjected to high current. It is intended to protect against abnormal conditions of current. A current-limiting device.

fuse, enclosed cartridge-type   a tubular fuse with terminals at each end and a casing that insulates the fusible element and contains the arc.

fuse, plug-type   a household-type fuse having a threaded Edison or S-type base. Rated up to 30 amperes at 125 volts.

fuse, puller   a specially insulated tool for removing cartridge-type fuses from the junction box.

fuse, replaceable element   a renewable cartridge fuse that has a replaceable link. When one of these fuses blows, the ends are unscrewed and a new link is inserted. Replacement links are available in current-limiting, slow, and fast-responding types.

fuse, S-type   a dual-element fuse which must be used with an adapter. Each size of fuse has a corresponding adapter which cannot be removed from the fuse holder after it

is installed. It is therefore not possible to replace it with a fuse with a higher rating. Amperage rating up to 30 at 125 volts.

fuse, time-delay-type   an enclosed fuse having two elements that protect against a temporary overcurrent condition.

fusible   able to be united by melting together.

fusible disconnect   an electric switch designed to isolate part of the system when required. Provided with fuses for the protection of the equipment.

fusible element   the metal link in a fuse that overheats and melts when excess current flows through it. This opens the circuit and stops current flow.

fusible link   a metal strip that will melt at a specified temperature to protect a heating element against burnout if the limit switch fails.

fusible load center   an electric panel that supplies circuits with power and protects them with fuses.

fusible plug   a plug or fitting made with a metal of a known and low melting temperature. It is used as a safety device to release pressures in case of fire.

fusion   the melting and joining together of separate objects. The use of heat to change a substance from the solid to the liquid or plastic state.

fusion temperature   the temperature at which fusion occurs. Fusion is either the active process of melting by heat or the state of being fused or melted. For coal, the fusion temperature is reported as initial deformation (IDT), ash softening (AST), and ash fusion (AFT), the test being performed under a reducing atmosphere.

G

g   gram.

gal   gallon.

GAMA   Gas Appliance Manufacturers Association.

GEA   Geothermal Energy Association.

gen   generator.

gfic   ground fault interrupter circuit.

gil   green indicator light.

gov   governor.

gph   gallons per hour.

gpm   gallons per minute.

gr   gram.

GRC   Geothermal Resources Council.

grd   ground.

GRI   Gas Research Institute.

gain   the ratio of signal output to input, frequently referred to as span; a main factor in amplification.

galvanic action   the corrosion action between two metals of different electronic activity. This action is increased by the presence of moisture.

galvanized   describes metal that has been zinc coated.

galvanometer   instrument which measures small electric currents.

ganged   refers to switches or controls mechanically linked together for identical operation.

gangrene   the death of tissue combined with putrefaction in an otherwise living organism.

gap   space between objects.

gas   the fluid form of a substance in which it can expand indefinitely and completely fill its container; form that is neither liquid nor solid; a vapor. Also, any mixture of inflammable gases used for lighting or heating. Also see *blast furnace;* and *flue, liquefied petroleum, manufactured, mixed, natural,* and *zero gas.*

gas burner   a burner for use with gaseous fuel. Also see *atmospheric, inshot, mechanical-draft, partial premix, premix, raw gas,* and *upshot burners.*

gas chromatography   a method of analyzing and measuring components in a gas mixture, both qualitatively and quantitatively.

gas constant   a factor describing the weight of a specific volume of gas at a specific pressure. The coefficient R in the perfect gas equation, $PV = RT$.

gas, discharge   the hot superheated refrigerant gas leaving the compressor.

gas, flash   the gas resulting from the instantaneous evaporation of refrigerant in a pressure-reducing device to cool the refrigerant to the evaporation temperature obtaining at the reduced pressure.

gas, flue   a gas which results from combustion.

gas, fuel   any substance that must be kept sealed in a container to prevent it from escaping into the air. There are two major types of fuel gases: natural and liquefied petroleum.

gas, inert   a gas that neither experiences nor causes chemical reaction nor undergoes a change of state in a system or process; e.g., nitrogen or helium mixed with a volatile refrigerant.

gas main   a pipe installed in a community to convey gas to individual services or other mains.

gas mixer   a device for mixing gas and air, such as a fan, aspirator, or inspirator. In an injection-type burner, it is the combination of mixer head, mixer throat, and mixer tube.

gas, noncondensable   a gas in a refrigerating system which does not condense at the temperature and partial pressure at which it exists in a condenser and, therefore, imposes a higher head pressure on the system.

gas/oil burner   a burner capable of burning either gas or oil. Some types can burn both simultaneously. Also see *combination burner.*

gas pack   typically a combination roof-top unit that heats in the winter by using gas as its fuel and cools in the summer by using electric power.

gas pressure regulator   a device for controlling and maintaining a uniform outlet gas pressure.

gas pressure switch   switch used to detect an adequate gas pressure before gas burners are allowed to ignite.

gas, residual   the gas remaining in the clearance space of a compressor cylinder after the piston has reached the top of the stroke.

gas tracer   a gas having a powerful odor. Sometimes used in small quantities with odorless refrigerants to give warning of a leak.

gas utilization equipment   any device that utilizes gas as a fuel or raw material or both.

gas valve   a device for controlling the flow of gas to the burner in a gas-fired furnace or heater.

gas velocity   the speed of the gas in piping or equipment. Usually stated in feet per minute or feet per second.

gas vent   the piping and fittings used to convey flue gases to the outside atmosphere. May be one of the following types:

1. Type "B" - a vent for venting listed gas appliances with draft hoods and other category I gas appliances listed for use with type "B" gas vents.
2. Type "BW" - a vent for venting listed gas-fired vented wall furnaces.
3. Type "L" - a vent for venting appliances listed for use with type "L" vents and appliances listed for use with type "B" gas vents.
4. Special gas vent - gas vents for venting listed category II, III, and IV gas appliances.

gas volume control   used to regulate the amount of gas needed to produce certain desired temperatures and conditions in domestic absorption automatic control refrigerators.

gases   natural gas, manufactured gas, and liquefied petroleum (LP) gas in the vapor phase only. Liquefied petroleum gas/air mixtures, and mixtures of these gases, plus gas/air mixtures within the flammable range, with the fuel gas or the flammable component of a mixture being a commercially distributed product.

gasket   a resilient or flexible material used between mating surfaces of refrigerating unit parts or of refrigerator doors to provide a leakproof seal.

gasket, foam   a joint-sealing device made of rubber or plastic foam strips.

gate   a device that has multiple inputs and a single output. There are five basic types of gates: and, or, nand, nor, and inverter. A gate can also be one terminal of some electronic devices, such as SCRs, triacs, and field effect transistors.

gate valve   a valve that opens to the full diameter of the pipe, thereby allowing unobstructed maximum flow.

gauge   (1) a term used to denote the physical size of a wire and sheet metal thickness. (2) An instrument for measuring pressure or liquid level.

gauge, compound   an instrument used for measuring pressures both above and below atmospheric pressure.

gauge, draft   a vacuum gauge used to determine the negative pressure of a heating unit vent.

gauge, gas manifold pressure   a direct reading gauge for measuring gas manifold pressure of a vapor-burning heating unit. A more convenient substitute for a "U" tube manometer. Measures in increments of inches of water.

gauge glass   often referred to as the water glass; arranged so that the water in the boiler stands at roughly the same level as the water in the glass. This glass is not found on hot water boilers. Actually, water in a boiler under pressure is about 4 inches higher because of expansion.

gauge, high-pressure an instrument used for measuring pressures in the range of 0 to 500 psig.

gauge, liquid level a gauge mounted on or in a vessel to indicate the liquid level within the vessel.

gauge, low-pressure an instrument used for measuring pressures in the range of 0 to 50 psig.

gauge lugs attached to the gauge ring on the receding die threader. Each lug has a size printed on its face. The lug size and the pipe size to be threaded must correspond. The positioning of the lug also positions the workholder jaws.

gauge manifold a device constructed to hold both compound and high-pressure gauges and equipped with valves to control flow of fluids through it.

gauge port opening or connection provided for a service technician to install a gauge.

gauge pressure pressure expressed in pounds per square inch gauge (psig). Readings in psig measure only pressures above atmospheric. Gauges are calibrated to read zero psig at atmospheric pressure.

gauge rings movable rings located at the rear of the workholder. A gauge ring has four lugs, one of each pipe size for which the threader can be used. Rotating the gauge ring will move the position of the workholder jaws.

gauge, standard an instrument designed to measure pressures above atmospheric.

gauge, vacuum an instrument used to measure pressures below atmospheric pressure.

gauss a unit of measurement of magnetic flux density.

gear a toothed wheel that transmits rotary motion from one shaft to another.

general-purpose area all areas where explosion-proof or intrinsically safe construction is not required and most areas where gas detection equipment is installed.

general-purpose motor a motor designed with standard operating characteristics and mechanical construction for use under usual service conditions. Has a service factor rating.

general-purpose relay a relay usually rated up to 10 amperes and intended for control circuit applications.

generator a rotating electric machine used to provide a large amount of electrical energy. A generator converts mechanical energy to electric energy.

generator, absorption the basic part of an absorption system; a heat exchanger provided with a means of heating used to drive refrigerant out of a solution.

generic name a designation or identification such as a code name, code number, or brand name used to identify a chemical by other than its original name.

geothermal well a drilled well in which the return water is returned to the same well from which the supply water is taken.

giga- a numerical prefix denoting one billion (for example, a gigacycle is one billion cycles).

gilbert a unit of measurement of magnetomotive force (MMF).

gland an adjustable part that compresses packing into a stuffing box.

glass, gauge device for showing liquid level.

glass, sight glass tube used to indicate the liquid level in tanks, bearings, and similar equipment.

glass stem thermometer a popular type of thermometer, it has a glass stem mounted in a metal case and can easily fit into a pocket. Glass stem thermometers will most often read from −30°F to 120°F. The tubes are filled with either mercury or a red fluid.

Glauber's salt   the most common type of eutectic salt. It is used to store solar energy.

glazing   the specialized coating applied to the surface of the absorber plates. This is what allows the absorber to collect heat efficiently.

glitch   an unwanted pulse or logic state, usually caused by poor design and/or propagation delays.

global warming   often called the greenhouse effect. In global warming, tropospheric pollutants like CFCs, HCFCs, HFCs, carbon dioxide, and carbon monoxide absorb and reflect the earth's infrared radiation. This causes re-radiation back to the earth and a gradual increase in the earth's average temperature.

globar   a conductive ceramic from which high-temperature flame rods are made. It has a maximum temperature rating of 2600°F (1425°C).

globe valve   a valve with a movable disc-type element and a stationary ring seat that changes the direction of the fluid flowing through it.

glow coil   a device that automatically reignites a pilot light if it goes out.

glycol water solution/forced-air furnace   furnace with a 50% glycol and 50% distilled water solution which passes through a tube-and-fin heat exchanger to distribute heat through the furnace duct system.

goggles   safety glasses with a side shield to prevent objects from getting into the eyes.

governor, zero   a regulating device that is normally adjusted to deliver gas at atmospheric pressure within its flow rating.

grace period   the time required to build up an explosive charge in a burner; the maximum time the unignited combustible reac-

tants can safely be put into and retained in a combustion chamber.

grades of fuel oil   voluntary commercial standards recommended by the U.S. Bureau of Standards for different classifications of fuel oil, based on characteristics such as specific gravity and viscosity.

gradual switches   manual switches used in a pneumatic control system to vary the air pressure in the circuit.

graduate relay   a pneumatic relay capable of maintaining in one air line, usually the branch line, an air pressure proportional to the pressure in another line, usually the pilot line. It may be direct acting, increasing branch line pressure in reaction to an increase in pilot line pressure; or it may be reverse acting, reducing branch line pressure on an increase in pilot line pressure.

graduate switch   a pneumatic manual switch for adjusting the air pressure in a line to any value from zero to full supply pressure.

graduated acting   a term applied to a control instrument or device which functions to give throttling control—that is, it operates between full on and full off positions.

graduated cylinder   device used for measuring an exact refrigerant charge. Such cylinders are very accurate. Commonly referred to as a Dial-a-charge.

grain   a unit of weight equal to one 7000th of a pound (.06480 grams). It is used to indicate the amount of moisture in the air.

gram   a metric unit of weight equal to .035 ounces.

graphic display   a master control panel which pictorially and colorfully traces the relationship of control equipment and the process operation. It permits an operator to check on the operation of a distance control system at a glance by noting dials, valves, scales, and lights.

graphite   a soft, black, shiny form of carbon used for pencil leads, lubricants, and electrodes.

grate area   grate surface area measured in square feet, used in estimating the fuel burning rate.

gravity   refers to the acceleration due to the force of gravity, which is 32.16 feet per second.

gravity convection   is the natural movement of heat through a fluid that occurs when a warm fluid rises and cool fluid sinks under the influence of gravity. Another term for this is thermosiphoning.

gravity feed   supplying oil to a burner from a gravity tank, using the force of gravity.

gravity furnace   a furnace which delivers heat by the natural tendency of warm air to rise and cold air to sink. A gravity-type furnace that contains no fans or filters.

gravity hot water   a hot water heating system in which circulation is promoted by the difference in density between hot and cold water.

gravity, specific   the specific gravity of a solid or liquid is the ratio of the mass of the body to the mass of an equal volume of water at some standard temperature. At the present time a temperature of 4°C (39°F) is commonly used by physicists, but the engineer uses 60°F. The specific gravity of a gas is usually expressed in terms of dry air at the same temperature and pressure as the gas.

greenfield   a flexible metallic conduit used in connection of electrical power to machinery and applications which require bends of the conduit at various angles.

greenhouse principle   a method of converting and trapping radiation from the sun in the form of heat. Also see *global warming*.

grille   an ornamental or louvered opening placed at the end of an airway. It permits airflow, but prevents large objects from entering the duct. It may be located in a sidewall, ceiling, or floor.

grind   to remove metal by means of an abrasive wheel, often made of carborundum. Used chiefly where accuracy is required.

grommet   a plastic, metal, or rubber doughnut-shaped protector for wire or tubing as it passes through a hole in an object.

gross capacity, heat pump   the gross capacity of a heat pump in the heating mode. It is the total amount of heat energy transferred to the inside air or material. This is made up of the heat energy picked up from a heat source (air or water) plus the heat energy equivalent of the electrical energy required to operate the heat pump.

gross output   a rating applied to boilers. It is the total quantity of heat which the boiler will deliver and at the same time meet all limitations of applicable testing and rating codes.

ground   an electrical term meaning to connect a circuit to the earth, or some other large conducting body serving as earth, thus making a complete circuit. A common return to a point of zero potential, such as a furnace or air conditioner's metal chassis.

ground clamp   a mechanical clamping device to connect a ground wire or conduit to ground.

ground coil (earth coil)   a heat exchanger buried in the ground which may be used either as an evaporator or as a condenser.

ground fault   a conducting connection, intentional or accidental, between any conductor of an electrical system and the conducting material (metal conduit, metal cabinet, etc.) which encloses the conductors, as well as any conductors which are grounded or may become grounded.

ground fault circuit interrupter (GFCI)   safety device designed to protect a circuit from overcurrent and to protect people from potentially hazardous ground faults arising from the use of defective appliances or portable tools.

ground loop, double-U-bend, vertical
a multiple-pipe system in vertical holes, connected to divide the liquid flow among the loops.

ground loop, four-layer, horizontal two two-layer pipe loops located in the same trench, one above the other.

ground loop, single-layer, horizontal
one continuous length of pipe laid horizontally in the earth.

ground loop, single-U-bend, vertical
a single run of pipe in one or more vertical holes, connected in series where all the liquid travels through all portions of the loop.

ground loop, two-layer, horizontal a single loop that doubles back on itself to reduce the earth area needed.

ground potential the potential of the earth. A circuit, terminal, or chassis is considered to be at ground potential when it is used as a reference point for other potentials in the circuit.

ground, short circuit a fault in an electrical circuit allowing electricity to flow into the metal parts of the structure.

ground wire an electrical wire which will safely conduct electricity from a structure into the ground.

grounded refers to the condition of having a proper ground.

grounded conductor a system or circuit conductor that is intentionally grounded.

grounding to remove the possibility of electrical shock. Protection against static charges which sometimes build up on operating equipment.

grounding conductor a conductor used to connect equipment or the grounded circuit of a wiring system to a grounding electrode or electrodes; usually colored green.

grounding electrode connection a conductor interconnecting the grounding electrode to the neutral bus of the service equipment.

Group 1 refrigerant a nontoxic, nonflammable refrigerant.

Group 2 refrigerant a toxic and moderately flammable refrigerant.

Group 3 refrigerant a very flammable refrigerant.

guide see *valve guide*.

guide vanes vanes used to produce capacity control in a centrifugal compressor. Also called prerotational guide vanes.

gun-type burner a power burner in which a fan, or blower, blows air at high velocity past turbulators. The gas, at regulated pressure, is released into the turbulent airstream—typically from a ring at the mouth of the burner (in which case it is also called a ring burner). The gas escapes through orifices around the periphery of the ring. Gas and air are adjusted simultaneously to maintain the proper air/fuel ratio as the firing rate changes. In high-pressure gun burners, the gas is ejected at pressures up to 15 psi from the spuds located in the center of the turbulent airstream instead of at the outside. Also see *forced-draft* and *raw gas burners*.

H

H abbreviation for magnetic intensity and henry.

HA Heating Alternatives, Inc.

HBI Healthy Buildings International.

HCFC hydrochlorofluorocarbons.

hdd65 heating degree-days base 65°F.

HEI Heat Exchange Institute.

hepa high-efficiency particulate arrestance.

HFC hydrofluorocarbons.

Hg mercury.

HI Hydraulic Institute or Hydronics Institute.

hlf heating load factor.

hp horsepower.

hsf high-side float.

hsi hot surface ignition.

hspf heating seasonal performance factor.

ht height.

H₂O water.

HUD U.S. Housing and Urban Development.

HVAC heating, ventilating, and air-conditioning.

HVI Home Ventilating Institute.

Hz hertz.

hacksaw a fine-toothed saw used to cut metal.

halide leak detector a device used to detect refrigerant leaks in a system. A burner is equipped with a source of fuel, a mixing chamber, a reactor plate, and an exploring tube. The reactor plate surrounds the flame. When the open end of the exploring tube is held near a refrigerant leak, some of the refrigerant is drawn into the mixing chamber where its presence changes the color of the flame. Also see *flame test for leaks*.

halide refrigerants the family of refrigerants that contain halogen chemicals. These refrigerants include R-22, R-500, and R-502.

halogen any of the five chemically related nonmetallic elements that include fluorine, chlorine, bromine, iodine, and astatine.

halogenated a term usually applied to hydrocarbons that are combined with fluorine, bromine, chlorine, iodine. Vinyl chloride, methyl chlorine, halon, chloroform and Freon are examples.

Halon (Freon 1301) a fire suppressant as well as a noncombustible gas frequently used in fire extinguishing systems.

hammer a hand tool used for striking another object.

hand notcher a tool used for cutting notches along the edge of a piece of sheet metal.

hand seam a tool used to form seams on a piece of sheet metal.

hand shutoff valves valves that make it possible to quickly isolate sections of a system for servicing.

hand truck a two-wheeled piece of equipment that can be used for moving heavy objects.

hanger device attached to walls or other structures for support of system piping.

hard copy any printed or plotter paper output.

hard-drawn copper wire copper wire that has been drawn to size and not annealed.

hard-drawn tubing copper tubing which has been specially hardened to keep it stiff.

hard flame a flame with a hot, tight, well-defined inner cone.

hard soldering see *brazing*.

hard solders silver-bearing brazing alloys that have a melting temperature that ranges from 1000°F to 1500°F (593°C to 816°C).

hard start kit a kit consisting of a start relay (potential relay) and a start capacitor used to provide high starting torque. When added to a PSC motor circuit, it changes it into a CSR motor circuit.

hard starting refers to the difficulty of a motor or compressor in starting; due either to low voltage or excessive pressure differential.

hard wiring permanent, line voltage wiring.

hardening the heating and cooling of certain iron-based alloys for the purpose of producing a hardness that is superior to that of the untreated metal.

hardness the measure of the amount of mineral salts dissolved in water.

hardware the mechanical, magnetic, electronic, and electrical devices from which a computer is fabricated; the assembly of material forming a computer.

harness a term used to describe a group of conductors laid parallel or twisted, usually with many breakouts, laced together or pulled into a rubber or plastic sheath; used to interconnect electrical circuits.

Hartford loop   the loop in the return main of the boiler piping that maintains the water level in the boiler.

Hastelloy   trade name for a hard, noncorroding metal alloy.

hazard communication rule   requires chemical manufacturers and importers to assess the hazards associated with the chemicals in their workplace. Material handling data sheets, labeling, and training are all the result of this law.

hazardous area   an area where combustible gases are usually present or likely to be; generally such areas are classified as hazardous and are the opposite of general-purpose areas. Reference National Electric Code (NFPA 70) Article 500 for hazardous areas.

hazardous material   is any substance or mixture of substances having properties capable of producing adverse effects on the health and safety of a human being. A hazardous material is one that has one or more of the following characteristics: (1) a flash point below 140°F, closed cup, or is subject to spontaneous heating; (2) a threshold limit value below 500 ppm for gases and vapors, below 500mg/m for fumes, and below 25 mppcf (million particles per cubic foot) for dusts; (3) a single dose oral LD_{50} below 50 mg/kg; (4) is subject to polymerization with the release of large amounts of energy; (5) is a strong oxidating or reducing agent; (6) causes first-degree burns to skin in short time exposure, or is systemically toxic by skin contact; or (7) in the course of normal operations, may produce dusts, gases, fumes, vapors, mists, or smokes which have one or more of the above characteristics.

head   another measure of pressure. Usually applies to centrifugal pumps. Indicates the height of a column of water being lifted by the pump, neglecting friction losses in piping. For water, divide head in feet by 2.31 to get pressure in pounds per square inch (psi). Usually expressed in feet of water, inches of mercury, or millimeters of mercury.

head, available   the pressure available to overcome friction in the system and to circulate the fluid.

head, friction   head required to overcome friction of the interior surface of a conductor and between fluid particles in motion.

head pressure   pressure which exists in the condensing side of the refrigerating system. Also called discharge pressure or high-side pressure. It is that pressure between the discharge side of the compressor and the inlet of the metering device.

head pressure control   the pressure-operated control which opens the electrical circuit if the high-side pressure becomes excessive.

head, static   the pressure of fluid expressed in terms of height of column of the fluid, such as water or mercury.

head, thermal   difference in pressure between the weight of the column of warmed water on the supply side and the equal column of cooler water on the return side of a hot water heating system. This is the only force in a gravity hot water heating system.

head, tool   the working end of a tool or implement; an attachment to or part of a machine that holds or contains the operative device.

head, total static   in flowing fluid, the sum of the static and velocity heads at the point of measurement. Static head from the surface of the supply source to the free discharge surface.

head, velocity   in a flowing fluid, the height of fluid equivalent to its velocity pressure.

header   a manifold or supply pipe to which a number of branch pipes are connected.

header, close, geothermal   a piping system where the supply and return headers for multiple-loop vertical systems are spaced close together with the multiple loops arranged in a circle around the headers.

header, reverse-return, geothermal   a piping system where the vertical loops are arranged in a straight line, and the headers between them are connected to supply and return from opposite ends. Supply is to the closest loop, return is from the most distant vertical loop.

heat   a form of energy which, when added, causes substances to rise in temperature. Heat always flows from a body of higher temperature to a body of lower temperature. Energy associated with random motion of molecules. Also see *latent heat, sensible heat, specific heat, total heat,* and *heat of the liquid.*

heat-affected zone   that portion of the base metal which has not been melted but has been altered by heating, welding, brazing, soldering, or cutting.

heat anticipator   a heater, either fixed or adjustable, in the thermostat that prematurely terminates the furnace on cycle to assure that room temperature does not exceed the thermostat set point due to thermal inertia. Must be set to the amp draw of the heating low-voltage circuit amperage. Designed to minimize system overshoot.

heat block   insulation material installed between the cell mount of an infrared flame detector and the sighting pipe to reduce heat conduction to the cell.

heat capacity   the amount of heat necessary to raise the temperature of a given mass one degree. Numerically, the mass multiplied by the specific heat.

heat coil   a device, made of tubing or piping, designed to transfer heat to a cooler substance by using transfer fluids.

heat conductor   a material capable of readily conducting heat. The opposite of an insulator or insulation.

heat content   the amount of heat, usually stated in Btu per pound (calories per gram), absorbed by a refrigerant in raising its temperature from a predetermined level to a final condition and temperature. Where change of state is encountered, the latent heat necessary for the change is included.

heat dissipation   conduction of heat away from a solid-state switch by use of a heat sink. This is necessary to prevent damage with currents of 3 or more amperes.

heat energy   total energy of all the molecules in a given substance.

heat exchanger   any device for transferring heat from one medium to another. A direct heat exchanger is a self-contained device which transfers heat generated in the combustion chamber directly through the walls of the heat exchanger to the heating medium. An indirect heat exchanger contains a heating medium and transfers heat to another medium separately contained in close contact with or directed through the heat exchanger.

heat exchanger, double-pipe   one in which two pipes are arranged concentrically, one within the other, and in which one fluid flows through the inner pipe and the other fluid through the annulus between the two pipes.

heat flow   the movement of heat from a warmer to a cooler substance. The rate depends upon the temperature difference, the area exposed, and the type of material.

heat gain   the rate at which a structure gains heat by infiltration, solar radiation, occupant respiration, and lighting (in Btu) for a space to be conditioned, at the local summer outdoor design temperature and a specified indoor design condition.

heat, humid   ratio of increase of enthalpy per pound of dry air with its associated moisture to raise the temperature under conditions of constant pressure and constant specific humidity.

heat intensity   heat concentration in a substance as indicated by the temperature of the substance through the use of a thermometer.

heat interchanger   a device used to transfer heat from the liquid refrigerant to the suction gas; also known as a heat exchanger.

heat lag   when a substance is heated on one side, it takes time for the heat to travel through the substance. This time is called heat lag.

heat, latent   heat characterized by a change of state of the substance concerned, for a given pressure and always at a constant temperature for a pure substance, i.e., heat of vaporization or fusion.

heat leakage   the flow of heat through a substance.

heat load   amount of heat, measured in Btu, which is added or removed during a period of 24 hours.

heat loss   the rate at which a structure loses heat (in Btu) from a space to be conditioned, at the local winter outdoor design temperature and a specified indoor design condition.

heat loss factor   the rate of heat transfer through a specific material for every one degree in temperature difference.

heat, mechanical equivalent of   an energy conversion ratio of 778.177 ft/lb = 1 Btu.

heat of compression   the mechanical energy of pressure transformed into energy of heat.

heat of condensation   the latent heat energy involved in the transition from the solid to the liquid state.

heat of fusion   the heat released in changing a substance from a liquid state to a solid state. The heat of fusion of ice is 144 Btu per pound.

heat of the liquid   the heat (Btu) contained in a liquid due to its temperature. The heat of the liquid for water is 0 at 32°F and increases approximately 1 Btu for every degree rise in temperature.

heat of reaction   heat per unit mass or per mole of one of the reagents or products of reaction in a chemical reaction. It is described as exothermal if given off, endothermal if absorbed.

heat of respiration   the process by which oxygen and carbohydrates are assimilated by a substance. Also, a process in which carbon dioxide and water are given off by a substance.

heat of vaporization   the latent heat energy required to change a substance from a liquid to a gas.

heat pipe   a heat exchanger capable of transferring heat over a relatively long distance at a low temperature difference.

heat pump   a compression-cycle system used to supply heat or cooling to a temperature-controlled space. This system may also remove heat from the same space.

heat reclaim   the process of reusing discharged heat from such sources as exhaust fans, condenser coils, and hot water drains to do useful work.

heat recovery system   produces and stores hot water by transferring heat from condenser to cooler water.

heat rejection effect, condensing   that portion of the total refrigerant heat-rejecting effect of a condenser which is used for condensing the entering refrigerant vapor to a saturated liquid at the entering refrigerant pressure.

heat rejection effect, subcooling   the total refrigerant heat rejection effect less the condensing heat rejection effect.

heat rejection effect, total refrigerant   total useful capacity of a refrigerant condenser for removing heat from the refrigerant circulating through it.

heat relay a device used to stage the elements of an electric heating system on and off.

heat, sensible a term used in heating and cooling to indicate any portion of heat which changes only the temperature of the substance involved.

heat sink a device, usually a metal plate or fin-shaped object, used to transfer a rise in temperature away from a switch into the surrounding air, into a liquid, or into a larger mass.

heat, specific the ratio of the quantity of heat required to raise the temperature of a given mass of any substance one degree to the quantity required to raise the temperature of an equal mass of a standard substance (usually water at 59°) one degree.

heat, total the sum of sensible and latent heat. Usually referred to as enthalpy.

heat transfer the movement of heat from one body or substance to another. Heat may be transferred by radiation, conduction, convection, or a combination of the three.

heat transfer coefficient the amount of heat passing through a given thickness and area of a material per unit of time and temperature difference.

heat transfer fluid the medium used to transfer heat from the collector to the heat storage tank.

heat transmission any time rate of heat flow; usually refers to conduction, convection, and radiation combined.

heat transmission coefficient any one of a number of coefficients used in calculating heat transmission through different materials and structures by conduction, convection, and radiation.

heat treatment the application of a series of heating and cooling cycles to a metal or alloy to bring about a desired condition.

heat unit a fixed amount of heat, such as Btu, calorie, or therm.

heat, vital heat generated by fruits and vegetables in storage due to ripening.

heated slab concrete slab-on-grade floor containing wires, cables, pipes, or ducts that transfers heat to the conditioned space.

heated space enclosed space within a building that is heated by a heating system whose output capacity exceeds 10 Btu/h × ft^2 or is capable of maintaining a space dry bulb temperature of 50°F or more at design heating conditions.

heater an apparatus for giving heat or warmth; a furnace, oven, stove, radiator, or similar device. Also see *air, booster, central, direct-fired, external, indirect-fired, internal, make-up air, radiant tube-type, space,* and *unit heaters.*

heater, infrared heater that converts flame energy into infrared radiant energy.

heater, make-up air a heat exchanger whose only function is to increase the temperature of outside make-up air to that of the air recirculating in the system.

heater, room a heater designed to warm only the room in which it is installed, without the use of ducts.

heater, unit a self-contained heater, designed to heat only the nonresidential space in which it is installed.

heating coil a heat transfer device which releases heat.

heating control a device which controls the temperature of a heat transfer unit which releases heat.

heating effect factor an arbitrary allowance added to the test output of some types of terminal units when establishing the catalog ratings. This allowance is intended to give credit for improved heat distribution obtained from the terminal unit.

heating element a unit assembly consisting of a resistor, insulated supports, and terminals for connecting the resistor to the electric power.

heating load　a heating load is the rate at which heat energy must be supplied to a space in order to maintain a certain condition designed for it.

heating medium　a substance such as air, steam, water, or a heat transfer fluid used to convey or transfer heat from the boiler, furnace, or other source of heat to the heating units from which the heat is dissipated.

heating mode　the operating phase of a system that adds heat energy to an occupied area.

heating, regenerative　a heat transfer process for utilizing heat which must be rejected or absorbed in one part of a cycle to perform a useful function in another part of the cycle.

heating seasonal performance factor (HSPF)　total heating output of a heat pump during its normal annual usage period for heating (in Btu) divided by the total electric energy input during the same period (in watt-hours).

heating surfaces　all surfaces which transmit heat directly from the flame or flue gases to the medium being heated.

heating system, direct-fired　a heating system in which combustion takes place in the air being blown into the building. The outdoor air temperature is increased by direct contact with the flame of the heater. Efficiency of this system is 100%.

heating system, duct heater　a heating system in which the heater is installed directly in the distribution duct of the central air-conditioning or heating system. May be electric, gas-fired, or oil-fired.

heating system, electric heater　a heating system that consists of one or more stages of resistive heating elements installed in a duct or central furnace.

heating system, high-pressure steam　a steam heating system employing steam at pressures above 15 psig.

heating system, high-temperature water　a heating system in which water having supply temperatures above 350°F is used as a medium to convey heat from a central boiler, through a piping system, to suitable heat distribution means.

heating system, hot water　a heating system in which water having supply temperatures lower than 250°F is used as a medium to convey heat from a central boiler, through a piping system, to suitable heat distribution means.

heating system, hot water coil　a heating system in which hot water is supplied by a central hot water boiler. Hot water coils are used to heat air.

heating system, indirect-fired　a heating system in which combustion takes place in a boiler or furnace. The fuel is burned in a combustion chamber, and the flue gases do not mix with the incoming air.

heating system, low-pressure steam　a steam heating system employing steam at pressures between 0 and 15 psig.

heating system, medium-temperature water　a heating system in which water having supply temperatures between 250°F and 350°F is used as a medium to convey the heat from a central boiler, through a piping system, to suitable heat distribution means.

heating system, panel　a heating system in which heat is transmitted by both radiation and convection from panel surfaces to both air and surrounding surfaces.

heating system, perimeter warm air　a warm air heating system of the combination panel and convection type. Warm air ducts embedded in the concrete slab of a house or structure that does not have a basement, around the perimeter, receive heated air from a furnace and deliver it to the heated space through registers placed in or near the floor. Air is returned to the furnace from registers near the ceiling.

heating system, radiant   a heating system in which only the heat radiated from panels is effective in providing the heating requirements. The term radiant heating is frequently used to include both panel heating and radiant heating.

heating system, split   a system in which the heating is accomplished by means of radiators or convectors supplemented by mechanical circulation of air (heated or unheated) from a central point. Ventilation may be provided by the same system.

heating system, steam   a heating system in which heat is transferred from the boiler or other source of heat to the heating unit by means of steam at, above, or below atmospheric pressure.

heating system, vacuum   a two-pipe steam heating system equipped with the necessary accessory apparatus which will permit operating the system below atmospheric pressure.

heating system, vapor   a steam heating system which operates under pressures at or near atmospheric and which returns the condensate to the boiler or receiver by gravity.

heating system, warm air   a warm air heating plant consisting of a heating unit (electric or fuel-burning furnace) enclosed in a casing, from which the heated air is distributed to various rooms in a building through ducts.

heating unit   radiators, convectors, baseboards, finned tubing; coils embedded in floor, wall, or ceiling; or any device which transmits the heat from the heating system to the room and its occupants.

heating value   the heat released by the combustion of a unit quantity of a fuel (usually one cubic foot of gas), measured in calories or Btu's.

heavy ends, hydrocarbon oils   the heavy molecules or larger molecules of hydrocarbon oils.

heavy fuel oil   Grades 5 and 6, used in commercial and industrial burners; generally requires preheating. Heating values range from 146,800 to 155,900 Btu's per gallon.

heel jaw   the bottom stationary serrated jaw of a pipe wrench.

height   linear measurement of one dimension, as from the base to the top of an object.

heliarc welding   joining of metal by using high-frequency electric current. An inert gas (usually helium) surrounds the welding to prevent oxidation.

helical stripe   a continuous, colored, spiral stripe applied over the outer perimeter of an insulated conductor for circuit identification purposes.

helix coil   a piece of bimetal formed into a helix-shaped coil that provides more surface area and a longer travel when heated.

henry   an electrical unit denoting the inductance of a circuit in which a current varying at the rate of one ampere per second produces an electromotive force of one volt. Its symbol is H.

hermetic   totally sealed, especially against the escape or entry of air. In HVAC/R applications, it means sealed by gaskets or welds, as in refrigeration compressors.

hermetic analyzer   this is an instrument that can be used for rocking frozen, wedged compressors free by reversing motor rotations. Has a bank of starting and run capacitors and has the ability to check motor windings for shorts, opens, continuity, and grounds. Some analyzers can be used as an ammeter, voltmeter, ohmmeter, and a capacitor or relay analyzer.

hermetic compressor   a compressor and electrically driven motor sealed within the same casing.

hermetic motor   compressor drive motor sealed within the same housing as the compressor.

hermetic system   a refrigeration system which has a compressor driven by a motor contained in a compressor dome or housing.

hermetically sealed unit   a sealed hermetic-type condensing unit is a mechanical condensing unit in which the compressor and compressor motor are enclosed in the same housing with no external shaft or shaft seal, with the compressor motor operating in the refrigerant atmosphere. The compressor and compressor motor housing may be of either the fully welded or brazed type, or the service-sealed type, and the housing is permanently sealed and is not provided with means of access for servicing internal parts in the field. In the service-sealed type, the housing is provided with some means of access for servicing internal parts in the field.

hertz (Hz)   a unit of frequency equal to one cycle per second.

hexagon   a six-sided figure with each of its vertices forming a sixty-degree angle.

hexagonal shoulder   a six-sided edge.

Hg   symbol for mercury. Heavy silver-white metallic element. It is the only metal that is liquid at ordinary room temperature. Symbol is Hg for the Latin term hydrargyrum.

hickey   a device used to bend conduit; also, a special fitting for attaching light fixtures to outlet boxes.

hidden lines   light dashed lines used on blueprints and plot plans to show edges that are not seen from a particular view. You have to look at another plan in the set to find these edges. Hidden lines are used to help the worker understand the drawing.

highboy furnace   a furnace in which air is drawn in through the sides or bottom and discharged out the top.

high-efficiency gas furnace   forced-air, gas-fired furnace which uses recycling of combustion flue gases through a secondary heat exchanger to achieve efficiencies above 85%.

high fire   the maximum firing rate of a burner or furnace.

high-fire interlock   an interlock which proves the damper is open for prepurge.

high-fire switch   see *high-fire interlock*.

high limit   a controller that features normally closed contacts and a sensing element inserted in a furnace (or boiler) that shuts down the burners or electric heater (regardless of room thermostat demand) when circulating air or water exceeds preset limits.

high-low fire   provision in a burner for either of two firing rates, high or low (no rate in between), selected according to load demand by the firing rate controller. A system is normally wired for guaranteed low fire start.

high-pressure appliance   an appliance that uses a refrigerant with a boiling point between –50°C and 10°C at atmospheric pressure.

high-pressure boiler (hot water or steam)   a boiler furnishing hot water at pressures in excess of 160 pounds per square inch (psig) or at temperatures in excess of 250°F (121°C); a boiler furnishing steam at pressures in excess of 15 psig.

high-pressure cutout   a normally closed electrical control switch operated by the high-side refrigerant pressure which automatically opens an electrical circuit if excessive head pressure or condensing pressure is reached.

high-pressure gauge   an instrument that measures pressures on the high side of the refrigeration system.

high-pressure gun burner   see *gun-type burner*.

high-pressure switch   see *pressure switch*.

high side   that part of a refrigerating system which is under condensing or high-side pressure. Also refers to the outdoor unit, which contains the condenser fan motor, compressor, outdoor coil, and possibly a receiver, mounted on a base unit.

high-side charging the process of introducing liquid refrigerant into the high side of a refrigeration system. The acceptable manner for placing refrigerant into a non-operating system.

high-side float a refrigerant control mechanism which controls the level of the liquid refrigerant in the high pressure of the mechanism.

high-speed fuses fuses with no intentional time-delay in the overload range and designed to open as quickly as possible in the short-circuit range. These fuses are often used to protect solid-state devices.

high-temperature boiler (hot water) a boiler furnishing hot water at temperatures over 350°F and usual pressures of about 300 psi.

high-temperature refrigeration a refrigeration temperature range starting with evaporator temperatures no lower than 35°F, a range usually used in air-conditioning cooling systems.

high vacuum a vacuum greater than 29 inches of mercury.

high-vacuum pump a machine which can create a vacuum in the 1000 to 10 micron range.

high-voltage circuit a circuit involving a potential of more than 600 volts; not defined by Underwriters Laboratories Inc.

high-voltage probe used to extend the range of a multimeter or oscilloscope to read up to 40 Kv AC or DC.

Hi-Re-Li system a patented heat pump cycle developed by Westinghouse Corporation.

holding charge the refrigerant charge that is supplied in a new condensing (high-side component) unit.

holding coil that part of a magnetic starter or relay that causes the device to operate when energized.

holding contacts a set of relay contacts used for the purpose of maintaining current flow to the coil of a relay. Generally used when the relay is initially energized by a momentary switch closure.

holding current the amount of current needed to keep an SCR or triac turned on.

holdover in an evaporator, the ability to stay cold after heat removal from the evaporator stops. A material used to store heat in latent or sensible form.

hole a vacancy that has been caused by a valence electron breaking its covalent bond and becoming a conduction electron. It has a positive charge.

hollow set screw (Allen) wrenches wrenches used to remove and install set screws that are recessed.

hollow tube gasket a sealing device made of rubber or plastic with a tubular cross section.

hone a fine grit stone used for precision sharpening.

hook jaw the top movable serrated jaw of a pipe wrench.

hoop stress the stress in a pipe wall, acting circumferentially in a plane perpendicular to the longitudinal axis of the pipe and produced by the pressure of the fluid in the pipe.

hopscotching a troubleshooting procedure for electric circuits that is accomplished by jumping from one component to another to determine which components are open or closed.

horizontal boiler see *water-tube boiler*.

horizontal flow a system with return air from one side flowing horizontally through a heat exchanger and out the other side as supply air.

horizontal furnace a forced-air, central furnace designed with essentially horizontal airflow.

horizontal return tube (HRT) boiler   see *fire-tube boiler.*

horizontal rotary oil burner   see *rotary oil burner.*

horizontal stripe   a colored stripe running horizontally with the axis of a conductor, sometimes called a longitudinal strip; used as a means of circuit identification.

horsepower (hp)   a unit of power equal to 550 foot-pounds per second, 33,000 foot-pounds per minute, or 746 watts.

$$hp = \frac{output\ (watts)}{746}$$

$$hp = \frac{torque\ (in/oz) \times rpm}{1,000,000}$$

horsepower, boiler   a measure of boiler capacity, equal to the production of 33,475 Btu's per hour.

hot   carrying a current or danger of electrical shock.

hot deck   the heating section of a multizone system.

hot gas   the refrigerant vapor leaving the compressor.

hot gas bypass   a piping system in a refrigerating unit which moves hot refrigerant gas from the condenser into the low side of the system.

hot gas defrost   a defrosting system in which hot refrigerant gas from the high side is directed through the evaporator for a short period of time and at predetermined intervals in order to remove frost from the evaporator.

hot gas line   the compressor discharge line in a refrigeration system which goes from the outlet of the compressor to the inlet of the condenser coil.

hot junction   that part of a thermocouple where the two wires that make up the thermocouple are joined together and heated to

produce electrical energy by the thermoelectric effect.

hot line   incoming, live (not grounded) wire(s) used to power a device, usually designed L1.

hot refractory hold-in test   a test for a flame safeguard control using a rectifying photocell, a cadmium sulfide cell, or an infrared flame detector, to make certain that hot refractory will not cause the flame relay to stay pulled in after the burner flame goes out.

hot refractory override test   see *hot refractory saturation test.*

hot refractory saturation test   a test for a flame safeguard control using an infrared flame detector. It is performed to make certain that radiation from hot refractory does not mask the flickering radiation of the flame itself. Also called hot refractory override test.

hot surface ignitor   a gas burner ignition system in which a ceramic resistive element is used as a heat source to ignite the gas.

hot water heating system   a heating system in which water is used as the medium by which heat is carried through pipes from the boiler to the heating units.

hot wire   an electrical lead which has a voltage difference between it and either another hot wire or a neutral wire.

hot-wire anemometer   an instrument which measures airspeed by changes in electrical resistance of a wire exposed to the air current.

hot-wire relay   a relay that is opened or closed by a thermal element that senses the starting current of the motor. The relay allows a starting capacitor or starting winding to drop out or drop in the starting circuit. This type of relay also has a built-in means of overload protection.

hot-wire valve   a heat-actuated valve in which the valve is opened and closed by expansion and contraction of a taut wire heated by an electric current passing through it.

housing   any protective shell or covering.

humid   damp, moist; containing much moisture.

humid climate   climate in which the following conditions occur: (a) 67°F or higher wet bulb outdoor ambient temperature for 3500 or more hours during the warmest six consecutive months of the year. (b) 73°F or higher wet bulb outdoor ambient temperature for 1750 or more hours during the warmest six consecutive months of the year.

humidification   the process of increasing the water vapor content of the conditioned air.

humidifier   a device used to add to and control the humidity in a confined space.

humidifier, central   a device which humidifies air to be circulated through ducts in an air-conditioning system.

humidifier fever   a respiratory illness that may be caused by exposure to toxins from microorganisms found in wet or moist areas in humidifiers and air conditioners. Also called air-conditioner or ventilation fever.

humidifier, room-spray-type   an air humidifier which sprays water directly into the room.

humidify   to add water vapor to the atmosphere; to add water vapor or moisture to any material.

humidifying effect   the latent heat of evaporation of water at the average evaporating temperature times the weight of the water evaporated per unit of time.

humidistat   a normally open electrical primary control device that is used to control humidity. It uses a moisture-sensitive element (usually nylon) to control a mechanical linkage that opens and closes an electric switch.

humidity   moisture or dampness. Relative humidity is the ratio of vapor present in air to the greatest amount possible at a given temperature.

humidity, absolute   weight of water vapor per cubic foot of dry air, expressed as grains of moisture per pound.

humidity, percentage   the ratio of the weight of water vapor associated with a pound of dry air to the weight of water vapor associated with a pound of dry air saturated at the same temperature.

humidity, ratio   see *humidity, specific.*

humidity, relative   the amount of moisture in the air expressed as a percentage of the maximum amount that the air is capable of holding at a specific temperature.

humidity, specific   weight of water vapor in one pound of dry air, expressed as grains of moisture per pound.

hunting   a continuous oscillation of the temperature, pressure, or relative humidity above and below the control point. Very rapid hunting is usually called oscillation.

HVAC/R circuit breaker   a circuit breaker with a built-in trip delay commonly used in air-conditioning installations due to the power surge on start-up.

hydraulic motor   a device which converts fluid power into mechanical force and motion. It usually provides rotary motion. Motors are either fixed displacement, in which the quantity of fluid per unit of output motion is constant, or variable displacement, in which the quantity of fluid per unit of output motion can be adjusted.

hydraulic pump   a device which converts mechanical force and motion into fluid power. Pumps are of either the fixed-displacement or the variable-displacement type.

hydraulics   branch of physics having to do with the mechanical properties of water and other fluids or liquids in motion.

hydrocarbons   organic compounds containing only hydrogen and carbon atoms in various combinations.

hydrochlorofluorocarbons (HCFC)   molecules created when some of the hydrogen atoms in a hydrocarbon molecule are replaced with chlorine or fluorine atoms. Because they have a shorter life than CFCs, HCFCs are less harmful than CFCs to stratospheric ozone.

hydrodynamic lubrication   lubrication that deals with the motion of fluids and the behavior of solid bodies immersed in them.

hydrofluorocarbons   molecules created when some of the hydrogen atoms in a hydrocarbon are replaced with fluorine. Because HFCs contain no chlorine, they don't destroy ozone but may contribute to global warming.

hydrolysis   the splitting of chemical compounds by reaction with water.

hydrolyzing action   the corrosive effect within a refrigeration system caused by the chemical reaction between moisture and the refrigerant.

hydrometer   a floating instrument used to measure specific gravity of a liquid. Specific gravity is the ratio of the weight of any volume of a substance to the weight of an equal volume of substance used as a standard.

hydronic   a type of heating system which circulates a heated fluid, usually water, through baseboard coils. The circulating pump is usually controlled by a thermostat.

hydronics   the science of heating and cooling with liquids.

hydrostatic pressure   extremely high and dangerous pressure created by the expansion of a liquid in an enclosed space, such as a cylinder.

hydrostatic test   a water test, not to exceed 1.5 times the maximum design working pressure, applied to a pressure vessel. The recommended water temperature for this test is 70°F.

hygrometer   (1) an instrument used to measure the degree of moisture in the atmosphere or (2) an instrument used to measure the specific gravity or "charge" of the electrolyte of a storage battery.

hygroscopic   the ability of a substance to absorb and retain moisture and change physical dimensions as its moisture content changes.

hygrostat   a control that actuates equipment when a specified humidity is attained.

hypersensitivity pneumonitis   a group of respiratory diseases, including humidifier fever, that involve inflammation of the lungs. Most forms of hypersensitivity pneumonitis are thought to be caused by an allergic reaction triggered by repeated exposures to biological contaminants.

hysteresis   a lag in the production of, or the collapse of, a magnetic field due to friction between the molecules of the magnetized substance.

hysteresis circuit   a special circuit in the differential thermostat which prevents the pump from being unnecessarily turned on and off immediately following an initial pump turn-on or turn-off event.

hysteresis loop   a graphic curve that shows the value of magnetizing force for a particular type of material.

hysteresis test   an electrical test used to check the integrity of centrifugal chiller-tube bundles.

I

I   symbol used to designate current.

IAEI   International Association of Electrical Inspectors.

IAPMO   International Association of Plumbing and Mechanical Officials.

IARW   International Association of Refrigerated Warehouses.

IBCA   Industry Bar Code Alliance.

IBEW   International Brotherhood of Electrical Workers.

IBR   Institute of Boiler and Radiator Manufacturers.

IC   integrated circuit.

ICBO   International Conference of Building Officials.

ICC   Interstate Commerce Commission.

ICE   a mnemonic device used to help remember that current (I) in a capacitive (C) circuit leads or is in front of voltage (E).

ICR   inductance, capacitance, resistance.

ICRA   International Compressor Remanufacturers Association.

id   inside diameter.

IDEA   International District Energy Association.

IDHCA   International District Heating and Cooling Association.

idlh   immediately dangerous to life and health.

IEEE   Institute of Electrical and Electronics Engineers.

IEQA   Indoor Environmental Quality Alliance.

IES   Illuminating Engineering Society or Institute of Environmental Sciences.

IFCI   International Fire Code Institute.

IFMA   International Facility Management Association.

IGSHPA   International Ground Source Heat Pump Association.

IGT   Institute of Gas Technology.

IHACI   Institute of Heating and Air Conditioning, Inc.

IHF   Industrial Health Foundation.

IIAR   International Institute of Ammonia Refrigeration.

IIE   Institute of Industrial Engineers.

IKECA   International Kitchen Exhaust Cleaning Association.

IMACA   International Mobile Air Conditioning Association.

IME   ice melting equivalent.

imp   impedance.

in   inch or inches.

in-lb   inch-pounds.

inv   inverse.

IOA   International Ozone Association.

ipt   iron pipe thread.

IR   infrared radiation.

ISA   Instrument Society of America.

ISB   Institute for Sick Buildings.

ISO   International Organization for Standardization.

ITSAC   International Thermal Storage Advisory Council.

I^2R   formula for power in watts. I = intensity of current measured in amps and R = resistance measured in ohms.

ice   frozen water; the state of H_2O below 32°F or 0°C.

ice bank   a thermal accumulator in which ice is formed during off-peak periods of refrigeration demand, and in which, during peak periods of refrigeration demand, compressor capacity is supplemented by melting ice.

ice can   a mold in which large blocks of ice are formed by suspension in a chilled brine tank.

ice cream cabinet   a commercial refrigerator which operates at approximately 0°F and is used for storage of ice cream.

ice harvest switch   located at the end of the water plate, it resets the timer on the status indicator card after each ice harvest. It is used only with a status indicator.

ice maker   a cyclic-type automatic ice making device which has separate and sequential water fill, freezing, and harvesting phases for the ice making process.

ice melting effect   see *ice melting equivalent.*

ice melting equivalent (IME)   The amount of heat absorbed by the melting of one ton of ice at 32°F. This would absorb 288,000 Btu's (144 latent heat of fusion × 2000 pounds) in a 24-hour period.

ice point   the freezing temperature of water. The freezing temperature of water is 0°C, 32°F, or 273.16°K.

ice ring   an accumulation of ice at the bottom of the outdoor coil due to incomplete defrost operation of a heat pump system.

ice storage bin rating   the capacity of the ice bin of an automatic ice maker storage bin. The average weight of ice contained in the bin when the bin fill device terminates the ice making process.

ice water thickness   a commercial classification applied to molded cork covering and similar insulation for refrigerant and chilled water lines. Somewhat thinner than brine thickness.

icebox   a refrigerator or cooler in which the heat absorber is ice instead of an evaporator.

identification plate   a metal plate or sticker that provides information such as manufacturer, part number, and specifications. Frequently mounted on the outside housing of compressors and motors.

identified   refers to equipment that is suitable for a specific purpose or application.

idler   a pulley used on some belt drives to provide the proper belt tension and to eliminate belt vibration.

ignite   to set fire to; to heat to a high temperature.

igniter   any electrical or mechanical device and related equipment used to ignite a fuel/air mixture. Also, a burner (like a pilot) using gas or oil to ignite very large gas, oil, or pulverized coal burners in very large water-tube boilers (normally field-erected).

ignition   the act of starting combustion. Also see *automatic, continuous, direct spark, electric, inherent, intermittent, interrupted, manual, proved, proved spark, torch,* and *unproved ignition.*

ignition, automatic   a heating-fuel ignition system which ignites fuel at the beginning of the cycle only, not constantly throughout the cycle.

ignition bracket assembly   this assembly is made up of a bracket, an ignition transformer, a solenoid gas valve, an electric igniter, a fire safety switch, a twist lock receptacle, a terminal block, and a burner latch.

ignition electrode   a metal conductor used to generate a spark across a narrow gap to ground in order to ignite a fuel/air mixture.

ignition interference   electrical noise, caused by ignition current feeding through the flame to the flame rod, which is superimposed on the flame signal (flame rod detectors only). The interference may be additive or subtractive (it may increase or decrease the flame signal). Subtractive interference may cause the flame relay to drop out; severe additive interference may damage the flame relay unless an arc gap protector is in the circuit.

ignition interference test   a test to make certain that ignition current is not interfering with the proper operation of a flame rod. See *ignition interference.*

ignition point   the temperature at which a fuel/air mixture will light and continue to burn.

ignition return   immediate restoration of ignition, without preignition purging or interlock checks, after loss of the main burner flame. If the main burner flame is not reestablished, safety shutdown occurs. Also called relight.

ignition spark response test a test for a flame safeguard control, using an ultraviolet flame detector, to make certain that the ignition spark is not actuating the flame relay.

ignition temperature a term generally used to mean the lowest temperature that will cause a gas to ignite and burn. It is not a precise term and is subject to several variables; it is used only as an indication.

ignition timing a period of time during which ignition means are on. This provides a means of establishing and stabilizing the flame to ensure proper burning of the fuel when the main burner is firing.

ignition transformer a device which provides a high-voltage spark (usually 6,000 to 10,000 volts) which will cause ignition.

ignition trials a period of time during which the pilot and main burner must be ignited (main burner only if using direct spark ignition). Also see *main burner flame-establishing period* and *pilot flame-establishing period.*

ignition velocity see *flame propagation rate.*

ignitor any device used to light gas. A spark ignitor uses an electric spark generated across an air gap for this purpose.

illumination the density of the luminous flux on a surface; it is the quotient of the flux by the area of the surface when the latter is uniformly illuminated.

immediately dangerous to life and health (IDLH) a descriptive term for chemical concentration levels used to determine selection of a respirator. The maximum concentration from which one could escape within 30 minutes without any escape-impairing symptoms or any irreversible health effects.

immerse to dip, stick, or plunge into, as into a liquid.

immersion the act of putting an object into a liquid so that it is completely covered by the liquid.

immersion-type controller a controller constructed with a flexible tube and a remote measuring element, immersed in a well in a pipe or tank.

impact pressure the total pressure of a flowing gas, including velocity and pressure above atmospheric.

impact tool a hand tool which converts a hammer blow to useful leverage.

impact tube the center tube of a pilot tube that measures both pressure and velocity.

impedance the total resistance to the flow of an AC current as a result of resistance, reactance, or capacitance in the circuit. It is expressed in ohms and designated by the symbol Z.

impedance-protected motor a motor designed to not burn out in less than 15 days under locked-rotor (stalled) conditions, in accordance with UL Standard 519.

impedance relay a single-pole, single-throw normally closed relay that has a high-resistance coil that is wired to prevent compressor start-up after a safety control opens. Equipment operation will not start until a manual reset is performed. Also called a lockout relay or control.

impeller a series of rotating blades or vanes similar to the old-fashioned paddle wheel. In an open impeller, the impeller blades rotate between the stationary walls of the blower housing. The walls tend to channel the air so that most of it flows out through the tips of the blades, but some air slips out sideways from between the blades and short-circuits back to the impeller inlet. A closed impeller has cover plate discs attached to the sides of the blades, and thus short circuiting is minimized.

impingement   a condition in a gas or oil furnace when the flame strikes the sides of the combustion chamber, resulting in poor combustion efficiency.

impingement target burner   a burner consisting simply of a gas orifice and a target, with the gas jet from the orifice entraining combustion air in the open and the mixture striking and burning on the target surface. No usual burner body is used.

impurities   dirt or other foreign matter mixed in a substance so as to make it unclean.

in contacts   those relay contacts which complete circuits when the relay coil is energized. They are also referred to as normally open contacts.

in-line ammeter   a current-measuring device that is connected in series with the circuit being tested.

in-line fan (tubular centrifugal fan)   a fan where airflow is developed as in a centrifugal blower, but after leaving the impeller the air is contained in a tubular housing and, by means of turning vanes, is discharged in an axial direction. Employs single-inlet centrifugal wheels, usually with backward-inclined blades. The tubular centrifugal fan has performance characteristics similar to a centrifugal blower and the compact physical configuration of the tubeaxial fan. Can be vertically or horizontally mounted, thus providing a simpler installation by minimizing the need for duct turns and transitions.

in-phase   describes two waveforms of the same frequency which pass through their minimum and maximum values at the same time and polarity.

incandescence   the state of a material with such a high temperature that it gives off light.

incandescent lamp   a lamp which gives light due to a filament glowing at a white heat.

inch-ounce   a measure of the torque for a small motor. One ounce of force applied at 1″ from the center line of the shaft.

inch-pound   the amount of power needed to raise one pound one inch.

inches of mercury   a unit used in measuring pressures. One inch of mercury column equals a pressure of 0.491 lb/in.

inches of water   a unit of pressure equal to the pressure exerted by a column of liquid water one inch high at sea level and at a temperature of 39.2°F. One inch of water column equals a pressure of 0.578 ounce per square inch (.036 psi). One inch of mercury column equals about 13.6 inches of water column. Approximately $1/28$ of one psi.

incinerate   to burn to ashes, burn up.

inclined   describes a line or plane that makes an angle with another line or plane.

inclined gauge   see *inclined manometer*.

inclined manometer   an instrument which measures low gas pressure by means of a diagonal column of water or a special specific gravity fluid.

incompatible   not suited to be used together; not in harmony or agreement.

incomplete combustion   combustion in which the fuel is only partially burned and capable of being burned further under proper conditions. It results from an inadequate amount of air for the quantity of fuel provided. It can also occur in excess air conditions if mixing is poor and/or the flame is chilled below the ignition temperature before the full combustion reaction can take place. An example is the burning of carbon, producing carbon monoxide (CO); with more air in the combustion mixture, carbon dioxide (CO_2) would result.

increment   amount of increase or addition.

independent lightoff   separate ignition of each burner in a multiburner system. Each burner can be started or stopped by itself.

indicating controller   a controller equipped with a scale and an indicating pointer. It often shows the set point as well as the actual temperature of the medium being controlled.

indicator (electrical)   the part of the electrical system that shows if it is on or off (a light bulb) or indicates a specific quantity (like an electrical meter).

indirect-fired external heater   any oven heating system in which the oven atmosphere is kept separate from the combustion gases, and in which the burners and combustion chamber are outside of the oven chamber. There are three types:

1. Recirculating - oven atmosphere is returned to the heater to be reheated.
2. Nonrecirculating - oven atmosphere is not returned to the heater.
3. Internal radiator - products of combustion from the heater are circulated through radiator tubes located within the oven chamber.

indirect-fired heater   a heater in which the products of combustion (flue gases) are not mixed with the medium being heated. Also see *indirect-fired external, indirect-fired internal,* and *radiant tube-type heaters.*

indirect-fired internal heater   any oven heating system in which the oven atmosphere is kept separate from the combustion gases, and in which the burners are contained in gas-tight radiators within the oven chamber. There are two types:

1. Explosion-resisting - constructed to withstand explosion pressure from ignition of a gas/air mixture in the radiators.
2. Nonexplosion-resisting - with gas-tight radiators which are not designed to withstand an internal explosion.

indirect system   a solar heating system in which the solar heat is collected outside of the building and moved inside through ducts or piping with fans or pumps.

indirect water heater   a coil or bundle of tubes, usually copper, surrounded by hot boiler water. The domestic water is within the tube and is heated by transfer of heat from the hot boiler water surrounding the tube.

indirectly conditioned space   enclosed space within a building that is not heated or cooled space, whose area-weighted heat transfer coefficient to heated or cooled space exceeds that to the outdoors or to unconditioned space, or through which air from heated or cooled space is transferred at a rate exceeding three air changes per hour.

indoor coil   a heat pump component that is either an evaporator or a condenser, depending upon whether the system is operating in the heating or cooling mode.

indoor design temperature   the indoor air temperature used when calculating the design heat loss. The indoor design temperature is usually assumed to be 70°F.

indoor fan relay   an electric relay that starts and stops an indoor fan on cooling, electric heating, and heat pump systems.

indoor-outdoor temperature difference   the temperature of the indoor air minus the temperature of the outdoor air.

induced air   air which flows into a furnace because the furnace pressure is less than atmospheric pressure. This includes air brought into a furnace by entrainment in a high-velocity stream.

induced current   the current that flows as the result of an induced electromotive force.

induced draft   air movement into and through the combustion chamber and breeching, produced by a partial vacuum within the combustion chamber created by a fan at the outlet of the chamber.

induced-draft burner   a gas burner which uses an induced draft to bring in combustion air. Also see *induced-draft* and *mechanical-draft burner.*

induced-draft cooling tower a cooling tower in which the flow of air is created by one or more fans drawing the saturated air out of the tower.

induced-draft fan a fan or blower that produces a negative pressure in the combustion chamber, causing a suction which draws in air.

induced magnetism the phenomenon where a magnetic field produces magnetism in a metal.

induced voltage the potential that causes induced current to flow through a conductor which passes through a magnetic field.

inductance the inherent property of an electrical circuit that opposes a change in current. The property of a circuit whereby energy may be stored in a magnetic field. Inductance is present only when the current is changing.

induction the phenomenon of a voltage, magnetic field, or electrostatic charge being produced in an object by lines of force from such fields near the object.

induction coil a device for obtaining high voltage. It contains a primary coil with only a few turns of heavy wire and a secondary coil with many turns of fine wire.

induction motor an alternating current motor which operates on the principle of a rotating magnetic field. The rotor has no electrical connection, but receives electrical energy by transformer action from the field windings.

inductive circuit any circuit that contains at least one magnetic load.

inductive heating a method of heating conductors in which the material to be heated is placed inside a coil of wire and high-frequency alternating current voltage is applied.

inductive load a lagging load; a load that is predominantly inductive, so that the alternating current lags behind the alternating voltage, i.e., the current does not change direction until after the voltage has changed. Power consumption for inductive loads is calculated by volts times amperes times the power factor of the load.

inductive pick-up the generation of a voltage in one conductor by induction from another nearby conductor.

inductive reactance the phenomenon where electromagnetic induction in a circuit creates a counter or reverse EMF (voltage) as the original current changes. It opposes the flow of alternating current.

inductor a coil of wire which has the property of inductance and is used in an electric circuit.

industrial air-conditioning air-conditioning to produce other than human comfort conditions.

industrial furnace a process-type heater which changes the characteristics of the material being processed. It is usually operated at temperatures above 1200°F.

industrial oven a process-type heater normally used for drying. It is generally operated at temperatures from 400°F to 800°F.

industrial process refrigeration complex, custom appliances used in the chemical, pharmaceutical, petrochemical, and manufacturing industries.

inert gas a gas, usually nitrogen, that is chemically inactive in a refrigeration system. Used as a substitute for refrigerant in drying a system or while shipping components.

inertia the property of a body (mass) at rest to resist movement and of a body in motion to continue in motion, so that some external force must be applied to move a body at rest and to slow down or stop a body in motion.

inerting introducing an inert medium into a furnace, pulverizer, or other enclosure to reduce the oxygen content of the resulting mixture below the limits of flammability.

inerts   noncombustible substances in a fuel.

infiltration   passage of outside air into buildings through doors, cracks, windows, etc.

inflammable   capable of being ignited and burned; synonym for flammable and combustible.

inflammation   a type of reaction produced in the tissues by an irritant, injury, or infection. It is characterized by redness and swelling caused by an influx of blood and fluids.

infrared flame detector   a detector that responds to the infrared radiation (wavelength between 0.75 and 1000 microns) emitted by a flame. Also see *lead sulfide cell*.

infrared heater   a heater that directs a substantial amount of its energy output in the form of infrared energy into the area to be heated. Such heaters may be of the vented or unvented type.

infrared lamp   an electrical device which emits infrared rays. These are invisible rays just below red in the visible spectrum.

infrared radiation (IR)   invisible, electromagnetic waves of low frequency (long wavelength—between 0.75 and 1000 microns). They are generated by thermal agitation and radiated by everything with a temperature above absolute zero (–273°C); the hotter the object, the greater the infrared radiation. Infrared radiation comprises about 90% of the light spectrum, ranging from the low end up to the white visible light range. Also see *hot refractory hold-in test* and *hot refractory saturation test*.

infrared rays   the rays that transfer heat by radiation.

ingestion   the taking in of a substance through the mouth.

inhalation   the breathing in of a substance in the form of a vapor, gas, fume, mist, or dust.

inherent ignition   feedback of part of the heat generated by the flame to ignite more of the combustible mixture; it must keep the fire going after ignition is terminated.

inherent protector   a temperature- and current-sensitive device placed in a hermetic compressor for motor overload protection.

inhibitor   a substance added to oil, water, gas, etc. It is used to prevent unwanted action such as rusting, foaming, etc.

initial resistance   a new, clean filter's resistance to flow.

initiate   to begin an action or sequence of events such as a defrost cycle.

injection burner   see *inspirating burner*.

inlet   that part of a valve through which a fluid enters.

inner cone   the smaller flame which does most of the heating in oxyacetylene brazing.

input combustion control   see *firing rate controller*.

input rate   (1) the power which is applied to a piece of equipment or to the terminals on the piece of equipment to which the power is being applied. (2) The fuel rate going into a heating appliance.

input rating   the gas-burning capacity of an appliance in Btu/h as specified by the manufacturer. Appliance input ratings are based on sea level operation up to 2000 feet elevation. For operation at elevations above 2000 feet, input ratings should be reduced at the rate of 4% for each 1000 feet above 2000 feet.

input signal   the variations of the input voltage or current. The alternating current portion of the signal.

input voltage   the amount of voltage connected to a device or circuit.

inrush current   in a solenoid or coil, the steady-state current drawn from the line when the armature is in its maximum open position. Allowable inrush can be up to 10 times the pilot duty rating (running current).

inscribe   to draw one figure within another figure.

insertion element   a tube-shaped thermostat sensing element designed for use in liquids or in air.

insertion-type controller   a controller mounted on a duct or pipe, with its rigid measuring element inside the duct or pipe.

inshot burner   a gas burner in which the gas is delivered from the side(s) of the combustion chamber, resulting in a horizontal flame.

inside calipers   a hand tool used to measure material on the inside. A hole diameter, for example, can be measured by placing a caliper inside of it.

inside diameter   measurement across the widest part of a circular object, from inside surface to inside surface.

inside micrometer   a hand tool used to measure the inside diameter of objects such as rings and cylinders.

inside stop   the inside edge of a double-hung window. The expandable partitions of a window air conditioner expand to touch each side of the inside stop.

inside wrench   a wrench which grips a pipe or fitting from the inside to prevent scoring of the outer surface (especially threads and chrome).

insolation   the solar energy received by a given surface.

inspection   the measuring and checking of equipment or installations to determine whether they have been serviced or installed per specifications.

inspection plates   handhole covers which, when properly removed, make possible the inspection of the internal parts of equipment.

inspirating burner   a gas burner which uses venturi action to bring in combustion air. Also called an injection burner or venturi mixing burner. Also see *atmospheric burner* and *venturi*.

inspirator mixer   a mixing device in which a jet of gas is used to entrain primary air at a rate proportional to the gas flow rate. Also see *inspirating burner*.

instability   the characteristic of a control system with just enough variation in maintaining the set point to distinguish it from sluggishness or cycling.

installation diagram   a diagram that shows little internal wiring but gives specific information as to terminals, wire, sizes, color coding, and breaker or fuse sizes.

instantaneous hot water heater   one that contains no more than one gallon of water per 4000 Btu/h of input.

instantaneous voltage   a voltage value at any instant (time) along a waveform.

instrument   used broadly to denote a device that has measuring, recording, indicating, and/or controlling abilities.

instrument piping   the tubing, piping, and electrical wiring used in pressure measuring, heat-sensing, and electrical instruments.

insulation   a material having a resistance to heat flow.

insulation, brine thickness   a commercial classification applied to molded core covering and similar insulation for refrigerant and brine lines.

insulation classes   electric motor insulation is rated by its temperature capability for reasonable motor life. The classes are Class A (105°C), Class B (130°C), Class F (155°C), and Class H (180°C). These are total temperatures, not temperatures over ambient.

insulation, electric   materials which are poor conductors of electricity and which are used to cover wires and components to prevent short circuits and accidental shock hazards.

insulation, fill   granulated, shredded, or powdered material, prepared from vegetable, animal, or mineral origin. It can come in bulb or batt form.

insulation, ice water thickness   a commercial classification applied to molded core covering and similar insulation for refrigerant and chilled water lines.

insulation resistance   that property of an insulating material which resists electrical current flow through the insulating material when a potential difference is applied.

insulation, sound   acoustical treatment of fan housings, supply ducts, and other parts of a system and equipment for isolation of vibration, or reduced transmission of noise.

insulation, thermal   a substance that is used to retard or slow down the flow of heat transfer through a wall or partition.

insulator   substances containing very few free electrons and requiring large amounts of energy to break electrons loose from the influence of the nucleus.

intake (valve)   opening through which a fluid is drawn into a component.

integral   describes a whole number. For example, integral horsepower motors are motors of one horsepower and larger.

integral tank   any fuel tank furnished by the manufacturer as a component part of the complete assembly; either attached to the appliance or intended for separate mounting adjacent to the appliance.

integrated circuit   a circuit that incorporates multiple transistors and other semiconductors in a single circuit. It is sometimes called a chip.

integrated circuit board   electronic circuit made from transistors, resistors, etc., all placed into a package called a "chip," since all circuits are on one base of semiconductor material.

integrated part load value (IPLV)   single number figure of merit, based on part-load EER or COP, expressing part-load efficiency for air-conditioning and heat-pump equipment on the basis of weighted operation at various load capacities for the equipment.

integrated system   a solar heating system in which the solar heat is absorbed in the walls or roof of a dwelling and flows to the rooms without the aid of complex piping or ducts.

interchangeable   describes a part that has been made to specific dimensions and tolerances and is capable of being fitted into equipment in place of a similarly made part.

interconnecting wire   a type of wire for external use in electronic equipment where it is exposed to physical abuse. Interconnecting wire encompasses both control and power circuits.

intercooler   the cooling coil between stages in a multistage compression system.

interface   the interrelationship or means of communication between any two (or more) functions, modules, components, or communication devices.

interlock   an automatic controller or switch which monitors the physical state of a required condition and furnishes proof to the flame safeguard control that the condition is proper for burner operation to start or to continue. Also see *high-fire, lockout, low-fire, preignition, recycle, running, start,* and *valve-closed interlocks.*

interlocking systems   an arrangement of interlocks to ensure that all interrelated parts of an air-conditioning or refrigeration system are operating properly together.

intermittent cycle   a cycle which repeats itself at different intervals.

intermittent ignition   ignition by an energy source which is automatically energized each time there is a call for heat, and which is maintained during the entire run period. This ensures that a means of igniting the incoming fuel will always be present.

intermittent pilot   a pilot automatically ignited each time there is a call for heat and maintained during the entire run period. It is shut off with the main burner at the end of heat demand.

internal combustion engine   an engine driven by expansion resulting from the burning of fuel confined within the engine.

internal compressor overload   an overload that is embedded in the windings of a motor. Some internal overloads break the power to the motor directly (direct style) while others merely open a set of contacts that is wired into an electric control circuit (pilot-duty style).

internal energy   the sum of all the kinetic and potential energy contained in a substance due to the states of motion and separation of its several molecules, atoms, and electrons. It includes sensible heat (vibration energy) and that part of the latent heat that is represented by the increase in energy during evaporation.

internal equalizer   in a thermostatic expansion valve, an integral part or passage which provides exposure of the actuating element (diaphragm or bellows) to pressure leaving the valve.

internal heat gain   heat produced within the conditioned space by people, electric appliances, and the like.

internal heater   a heater in which the burner(s) and combustion chamber are within the oven chamber and in contact with the medium being heated. Also see *direct-fired internal* and *indirect-fired internal heaters*.

internal-mix oil burner   see *atomizing oil burner*.

internal overload   a heat-sensitive control embedded in motor windings; opens in case of excessive winding temperatures or current draw.

internal threads   female threads; threads that are not exposed.

internally equalized   describes a thermostatic expansion valve which senses evaporator inlet pressure under its diaphragm.

internally fused   with a fusible link built inside of the run capacitor that helps stop motor winding damage if a capacitor shorts out.

interrupted ignition   ignition by an energy source which is automatically energized each time there is a call for heat and is cut off automatically after flame is proved or at the end of a predetermined time.

interrupted pilot   a pilot automatically ignited each time there is a call for heat and is cut off automatically at the end of the main burner flame-establishing period.

interrupter   a switching device which opens and closes a circuit.

interruptible supply   refers to a fuel supply agreement whereby the customer's supply may be cut off in case of shortage. Fuel is usually available at a reduced rate.

interrupting capacity   the maximum short-circuit current that a circuit breaker can safely interrupt.

interrupting rating   the highest current that a fuse or circuit breaker will permit under ideal or test conditions.

interstage differential   in a multistage HVAC system, the change in temperature at the thermostat needed to turn additional heating or cooling equipment on.

Interstate Commerce Commission (ICC)   a government body which controls the design and construction of pressure containers.

intrinsic semiconductor   a semiconductor that has no impurities in its crystal structure.

intrinsically safe   describes an instrument designed and constructed to practically preclude the possibility of igniting a combustible mixture.

Invar   a metal that is an alloy of iron and nickel. Used as a bimetal for thermostats and temperature-sensing devices.

inventory   itemized list of goods, property, etc.; for example, a stock listing or store of goods.

inverse   the value of one divided by some quantity (such as $1/R_t$, for finding parallel resistances).

inversely proportional   describes a relationship where one quantity increases or decreases, causing another quantity to do the opposite.

inverted trap   a trap in refrigeration piping to prevent slugging of refrigerant or oil back to the compressor.

invoice   an itemized statement of charges for billing.

in-wall evaporator   this type of evaporator is used mainly on domestic freezers where the tubing is attached to the outside walls of the inner liner.

I/O device   input/output device. A keyboard, magnetic disk, printer, CRT terminal, or similar device that transmits data to or receives data from a computer or secondary storage device. In a more general sense, any digital device, including a single integrated circuit chip, that transmits data to or receives data or strobe pulses from a computer.

ion   an atom which has lost or gained some electrons. It may be positive or negative, depending on the net charge.

ion exchange   the phenomenon where one ion or group of ions replaces another ion or group of ions in a solution.

ionic bonding   a type of atomic bonding that occurs when one atom donates valence electrons to another atom.

ionization   a process by which electrons are detached from atoms or molecules, thus originating ions and free electrons. This is achieved by collisions or by high-energy radiation.

ionization voltage   the potential at which a material ionizes. The electrical potential at which an atom gives up an electron.

IR drop   an electrical term indicating the loss in a circuit expressed in amperes times resistance ($I \times R$) or voltage drop.

iris slide   a thin plate with a small aperture.

is-, iso-   prefix meaning constant; as isothermal, constant temperature; isentropic, constant entropy; isobaric, constant pressure; etc. In chemistry, isomers have different characteristics but the same number and kinds of atoms.

isentropic   a process carried out reversibly without energy interchange as heat. Also a process carried out with no entropy change.

isolate   to set apart from others, place alone; separate. To find the problem in an electrical circuit.

isolated   not easily accessible; requiring special ways of clearance to obtain entry.

isolated contacts   a term usually applying to relays (or switches) which are supplied with no instrument power to them and are available to the user for switching power circuits of the person's choice.

isolated limited secondary circuit   a circuit of limited energy derived from an isolated secondary winding of a transformer having a maximum capacity of 100 volt-amperes (va) and an open circuit secondary voltage rating not exceeding 1000 volts.

isolation relays   components used to prevent stray unwanted electrical feedback that can cause erratic operation.

isolation transformer   a transformer with a 1:1 turn ratio used to isolate an AC power line from equipment with a chassis ground. A transformer whose secondary winding is electrically isolated from its primary winding.

isomers   molecules that have the same numbers of the same atoms that another molecule has, but the atoms are arranged differently in their structure. Even though isomers of the same compound have equal numbers of atoms of the same element, they have very different physical properties. An example would be refrigerants R-134 and R-134a.

isometric   describes a process carried out at a constant volume.

isometric drawing   a pictorial in which the sides of the object are shown 120° apart.

isopiestic process   a process carried out at constant pressure.

isothermal   describes changes of volume or pressure under conditions of constant temperature.

isothermal process (expansion and contraction)   an action which takes place without a temperature change.

Isotron   trademark name of refrigerant manufactured by Pennsalt chemicals.

J

J box   a metal or plastic box where electrical connections are made.

jacket   the outer nonmetallic coating or covering applied over insulated wire or cable.

jacketing   surrounding an object with a control bath or stream of fluid for temperature control or heat absorption.

jaw-type pipe wrench   wrench with serrated jaws to grip pipe.

Jellif alloy "K"   a chromium aluminum alloy iron wire which is resistant to oxidation up to 2200°F (1200°C); used for flame rods in flame detectors.

jet burner   a burner in which streams of gas or air/gas mixtures collide in air at some point above the burner ports and burn there.

jet cooling system   a system in which a jet pump is used to produce a vacuum so water or refrigerant may evaporate at relatively low temperatures. These systems usually require a large condenser and have a low efficiency to remove heat.

jet velocity   this is the maximum velocity of air coming out of an outlet.

jogging   the quickly repeated closure and opening of the circuit to start a motor from the rested position for the purpose of accomplishing small movements of the driven machine.

joint, adhesive   a joint made in plastic pipe by the use of an adhesive substance that forms a continuous bond between the mating surfaces without dissolving either one of them.

joint, bellows   an item of equipment used to compensate for the expansion and contraction of a run of pipe. The device is built with a flexible bellows that stretches or is compressed as necessary to accept the movement of the piping.

joint, brazed, high-temperature   a gas-tight joint obtained by the joining of metal parts with metallic mixtures or alloys which melt at temperatures below 1500°F, but above 800°F.

joint clearance   the space between two surfaces of a joint.

joint compound   a substance applied to threaded fittings to ensure a leakproof joint.

joint, insulating   a fitting made of material which will not conduct electricity, thereby preventing the flow of current through a piping system.

joint, leaded   a joint that is sealed with poured hot lead.

joint, mechanical   a gas-tight joint obtained by the joining of metal parts through a positive holding mechanical construction (such as flanged joint, screwed joint, or flared joint).

joint, slip   a joint in which the provision for expansion and contraction consists of a cylinder that moves in and out of the main body of the device.

joint, soldered   a gas-tight joint obtained by the joining of metal parts with metallic mixtures or alloys which melt at temperatures below 800°F.

joint, solvent cement   a joint made in thermoplastic piping by the use of a solvent or solvent cement that forms a continuous bond between the mating surfaces.

joint, welded   a gas-tight joint obtained by the joining of metal parts in the plastic or molten state.

joule   a scientific unit of heat. The amount of heat needed to raise the temperature of 1 kilogram of water 1°C is 4.187 kilojoules. The quantity of heat equal to one watt-second.

Joule-Thomson effect   a change in temperature of a gas on expansion from a high pressure to a low pressure through a porous plug.

Joule's law   the law which states the relationship between the heat produced by current flow and the amperage, resistance, and time span involved.

journal, crankshaft   the part of the crankshaft which contacts the bearing.

journeyman   a tradesperson who has served his or her apprenticeship training or learning of 3 to 5 years and is capable of completing an installation without supervision.

jumper   a short length of wire used to complete a circuit temporarily or to bypass part of a circuit. Also, the action of using a jumper.

jumper out   to temporarily remove an electrical component from an electrical circuit, for test purposes only, by connecting a wire across the component's contacts.

junction   a point in a circuit where the current branches out into other sections.

junction box   a box used to connect sections of electrical conduits or wires, at the same time providing access to the enclosed conductors through a removable cover on the junction box for connecting and branching the enclosed conductors.

junction capacitance   the effective capacitance that a P-N junction produces.

junction field effect transistor   a field-effect device that uses a reversed-biased P-N junction gate.

K

K   Kelvin.

Kg   kilogram.

Kv   kilovolt.

Kva   kilovolt amps.

Kvah   kilovolt ampere hour.

Kvar   kilovar.

Kw   kilowatt.

Kwh   kilowatt-hour.

K factor   the ability of a material to conduct heat. Expressed in Btu's per hour, per square foot, per inch of thickness of the material.

Kanthal A-1   a stainless steel alloy used in the manufacture of flame rods. It has a maximum continuous operating temperature rating of 2462°F (1350°C).

Kata thermometer   a large bulb alcohol thermometer used to measure air velocities or atmospheric conditions by means of the cooling effect.

Kelvin scale   the thermometer scale on which the unit of measurement equals the centigrade degree and according to which absolute zero is 0° degree, the equivalent of –273.16°. Water freezes at 273.16° and boils at 373.16°.

kerf   a groove or cut made by a saw.

key   a small piece of metal partially in the shaft and partially in the pulley to prevent separation of the shaft and the pulley from each other.

keyboard   a device with keys or switches that is used with digital equipment.

keyway   the recess or slot in a shaft that holds the key.

kickback diode   a diode that is made by joining together two pieces of semiconductor material.

kiel   a crayon used for making marks on pipe. Kiel, unlike ordinary chalk, will not crumble.

kilo-   prefix meaning one thousand. Twenty kilovolts means twenty thousand volts.

kilocycle   one thousand cycles.

kilogram   one thousand grams.

kilohertz   one thousand hertz.

kilojoule   in refrigeration work, the unit used to measure quantities of heat.

kilometer   a metric unit of linear measurement that equals 1000 meters.

kilopascal   a metric unit of measurement for pressure used in the HVAC industry. There are 6.89 kilopascals in 1 psi.

kilovolt (Kv)   one thousand volts.

kilovolt-amperes (Kva)   the product of voltage and amperes (power) multiplied by 1000.

kilowatt   a unit of electrical power equal to 1000 watts. Equivalent to 3,414 Btu/h.

kilowatt-hour   1000 watts per hour. Common unit of measurement of electrical energy for home and industrial use. Power is priced by the Kwh.

kinetic energy   energy that exists in the form of movement.

king valve   a manual liquid line service valve located at the outlet of the receiver.

Kirchhoff's current law   the sum of the currents flowing into any point or junction of conductors of a circuit is equal to the sum of the currents flowing away from that point.

Kirchhoff's voltage law   in any current loop of a circuit, the sum of the voltage drops is equal to the voltage supplied to that loop; or, taken with proper signs (– or +), the algebraic sum of the voltage sources and voltage drops in a circuit is equal to zero.

knife switch   a manual-open electrical circuit control, with lever mounted poles. Used mainly in experimentation.

knockout   a removable portion in the side of a box or cabinet. During installation, it can be readily taken out with a hammer, screwdriver, or pliers so wires, cables, or fittings can be attached.

knurl   a pattern of dents produced by a knurling tool in a turned surface to produce a better hand grip.

Kw demand   the maximum rate of electrical power usage for a 15- or 30-minute interval in a commercial building for each billing period. A utility meter records this maximum rate, and customers are billed for this peak rate, usually once per month.

Kwh consumption   the amount of electrical energy used over a period of time. The number of Kwh used per month. Often called consumption.

L

L   symbol for inductance.

lb   pound(s).

LCD   liquid crystal display.

LED   light emitting diode.

LEL   lower explosive limit.

lgth   length.

LNG   liquefied natural gas.

lpc   low-pressure control.

LPG   liquefied petroleum gas.

lr   locked rotor.

lrA   locked rotor amps.

LRSV   liquid receiver service valve.

lsf   low-side float.

L1   incoming power line. Usually 120 volts.

L1-L2   incoming power supply. Usually 240 volts.

L1, L2, L3   incoming three-phase power supply lines.

label   any written, printed, or graphic material displayed on or affixed to containers of hazardous chemicals. A label should contain the identity of the hazardous chemical; appropriate hazard warnings; and name and address of the chemical manufacturer, importer, or other responsible party.

label diagram   a type of circuit diagram that contains the component arrangement diagram, a wiring diagram, and a legend. Label diagrams are generally placed in a convenient location inside the unit, such as on the inside of the control panel.

labeled   describes equipment or materials to which a label or other identifying means has been attached which is accepted by the authority having jurisdiction concerning the product's use and evaluation.

lacquer   a protective coating or finish which dries to form a film by evaporation of a volatile constituent.

ladder diagram   a schematic circuit diagram drawn in the form of a vertical ladder. The outer vertical lines represent the electrical supply conductors. The horizontal steps represent individual circuits with all component devices.

lag   a delay in the effect of a changed condition, at one point in the system, on some other condition to which it is related. Also, the delay in action of the sensing element of a control, due to the time required for the sensing element to reach equilibrium with the property being controlled; i.e., temperature lag, flow lag, etc.

lagging   the thermal insulation applied directly to pipes, ducts, and boiler jackets.

lagging phase angle   the angle by which current lags voltage (or voltage leads current) in an inductive circuit.

laminations   thin sheets of soft iron or steel used in the construction of electrical machines and components to reduce heat losses due to eddy currents.

lamp   an electrical load device that converts electrical energy into light energy.

lamp, steri   a lamp which gives off high-intensity ultraviolet rays and is used to kill bacteria. It is often used in food storage cabinets.

lantern gland (packing)   a packing ring inside a stuffing box that has perforations for the introduction or removal of oil.

lapping   smoothing a metal surface to a high degree of refinement or accuracy using a fine abrasive.

large-port burner   see *spreader burner*.

latching   a characteristic of a P-N switch that allows it to remain in the on position after the triggering signal has been removed.

latching current   the amount of current applied to an SCR at the turn-on point so that the silicon-controlled rectifier will latch on.

latching relay   a relay which must be reset either manually or electrically after being energized. Another common term for it is an impedance relay.

latent heat   a term used to express the heat energy required to change the form of a substance without changing its temperature. The heat energy used to change water to steam, ice to water, water to ice, and to remove moisture from the air is latent heat. It requires 970 Btu to change one pound of water to steam. It also takes 970 Btu to remove one pound of moisture from the air. It cannot be measured by a thermometer. Hidden heat.

1. Fusion - change of state of element or compound from solid to liquid, or reverse.
2. Vaporization - change of state from a liquid to a gas.
3. Sublimation - change of state from a solid to a gas.

latent heat of condensation amount of heat released (lost) by a pound of a substance in changing its state from a vapor (gas) to a liquid.

latent heat of fusion the amount of heat energy, in Btu's, required to change one pound of a liquid to one pound of solid at the same temperature.

latent heat of melting the amount of heat energy, Btu's, that must be added to change the state of one pound of solid to one pound of liquid at the same temperature.

latent heat of sublimation the process in which a substance changes directly from a solid to a vapor, without passing through the liquid phase.

latent heat of vaporization amount of heat required, per pound of substance, to change its state from a liquid to a vapor (gas).

lathe a machine used to shape metal or other materials by rotating it against a tool.

law of conservation of energy the amount of energy in existence in the universe is constant. The machines that we build and operate do not produce energy; they merely change it from one form to another.

law of corresponding states all gases having the same reduced properties are at the same state.

law of electric charge see *law of magnetism*.

law of magnetism the law that states that like magnetic poles repel and unlike magnetic poles attract.

layout tools sheet metal tools that are used to mark, measure, and square sheet metal.

lead the phase of one alternating quantity that is ahead of the other, measured in angular degrees. Also, a wire connection.

lead-acid cell a secondary cell that has positive and negative plates made of lead peroxide and lead and has a liquid electrolyte of sulfuric acid mixed with water.

lead end end of motor where the electrical connections are located.

lead sulfide cell an infrared sensor using lead sulfide (PbS) as the sensing material. The resistance of the lead sulfide decreases when exposed to infrared radiation, resulting in increased current flow.

leading phase angle the angle by which current leads voltage (or voltage lags current) in a capacitive circuit.

leak check an operation performed on a complete gas piping system, and connected equipment, prior to placing it into operation following initial installation and pressure testing, or interruption of gas supply to verify that the system does not leak.

leak detector a device or instrument such as a halide torch, an electronic leak detector, or soap solution used to detect leaks.

leakage path a path, normally of high resistance, through which an undesirable stray current (leakage current) flows to ground; caused by buildup of moisture, soot, or accumulated dirt.

lean mixture an air/fuel mixture in which an excess of air is supplied in proportion to the amount of fuel. Also see *air-rich*.

LED a light emitting diode that will produce light when current flows through it.

left-hand rule (1) to determine the direction of the magnetic field around a single conductor, point the thumb of the left hand in the direction of current flow (– to +) and the fingers will extend around the conductor in the direction of the magnetic field; (2) to determine the polarity of an electromagnetic coil, extend the fingers of the left hand around the coil in the direction of current and the thumb will point to the north polarity; (3) to determine the direction of the induced-current flow in a generator conductor, hold the thumb, forefinger, and middle finger of the left hand at right angles to one another, point the thumb in the direction of motion of the conductor, the forefinger in the direction of the magnetic field (N to S), and the middle finger will point in the direction of induced voltage.

left-handed threads   left-handed threads are turned counterclockwise or backwards to tighten, and clockwise to loosen.

legend   an explanation of the component abbreviations on a diagram.

Legionnaire's disease   disease named after an outbreak of the illness at an American Legion Convention in July of 1976.

Lenz's law   the induced counterelectromotive voltage in any circuit is always in such a direction that it will oppose the force that produces it.

level   a tool used to establish a true horizontal or vertical line.

lever truck   a long-handled, two-wheeled device that can be used to lift and assist in moving heavy objects.

lever-type tubing bender   tool calibrated to allow the making of accurate short-radius bends up to 180°.

life cycle   a test performed on a material or configuration to determine the length of time before failure in a controlled, usually accelerated, environment.

lift   (1) valve stem travel or the height of a vertical riser or length of tubing. (2) To elevate a fluid from one level to another.

lift, pressure drop due to   the difference in pressure between the top and the bottom of a column of fluid due to the weight of the fluid.

lifting flames   flames which lift from or blow off the pilot or main burner ports. Caused by an overrating of the burner, too hard a primary air adjustment, or both.

light emitter   the device that converts electrical energy into light energy.

light emitting diode   a semiconductor device that emits incoherent light formed by the P-N junction. Light intensity is roughly proportional to the electrical current flow.

light fuel oil   Grades 1 and 2, which are distillate fuel oils used predominantly in domestic heating equipment. Heating values range from 132,900 to 141,800 Btu per gallon.

lightoff   the procedure of igniting a burner or system of burners. Also see *independent, sequential,* and *unison lightoff.*

limit action   the opening of the contacts of a limit controller to shut down a burner (and in some instances make an alarm circuit) because of an abnormal or unsafe condition.

limit control   a controller which continuously monitors a condition (such as temperature, pressure, or liquid level) in a controlled medium and responds immediately to shut down the system if a dangerous, predetermined condition occurs. It is normally set beyond the operating range of the controlled equipment.

limit of flammability   the minimum and maximum limits of concentration by volume of a flammable substance in air below and above which flame propagation does not occur upon contact with a source of ignition.

limit shutdown   a condition in which the system has been stopped because the value of the temperature or pressure has exceeded a preestablished limit.

limit switch   an electrical safety switch, usually on a heater, that will open to turn off a heat source if the sensed temperature rises to the set point.

line   a colloquial term for power line or the conductors carrying power from the generating equipment. In general, any wire, pipe, etc., or system of these, carrying fluid, electricity, etc.

line break overload   an overload that breaks the power going to the motor and is most commonly used on small motors.

line charge   the amount of refrigerant that must be added to a system's normal charge to compensate for the added length of its lines.

line, condenser drain   that part of the refrigerant piping between the outlet of the condenser and the inlet to the liquid receiver.

line cord   the power supply cable from the appliance to a wall outlet.

line, discharge   that part of the refrigerant piping between the outlet of the compressor to the inlet of the condenser.

line drop   the voltage drop due to resistance, reactance, or leakage in an electrical conductor.

line duty device   a protective device that opens the motor winding circuit under conditions of excess current or temperature.

line set   a term used for the insulated suction and liquid line premade by the manufacturer.

line starter   a contactor that has built-in overload protection. It is used to operate and protect single- and three-phase motors.

line, suction   that part of the refrigerant piping between the outlet of the evaporator and the inlet of the compressor.

line tap   a valve that can be attached to a straight run of pipe to tap into that line for pressure testing, charging, and evacuation procedures.

line valve   a three-way stem-type service valve that may be placed in a liquid line to service the line and used to pump down the system. Line valves may also be placed in the suction line. See *service valve.*

line voltage   the voltage of the power supply to the building, as distinguished from control voltage. In homes this is usually 120 or 240 volts.

line voltage circuit   a circuit involving a potential of more than 30 volts and less than 600 volts (generally 120 or 240 volts

AC). Underwriters Laboratories Inc. also calls this a high-voltage circuit.

linear characteristic   a valve flow characteristic, approximating a straight line relationship, which results in equal volume changes for equal movements of the valve stem, regardless of the percentage of valve opening. The output varies in direct proportion to the input.

linear, meter   generally used to mean a readout of a meter in which all divisions are equal.

linearity   the deviation from a straight line. A change in one quantity that is directly proportional to the change in another quantity.

liner   see *radiation shield.*

liner, refrigeration   the enclosure forming the interior of a general refrigerated compartment and/or some freezer compartment(s). The complete liner comprises the compartment liner in the cabinet, the exposed breaker strip surfaces, and the door liner(s).

lines of force   same as magnetic flux. See *flux.*

lining   those interior surfaces of a combustion chamber which are exposed to combustion during use of the device.

linkage   a mechanical arrangement for transferring motion in a desired manner, consisting of solid pieces with movable joints. An example of this would be the connections through which an actuator opens, closes, or positions a valve or damper (usually a push rod, two crank arms, and two ball joints).

liquefaction   change of state to liquid, generally used instead of condensation in the case of substances ordinarily gaseous.

liquefied natural gas   natural gas which has been cooled until it becomes a liquid.

liquefied petroleum (LP) gas   fuel gases, including commercial propane (predominantly propane or propylene) or commercial butane (predominantly butane, isobutane, and/or butylene), which are sold in bottles under pressure as a liquid and called bottled gas. These gases are higher hydrocarbon gases normally obtained as a by-product of oil refineries or by stripping natural gas.

liquid the fluid form of a substance in which it can assume the shape of its container while retaining its independent volume; state that is neither gas nor solid.

liquid absorbent a chemical in a liquid form which has the ability to take on or absorb moisture.

liquid charge bulb usually refers to the power element of temperature controls and thermostatic expansion valves. The power element and remote bulb are sometimes charged with a liquid rather than a gas.

liquid desuperheater valve that permits a small flow of refrigerant to enter the low side of systems to cool suction gas.

liquid eliminator a device for the separation of liquid droplets entrained in a flowing gas stream.

liquid filter a very fine strainer placed in the liquid line to remove foreign matter from the refrigerant.

liquid indicator a device located in the liquid line which provides a glass window through which liquid may be observed.

liquid line the tube which carries liquid refrigerant from the condenser outlet or liquid receiver outlet to the inlet of the refrigerant metering control device.

liquid nitrogen nitrogen in liquid form which is used as a low-temperature refrigerant in chemical (or expendable) refrigerating systems.

liquid receiver cylinder connected to the condenser outlet for the storage of liquid refrigerant in the system.

liquid receiver service valve a two- or three-way manually operated valve located at the receiver outlet used for installation and service operations. Also called a king valve.

liquid refrigerant charging the process of allowing liquid refrigerant to enter the refrigeration system through the liquid line to the condenser and evaporator.

liquid return line the line that carries the liquid refrigerant from the outlet of the condenser to the inlet of the receiver. Also see *condenser drain line.*

liquid sight glass a glass bull's-eye installed in the liquid line to permit visual inspection of the liquid refrigerant. Used primarily to detect bubbles in the liquid, indicating a shortage of refrigerant in the system. Also called a liquid indicator.

liquid slugging the presence of a large amount of refrigerant liquid in the compressor cylinder clearance space, usually causing immediate damage.

liquid stop valve a magnetically operated valve which is generally used to control the flow of liquid to an evaporator, but which may also be used whenever on-off control is permissible. An electrical solenoid winding controls the action of the valve. Also called a pump-down valve.

liquid to suction heat exchanger a heat exchanger where warm liquid is cooled by cold gas to increase subcooling.

liquid-vapor valve, refrigerant cylinder a dual hand valve on refrigerant cylinders which is used to release either gas or liquid refrigerant from the cylinder.

liquid, volatile one which evaporates readily at atmospheric pressure and room temperature.

liquidus the point where melted solder or brazing filler material starts to flow.

liquor solution used in absorption refrigeration. Solvent can have a relatively high or low concentration of solute.

listed   a term describing equipment or materials included in a list published by an organization acceptable to an authority having jurisdiction and concerned with product evaluation that maintains periodic inspection of production of listed equipment or materials, and whose listing states either that the equipment or material meets appropriate standards or has been tested and found suitable for use in a specified manner.

liter   metric unit of volume which equals 61.03 cubic inches.

litharge   lead powder mixed with glycerin to seal pipe thread joints.

lithium bromide   chemical commonly used as the absorbent in absorption cooling systems. Water would then be used as the refrigerant.

live steam   superheated high-energy steam direct from the boiler.

living unit   one or more rooms designed to be used as living quarters and providing complete, independent living facilities for one or more persons, including permanent provisions for living, sleeping, eating, cooking, and sanitation.

load   the power consumed by a machine or circuit in performing its function. A device that absorbs power and converts it into the desired form. The impedance to which energy is being supplied. A device that converts electrical energy into another form of energy such as heat, light, sound, or magnetism. Also see *capacitive, full, inductive,* and *net loads.*

load center   generally the service entrance. A point from which branch circuits originate.

load change   the change in the usually uncontrollable heat gain or loss caused by lights, machinery, people, outside air temperature variations, or solar effect.

load factor   the ratio of the average load in kilowatts supplied during a designated period to the peak or maximum load occurring in that period. Typical formula is expressed as the kilowatt-hours consumed over the specified period divided by the product of the kilowatt peak demand registered times the number of hours in the period. The kilowatt-hours and peak generally are on a net output basis. The peak generally is for a 60-minute demand interval.

load management   the control of electrical loads to reduce Kw demand and Kwh consumption.

load management system   the set of devices that, when installed, effectively reduces Kw and Kwh consumption.

load programmer   any device that turns loads on and off on a real-time, time interval, or Kw demand basis.

load, refrigeration   the amount of heat per hour that the refrigeration system is required to remove at design conditions.

load relay   a relay in a flame safeguard control circuit that starts the burner operating sequence.

load shedding   shutting down noncritical electrical equipment to a preselected level when a peak electric use period approaches. This is done to prevent paying an excessive electric rate which is based on the highest electric usage during a preset billing period.

load usage   the sum of the air change, product, and miscellaneous loads on a refrigerator; the sum of the loads exclusive of the wall heat gains.

loading   the effect when a meter is connected into a circuit that causes the meter to draw current from the circuit.

localized controllers   independent energy control device located near the system it is controlling.

locked rotor   in a motor, the steady-state current taken from the line while the rotor is locked and the rated voltage (and frequency in alternating current motors) is applied to the motor. Allowable locked-rotor current can be up to 6 times the running load amps.

locked-rotor amperage the amperage flowing in the circuit to a motor-driven apparatus when the motor is locked to prevent its movement. This amperage is with rated voltage and frequency applied and is typically as much as six times the full load current of the motor, and four to five times the full load current in hermetic compressors.

locked-rotor current the amount of current produced when voltage is applied to a motor and the rotor is not turning.

locked-rotor torque the amount of torque produced by a motor at time of initial start.

locking cam a device that secures the workholder on the pipe when pushed away from the threader and releases the workholder when pushed toward the threader.

lockout (control) a control feature which, when the control reaches its cutout point, stays cut out until manually reset. Also see *safety shutdown*.

lockout (safety) the process of locking the main electrical switch in the open position to safely perform equipment maintenance.

lockout interlock a running interlock used with a primary or programming control which will cause safety shutdown (will not recycle) if an improper condition occurs. The interlock may be a combustion air controller (airflow switch) or a fuel pressure switch. See *running interlock*.

lockout switch a time delay device in a flame safeguard control which trips and locks out the control (safety shutdown) if improper conditions occur. It must be manually reset to restart the system.

lockout switch timing the length of time (usually 15 or 30 seconds nominal) that the heater in a lockout switch must be energized before it causes the switch to trip (pop out).

lockout tagout see *lockout (safety)*.

lockout time the time a flame safeguard control takes to be electrically inoperative. See *lockout switch timing*.

lodestone the name used for natural magnets in early times.

logarithm a mathematical expression dealing with exponents showing the power to which a value called the base must be raised in order to produce a given number.

logic a decision-making capability of computer circuitry.

long-flame burner a burner which purposely has poor mixing of fuel and air (using secondary air only) so that the fuel takes more time to burn, thus producing a long, luminous flame. Also called a diffusion flame burner, luminous flame burner, or yellow flame burner. Also see *delayed mixing*.

longitudinal-drum boiler see *water-tube boiler*.

longitudinal section a section through the wider or longer part of the building.

loop see *closed loop* and *open loop*.

loss factor the loss factor of an insulating material is equal to the product of its dissipation and its dielectric constant.

louver a series of vanes that permit directional adjustment of airflow. It is usually installed on outside grilles or intake openings to impede water entry into ducts or elbows and to minimize turbulence. It may also include an indoor grille to eliminate light penetration.

louver-type damper a damper consisting of several blades, each pivoted about its center, and all linked together for simultaneous operation. Also see *opposed-* and *parallel-blade dampers*.

low ambient control a device for maintaining adequate head pressure when the temperature of an air-cooled condenser falls below normal due to low ambient temperatures.

low fire the minimum firing rate of a burner or furnace.

low-fire interlock an interlock which proves the damper is closed prior to ignition trials.

low-fire start the firing of a burner with the fuel controls in a low-fire position to provide a minimum of incoming fuel from the main fuel valve(s) to facilitate a smooth start and to provide a safe operating condition during lightoff. In a system with guaranteed low-fire start, interlocks are used to prevent start-up if the burner is not in the low-fire start position.

low-fire start/high-fire run operation sequence in which the burner starts in the low-fire position. After the flame is proven, the burner goes to the high-fire rate for the duration of the run period.

low-fire switch see *low-fire interlock*.

low head boiler see *water-tube boiler*.

low/high low prepurge a prepurge period during which the air damper is driven open for the purge period and then back to low-fire position for the burner lightoff. This is called low/high low proven prepurge if suitable interlocks indicate that the damper actually reached the open position during prepurge, and then closed again before ignition trials.

low limit a controller which shuts down the system if a condition drops below its minimum value for safe operation. When the boiler also heats the domestic hot water supply, this control maintains adequate boiler water temperature at times when the thermostat is not calling for heat.

low limit, chiller a protective device to prevent a system, or any part of it, from operating below the setting of that device. Used to prevent freeze-up in a water chiller or excessively low temperature in ductwork.

low link control a switch operated by the temperature of the water in a boiler and used to start the burner at any time the water temperature drops to some prescribed minimum. This control is used if the boiler is supplying domestic hot water as well as heat for the building.

low-loss refrigerant fittings any device that connects hoses, appliances, or recovery or recycling machines, and is designed to close automatically or to be closed manually when it is disconnected.

low oil temperature switch a temperature-actuated device arranged to effect the safety shutdown of a heavy oil burner or to prevent it from starting when the fuel oil temperature falls below the limits required to maintain the viscosity range recommended by the burner manufacturer.

low-pressure appliance any appliance that uses a refrigerant with a boiling point above 50°F at atmospheric pressure.

low-pressure boiler (hot water or steam) a boiler furnishing hot water at pressure not exceeding 160 pounds per square inch (psig) and at temperatures not more than 250°F (121°C); a boiler furnishing steam at pressures not more than 15 psig.

low-pressure control motor protection device that senses low-side pressure. Control is wired in series with the motor and will shut off during periods of excessively low suction pressure.

low-pressure switch see *low-pressure control*.

low side that portion of a refrigerating system which is under the lowest evaporating pressure. This is from the metering device outlet to the compressor suction valve.

low-side charging the process of introducing refrigerant vapor or gas into the low side of the system. Usually reserved for the addition of a small amount of refrigerant after service repairs.

low-side float valve   a refrigerant control valve operated by the level of liquid refrigerant in the low-pressure side of the system.

low-side pressure   pressure in the cooling side (evaporator) of the refrigerating system.

low-side pressure control   a device used to keep the low-side evaporating pressure from dropping below a certain preset pressure.

low-temperature refrigeration   a refrigeration temperature range starting with evaporator temperatures no higher than 0°F for storing frozen foods.

low-temperature water system   a hot water heating system operating at design water temperatures of 250°F or less and a maximum working pressure of 160 psi.

low voltage   control voltage usually used for domestic room thermostats. It is usually 18 to 30 volts.

low-voltage circuit   a circuit involving a potential of not more than 30 volts AC (42.4 volts peak) or 30 volts DC in which the current is supplied by a primary battery, by a standard Class 2 transformer or other suitable transforming device, or by a suitable combination of transformer and fixed impedance having the output characteristics of a Class 2 transformer. A circuit derived from a line voltage or a high-voltage circuit, by connecting series resistance to limit the voltage and current, is not considered to be a low-voltage circuit.

low-voltage control   a control used to open or close electrical circuits as temperature or pressure limits are reached.

low-voltage protection   a magnetic relay circuit connected so that a drop in voltage causes the motor starter to disconnect the motor from the line.

low-water cutoff   a device to shut down the burner when the water level in a boiler falls to a predetermined, dangerously low level.

lowboy furnace   a short upflow furnace.

lower explosive limit   denotes the minimum concentration of combustible gas or vapor (% by volume in air) that will ignite and burn if an ignition source is present.

lower sash bottom rail   the part of a double-hung window that closes down on the top of an installed window air-conditioner unit.

lower sash top rail   this is part of a double-hung window where at the inside stop a bracket is placed when a window air-conditioner unit is installed. This bracket pushes against the lower sash top rail and keeps the window from being raised.

LP gas   liquified petroleum, a substance used as a gas for fuel. It is transported and stored in the liquid state.

LP gas-air mixtures   liquefied petroleum gases distributed at relatively low pressures and normal atmospheric temperatures which have been diluted with air to produce desired heating value and utilization characteristics.

L-type copper   medium-thickness tubing suitable for low-pressure applications.

lubricant   anything that reduces friction.

lubricated plug valve   a manual shutoff valve with a tapered plug, which uses a lubricant to hydraulically lift the plug from its seat and to seal the valve against leakage in the closed position.

lubrication   the act of making an object slippery or smooth in order to reduce friction. This is usually done with an oil or grease.

lubrication, force-feed   a lubricating system in which the lubricant is forced to the various bearing surfaces by an oil pickup or pump, as opposed to splash lubrication.

lug   mounting or brackets (usually three) extending from a motor shell.

lugs terminals or terminal places on the end of a wire or equipment to facilitate rapid connection.

lumen a unit of measurement for the intensity of light.

luminous flame burner see *long-flame burner.*

M

M meter, mutual inductance.

ma milliampere (one-thousandth of an ampere).

MACS Mobile Air Conditioning Society.

man manual.

MANA Manufacturers Agents National Association.

max maximum.

MBH thousands of British thermal units (45 MBH = 45,000 Btu).

MCAA Mechanical Contractors Association of America, Inc.

mech mechanical.

meg- prefix meaning one million (1,000,000).

mega- prefix meaning one million (1,000,000).

mep mean effective pressure.

mfd microfarad.

MHANA Masonry Heater Association of North America.

mho an electrical unit of conductivity of a body with the resistance of one ohm. The reciprocal of ohm.

MICA Midwest Insulation Contractors Association.

min minimum.

misc miscellaneous.

mmf magnetomotive force.

mop maximum operating pressure.

mopd maximum operating pressure differential.

mot motor.

MSCA Mechanical Service Contractors of America.

msd most significant digit. The left-most digit in a display.

msds material safety data sheet.

mss minimal stable signal.

MSSVFI Manufacturer's Standardization Society of the Valve and Fittings Industry, Inc.

mtg mounting.

mtw machine tool wire.

mv millivolt.

Mach number ratio of the velocity at a point in a fluid to the velocity of sound at that point at a given instant of time.

machine room the area where commercial and industrial refrigeration and heating machinery—except for evaporators—is located.

machine tool a power-driven tool that is used to cut and shape metal such as in making ductwork.

machined seat a surface which has been ground to a perfectly level plane.

machinist's file a tool used for filing and finish work.

magnesium (Mg) a metallic element that is light silver-white, easy to work with, and burns with a hot, white light. It is used in photographic flashbulbs.

magnet a body which has the property of attracting or repelling magnetic materials.

magnetic across-the-line starter a motor starter or switch that allows full-line voltage to the motor windings when engaged.

magnetic circuit a complete path for magnetic lines of force from a north to a south polarity.

magnetic clutch a device operated by magnetism to connect or disconnect a power drive.

magnetic contactor   a multiple switch assembly that includes an electromagnetic coil which, when energized, closes all switches in unison. Magnetic contactors are used with single- and three-phase motors that have overload devices built into their windings.

magnetic field   magnetic lines of force which extend from a north polarity and enter a south polarity to form a closed loop around the outside of a magnetic material.

magnetic field strength   amount of magnetomotive force per unit length. Other terms for magnetic field strength are magnetic field intensity and magnetizing strength.

magnetic flux   the rate of flow of magnetic energy across or through a surface (real or imaginary).

magnetic gasket   a sealing material which adheres due to small magnets inserted in the gasket.

magnetic hysteresis   internal friction resulting from subjecting a ferromagnetic substance to a varying magnetic field.

magnetic materials   metallic materials such as iron, nickel, and cobalt which exhibit magnetic properties.

magnetic overload   an overload device that senses the current draw of a load by the magnetic field produced, which is proportional to the current draw. The device will open a set of contacts on the high current draws and allow them to close when the ampere draw returns to normal.

magnetic poles   area of concentrated lines of force on a magnet which produce north and south polarities.

magnetic saturation   a condition that exists in a magnetic material when an increase in magnetizing force does not produce an increase in magnetic flux density around the material.

magnetic starter   (1) a multiple switch assembly that includes overload devices. An electro-

magnet is included to activate the switches in unison. If the overload devices sense an overload condition at the motor, they will open the circuit to the coil, opening all switches to stop the motor. Magnetic starters include a reset button to reinstate motor operation after it has been shut down by the overloads. (2) An on-off switch that electrically opens and closes a contact in much the same way as a relay. Has provisions for overload protection.

magnetic valve   see *solenoid valve.*

magnetism   a force which causes a magnetic field to attract ferrous metals, as in when like poles of a magnet repel, and unlike poles attract each other.

magnetize   to bring about a molecular rearrangement in a material which converts it into a magnet.

magnetomotive force (mmf)   a force that produces a magnetic field around a magnetic device.

main   the primary circuit which supplies all the others. In relation to air ducts, electrical, plumbing, and piping.

main air   see *combustion air.*

main burner   the burner (as distinguished from the pilot burner) which delivers fuel to the combustion chamber (and mixes it with the air) where it is burned to provide heat to the desired space.

main burner flame-establishing period   the period of time in ignition trials during which the flame safeguard control permits the main fuel valve(s) to be open before the flame detector is required to detect the main burner flame.

main circulating loop   the section of an oil handling system which delivers the oil from storage to the branch circuits and returns the unused oil to the storage tank.

main distribution cabinet   the enclosure in a facility that houses utility metering equipment, the main electrical disconnect switch, and the branch circuit overcurrent protection. Electrical service is distributed throughout the building from this cabinet.

main flame trial see *main burner flame-establishing period.*

main fuel valve(s) an automatic, or manually reset, safety shutoff valve(s) which controls the fuel input to the main burner and is energized by the flame safeguard control. Also see *manual reset, motorized, solenoid,* and *safety shutoff valves.*

main line a large pipe that distributes fluid to smaller branch pipes.

main object lines these are the heavy lines used to outline an object or structure. They are continuous lines which show all edges and surfaces.

main truck line pipe or duct for distributing fluids such as air, water, or steam to various branch ducts and for collecting fluids from various branches.

main vent the principal pipe of a plumbing venting system.

main windings the run winding of an electric motor.

mains when referring to pneumatic controls, this term usually refers to the air lines which supply primary air pressure at 15 to 20 psig.

maintaining contact also known as a holding or sealing contact. It is used to maintain the coil circuit in a relay control circuit. This contact is connected in parallel with the start push button.

maintenance time reminders a computer program which monitors the time a machine has been operating since its last maintenance check and produces an appropriate report to the operator.

major diameter the widest measurement from the outside edges of the threads.

majority carrier the carrier, either an electron or a hole, having the greatest number in a semiconductor material.

majority carrier diffusion current the current flow carried by the diffusing majority carriers and crossing a P-N junction.

make to complete an electrical circuit by closing a switch either manually or by automatic means.

make-up air air drawn into a conditioned space to replace that which has been removed by an exhaust system.

make-up heater a heater which raises the temperature of outdoor air that is brought into a building to compensate for air removed by exhaust fans or by other methods.

make-up water water which is added to a boiler, tank, or some other container to replace water which has been lost, thus maintaining the proper water level.

make-up water line the water connection to the boiler or system for filling or adding water when necessary.

male thread external thread on pipes, fittings, and valves for making connections that screw together.

malfunction the failure of a device to operate as it should.

malignancy abnormal mass of new tissue growth that serves no function in the body and that threatens life or health.

malleable term used to describe pipe fittings that are made of annealed cast iron.

mandatory required, necessary, commanded by authority.

manifold a pipe with one inlet and several outlets, or with one outlet and several inlets, for connecting with other pipes. In a multi-burner system, the pipe which distributes fuel to the individual burners. Also see *header.*

manifold, discharge a device used to collect compressed refrigerant from the various cylinders of a compressor.

manifold, gas the conduit of an appliance that supplies gas to the individual burners.

manifold gauges   see *manifold, service.*

manifold pressure   the gas pressure in an appliance manifold, upstream of burner orifices.

manifold, service   a device, equipped with gauges and manual valves, used by service technicians to charge, evacuate, or recover refrigerant; measure system pressure; and analyze system operation in refrigeration systems.

manifolding   in direct-expansion or dry evaporators, the method of circulating the refrigerant through separate rows of tubes.

manipulated variable   that quantity or condition which is regulated by the automatic control system in such a manner that it causes the desired change in the controlled variable. The manipulated variable is a characteristic of the control agent.

manometer   an instrument for measuring the pressure of gases or vapors. A column of incompressible liquid, such as mercury, is displaced an amount proportional to the magnitude of the gas pressure. Thus, the height of the column indicates the pressure.

manometer, inclined   a manometer on which the liquid tube is inclined from horizontal to produce wider, more accurate readings over a smaller range.

manometer, U-tube   an instrument used for measuring pressures only slightly above or below atmospheric. This instrument is partially filled with liquid, usually water, mercury, or a light oil, and constructed so that the amount of displacement of the liquid indicates the pressure being exerted on the instrument.

manual   a term meaning done by hand; not automatic. Also, any reference book used for service work.

manual controller   a controller operated by hand at the location of the controller.

manual ignition   ignition by an energy source which is manually energized, where the fuel to the main burner is turned on only by hand and ignited under supervision of the operator.

manual ranging   the process in which the operator selects the proper range on a measurement instrument.

manual reset   the manual operation required after safety shutdown before the system can be restarted. This is preferred where unexpected restarting would be hazardous, as on saws, conveyors, or compressors.

manual reset valve   a safety shutoff valve which is opened manually and held in the open position electrically or pneumatically. It is closed automatically by the control system and cannot be opened manually until power is restored by the control system.

manual shutoff valve   a manually operated valve in a fuel line (main or pilot) for the purpose of completely turning on or shutting off the fuel supply. Also see *lubricated plug valve.*

manual start   a process in which the burner is started by operator action, such as pushing the start button on a controller. This is sometimes required by local codes to ensure that an operator is actually present on start-up.

manual starter   a switch that is operated manually and used to start motors. The switch includes an overload device that will disengage the electrical circuit to the motor in the event the motor becomes overloaded.

manual system   a system which requires all manual operation; a system in which the burner is purged, started, ignited, sequenced, modulated, and stopped manually.

manually ignited burner   a burner in which fuel to the main burner is turned on only by hand and ignited under supervision.

manufactured gas   a gas made artificially for use as fuel by distillation, cracking of oil or coal, the steam-carbon reaction, or by a combination of these three processes. Examples are coke oven gas and carbureted water gas.

mapp gas methylacetylene-propadiene stabilized fuel gas. Used in the soldering and brazing process.

mar to bruise or damage.

masonry anchors expanding devices that accept a fastener for mounting objects on a masonry surface.

mass a quantity of matter cohering together to make one body which is usually of indefinite shape.

mass spectrum analysis an absorption machine factory leak test performed using helium.

master a tradesperson possessing the qualifications of a journeyman and also the knowledge of the physical laws affecting his/her work and installations. An expert in his/her field.

master controller an instrument whose variable output is used to change the set point of a submaster controller. The master may be a humidistat, pressure controller, manual switch, transmitter, or thermostat.

master fuel trip a device for rapid automatic shutoff of all fuel, including igniters. It may have manual or automatic initiation.

master switch the manual switch through which power is applied to a flame safeguard control; the principal disconnect means. Also called a disconnect switch.

material safety data sheet an OSHA form that must be in English and include material identity (chemical and common names); ingredients in mixtures, if they are hazardous; physical and chemical characteristics; physical hazards (fire, reactivity); health hazards (signs and symptoms of exposure); medical conditions aggravated by exposure; primary route(s) of entry into the body; OSHA, ACGIH, and ventor exposure levels and TLVs; carcinogenicity statement per NTP, IARC, or OSHA; general precautions for safe handling and use; emergency response procedures and first aid; and appropriate work practices.

matter any material that makes up the world; anything that occupies space and has weight; can be a solid, a liquid, or a gas.

maximum operating pressure limits the pressure to the compressor to protect it from overloading or over-amping the compressor after a defrost or pull down.

maximum power rating the maximum power that a device can handle safely. Measured in watts.

maximum working pressure the maximum pressure at which a piping system may be operated in accordance with the provisions of the piping code. It is this pressure that is used in determining the setting of pressure-relieving or pressure-limiting devices installed to protect the system from accidental excessive pressure.

mean the midpoint in any ranked series of numbers. The midpoint between the maximum and the minimum values of any event.

mean annual earth temperature the mean or average temperature of the earth as it changes throughout the year. The largest factor for earth temperature change is sunshine.

mean effective pressure (mep) the average pressure on a surface when a changing pressure condition exists.

measurable resistance the actual resistance of a circuit or component as measured with an ohmmeter.

measured variable the variable such as temperature, relative humidity, or pressure being measured by a sensing element.

mechanical atomizer a device which breaks fuel up into tiny droplets without using an atomizing medium. Also see *atomizer.*

mechanical-atomizing oil burner   see *atomizing oil burner.*

mechanical bender   a tool that provides extra leverage for bending tubing while preventing crimping.

mechanical cycle   a cycle which has a repetitive series of mechanical events.

mechanical draft   the pressure difference, created by machinery such as a fan or blower, sufficient to supply all, or part of, the required combustion air into the combustion chamber. Also see *forced* and *induced drafts.*

mechanical-draft burner   a gas burner relying on machinery to bring in combustion air. They are classified by the methods used to get air into the combustion chamber.

1. Forced-draft burner (commonly called a power burner) - combustion air is blown in by a motor-driven fan. Examples are aspirating, gun-type, mechanical-premix, and zero governor burners.
2. Induced-draft burner - a fan at the outlet of the combustion chamber creates a slight partial vacuum within the chamber; the higher atmosphere pressure outside will force air into the combustion chamber.
3. Fan-mix burner - air is drawn in by a fan, which is driven by high-pressure fuel gas escaping from the small orifices in driver arms attached to the fan blades.

mechanical drawings   these show the plans for the heating, ventilation, cooling, and plumbing systems. Sometimes these plans will be shown on separate drawing sheets.

mechanical duty (motors)   cooling by means of a fan inside the motor housing.

mechanical efficiency   the ratio of work done by a machine to the energy used to do it.

mechanical equivalent of heat   the ratio of heat energy to mechanical energy. 1 Btu = 778 foot pounds. This is sometimes called Joule's equivalent.

mechanical exhaust system   equipment installed in and made a part of the vent, which will provide a positive induced draft.

mechanical joint   a tubing connection that can be made and broken with wrenches, i.e., without the application of heat.

mechanical-premix burner   a power burner in which the air and gas are mixed, under pressure, in a motor-driven blower. Simultaneous modulation of air and gas allows adjustment of the air/fuel ratio over a wide range, so an extremely short, hot flame can be produced. Also see *forced-draft* and *premix burners.*

mechanical refrigeration   a term usually used to distinguish a compression system from an absorption system.

mechanical seal   a device mounted in the pump housing and/or on the pump shaft to prevent leakage from the pump. It has a rotating part and a stationary part with highly polished touching surfaces. Has excellent sealing capability and life but can be damaged by dirt or grit.

mechanic's lien   a legal claim to ownership of repaired equipment if payment for the repair is not made.

media   the material in a filter that traps and holds the impurities.

medium, heating   a solid or fluid, such as water, steam, air, or flue gas, used to convey heat from a boiler, furnace, or other heat source, and to deliver it, directly or through a suitable heating device, to a substance or space being heated.

medium-temperature refrigeration   refrigeration where evaporator temperatures are 32°F or below, normally used for preserving fresh food.

medium-temperature water system   a hot water system operating at temperatures of 350°F or less, with pressures not exceeding 150 psi.

megacycle   one million cycles.

megavolt   one million volts.

megawatt   one million watts.

megger   an instrument (megohmmeter) that can detect very high resistances, in millions of ohms. The name is derived from megohm or 1,000,000 ohms.

megohm   a measure of electrical resistance equal to a million ohms.

megohmmeter   an instrument for measuring extremely high resistances (in the range of millions of ohms).

melt   to change state from a solid to a liquid.

melting point   the temperature, at atmospheric pressure, at which a substance will melt.

melting time   the amount of time required to melt the fuse link during a specified overcurrent.

memory   any device that can store logic 0 and logic 1 bits in such a manner that a single bit, or group of bits, can be accessed and retrieved.

mercoid bulb   see *mercury bulb*.

mercury   electrically conductive, silver-colored metal that is liquid at room temperature. Liquid commonly used in a liquid thermometer. Symbol is Hg.

mercury barometer   a device for measuring atmospheric pressure. It consists of a hollow glass tube, sealed on one end and open at the other, that is filled with mercury and turned upside down; the open end is placed in a dish half-filled with mercury.

mercury bulb   an electrical circuit switch which uses a small quantity of mercury in a sealed glass tube to make or break an electrical contact with the terminals inside the tube.

mercury switch   an electric switch made by placing a large globule of mercury in a glass tube having electrodes arranged in such a way that tilting the tube will cause the mercury to make or break the circuit.

met   unit employed to describe the rate at which the human body generates heat. Metabolic rate depends mostly on our level of muscular activity, partly on what we eat and drink (and when), and partly on where we are in our normal daily cycle. One met is defined as 58.2 W/m^2, or 18.4 Btu/h · ft^2. It is the energy produced per unit of surface area by a seated person at rest. The total heat thus produced by a normal adult is about 117 W, or 400 Btu/h. The more active we are, the more heat we produce. The flow of this heat is regulated chiefly by the skin.

metal fatigue   a weakening of metal due to repeated bending or constant vibration.

metallic bonding   the manner in which loosely held atoms are bound together in metals.

metallurgy   is the term for the science and technology of metals and their characteristics.

meter   a metric unit of linear measurement equal to 39.371 inches. Also, an instrument for measuring rates or integrating rates over a period of time.

meter, electrical   an instrument used to measure various characteristics of an electric circuit such as ohms and volts.

meter, flow   an instrument used to indicate the rate of a liquid's flow in the system. The instrument is calibrated for the specific application.

meter multiplier   a resistor connected to a meter (in series) for the purpose of providing greater range capacity.

metering device   a valve or small-diameter tube that restricts fluid flow. Meters refrigerant to the evaporator to match the evaporator's capacity. The metering device separates the high and low sides of the refrigeration system. The coldest point in the refrigeration system.

metering valve   see *firing rate valve.*

methane   a hydrocarbon gas with the formula CH_4; the principal component of natural gas.

methanol drier   an alcohol-type chemical used to change water in a refrigerating system into a nonfreezing solution.

methyl chloride (R-40)   a chloromethane chemical once commonly used as a refrigerant. The chemical formula is CH_3Cl. Cylinder color code is orange. The boiling point at atmospheric pressure is –10.4°F.

metric system   a decimal system of measures and weights, based on the meter and gram. The length of one meter is 39.371 inches.

micro-   one-millionth part of the unit specified.

microamp   one millionth of an ampere.

microcomputer   a computer system based on a microprocessor that contains all memory and interface hardware necessary to process software.

microfarad   unit of capacitance equal to one millionth of a farad. A common rating for both start and run capacitors. The "electrical size" of the capacitor rating refers to the size of the plate area of the capacitor. Its symbol is mfd.

microgram   one millionth of a gram.

microhenry   one millionth of a henry.

microinch   one millionth of an inch.

micrometer   an instrument used to measure the outside of an object. An object is placed inside the micrometer structure, then the thimble is tightened down to place the object against the anvil. The micrometer is read by reading the highest figure visible in the thimble: 1 = 0.100, 2 = 0.200, and so on. To this number is added the visible vertical number: 1 = 0.025, 2 = 0.050, and so on. Then these two numbers are

added together to arrive at the total thickness of the material being measured.

micron (μ)   a metric unit. For length it is one millionth (1/1,000,000) of a meter. There are 25,400 microns in one inch. For pressure it is one 25,400th (1/25,400) of an inch of mercury.

micron gauge   instrument for measuring vacuums very close to a perfect vacuum. These instruments measure the last part of an inch of vacuum in microns.

microprocessor   an electrical component consisting of integrated circuits, used either in computers or as a stand-alone unit, which may accept information, store it, and control an output device.

microsecond   one millionth of a second.

microswitch   an electrical circuit control which opens and closes on a very slight motion.

mid-seated (cracked)   describes a position on a valve that allows refrigerant flow in all directions.

migrate   to move from one area to another.

mil $\frac{1}{1000}$ of an inch.

mill files   mill files are always single cut. They are used primarily for sharpening.

milli- $\frac{1}{1000}$. 1000 millivolts equal 1 volt.

milliammeter   a meter which measures in the milliampere range of current.

milliampere   a unit of electrical current equal to one thousandth of an ampere.

milligram $\frac{1}{1000}$ of a gram.

millimeter $\frac{1}{1000}$ of a meter.

millimeter of mercury   a unit of pressure equal to the pressure exerted by a column of mercury one millimeter high at sea level and at a temperature of 0°C (32°F).

millisecond $\frac{1}{1000}$ of a second.

millivolt   a unit of electrical voltage equal to one thousandth ($\frac{1}{1000}$) of a volt.

minimum firing rate   the lowest input rate for a burner or a process.

minimum fresh air requirements   the smallest amount of fresh outdoor air needed to replenish interior space air to satisfy local legal codes.

minimum on-time   the shortest period of time that a load can be energized when it is being duty cycled.

minimum stable signal (MSS)   the best superheat setting which will provide constant or little temperature change at the thermostatic expansion valve temperature-sensing element while the system is running.

Minipeeper   a Honeywell trademark; a compact ultraviolet flame detector which consists mainly of a high-power sensing tube called a UV power tube.

minor diameter   the smallest diameter, measuring from the inside of the threads.

minority carrier drift current   the current flow across a P-N junction carried by the minority carriers which are accelerated by the potential barrier.

minority carriers   the carriers of the least number in a semiconductor material.

misalignment   the condition of not being properly aligned, not straight.

miscibility   in refrigeration, the ability of oil to mix with refrigerant.

miscible   describes the extent to which liquids and gases can be mixed or blended. Also refers to substances capable of being mixed in all proportions.

mist   suspended liquid droplets in the air generated by condensation from the gaseous to the liquid state or by mechanically breaking up a liquid by splashing or atomizing.

mixed air   the air in a ventilation system that is composed of return air and outdoor air before it has been conditioned.

mixed gas   a mixture of natural and manufactured gases. Mixed gases result from the increased distribution of natural gas through transcontinental pipelines into areas having existing manufactured gas facilities.

mixer   a device which combines things so that the resulting substance is uniform in composition, whether or not the separate elements can be distinguished. See *gas mixer*. Also see *aspirator, fan,* and *inspirator mixers*.

mixer face   the air inlet end of the mixer head.

mixer head   that portion of an injection-type burner, usually enlarged, into which primary air flows to mix with the gas stream.

mixer throat   that portion of the mixer which has the smallest cross-sectional area and which lies between the mixer head and the mixer tube.

mixer tube   that portion of the mixer which lies between the mixer throat and the burner head.

mixing box   a container, located at the room being conditioned, in which hot and cold air are mixed as required to maintain the desired room temperature.

mixing dampers   two interlinked sections of a damper. As one section opens, the other section closes.

mixing valve   a three-way valve with two inlets and one outlet, designed specifically for mixing applications. The proportions of the fluid leaving the outlet can be varied by moving the valve stem. It cannot be used for diverting applications because it has only one disc and two seats.

mixture   a blend of two or more components that do not have a fixed proportion relative to each other, and that, however well blended, keep their individual chemical characteristics. Unlike compounds, mixtures can be separated by physical methods like distillation. One example is a near-azeotropic blend of refrigerants.

mm Hg millimeters of mercury. Measures pressures.

mode a particular functioning arrangement or condition.

mode door a baffle that directs incoming air through either the heating or cooling coil, depending upon the function desired.

model number a number that identifies a set of identical products or components.

modulate to adjust by increments and decrements; to modify by varying a second condition. Also, the firing rate position during which the firing rate motor is under the control of an external series 90 controller.

modulating describes a type of device or control which tends to adjust by increments (minute changes) rather than by either full on or full off operation.

modulating control a method of control in which the controlled device (in this case a valve or damper) may assume any position between fully open and fully closed. Also see *proportioning control*.

modulating controller a proportioning controller which automatically positions the device it controls anywhere between its extreme positions in response to changes in the controlled medium. Also see *firing rate* and *proportioning controllers*.

modulating fire varying the firing rate as the load varies. This results in longer burner operation because the firing rate is lowered as temperature or pressure builds up toward the cutoff point. It decreases on/off operation and increases the efficiency of the system.

modulating motor an electric motor, used to drive a valve or damper, which can position the valve or damper anywhere between fully open or fully closed in proportion to changes in the controlled medium. Also see *firing rate motor*.

modulating range the change in the controlled condition necessary for the controller to position the modulating actuator from one extreme to the other.

modulating refrigeration cycle a term referring to a refrigerating system of variable capacity.

modulating valve an automatic control valve designed so that the valve opening is varied within narrow limits throughout the entire range from high-fire to low-fire position by means of a proportional actuator. Also see *firing rate valve*.

module a group of components in a circuit that are combined in a replacement package. Replacement is by the module in its entirety, not by the individual components.

Modutrol motor Honeywell trademark; see *modulating motor*.

moisture barrier a substance that will prevent the flow of water, but not water vapor.

moisture content the amount of water vapor in a given amount of air, usually expressed in grains of moisture per pound of dry air. (There are 7000 grains of moisture per pound of moisture.)

moisture determination the use of instruments and calculations to measure the relative or absolute moisture in an air-conditioned space.

moisture indicator an instrument containing a chemical disk that is sensitive to moisture and gradually changes color to reflect these changing conditions. Used to measure and indicate moisture content of a refrigerant.

moisture vapor seal a tight barrier located on the interior of a wall section placed on the outside of the insulation to prevent pushing of moisture through the insulation by vapor pressure.

mole a unit of weight or mass.

molecular pertaining to or consisting of molecules.

molecular motion the movement of molecules within a substance.

molecular sieve a refrigerant drying method employing an adsorbent having pores of uniform molecular dimensions to aid in the collecting of unwanted water.

molecular weight an expression of the weight of a substance in terms of the weight of one molecule; the sum of the atomic weights of the atoms in the molecule.

molecule the smallest particle that a compound can be reduced to before being broken down into its basic elements.

molex connectors separable connectors that provide an easy means of disconnecting and connecting wires. Can be used over and over.

Mollier diagram graph showing the relationship between the thermal properties of fluids. These properties include refrigerant pressure, heat, and temperature. Also known as an enthalpy chart.

molly bolts expanding metal fasteners used to anchor light loads to hollow wall sections.

molten alloy relay an overload device that opens a set of contacts by thermal energy. This type of device allows the temperature produced by the starting current of a load to be transferred to a molten alloy device. When it reaches a certain temperature, it will melt the solder around the device, causing it to slip and open the contacts; when it cools it will harden again, and the relay must be manually reset.

momentary loss of power a short interruption of power to a circuit or system.

momentary switch a spring-loaded electrical control that will make or break a circuit only when it is held in place.

Monel a trademark name for a metal alloy consisting chiefly of copper and nickel.

monitor a device which senses a condition requiring attention and gives an alarm without initiating corrective action.

monitor top a refrigeration unit built by General Electric which has a cylindrical condenser surrounding the motor compressor mounted on the top of the cabinet.

monochlorodifluoromethane a HCFC refrigerant known as R-22. Chemical formula is $CHClF_2$. Cylinder color code is green. Boiling point is $-41.4°F$ at atmospheric pressure.

monoflo fitting a fitting used in one-pipe heating systems to divert hot water from the supply line to the individual heaters or radiators.

monoxor an instrument used to measure the concentration in parts per million (ppm) of carbon monoxide (CO) in a vapor sample.

Montreal Protocol an agreement signed in 1987 by the United States and 22 other countries, and updated several times since then, to control releases of ozone-depleting substances like CFCs and HCFCs and eventually phase out their use.

motive power term used to express the source from which a device such as a diaphragm valve, relay, or motor obtains its power (electric or fluid).

motor a device used to create a rotating motion with drive components that require rotating motion. Electrical energy is changed to mechanical energy by magnetism, which causes the motor to turn.

motor, 2-pole a 3600 rpm electric motor (synchronous speed). Full load speed of 3450 rpm.

motor, 4-pole a 1800 rpm electric motor (synchronous speed). Full load speed of 1725 rpm.

motor, 6-pole a 1200 rpm electric motor (synchronous speed). Full load speed of 1150 rpm.

motor burnout a condition in which the insulation of an electric motor has deteriorated by overheating.

motor, capacitor   a single-phase induction motor with an auxiliary starting winding connected in series with a capacitor for better starting characteristics.

motor, capacitor-start, capacitor-run   a motor similar to the capacitor start motor except that the run capacitor and run winding are designed to remain in the circuit at all times.

motor, capacitor-start, induction-run   a motor having high starting and breakdown torque, medium starting current. Used on hard starting applications; compressors, positive displacement pumps, farm equipment, etc.

motor control   device to start and/or stop a motor at certain temperature or pressure conditions.

motor, induction   the most common motor type. Speed remains relatively constant as load changes. There are several kinds of induction motors including: shaded-pole; permanent split-capacitor; split-phase-start, induction-run; capacitor-start, induction-run; and capacitor-start, capacitor-run.

motor mounting   manner in which motor is attached to equipment. Can be one of the following types:

1. Bolted - motor is attached to frame with removable bolts.
2. Rigid - motor is solidly fastened to equipment through a metal base that is bolted, cast, or welded to the motor shell or frame.
3. Resilient or cradle - motor shell is isolated from the base by rubber rings on the end shields to reduce transmission of vibration to the driven equipment.
4. Face or flange - drive end has a flat mounting surface, machined to standard dimensions, with holes to allow easy, secure mounting to driven equipment. Commonly used on pumps, oil burners, and gear reducers.
5. Stud - extended through bolts: motor has bolts extending from the front or rear, by which it is mounted. Often used on small direct-drive fans and blowers.
6. Yoke - tabs or ears are welded to motor shell to allow bolting of a motor to a fan column or bracket.

motor, permanent split-capacitor (psc)   a motor with performance and applications similar to shaded-pole motors but more efficient, with lower line current and higher horsepower capabilities.

motor service factor   a factor over and above an electric motor's normal operating design parameters, indicated on the nameplate, under which it can operate for a limited time.

motor, shaded-pole   a small induction motor with a shaded pole used for starting. This type of motor has a very low starting torque.

motor, split-phase start, induction-run   this type of motor has moderate starting torque, high breakdown torque. Used on easy starting equipment, such as belt-driven fans and blowers, grinders, centrifugal pumps, etc.

motor starter   high-capacity electrical switching device that contains a coil, contacts, and overload protective devices.

motor, three-phase   operates on three-phase power only. Has high starting and breakdown torque, high efficiency, medium starting current, simple and rugged design, and long life. Designed for commercial applications.

motorized valve   an automatic control valve which is completely opened by the rotation of an electric motor and is generally automatically closed by a spring or other mechanical means when the electrical circuit is broken. Also see *firing rate motor, firing rate valve,* and *safety shutoff valve.*

mount   a support leg.

mouse trap   another name for the balancing relay in a modulator motor. See *balancing relay.*

movable contact the member of a contact pair that is moved directly by the actuating system.

muffler sound-absorbing chamber in a mechanical system used to reduce the sound of gas pulsations.

mullion stationary part of a structure between two doors.

mullion heater an electrical heating element mounted in the mullion and used to keep the mullion from sweating or frosting.

multiburner system a heating system with more than one main burner.

multiconductor more than one conductor within a single cable complex.

multidrop a form of digital communication in which all digital devices are connected in parallel to a common bus.

multifamily structure building of three stories or fewer above grade containing three or more living units other than townhouses, including a manufactured building (modular).

multiflame tip brazing tip that produces several small flames which tend to wrap around the object or tubing being heated.

multifuel burner see *combination burner.*

multifunction counters instruments that measure alternating electrical signals. Provide frequency, period, frequency ratio, time interval, and totalize functions. Key parameters include frequency range, least significant digit displayed, resolution, accuracy, and stability.

multimeter a meter that measures two or more electrical quantities, such as volts, ohms, and milliamperes. There are two types: analog and digital. Either type is available in bench or hand-held models. Also called a VOM or DVOM.

multipass boiler a horizontal fire-tube boiler in which the flue gases are passed back and forth through the boiler shell two or more times by means of a tube arrangement or baffles. Each change in direction is called a pass. In order to maintain the flue gas velocity, each succeeding pass is reduced in total cross section to compensate for the reduced flue gas volume as the gases cool. Also see *firebox, fire-tube,* and *scotch boilers.*

multiple evacuation a procedure for removing the refrigerant from the system. A vacuum is pulled, a small amount of refrigerant is allowed into the system, and the procedure is repeated. This is also called a "triple evacuation" because the procedure is usually done three times.

multiple-evaporator system a refrigerating system with two or more evaporators connected in parallel. Also referred to as multiplexing.

multiple loop control one controller used to control several independent HVAC systems.

multiplexing system a refrigerating mechanism in which several evaporators are connected to one condensing unit.

multiplier (ohmmeter) the multiplying factor used to determine the actual resistance value of the item being tested. For example, the actual ohmic value measured by the meter is 35 ohms and the meter is being used on the R times 100 scale. The actual resistance would then be 3500 ohms. (35 × 100 = 3500)

multiplier (voltmeter) a resistance placed in series with the movement of a voltmeter to increase the measuring range of the instrument.

multiport burner a burner having a number of nozzles from which fuel and/or air is discharged into the combustion chamber; as distinguished from a single-port burner.

multiposition a control arrangement that provides two or more points of control between full off and full on.

multirange meter   a meter that has two or more ranges to measure an electrical quantity.

multispeed motor   one which can be operated at any of two or more definite speeds, each being practically independent of the load. In the case of multispeed permanent split-capacitor (psc) and shaded-pole motors, the speeds are dependent on the load. Speed changes are used to vary the output of the conditioning equipment. Speed changes can be achieved by regulation of internal or external resistance or by frequency changes.

multistage thermostat   a temperature control that sequences two or more switches in response to the amount of heating or cooling demand.

multizone   describes a heating and cooling unit that is equipped to condition more than one zone in a structure.

muntins   these are the parts of a casement window that separate panes of glass. They may be made of metal or wood.

muriatic acid   a cleaning solution; also known as hydrochloric acid.

mushroomed   term used to describe the head of a chisel or other tool that is flattened and spread out from being struck.

mutual inductance (M)   when two coils are located close together so that the magnetic flux of each coil affects the other coil in terms of their inductance properties.

N

NAAMM   National Association of Architectural Metal Manufacturers.

NAC   National Asbestos Council.

NACE   National Association of Corrosion Engineers.

NADCA   National Air Duct Cleaners Association.

NAFA   National Air Filtration Association.

NAFEM   North American Association of Food Equipment Manufacturers.

NAHB   National Association of Home Builders.

NAIMA   North American Insulation Manufacturers Association.

NAM   National Association of Manufacturers.

NAOHSM   National Association of Oil Heating Service Managers.

NAPE   National Association of Professional Engineers or National Association of Power Engineers.

NAPHCC   National Association of Plumbing Heating Cooling Contractors.

NARI   National Association of the Remodeling Industry.

NAS   National Academy of Sciences.

NASM   National Association of Service Managers.

NATT   National Association of Trade and Technical Schools.

NAWD   National Association of Wholesaler-Distributors.

NAWIC   National Association of Women in Construction.

NBBPVI   National Board of Boiler and Pressure Vessel Inspectors.

nc   national course thread.

n/c   normally closed.

NCAC   National Council of Acoustical Consultants.

NCIAQ   National Coalition on Indoor Air Quality.

NCPWB   National Certified Pipe Welding Bureau.

NCRSA   National Commercial Refrigeration Sales Association.

NCSBCS   National Conference of States on Building Codes and Standards.

NEBB   National Environmental Balancing Bureau.

NEC   National Electric Code.

NECA   National Electrical Contractors Association.

NEDA   National Environmental Development Association.

neg   negative.

NEHA   National Environmental Health Association.

NEIC   National Energy Information Center.

NEMA   National Electrical Manufacturers Association.

NEMI   National Energy Management Institute.

NESA   National Energy Specialist Association.

nf   national fine thread.

NFPA   National Fire Protection Agency or National Fluid Power Association.

NFSA   National Fire Sprinkler Association.

NGA   National Geothermal Association.

NGWA   National Ground Water Association.

NHRAW   North America Heating Refrigeration Air Conditioning Wholesalers.

NIACA   National Insulation and Abatement Contractors Association.

NIBS   National Institute of Building Sciences.

NIOSH   National Institute of Occupational Safety and Health.

NIST   National Institute of Standards and Technology.

n/o   normally open.

no   number.

nom   nominal.

NRCA   National Roofing Contractors Association.

nre   net refrigeration effect.

NSC   National Safety Council.

NSF   National Sanitation Foundation.

NSPE   National Society of Professional Engineers.

NSPI   National Spa and Pool Institute.

NSWMA   National Solid Wastes Management Association.

NTC   negative temperature coefficient thermistor.

NUCA   National Utility Contractors Association.

NWSA   National Welding Supply Association.

National Electric Code (NEC)   a national code written for the purpose of safeguarding persons and property from the hazards arising from the improper use of electricity. Sponsored by the National Fire Protection Association. The NFPA 70 is used by insurance inspectors and many government bodies regulating building codes.

National Electrical Manufacturers Association (NEMA)   sets standards for motors, controls, and most electrical machines in the United States.

national fine threads   threads which conform in shape and dimension to standards established by the industry.

national pipe taper   the standard designation for a standard tapered pipe thread.

natural convection   movement of a fluid caused by temperature differences (density changes).

natural draft   the pressure difference resulting from the tendency of hot gases to rise up a vertical flue or chimney, thus creating a partial vacuum in the furnace. Natural draft is primarily a function of the vertical flue height and the temperature difference between the inlet and outlet points of the flue.

natural-draft burner   a gas burner which depends on a natural draft to bring in combustion air. Also see *atmospheric burner* and *natural draft*.

natural-draft cooling tower   a cooling tower in which the flow of air depends on natural air currents or a breeze. Generally applied where the spray water is relatively hot and will cause some convection currents.

natural gas   a mixture of several combustible gases and, usually, a small percentage of inert gases, obtained from geologic formations in nature. These gases consist mostly of a mixture of organic compounds (normally methane, butane, propane, and ethane). The heating value of natural gases varies between 900 to 1400 Btu per cubic foot; the usual range for use is 1000 to 1050 Btu per cubic foot. Properties include an ignition temperature of 1170°F, maximum burning speed of 25 inches per second, upper explosive limit (UEL) of 14% by volume, lower explosive limit (LEL) of 4% by volume, and a specific gravity of .4 to .8. Chemical formula is CH_4.

natural magnet   metallic material that has magnetic properties in its natural state.

natural ventilation   the unaided movement of air into and out of an enclosed space through intentionally provided openings, such as open windows and doors.

nausea   a tendency to vomit; a feeling of sickness in the stomach.

near-azeotropic blend   a blend that acts like an azeotrope, but has a small volumetric composition change and temperature glide as it evaporates and condenses.

NEC Class 1 wiring   wiring methods and materials required by the National Electric Code for voltages not exceeding 600 (line voltage) except where specifically permitted. This does not involve remote control, low-voltage relay switching, low-energy power and signal systems, or communications systems as defined by the code.

needle nose pliers   pliers with long, tapering jaws used for gripping small objects, especially wires.

needle point valve   type of valve having a needle point plug and a small seat orifice for low-flow metering.

negative   a nonpositive, below-zero value. Also, an electric polarity sign indicating an excess of electrons.

negative electrical charge   the charge that results from electrons being added to neutral atoms.

negative pressure   a pressure less than atmospheric pressure. Also see *furnace pressure*.

negative temperature coefficient thermistor (NTC)   electronic thermistor which decreases in resistance as temperature increases.

neon test light   a lamp consisting of a glass bulb filled with neon and two or more insulated electrodes. When the neon is ionized by a potential difference, current flows through the neon, creating a red glow. Used to check for the presence of voltage in a circuit.

neoprene   a synthetic rubber which is resistant to hydrocarbon oil and gas.

net load   heat requirements exclusive of piping losses and pickup.

net oil pump pressure   the difference between crankcase pressure and oil pump pressure.

net rating   the rating of a boiler which indicates the net load that may be connected to it, provided the piping losses and pickup load do not exceed the standard allowances.

network   a series-parallel circuit.

neutral   neither positive nor negative.

neutral conductor   the circuit completion wire in a two-wire system.

neutral flame   the flame that results from supplying equal amounts of oxygen and fuel.

neutral point   a predetermined point in the range of a control instrument at which no action takes place.

neutral pressure   a pressure equal to atmospheric pressure. Also see *furnace pressure.*

neutral wire   the balance wire in a three-wire electrical distribution system. The grounded conductor.

neutralizer   a substance used to counteract the effects of corrosive acids and render them chemically harmless.

neutron   a particle in the nucleus (center) of an atom which has no electrical charge or is neutral.

newton   force exerted on an object that has a mass of 1 kilogram and a gravitational acceleration of 1 m/sec^2.

newton/meter^2   metric unit of measurement for pressure. Also called a pascal.

nichrome   nickel chromium alloy used to make resistance heating elements.

nickel cadmium cell   an alkaline cell which has a longer life than carbon/zinc dry cells.

night set-back   adjustment of a temperature control to a lower or higher temperature to save operating costs.

nipple   a short pipe that is threaded on the outside on both ends.

nitric oxide (NO)   a colorless gas, formed during combustion, that is irritating to skin, eyes, and the respiratory tract.

nitrogen   a colorless, odorless gas used in pressure testing and purging of refrigerant piping. Symbol is N_2. It is used in the brazing process because it replaces the oxygen in the air in the tube or pipe and reduces the formation of scale (copper oxide).

nitrogen dioxide (NO$_2$)   a reddish-brown, mildly poisonous gas formed through combustion that is highly irritating and damaging to the respiratory tract. Often found in smog or transportation exhaust fumes.

nitrogen oxides (NO$_x$)   the class of compounds, including nitrogen dioxide and nitric oxide, that are formed through combustion of fuels.

no-frost freezer   a low-temperature refrigerator cabinet in which no frost or ice collects on produce stored in the cabinet.

noise   electrical or electronic interference with the signal of interest.

noise criteria   the outlet sound rating. It is based on the sound absorption value of a specific room and other set standards.

noise dosimeter   an instrument used to measure sound in dBa.

noise reduction   a reduction or loss in sound transmission from one space to another space, through one or more parallel paths of ceiling furred, plenum ceiling, through partitions, or along ventilation ducts.

nomenclature   a system of special terms or symbols, like those used in science.

nominal   the average rating of voltage, current, power, etc., during normal operation of an electric circuit.

nominal body rating   see *valve body rating.*

nominal size   an approximate size which may be greater or less than the actual size.

nominal-size tubing   tubing of a measurement which has an inside diameter the same size as iron pipe of the same stated size.

nominal voltage   value assigned to a circuit or electrical system to designate its voltage (for example 120, 208, 240, 277, etc.).

noncode installation   a functional refrigerating system installed where there are no local, state, or national codes in force.

noncondensable gas   a gas which does not change into a liquid at operating temperatures and pressures.

nonconductor   an insulator or material which does not conduct electricity.

nonferrous   describes a group of metals and metal alloys which contain no iron.

nonflammable   describes a material that will not support combustion.

nonfrosting evaporator   an evaporator which never collects frost or ice on its surface.

noninductive load   a load that has only resistive qualities with no inductive qualities. An electric heater and incandescent lighting are two common types of noninductive loads.

nonmiscible   a term describing two substances, such as water and oil, which are incapable of mixing.

nonpolar   describes a system or substance without opposite extremes, as of magnetism or electric charge.

nonrecycling control   a flame safeguard control which does not recycle after shutdown. See *cutoff.*

nonreversing   a term applied to a device that can be operated in only one direction.

nonsinusoidal wave   any wave that is not a sine wave, such as a triangular, square, or pulse wave.

normal care   the periodic tasks usually performed to operate and maintain an appliance, such as air, fuel, pressure, and temperature regulation; and cleaning, lubrication, and resetting of controls.

normal charge   the prescribed volume of refrigerant in a refrigeration system.

normal fuel supply pressure   the pressure at the fuel service connection for which the fuel burning system is designed.

normally closed   describes a controlled device which automatically assumes a closed position when no operating force is applied. It is the opposite of normally open. For example, a control valve which automatically closes when the air pressure or electrical current is removed is described as normally closed.

normally open   describes a controlled device which automatically assumes an open position when no operating force is applied. For example, a control relay that requires electrical current to close it.

north pole, magnetic   that end of a magnet from which magnetic lines of force flow.

NO_x   oxides of nitrogen (NO, NO_2, and N_2O_4). They react with the moisture in the respiratory tract to produce acids that corrode and irritate tissue, causing congestion and pulmonary edema. Symptoms of acute exposure can develop over six to twenty-four fours. Chronic exposures to low levels can cause irritation, cough, headache, and tooth corrosion.

nozzle   the device on the end of a fuel oil pipe used to form the oil into fine droplets by forcing the oil through a small hole to cause the oil to break up. The oil is also forced into definite swirl patterns to mix with air for complete combustion.

nozzle mixing burner   a burner in which the fuel and air are not mixed until just when they leave the burner port, after which mixing is usually very rapid. The flame cannot flash back in this type of burner.

N-type impurities   impurities that have more than four valence electrons and will donate free electrons to a semiconductor.

nucleus   the core or center part of an atom, which contains protons having a positive charge and neutrons having no electrical charge.

null   zero.

nut driver   a hand tool that has a socket head used primarily to drive hexagonal head screws on equipment.

nuts   internally threaded metal pieces, usually square or hexagonal in shape, that are used with bolts.

nylon strap fastener   this tool is used to install nylon strap clamps around flexible ducts. It automatically cuts the strap off when a preset tension is reached.

 O

oc   on center.

od   outside diameter.

oem   original equipment manufacturer.

opao   open, air-over.

OPEI   Outdoor Power Equipment Institute.

OSHA   Occupational Safety and Health Administration.

oz   ounce.

obsolete   out of date; no longer in use or practice.

obtuse angle   an angle of more than 90°.

occupants   people or animals in a space.

Occupational Safety and Health Administration   a law passed by Congress in 1970 to maintain occupational safety and to protect persons in places of employment.

occupied zone   an area controlled by one thermostat that is said to be occupied.

octagon   an eight-sided figure with each vertex forming a 45° angle.

octal plug   an eight-pin male connector with a location key for proper orientation.

octave   frequency difference between harmonic vibrations.

octyl alcohol-ethyl hexanol   additive in absorption machines that reduces surface tension in the absorber.

odor   that property of air contaminants that affects the sense of smell.

odor threshold   the lowest concentration of a material's vapor (or a gas) in air that can be detected by smell.

odorant   a substance added to an otherwise odorless, colorless, and tasteless gas to give warning of gas leakage and to aid in leak detection.

off cycle   that part of a refrigeration cycle when the system is not operating.

off-cycle defrost   a defrosting method in which the fan runs continuously while the system is off, so warm air melts accumulated frost from the evaporator.

off delay timer   a timer that delays changing its contacts back to their normal position when the coil is de-energized.

off period   a period of time, other than safety shutdown, during which the burner is not firing.

offset   a sustained deviation between the actual control point and the set point under stable operating conditions. Offset is caused by load changes affecting the system. Offset is also referred to as drift, deviation, or droop.

ohm   a unit of measurement of electrical resistance. The resistance of a circuit in which a potential difference of one volt produces a current of one ampere. Its symbol is Ω.

ohmmeter   an instrument for measuring resistance in ohms.

Ohm's law   the mathematical relationship among the voltage, current, and resistance in an electric circuit. Discovered by Georg Simon Ohm. It is stated as voltage equals current times resistance.

oil   a liquid lubricant; a heavy liquid fuel.

oil binding   physical condition when an oil layer on top of the refrigerant liquid hinders it from evaporating at its normal pressure/temperature condition.

oil bleed   a bypass through or around a valve or other component in a refrigeration system that aids in returning oil to the compressor.

oil burner   a burner for burning oil. Also see *atomizing oil, rotary oil,* and *pressure-atomizing gun-type burners.*

oil burner relay   a special multipurpose control used with oil burners. This device controls the operation of the oil burner and also acts as a safety to prevent operation in the event of malfunction.

oil check valve   a check valve installed between the suction manifold and the crankcase of a compressor to permit oil to return to the crankcase, but to prevent the exit of oil from the crankcase upon starting.

oil, compressor lubricating   a highly refined lubricant made especially for refrigeration compressors. May be synthetic or mineral based.

oil cooler   a heat-exchanging coil for dissipating heat from lubricating oil.

oil, entrained   oil droplets carried by high-velocity refrigerant gas.

oil equalizer   a pipe connection between two or more pieces of equipment made in such a way that the pressure, or fluid level, in each piece is maintained equally.

oil-filled capacitor   a run capacitor that is filled with an oil dielectric designed to dissipate internal heat.

oil filter   a device located to prevent the passage of foreign material through it from doing harm to those devices downstream. For example, a refrigeration oil filter to prevent damage to the bearing surfaces or fuel oil filter to prevent damage to the pump or nozzle.

oil-free air compressor   an air compressor used for all consumer users from light to heavy duty and most commercial applications as well.

oil groove   a channel in bearings, or other closely machined parts, that permits the flow of lubricant.

oil level   the level of the oil in a compressor crankcase at which it must be carried for proper lubrication. This level is determined by the manufacturer of the compressor.

oil-logged   clogged or saturated with oil.

oil loop   a loop placed at the bottom of a riser to force oil to travel up the riser due to increased velocity of a smaller area.

oil lube air compressor   an air compressor for heavier duty use that has cast iron cylinder sleeves and an aluminum crankcase and head for heat dissipation.

oil passages   lubrication holes drilled in the crankshaft, connecting rods, and other components of a pump or compressor.

oil pressure gauge   a device used to show the pressure of oil developed by the pump.

oil pressure safety cutoff   a motor protection device that senses oil pressure in the compressor. It is wired in series with the compressor contactor and will shut off the motor during periods of low oil pressure. It is usually a manual reset controller.

oil pump   a device that provides the source of power for force-feed lubrication systems in refrigeration systems, or the oil pump in a fuel-oil-fired furnace.

oil, refrigeration   specially prepared oil used in refrigeration systems. The oil must be dry, otherwise, moisture will condense out and freeze in the metering device and cause the refrigeration mechanism to fail. An oil is classified according to viscosity of 150, 300 or 500.

oil reservoir   that area in the base of the oil separator where oil is accumulated prior to its return to the compressor.

oil return line   the line that carries the oil collected by the oil separator back to the compressor crankcase.

oil rings   expanding rings mounted in grooves of the piston, designed to prevent oil from moving into the compressor clearance space.

oil safety switch   see *oil pressure safety cutoff.*

oil separator   a device piped into the hot gas discharge line that is used to remove oil from the gaseous refrigerant.

oil sight glass   a glass "bull's-eye" in the compressor body that permits visual inspection of the compressor oil level.

oil sludge   usually a thick, slushy substance formed by contaminated oils.

oil still   a device used to recover refrigerant from oil by distillation.

oil trap   a means of accumulating minute droplets of oil and accelerating their return to the compressor. Usually consists of no more than a U-bend at the lowest point in the suction line. It can also be improperly installed refrigerant suction lines.

on cycle   the period when equipment, specially refrigeration equipment, is in operation.

on delay timer   a timer that delays changing the position of its contacts when the coil is energized.

on/off control   a type of control in which the controlled device is moved from one of two fixed positions to the other by the action of the controller. For example, a valve which is moved from its open to its shut position, or a relay whose contacts are either open or closed.

on/off valve   see *two-position valve.*

one-pipe fitting   a specially designed tee for use in a one-pipe hot water system to connect the supply or return branch into a circuit. These fittings cause a portion of the water flowing through the circuit to pass through the terminal unit.

one-pipe supply riser (steam)   a pipe which carries steam to a heating unit and also carries the condensate from the heating unit. In an up-feed riser, steam travels upward and the condensate travels downward, while in a down-feed both steam and condensate travel down.

one-pipe system (hot water)   a hot water heating system in which one pipe serves both as a supply main and also as a return main. The heating units have separate supply and return pipes, but both are connected to the same main.

one-pipe system (oil)   an oil supply line that is used to bring the supply of fuel oil from the tank to the burner. This system has no return line.

one-pipe system (steam)   a steam heating system consisting of a main circuit in which the steam and condensate flow are in the same pipe. There is one connection to each heating unit which must serve as both the supply and the return.

one-time fuse   generic term used to describe a class H nonrenewable cartridge fuse, with a single element.

one ton of cooling   the removal of heat from the conditioned space at the rate of 12,000 Btu/h.

opacity   the state or quality of being opaque; smoke density measured in Ringelmanns. Smoke opacity which exceeds a preset level will cause a stack smoke detector to pull in an alarm relay.

open circuit   a circuit which does not provide a complete path for the current to flow. A noncontinuous circuit. An interrupted electrical circuit which stops the flow of electricity.

open compressor   term used to indicate an external drive compressor. Not fully hermetic.

open damper purge   the process in which, during prepurge, the damper opens to high-fire position and the burner motor drives air through the combustion chamber to remove any potentially explosive fuel or fumes. The damper closes to low-fire position for ignition trials, and opens again to high-fire position for the run period.

open delta circuit   a type of three-phase service connection that uses only two transformers to provide 240-volt three-phase power and 120- or 240-volt single-phase power.

open display case   a commercial refrigerator designed to maintain its contents at refrigerating temperatures even though the contents are in an open case.

open-end adjustable wrench   a wrench similar in shape to an open-end wrench, but with adjustable jaws.

open-end wrench   a wrench with open jaws to fit over a nut or a bolt of a fixed size from either end. Used in close quarters where the box end or socket will not allow.

open loop   a control system in which the controller controls the actuator, in a definite sequence, and the results are not reflected back to the controller. For example, an outside air controller on the intake side of a steam coil operates a steam valve to allow a definite quantity of steam to enter the coil in accordance with outside air temperatures. The open loop is seldom used in air-conditioning control systems today.

open-type compressor system   a refrigerating system which uses a belt-drive compressor or a coupling-driven compressor.

open winding   a broken wire in the motor winding that is not touching the motor shell.

operating control   a control (other than a safety control or interlock) which starts, stops, and regulates burner firing according to load demand. It may also actuate auxiliary equipment.

operating costs   the total cost of operating and maintaining an air-conditioning system including energy, maintenance, and depreciation.

operating cycle   the complete sequence of operations required in the normal functioning of an item of equipment. For a flame safeguard control, the operations performed between a call for heat and satisfaction of the call for heat (when the operating set point is reached). Also see *timer cycle.*

operating differential   the overall swing (high point minus low point) of a controlled variable that is necessary to activate a controller.

operating pressure   actual pressure at which the system works under normal conditions. This pressure may be positive or negative (vacuum).

operating range   the region between the maximum fuel input and minimum fuel input in which the burner flame can be maintained, continuous, and stable.

operating recorder   a machine that makes a graphic record for diagnosis of equipment performance, temperature, pressure, voltage, or any other measurable condition, in a given operating time.

operating speed   the switching speed of a transistor expressed as the turn-on time, the turn-off time, the rise time, or fall time. The amplifying speed is expressed in terms of the maximum frequency of the input signals that can be satisfactorily amplified. The operating speed of the device is dependent mainly upon the system capacitance. This specification implies both switching and amplifying speeds of the transistor.

operational amplifier   a type of amplifier used in integrated circuits that is characterized by very high voltage gains and differential inputs.

operator   one of two functional components in a controlled device. The operator converts a signal from the controller into a useful local action. Also see *final control element.*

opposed-blade damper   a flap or louver-type damper in which alternate blades rotate in opposite directions. This type provides an equal percentage flow characteristic of successive equal increments of rotation, producing equal percentage increases in flow. This is particularly useful for throttling applications where accurate control at low flow rates is required.

optical flame detector   a detector that responds to light (visible or otherwise) emitted by a flame. Also see *infrared, rectifying photocell,* and *ultraviolet flame detectors.*

optimum air supply the quantity of air which will give greatest thermal efficiency under actual conditions. With perfect mixing of fuel and air, the optimum air supply is equal to the chemically correct amount of air. Also see *air/fuel ratio.*

optoelectronics a technology that employs devices that will operate optically as well as electrically.

orbit the path along which electrons travel around the nucleus of an atom.

organic pertaining to or derived from living organisms. Chemical compounds that contain carbon and hydrogen, with or without oxygen, nitrogen, or other elements. Volatile organic compounds vaporize at room temperature and pressure. They are found in many indoor sources, including many common household products and building materials.

orifice an opening or window, such as in an aperture disc or iris slide. In a burner, the opening in a cap, spud, or other device whereby the flow of fuel is limited and through which the fuel is discharged to the burner.

orifice cap (hood) a movable fitting having an orifice which permits adjustment of the flow of fuel by the changing of its position relative to a fixed needle or other device.

orifice, oil-metering a small hole in the pickup tube of the accumulator used to ensure oil return to the compressor in small, easily handled quantities.

orifice spud a removable plug or cap containing an orifice which permits adjustment of the fuel flow, either by substitution of a spud with a different sized orifice or by the motion of a needle with respect to it.

orifice tube a metering device consisting of a restricting tube with inlet and outlet screens.

orificing a procedure used to reduce the field of view of a detector by means of an opaque plate or card with a selected-size opening. This is frequently required to reduce refractory interference to acceptable levels.

original equipment manufacturer (OEM) same as the original part.

o-ring sealing device used between parts where there may be some movement.

oscillation fluctuation, instability. A single swing of a swinging object. The variation between maximum and minimum values, as electrical current.

oscillator a device used to change DC voltage into AC voltage.

oscilloscope a fluorescent-coated tube which visually shows an electrical sine wave.

out contacts those relay contacts which complete circuits when the relay coil is de-energized. Also referred to as normally closed or out contacts.

out-of-phase the condition in which two components do not reach their positive or negative peaks at the same time.

out position those relay contacts which complete circuits when the relay coil is de-energized. Also referred to as normally closed or out contacts.

outage flame failure in heating equipment.

outdoor air air that is brought into the ventilation system from outside the building, and, therefore, not previously circulated through the system.

outdoor coil heat pump component that is either an evaporator or a condenser, depending upon whether the system is heating, cooling, or defrosting.

outdoor design temperature the outdoor temperature on which design heat losses are based.

outdoor thermostat a control device used in conjunction with a regular indoor thermostat to stage the heating elements (or auxiliary heat) in a two- (or more) stage heating system.

outgassing the emission of gases by materials and components usually during exposure to elevated temperature or reduced pressure.

outlet (1) a point at which current may be supplied to a dedicated load. (2) That part of a valve through which fluid discharges.

outlet box a box used to terminate a cable or conduit. Electrical connections are made within the box. A variety of covers and plates are available to close the box.

outlet, ceiling a round, square, rectangular, or linear air diffuser located in the ceiling, which provides a horizontal distribution pattern of primary and secondary air over the occupied zone and induces low-velocity secondary air motion through the occupied zone.

outlet, slotted a long, narrow air distribution outlet, comprised of deflecting members, located in the ceiling, sidewall, or sill, with an aspect ratio greater than 10. It is designed to distribute supply air in varying directions and planes and arranged to promote mixing of primary air and secondary room air.

outlet, vaned a register or grille equipped with vertical and/or horizontal adjustable vanes.

outlet velocity the average air velocity emerging from a grille or diffuser.

output the power or energy that a machine produces.

output signal a signal produced in response to a given input.

outside air external air. Atmosphere exterior to refrigerated or conditioned space. Ambient (surrounding) air.

outside air opening any opening used as an entry for air from the outdoors.

outside design temperature the outdoor temperature on which design heat losses are based.

outside diameter the largest diameter of a tube or pipe.

oven a compartment or receptacle for heating, baking, or drying by means of heat. Also see *industrial oven.*

overall coefficient of heat transfer (thermal transmittance) the time rate of heat flow through a body per unit area, under steady conditions, for a unit temperature difference between the fluids on the two sides of the body.

overcharge to fill a system with refrigerant beyond its design capacity.

overcurrent a condition which exists in an electrical circuit when the normal current is exceeded. Overcurrents take on two separate characteristics—overloads and short circuits.

overfire draft the draft measured over the flame within the combustion chamber.

overhead system any steam or hot water system in which the supply main is above the heating units. With a steam system the return must be below the heating units; with a hot water system, the return may be above the heating units.

overload can be classified as an overcurrent which exceeds the normal full-load current of a circuit. Also characteristic of this type of overcurrent is that it does not leave the normal current-carrying path of the circuit—that is, it flows from the source, through the conductors, through the load, back through the conductors, and to the source again.

overload heater an electrical device used in motor starters that will shut off the motor if the motor load exceeds acceptable amperes.

overload protector   a device, whether temperature, pressure, or current operated, which will stop operation of the unit if dangerous conditions arise. Can be either low or line voltage, pilot or direct duty.

overload relay   a thermal device that opens its contacts when the current through the heater coil exceeds the specified value for a specified time.

overrate firing   firing a boiler at an input rate in excess of its rated capacity. The rated capacity of the boiler is based upon its heat transfer surface area.

override   a manual or automatic action taken to bypass the normal operation of a device or system.

overshoot   the greatest amount a controlled variable deviates from its desired value, before stabilizing, after a change of input.

oversized   having more heating or cooling capacity than the minimum needed.

oxidation   literally, oxidation is a reaction in which a substance combines with oxygen provided by an oxidizer or oxidizing agent. According to modern atomic theory, oxidation is a reaction brought about by an oxidizing agent in which atoms, molecules, or ions lose electrons. Therefore, an oxidation reaction may occur even when oxygen is not present. However it may be defined, an oxidation reaction is always accompanied by an offsetting (balancing) reduction reaction in which (1) oxygen is removed from a compound, or (2) atoms, molecules, or ions gain electrons.

oxidize   to cause a corrosive chemical reaction by exposure to oxygen gas, forming a product like rust (iron oxide) or copper oxide (which forms on or inside copper tubing).

oxidizer   a material that yields oxygen readily to stimulate the combustion (oxidation) of organic matter.

oxidizing agent   a chemical or substance that brings about an oxidation reaction. The agent may (1) provide the oxygen to the substance being oxidized (in which case the agent has to be oxygen or contain oxygen) or (2) receive electrons being transferred from the substance undergoing oxidation.

oxidizing flame   a lean flame or fire resulting from combustion of a mixture containing too much air (or too little fuel). This kind of flame produces an oxidizing atmosphere, which tends to oxidize materials placed in it.

oxyacetylene torch   a type of torch that produces a flame by the combustion of acetylene and oxygen. It consists of a torch handle with tip, regulators, hoses, and oxygen and acetylene tanks. When these two gases are mixed together in the proper ratio, a very hot flame is produced.

oxygen   an elemental gas that comprises approximately 21% of the atmosphere by volume. Oxygen is one of the elements required for combustion.

oxygen-deficient   describes a mixture of gases containing too little oxygen to adequately support life. OSHA standard set at 19.5%.

oxygen-enriched   describes a mixture of gases having oxygen concentration greater than air. Normally any mixture of gases having over 21% oxygen.

ozone (O_3)   triatomic oxygen; a bluish gaseous form of allotropic oxygen derived or formed from diatomic oxygen by silent discharge of electricity or exposure to ultraviolet radiation. It is an unstable, powerfully bleaching, poisonous oxidizing agent with a pungent odor.

ozone depletion   a condition that happens when ultraviolet radiation in the stratosphere breaks CFC and HCFC refrigerants into their atomic elements—chlorine, fluorine, and hydrogen atoms. Chlorine atoms react with and destroy stratospheric ozone, which protects earth's human and other life forms from the sun's harmful ultraviolet radiation.

ozone layer the outermost layer of the earth's atmosphere, which absorbs ultraviolet light from the sun and shields the lower layers and the earth from harmful rays. The thinning of the ozone layer is believed to be caused by chlorine. Chlorofluorocarbons (CFCs) contain chlorine and, when released to the atmosphere, may cause deterioration of the ozone layer.

ozone test exposure of material to a high concentration of ozone to give an accelerated indication of oxidation in normal environments and in proximity to ozone-producing apparatus.

P

par parallel.

PATMI Powder Actuated Tool Manufacturers' Institute.

pb push button.

PCB polychlorinated biphenyl.

PDI Plumbing and Drainage Institute.

PEC Piping Education Council.

pel permissible exposure limit.

PEMAEC Process Equipment Manufacturers' Association and Environmental Council.

PF power factor.

PFI Pipe Fabrication Institute.

ph phase.

PLCA Pipe Line Contractors Association.

PMAA Petroleum Marketers Association of America.

PMI Plumbing Manufacturers Institute or Project Management Institute.

poa pressure-operated altitude.

pos positive.

pot potential.

ppb parts per billion.

PPFA Plastic Pipe and Fittings Association.

PPI Plastic Pipe Institute.

ppm parts per million.

ppt parts per trillion.

pri primary.

prot protection.

psc permanent split-capacitor.

PSC Piping System Council.

psi pounds per square inch.

psia pounds per square inch absolute.

psig pounds per square inch gauge.

ptc positive temperature coefficient.

pvc polyvinyl chloride.

packaged boiler a steam or hot water boiler in which the pressure vessel, furnace, and controls are designed, assembled, wired, and shipped as an integral unit. Packaged boilers are normally compact and efficient, delivering about one boiler horsepower (Bohp) for every five feet of heating surface. They are available in both fire-tube and water-tube types. Fire-tube packaged boilers range in size from about 500,000 to 30 million Btu/h (10 to 600 Bohp); water-tube packaged boilers range in size from about 12.5 million to 75 million Btu/h (250 to 1500 Bohp). Also called a steam generator.

packaged multizone units a packaged heating, ventilating, and air-conditioning unit that simultaneously maintains separate temperatures on a hot and cold deck. Each zone within the building then mixes air from these two decks to maintain space temperature.

packaged-terminal air conditioner (PTAC) an electrical heating and cooling system often found in the guest rooms of hotel/motels. The unit is installed through the wall of the room.

packaged-terminal heat pump (PTHP) a PTAC capable of using the refrigeration system in a reverse-cycle or heat pump mode to provide heat.

packaged units heating and cooling systems that include controls, air-moving devices, and other accessories to provide complete performance as desired by the designer.

packing sealing device consisting of soft material or one or more mating soft elements. Reshaped by manually adjustable compression to obtain or maintain a leakproof system.

packless valve a valve which uses a flexible membrane, rather than stuffing material, to seal the stem.

panel box an electrical junction box containing fuses and switches.

panel filter an unpleated, flat media filter.

panel heating a heat delivery method in which elements or water pipes are embedded in the ceiling, floors, or walls of the heated space.

panel power failure relay a relay that sheds noncritical loads to the load management panel during a power failure. Used to avoid setting a demand peak when power is lost to the load management panel.

panel radiator a heating unit placed on, or flush with, a flat wall surface and intended to function essentially as a radiator. Do not confuse with panel heating.

panel systems a heating system in which the ceiling or floor serves as the terminal unit.

panelboard a single panel, or a group of panel units, designed for assembly in the form of a single panel; including buses, and with or without switches and/or automatic overcurrent protective devices for the control of light, heat, or power circuits of small individual as well as aggregate capacity; designed to be placed in a cabinet or cutout box placed in or against a wall or partition and accessible only from the front.

paper capacitor capacitor in which the dielectric is made of waxed paper.

parallel-blade damper a flap or louver-type damper in which all blades rotate in the same direction. This type provides a fairly linear flow characteristic—the flow is nearly proportional to the damper shaft rotation. This is particularly useful in mixing applications where two different flow rates must be combined.

parallel circuit an electrical circuit in which the identical voltage is presented to all components, with current dividing among the components according to the resistances or the impedances of the components.

parallel connection a type of circuit in which there are two or more separate paths or branches for flow; a circuit in which all the components are not in series.

parallel flow in heat exchange between two fluids, the hottest portion of one meeting the coldest portion of the other.

part number the manufacturer's unique identification number for any part, usually marked on the part itself.

partial premix burner a gas burner in which part of the combustion air is mixed with the gas before the mixture is introduced into the combustion chamber, usually by venturi action. The required secondary air reaches the combustion chamber through spaces between the burner heads. Examples are inspirating, spreader, and tunnel burners.

partial pressures a condition where two or more gases occupy a space and each one creates part of the total pressure.

partial vacuum any pressure less than atmospheric.

partially halogenated HCFC an HCFC in which not every hydrogen atom in the molecule is replaced with chlorine or fluorine atoms.

particle count   concentration expressed in terms of the number of particles per unit volume of air.

particles   matter in which solid or liquid substances exist in the form of aggregated molecules. Airborne particulate matter typically ranges in size from 0.01 to 20 micrometers.

particulate   small, separate pieces of an airborne material. Dusts, fumes, smokes, mists, and fog are examples. Generally, anything that is not a fiber and has an aspect ratio of 3 to 1.

parts per million (ppm)   parts of vapor or gas per million parts of contaminated air by volume at 25°C and 1 torr pressure.

pascal (Pa)   also kilopascal (kPa). The unit of force per unit area.

Pascal's law   the law that states that the pressure applied to any part of a fluid is transmitted equally in all directions.

passive solar design   the use of nonmoving parts of a building to provide heat or cooling or to eliminate certain parts of a building that cause inefficient heating or cooling.

passive solar system   solar system which uses the walls of the building as the collector and the heat storage medium.

passivity   the tendency of certain metals to develop coatings of corrosion that protect the metal from further corrosion.

path   the part of the electrical system through which electrons travel from a source to a load, such as the electrical wiring used in a building or a piece of HVAC equipment.

pattern   refers to the uniform spray configuration of the fuel oil by the oil nozzle for an atomizing-type gun burner. Nozzle patterns can be either solid, semi-hollow, or hollow.

payback   total investment divided by one year's savings. This gives the number of years it will take to recover the investment with no regard to interest rates or taxes.

PCB   polychlorinated biphenyl.

peak   the maximum sine-wave amplitude reached during an electrical cycle. Maximum load or performance.

peak demand   the greatest amount of kilowatts needed during a demand interval.

peak let-through current   the instantaneous value of peak current let through by a current-limiting fuse, when it operates in its current-limiting range.

peak load   the maximum load carried by a system or a unit of equipment over a designed period of time.

peak-to-peak voltage   the value of AC sine-wave voltage from positive peak to negative peak.

peak voltage   the maximum positive or negative value of AC sine-wave voltage; $E_{peak} = E_{eff} \times 1.41$. The maximum instantaneous voltage.

pecking relay   see *checking relay*.

Peltier effect   where direct current is passed through two adjacent metals, one junction will become cooler and the other will become warmer. This is the basis of thermoelectric refrigeration.

penetrating oil   special lubricant that penetrates tight spaces to free rusted or locked parts.

penetration   this is the depth of a weld into the base metal.

pentagon   a five-sided figure with each vertex forming a 72° angle.

people skills   one of the most misunderstood applications of the HVAC industry. These are the skills that are necessary to work well with and for others.

percent   amount equal to $1/100$ of a number.

percent conductivity   the conductivity of a material expressed as a percentage of that of copper.

percentage regulation   the percentage of decrease in output voltage from a power supply from no-load to full-load conditions.

percolator   the section in an absorption refrigeration system through which heated solution from the generator is pumped to the separator by the buoyancy of the entrained refrigerant gas.

perfect combustion   burning with exactly the correct proportion of air to fuel so that all of the fuel and oxygen is burned. Also referred to as stoichiometric burning and theoretical combustion.

perfect gas   a hypothetical gas obeying the relation $PV = RT$.

perfect vacuum   theoretical state in which all atmospheric pressure is removed.

performance   output or efficiency.

performance chart   a table showing output or efficiency under various load conditions.

performance factor   efficiency of a unit based on Btu's per watt; same as EER. The ratio of the useful refrigerating effect of the system to the power input.

perimeter   the outer boundary of a geometric figure.

perimeter system   an air-conditioning system in which the radiators or registers for heating and cooling are located at the outer walls of the conditioned space.

period (time)   the time required to complete one AC cycle; time = 1/frequency.

perm   the unit of permeance. A perm is equal to 1 grain per (sq ft) (hr) (inch of mercury vapor pressure difference).

permanent magnet   a material which has its molecules magnetically aligned and has its own magnetic field. More specifically, a bar of metal which has been permanently magnetized.

permanent split-capacitor motor (psc)   a single-phase induction motor which has a capacitor continuously in the auxiliary windings. Unlike the split-phase or capacitor-start-type motors, there is no centrifugal switch to disconnect the auxiliary winding. This type of motor has low starting torque and is best suited for direct-drive applications such as fans, blowers, and some compressor motors. Psc motors are much more efficient than shaded-pole motors.

permeability   (1) water vapor permeability is a property of a substance which permits passage of water vapor, and is equal to the permeance of a 1-inch thickness of the substance. When permeability varies with psychrometric conditions, the spot or specific permeability defines the property at a specific condition. Permeability is measured in perm-inches. (2) The ability of one substance to allow another substance to pass through it. (3) The ability of a material to conduct magnetic lines of force as compared to air; the ability of a material to magnetize or demagnetize.

permeance   a measure of the ability of moisture to pass through a material. Permeance is measured in perms.

permissible exposure limit   an exposure limit established by OSHA. This may be time-weighted average (TWA) limit or a maximum-concentration exposure limit.

perpendicular   a line at a right angle (90°) to another line.

perpetual motion   the motion of a hypothetical machine which, once started, would operate indefinitely by creating its own energy.

perspective drawing   a pictorial drawing showing an object as it appears to the eye.

petcock   a small, manually operated faucet or valve used for draining unwanted or excess liquid or gas from the main system or for tapping a small amount for testing.

petroleum   see *crude oil*.

pH   a term referring to the percentage of hydrogen ion concentration in water, which denotes whether a substance is acid, alkaline, or neutral. A ph value of 8 or more indicates a condition of alkalinity; of 6 or less, acidity. A ph of 7 means a substance is neutral.

phase angle   the difference, in degrees, between two AC waveforms.

phase, electrical   a particular stage or point of advancement in an electrical cycle. The fractional part of the period through which the time has advanced measured from some arbitrary point usually expressed in electrical degrees, where 360° represents one cycle.

phase loss monitor   motor protection device for polyphase motors that measures current flow to detect phase loss.

phase, physical   a phase is any physically and chemically homogeneous quantity of matter. Can be in a solid, liquid, or vapor phase.

phase relationship   the relationship between voltage and current in an AC circuit. If the peaks of voltage and current are reached at the same time, the current is said to be in phase with the voltage. If these peaks occur at different times, the current is said to be out of phase with the voltage.

phase shift   a change in phase of a voltage or current after passing through a circuit or cable.

phase winding   an auxiliary winding, used for starting, that is out of phase with the run winding.

phial   term sometimes used to denote the power element sensing bulb on a thermostatic expansion valve.

phillips screw   a screw head configuration utilizing two crossed slots for extra leverage.

phosgene   a poisonous gas ($COCl_2$) formed when halide refrigerants are burned or exposed to an open flame.

photocell   see *rectifying photocell flame detector.*

photochemical reaction   a chemical reaction caused by light or ultraviolet radiation.

photoconductive   describes a substance that will conduct electricity when a light is shown on the P-N junction and that will block the flow of current when no light is present.

photoconductive cells   those devices whose resistance varies in proportion to the amount of light directed on them.

photodetectors   those devices that convert light energy into electrical energy.

photodiodes   those P-N junction diodes whose reverse current will vary according to the amount of light shining on them.

photoelectricity   a physical phenomenon where an electrical flow is generated by light waves.

photon   particle of electromagnetic energy found in solar radiation.

photostatically   describes the manner in which the molecular formation of an element changes due to light.

phototransistor   a transistor whose base collector responds to light to produce an electrical current used to energize the working circuit through a transistor. A much larger amount of current is produced than when a photodiode is used.

photovoltaic   describes the generation of electrical potential across a cell by the conversion of light energy to electrical energy.

photovoltaic material   a type of material that will develop voltage across its surface when a light is shined on its surface.

physical states   the three forms in which most substances can exist. These are solid, liquid, and gas.

pi   the ratio of a circle's circumference to its diameter, approximately 3.1416.

pickup allowance   that portion of the gross boiler output that is allowed for warming up the heating system and for taking care of the heat emission from a normal amount of piping.

pickup tube   the liquid drainage tube in a tank; especially a liquid receiver.

pickup voltage   the back electromagnetic force at which a potential relay (start relay) has a voltage high enough to open its contacts.

picofarad   one micro-microfarad.

pictorial wiring diagram   a style of electrical diagram that shows the approximate physical relationship of components and wiring.

piezoelectric   property of quartz crystal that causes it to vibrate when a frequency of 500 kHz or higher voltage is applied.

piezoelectric crystals   certain crystals which develop a potential difference between two faces of the crystal when it is mechanically distorted by pressure.

piezoelectric effect   the generation of electrical potential across a given material by application of pressure across the material.

pig tail   a flexible, usually heavy-duty, electrical lead attached to a component or appliance.

pillow block bearing   a bearing with a built-in resilient support for a rotating shaft.

pilot   a small burner (or a flame, smaller than the main burner flame) which is used to light off the main burner or burners. Also see *continuous* (constant, standing), *expanding, intermittent, interrupted,* and *proven pilot.*

pilot and main flame supervision   the pilot and main burner flame are supervised simultaneously by one detector.

pilot burner assembly   a combination gas pilot burner and flame rod flame detector; may also include an ignition electrode for spark ignition of the pilot, or a thermocouple adapter. Also called a rectification pilot or flame rectifier pilot.

pilot control   a valve arrangement used in an evaporator pressure regulator to sense the pressure in the suction line and to regulate the action of the main valve.

pilot control, external   a method by which the internal connection of the pilot is plugged and an external connection is provided to make it possible to use an evaporator pressure regulator as a suction stop valve as well.

pilot duty   a rating applied to inductive loads (usually a solenoid or coil) with a maximum power factor of 35%. Allowable inrush can be up to 10 times the pilot duty rating (running current).

pilot duty rating   the contact rating of a relay designed to switch the coil of electromagnetic devices such as solenoids, relays, contactors, or motor starters. The VA ratings of the controlling contacts must be equal to or greater than the sealed VA, not the inrush VA of the controlled coil, to prevent excessive contact wear or contact welding.

pilot flame   a small flame used to ignite a main flame.

pilot flame-establishing period   the period of time in ignition trials during which the flame safeguard control permits the pilot valve to be open before the flame detector is required to detect the pilot flame.

pilot generator   a series of thermocouples together in one unit that generates the voltage required to operate a gas valve.

pilot light   the flame that ignites the main burner on a gas furnace.

pilot link   a jumper screw or jumper wire which bypasses a normally open load relay contact in the flame detection circuit of some flame safeguard controls. If removed, it allows the control to be used with a continuous pilot (safe start check is not applicable).

pilot only   see *early spark termination.*

pilot positioner   a pneumatic balancing relay used in conjunction with a valve operator or damper operator to assist the controller in attaining a precise movement of the valve or damper operator being controlled. It has a separate source of supply air and can vary the pressure applied to the valve or damper operator over the full range of pressure, as needed, to achieve the required valve or damper position.

pilot safety valve   a valve which will close when pilot flame failure occurs, shutting off the gas supply to the main and pilot burner. Usually integral to the gas valve.

pilot solenoid   controls the flow of refrigerant by controlling the pressure to the equalizer of the thermostatic expansion valve.

pilot stabilization period   a timed interval starting with the proof of the pilot and ending with the opening of the main fuel valve(s). This period permits the pilot to establish itself before permitting the inrush of main fuel.

pilot supervision   detecting the presence or absence of a pilot flame.

pilot switch   a control used in conjunction with gas burners. Its function is to prevent operation of the burner in the event of pilot failure.

pilot trail   see *pilot flame-establishing period.*

pilot tube   a small-diameter tube that goes from the gas valve (if 100% shut off) or the B-cock (if not 100% shut off) to the pilot assembly. Usually made of aluminum.

pilot turndown test   a test to determine if the smallest pilot capable of holding in the flame relay is large enough to safely light off the main burner.

pilot valve   an automatic safety shutoff valve which controls the fuel input to the pilot.

pin   denoting an electrical terminal, usually in a connector. Normally a smaller termination than a lug.

pinch-off tool   a device used to press the walls of tubing together until fluid flow ceases.

pipe   a seamless tube conforming to the particular dimensions commercially known as standard pipe sizes; usually made of copper, steel, PVC, aluminum, or brass.

pipe die   a special tool used to cut threads on the outside of a pipe.

pipe dope   a paint-like compound with a sealant added to it, applied to male threads only, used to lubricate the threads and to prevent leakage.

pipe, equivalent length   the resistance of valves, controls, and fittings to flow, expressed as equivalent length of straight pipe for the convenience in calculating pipe sizes.

pipe fittings   components used to join sections of pipe. These include, but are not limited to, tees, elbows, reducers, and caps.

pipe friction loss   the flow resistance of liquid through the pipe. It is dependent on pipe size and flow quantity. Expressed in feet of head (ft hd) per 100 feet of pipe.

pipe rest   supports long lengths of pipe which would otherwise cause the vise stand to tip over.

pipe vise   a special tool used to securely hold steel pipe in position for cutting and threading.

pipe wrench   an adjustable wrench with a movable jaw and a stationary jaw, both having serrated teeth to grab onto round objects such as pipe; used to tighten or loosen pipe and fittings. Also called a Stillson wrench.

piping and pickup allowance   heat stored in the boiler and piping during warm-up and after shutdown and therefore deducted from gross boiler output since it is not available to the terminals.

piping system   all piping, valves, and fittings from the outlet of the point of delivery from the supplier to the outlets of the equipment shutoff valves.

piston   a close-fitting part which moves up and down in a cylinder or a type of metering device.

piston displacement volume displaced by a piston as it travels the full length of its stroke.

piston pin the part of a compressor that connects the connecting rod to the piston.

piston ring a circular metal ring that fits around the outside of a piston, filling the space between the piston and the cylinder wall to prevent leakage in either direction.

pitch (1) the angle or slope of a fan blade. (2) The distance from a point on one thread to a point on the next thread. (3) The slope of a pipe used to enhance removal of waste products.

pitot tube a device measuring total pressure and consisting of a small-diameter orifice projecting directly into an airstream and surrounded by an annular section with small-diameter entrances normal to the airflow, measuring static pressure. Both sections are usually connected to a manometer to indicate velocity pressure.

pivot a point, shaft, etc. on which something turns; to turn as if mounted on such a point.

placard an easily seen tag or label that usually indicates warning or caution.

planar diffusion a method by which all junctions of a diode are in a single plane when the manufacturing process is complete.

planned defrost shutting the compressor off with a timer so that the space temperature can provide the defrost.

plastic range the range of temperature between the solidus and liquidus points of a solder.

plate one of the electron-storing electrodes of a capacitor.

plate condenser a type of condenser used in refrigerators where the tubing is attached to a plate of sheet metal and is cooled by static air.

plate evaporator a flattened, solid cooling coil through which no air circulates.

play looseness between connected parts.

plenum an air compartment mixing chamber which is part of a distributing system, to which one or more ducts are connected. It may be attached to, or be an integral part of, the supply outlet or the return air inlet of a furnace.

plenum chamber a chamber or container for moving air or other gases under a positive pressure.

pliable easily bent, flexible.

pliers a hand tool that holds, cuts, bends, or removes objects. The name of the pliers usually tells what job they are intended for.

plug the end of a conductor which is designed to be inserted into an electrical receptacle.

plug cock see *cock*.

plug tap the plug tap is used after the taper tap has threaded. It tapers back three of four threads before the entire threading is reached. A plug tap is used to do most of the cutting. It can be used to thread a blind hole.

plug-type fuse a round, Edison base screw-in fuse.

plumbing system plan this plan shows the layout for the piping system that supplies the hot and cold water, the sewage disposal system, and the location of plumbing fixtures. Plans for smaller homes may include the entire plumbing system on one drawing, usually on the floor plan. But for complex structures, separate plans for each system may be used. These plans will tell you where the main pipe and shutoff valve are located, along with such fixtures as sinks, bathtubs, and toilets.

P-N junction where the P region and the N region are joined and formed into a single crystal in a semiconductor device.

P-N junction diode a type of semiconductor device that allows the electrons to flow through it in only one direction.

pneumatic operated by or filled with compressed air.

pneumatic timer   a device that uses the displacement of air in a bellows or diaphragm to produce a time delay.

point, critical   of a substance, the state point at which liquid and vapor have identical properties.

point, triple   the state point at which three phases of given substance (i.e., solid, liquid, and gas) exist in equilibrium.

pointer flutter   pressure pulsations that cause a gauge pointer to swing above and below the actual pressure reading.

points   teeth around the opening of a box end or socket wrench that grip the edges of the nut or the bolt head.

poison, Class A   a DOT term for extremely dangerous poisons, i.e., gases or liquids of such a nature that a very small amount of the gas or vapor of the liquid mixed with the air is dangerous to life. Examples include phosgene, cyanogen, hydrocyanic acid, and nitrogen peroxide.

poison, Class B   a DOT term for liquid, solid, paste, or semisolid substances other than Class A poisons, or irritating materials that are known, or presumed on the basis of animal tests, to be so toxic to man as to afford a hazard to health during transportation.

polar   describes molecules that have a positively charged end and a negatively charged end, each of which attracts its opposite.

polarity   the direction of electrical current flow direction or a magnetic charge (north or south).

pole   one set of electric contacts either in an automatic device or a manual switch. Electric devices such as relays, contactors, switches, and breakers can be purchased with one or more poles.

poles   two or more stationary electromagnets positioned at opposite sides of a circle inside the motor. They have opposing magnetic polarity.

polish   to produce a highly finished or polished surface by friction using a very fine abrasive.

pollen   an airborne irritant produced by plants.

polyalkylene glycols (PAGS)   a very hygroscopic (moisture-absorbing) refrigeration lubricant used with HFC refrigerants. Often used in automotive air-conditioning systems with HFC refrigerants. PAGS are incompatible with chlorine and have high molecular weights.

polybutylene   a plastic used for pipe material that has excellent creep resistance as well as high resistance to stress cracking. Recommended for earth loops.

polychlorinated biphenyl (PCB)   dielectric fluid used in capacitors and transformers that is very toxic. Use of PCBs in transformers and capacitors is strictly regulated by the EPA.

polycyclic organic matter   by-products of wood combustion found in smoke and considered to be a health hazard.

polyethylene   a family of insulating materials derived from the polymerization of ethylene gas. They are basically pure hydrocarbon resins, with excellent dielectric properties, and are used for tubing in ground loop systems, cold water lines, and heat pump piping.

polymer   a material having molecules of high molecular weight formed by polymerization of lower molecular weight molecules.

polyolester   a wax-free, ester-based synthetic oil lubricant used with HFC refrigerants. These oils have been used for years as jet engine lubricants.

polyphase   describes a motor of more than one phase; usually three-phase.

polyphase generation   electric power production using a generator that rotates three different conducting loops at the same time.

polyphase motor   an electrical motor designed to be used with three-phase electrical current.

polystyrene   plastic used as an insulation in some refrigerator cabinet structures.

polyurethane   any synthetic rubber polymers produced from the polymerization of an HO and NCO group from two different compounds. Often used in insulation and molded products.

polyvinyl chloride (pvc)   plastic pipe used in pressure applications for water and gas as well as for sewage and certain industrial applications.

ponded roof   a flat roof designed to hold water which acts as a cooling device.

porcelain   ceramic china-like coating applied to steel surfaces. Also used as an insulator for ignition leads on fuel oil-fired equipment.

port   an orifice or opening in a burner head through which fuel or an air/fuel mixture is discharged for ignition.

port loading   the input rate of a gas burner per unit of port area, obtained by dividing input rate by total port area. Usually expressed in terms of Btu per hour per square inch of port area.

portable dolly   a small platform with four wheels on which heavy objects can be placed and moved.

portable service cylinder   container used to store refrigerant. The two most common types are disposable and refillable.

posistor   a thermally sensitive resistor which has a positive temperature coefficient of resistance. Also see *thermistor*.

positive   a nonnegative, greater-than-zero value which has a deficiency of electrons.

positive displacement compressor   a compressor that raises vapor pressure by decreasing its volume.

positive displacement pump   a pump where the pumping action is created by moving chambers or pistons. The flow rate of this pump is almost the same at any pressure level. Generally self-priming. Should never be operated dry, because of internal wearing of rubber parts. As discharge flow is restricted (higher pressure or head) drive horsepower requirement increases. A relief device should be provided on the discharge line to prevent overpressure and damage to the pump motor if discharge line is closed off or severely restricted. The most common positive displacement pump types are diaphragm, gear, flexible impeller, rotary screw, roller or vane, piston, jet pump, and deep well submersible pump.

positive electrical charge   the charge that results from electrons leaving a neutral atom.

positive pressure   greater than atmospheric pressure. Also see *furnace pressure*.

positive temperature coefficient thermistor (PTC)   electronic thermistor which increases in resistance as temperature increases. Used to provide start assistance to a permanent split-capacitor motor.

post   two pin-like objects on either side of a threader. The posts fit through openings in the change plate which hold them securely. Moving the post will change the position of the dies.

postpurge   a period of time after the run period during which the burner motor (blower or fan) continues to run, driving all the products of combustion and any unburned fuel from the combustion chamber, and supplying air to burn fuel being purged from the fuel line downstream from the safety shutoff valve.

pot   short for potentiometer.

pot-type burner   a nonpressurized burner, in which fuel must evaporate to support combustion.

potable water   water that is suitable for human consumption. Domestic water.

potassium permanganate   used in carbon filters to help reduce unpleasant odors.

potential difference   the electrical force which moves, or attempts to move, electrons along a conductor or resistance.

potential, electrical   electrical force which moves, or attempts to move, electrons along a conductor or resistance.

potential energy   the energy present in a substance, or energy present because of position.

potential head   the energy created by, or of, position. It is measured by the work possible in dropping a vertical distance.

potential relay   a normally closed electrical switch which is operated by back EMF generated across the start windings.

potential transformer   a voltage transformer. The voltage supplied to a primary coil induces a voltage in a secondary coil according to the ratio of the wire windings in each of the coils.

potentiometer   an electromechanical device consisting of a resistive element with a terminal at each end, and a third terminal connected to the wiper contact. As the wiper moves along the element, it changes the resistance in each leg (portion of the element between each end terminal and the wiper). Thus the electrical input or output can be changed mechanically. Also see *auxiliary* and *feedback potentiometers*.

pound force   force applied to a one-pound mass. Has an acceleration of 32.173 ft/s^2.

pounds per square inch   a measure of air pressure.

pour point   the lowest or minimum temperature at which fuel oil can be pumped or flows readily.

power   the amount of work per unit of time. Source or means of supplying energy. In electricity its symbol is P and its units are the watt and kilowatt. Formula is P = volts × amps.

power burner   a gas burner in which combustion air is blown in by a motor-driven fan. Also called a forced-draft burner. Examples are aspirating, gun-type, mechanical-premix, and zero governor burners. Also see *mechanical-draft burner.*

power circuit   that portion of the total circuitry allocated to the distribution of primary AC power.

power consumption   power used multiplied by time, i.e., kilowatt-hour.

power element   the sensitive fluid-filled feeler bulb, capillary tube, and diaphragm element of a temperature-operated TXV control.

power factor (PF)   a comparison of the true power (watts) to the apparent power (volt amps) in an AC circuit. The cosine of the angle between voltage applied and the current reading.

power factor charge   a utility charge for a "poor" power factor. It is more expensive to provide power to a facility with a poor power factor (usually less than 80% efficiency).

power factor correction   installing capacitors on the utility service's supply line to improve the power factor of the building.

power loss   power consumed by resistance in a circuit; voltage drop.

power rating   the rating of a device that indicates the amount of current flow and voltage drop that can be permitted.

power relay   a relay generally rated up to 30 amperes and intended for use on direct switching of small motors and heating applications that do not have a high cycle rate.

power source   a source of electrical energy. It can be a battery, generator, piezoelectric crystal, thermocouple, or another source from which an electrical load draws its electrical energy.

power supply   the voltage and current source for an electrical circuit. A battery, a utility service, and a transformer are power supplies.

power tube   see *ultraviolet power tube.*

power unit   that part of the control instrument which causes the instrument to function.

power vent   furnace with integral means of venting products of combustion using an induced-draft fan motor.

powerpile   a thermocouple generator that has a normal volts open circuit (VOC) of 500 to 750 millivolts.

precharged lines   refrigerant tubing that comes from the manufacturer with a refrigerant charge sealed within it.

precipitate   to condense, as with vapor or gases, and cause free water to form. To separate a dissolved substance out from a solution.

precipitator, electrostatic   a device that removes particles from the air by electrically charging them and then collecting them on a plate of the opposite charge.

precision resistor   a resistor that has a high degree of accuracy.

precooler   a cooler used to remove sensible heat before shipping, storing, or processing.

precooler condenser   used to cool the refrigerant prior to entering the main condenser.

prefilter   a wide-mesh filter for trapping large particles before they reach and clog the fine-mesh, high-efficiency filter.

preheat   a process of raising the temperature of outdoor air before incorporating it into the rest of the ventilating system. Used when large amounts of very cold outdoor air must be used.

preheat flame   this is the flame of the torch tip that preheats the base metal to be cut, soldered, or brazed.

preheated air   air heated prior to its use for combustion; frequently the heating is done by hot flue gases.

preignition interlock   an interlock which proves a condition is proper for burner start-up and operation through prepurge, prior to ignition trials. It usually proves the main fuel valve(s) is closed. It may also be a damper position indicator (low- or high-fire proving switch), fuel pressure switch, or oil preheater controller. Also see *valve-closed interlock.*

premix burner   a gas burner in which the gas and air are mixed before they are introduced into the combustion chamber. Usually, the gas and air are both fed into a fan or blower, and the mixture is then blown into the combustion chamber. A premix burner burns with a short, hot flame with high heat release. Examples are mechanical-premix, fan-mix, and zero governor burners.

premixer   a device to mix gas and air before delivery to a burner, such as an aspirator, an inspirator, or a fan mixer.

prepurge   a period of time after burner start-up (call for heat) during which the burner motor (blower or fan) runs to expel the air of the combustion chamber breeching prior to ignition trials. This removes any unburned fuel so only the incoming fuel will be present for ignition.

prescriptive design   design of a living unit or building of the same size and occupancy type as the proposed design which complies with the prescriptive requirements of this standard. The prescriptive design includes specified assumptions concerning shape, orientation, HVAC, and other system design features. The prescriptive design is used to generate the compliance requirement for the annual energy cost method.

prescriptive requirements   specified values or rules representing the requirements that must be met in order to achieve compliance with the standard.

pressure force per unit area; usually measured in pounds per square inch (psi), or by the height of the column of water or mercury which the force will support (in feet, inches, or millimeters). Also see *absolute, atmospheric, furnace, gauge, normal fuel supply,* and *static pressure.*

pressure, absolute pressure figured from a perfect vacuum.

pressure, atmospheric the amount of pressure exerted by the air. Usually figured to be 14.696 psi (14.7) at sea level.

pressure-atomizing gun-type burner the simplest, and probably the most common, mechanical-atomizing oil burner. Light oil under pressures of up to 150 pounds per square inch is discharged through a nozzle or orifice producing a cone-shaped spray. The action of the nozzle, plus the impact of a rotating airstream from a fan, mixes the oil and air. Also see *atomizing oil burner.*

pressure-atomizing oil burner synonymous with mechanical-atomizing oil burner. See *atomizing oil burner* and *pressure-atomizing gun-type burner.*

pressure, back see *back pressure.*

pressure burner a burner in which an air and gas mixture under pressure is supplied, usually at 0.5 to 14 inches water column.

pressure controller a controller which monitors the pressure of steam, air, gases, or liquids and operates to keep the pressure within predetermined limits. It may operate as a pressure switch (on-off), or it may be a proportioning controller. Also see *pressure switch* and *proportioning controller.*

pressure, crankcase the pressure in the crankcase of a reciprocating compressor.

pressure, critical vapor pressure corresponding to the critical state of the substance at which the liquid and vapor have the same properties.

pressure, discharge the pressure against which the compressor must deliver the refrigerant vapor.

pressure drop (PD) the difference between the pressures at two points. Also resistance to flow caused by a restriction, like friction, vertical lift, and accessories.

pressure-enthalpy-heat diagram a graph of refrigerant pressure, heat, and temperature properties. See *Mollier diagram.*

pressure equalizing allowing the high-side and low-side pressures of a refrigeration system to become equal on the off cycle. This reduces starting load when beginning the new cycle.

pressure, gauge an instrument that measures pressure in psi (pounds per square inch). Primary tool used by service personnel for servicing and troubleshooting the system. Also called manifold gauge.

pressure, head force caused by the weight of a column of fluids. Expressed in feet, inches, or psi.

pressure, hydrostatic the normal force per unit area that would be exerted by a moving fluid on an infinitesimally small body immersed in it if the body were carried along with the fluid.

pressure-imposing element any device or portion of the equipment used for the purpose of increasing the pressure upon the refrigerant.

pressure limiter a device which remains closed until a certain pressure is reached and then opens and releases fluid to another part of the system.

pressure-limiting device a control that automatically stops the compressor at a predetermined pressure.

pressure motor control   a device which opens and closes an electrical circuit as the pressures change to desired pressures.

pressure null switch   a pressure-switching device with a single-pole, double-throw switch. The switch is activated by a diaphragm which senses pressure differential. The SPDT switch has a floating contact which may be positioned against either pole or can be positioned for no circuit at all. Used with non-spring-return damper motors.

pressure-operated altitude valve (POA)   a device which maintains a constant low-side pressure independent of altitude of operation.

pressure, operating   the pressure at which a system is operating.

pressure, partial   pressure attributable to each gas when the gases are in a mixture.

pressure-reducing valve   a diaphragm-equipped valve in the make-up water line of a hot water system that protects the system from city water pressures higher than the working pressure of the boiler.

pressure regulator   a device used to maintain a constant pressure in a fuel supply line regardless of the flow. It cannot maintain a pressure greater than its inlet pressure.

pressure regulator, evaporator   an automatic pressure-regulating valve that is mounted in the suction line between the evaporator outlet and the compressor inlet. Its purpose is to maintain a predetermined pressure and temperature in the evaporator.

pressure relief valve   a safety device that opens at a preset point to protect a boiler or hot water tank from excessive pressure.

pressure, saturation   at a given temperature, the pressure at which a liquid and its vapor, or a solid and its vapor, can coexist in stable equilibrium.

pressure, static   measure of the potential energy in a fluid. The force necessary to overcome the resistance to airflow presented by ducts, dampers, filters, etc.

pressure, suction   the pressure in the low-pressure side of the refrigeration system.

pressure switch   a switch that monitors the pressure of steam, air, gases, or liquids, and breaks a circuit when the pressure either rises or falls to a preset value. It is also used as a limit or interlock with a flame safeguard control to shut down the burner if the pressure exceeds high pressure switch or falls below low pressure switch a preset value. It may reset automatically when the pressure returns to normal, or it may require manual resetting.

pressure tap   opening used to check pressure.

pressure tap plug   threaded plug used to prevent leakage of material after taking a pressure reading.

pressure-temperature relationship   the constant, predictable relationship between the pressure and temperature of a given liquid and gas mixture under saturated conditions. An increase in pressure results in a temperature increase. A decrease in temperature results in a pressure decrease.

pressure test   an operation performed to verify the integrity of piping or tubing following its installation or modification.

pressure, total   sum of the static pressure and the velocity pressure at a given point.

pressure tube   a small line carrying pressure to the sensitive element of the pressure controller.

pressure, vapor   the pressure exerted by a vapor. If a vapor is kept in confinement over its liquid so that the vapor can accumulate above the liquid, the temperature being held constant, the vapor pressure approaches a fixed limit called the maximum, or saturated, vapor pressure, dependent only on the temperature and the liquid. The term vapor pressure is sometimes used as synonymous with saturated vapor pressure.

pressure, velocity   force necessary to move the mass of air to the required speed, a measure of the kinetic energy in a fluid.

pressure vessel   the steel drum or collector where generated steam or hot water is accumulated.

pressure water valve   a device used to control the water flow which responds to head pressure of the refrigerating system.

Pressuretrol   Honeywell trademark; see *pressure controller.*

pressurize   to introduce refrigerant or inert gas into a system to check for leaks.

preventive maintenance   scheduled inspection and replacement of short-lived components in order to avoid untimely and expensive replacement on an emergency basis.

primary   the input windings of a transformer.

primary air   the combustion air introduced into a burner which mixes with the fuel before it reaches the combustion chamber. Usually expressed as a percentage of the air required for complete combustion.

primary air inlet   the opening or openings through which primary air is admitted into a burner.

primary cell   a cell that cannot be recharged.

primary coil   a tube-and-fin circular coil that contains a water glycol solution which surrounds the ignitor and burner. This coil is used in a water glycol gas forced-air furnace.

primary control   a flame safeguard control which starts the burner in the proper sequence, proves that the burner flame is established, and supervises the flame during burner operation. It causes safety shutdown on failure to ignite the pilot or main burner, or on loss of flame.

primary controls   in air-conditioning and refrigerating systems, those controls that are used to start and stop the cycle when certain temperatures or pressures are reached.

primary element   that portion of the controller which feels the change in the controlled variable and initiates the change in energy which causes the controller to operate.

primary heat exchanger   that portion of the furnace where combustion takes place. Common heat exchanger conductor materials are steel, aluminum, and cast iron.

primary voltage   the voltage of the circuit supplying power to a transformer is called the primary voltage, as opposed to the output voltage of a load supply voltage which is called the secondary voltage. In power supply practice, the primary is almost always the incoming-voltage side of the transformer and the secondary is the outgoing-voltage side.

primary winding   the coil of a transformer to which AC source voltage is applied.

prime   a charge of liquid required to begin pumping action of centrifugal pumps when the liquid source is lower than the pump. May be held in pump by a foot valve on the intake line or by a valve or chamber within the pump.

prime mover   a system that supplies the mechanical energy to rotate an electrical generator.

prime surface   in describing a finned tube, the tube is the prime surface, and the fins are the secondary surfaces.

priming (boiler)   priming occurs in a boiler when the water level is so high that water mixes with steam.

priming (oil)   the act of bleeding the air from oil lines or a pump mechanism.

printed circuit card   a circuit card in which the interconnecting wires have been replaced by conductive strips painted or etched onto an insulating board in a manner similar to a photograph.

probe   any device that senses a condition that is remote from the meter or instrument and relays the effect back to the instrument.

process tube   a tube that extends from the compressor or filter drier of a hermetic system. It is used to gain access to the sealed system.

profit margin   the difference between cost and selling price. Also called markup.

program relay   a relay that provides multiple switching action in an electric control system, either in a fixed time sequence or in a variable sequence, depending upon signals received from two or more controllers.

programmer   see *programming control.*

programming control   a flame safeguard control that adds a timing function to the primary control to sequence additional burner functions such as prepurge, post-purge, timed trials for pilot and main burner flame, and firing rate switching.

propagation   the spread of flame through a flammable mixture from a source of ignition.

propane   an easily liquefiable hydrocarbon gas. Propane is one of the components of raw natural gas, and it is also derived from petroleum refining processes. Chemical formula is C_3H_8, maximum burning speed is 32 inches per second, specific gravity is 1.5, and ignition temperature is 900°F. Refrigerant 290 is used for low-temperature applications.

propane gas torch   a gas torch that has a throwaway tank and is easy to use. The flame adjusts easily and can be used for many operations.

propeller fan (axial)   an air-moving device in which the air flow is parallel or axial to the shaft on which the propeller is mounted. These fans have good efficiency, near-free air delivery, and are used primarily in low-static-pressure, high-volume applications. As static pressure is increased, horsepower increases and cfm decreases. Usually mounted in a venturi, ring, or other housing featuring simple construction and low cost.

properties, thermodynamic   basic qualities used in defining the condition of a substance, such as temperature, pressure, volume, enthalpy, and entropy.

proportional action   an output signal changing in proportion to the amount of change in the controlled or measured variable (contrast to two-position).

proportional actuator   an actuator which can position a damper or valve anywhere between fully open or fully closed in proportion to changes in the controlled medium. When this action is done automatically, it is called modulation. Also see *actuator.*

proportional band   the change in the controlled variable required to move the controlled device from one of its extreme limits of travel to the other. It is normally used in conjunction with recording and indicating controllers and is expressed in percent of the chart or scale range.

proportional control   a control that can be used to blend two streams of fluid in varying proportions.

proportional control action   a control action in which a manipulated variable is proportionate to any deviation from the set point.

proportional control plus derivative function   a time-proportioning controller that has a derivative function. The derivative function monitors the rate at which a system's temperature is either increasing or decreasing and adjusts the cycle time of the controller to minimize overshoot or undershoot.

proportional control with integral and derivative functions   a time-proportioning controller that has integral and derivative functions. The integral function automatically raises the stabilized system temperature to match the set point temperature to eliminate the difference caused by the time proportioning function. The derivative function monitors the rate of rise or fall of the system temperature and automatically adjusts the cycle time of the controller to minimize overshoot or undershoot.

proportional plus automatic reset action a combination of proportional action and a response which continually resets the control point back toward the set point to reduce the offset.

proportional plus rate action a combination of proportional action and a response that precedes the normal proportional response. The combined response is proportional to the rate of change or speed at which the controlled variable deviates from the set point.

proportioning controller a controller which includes a potentiometer to permit the device it controls to be set anywhere between its extreme positions. When this action is done automatically in response to changes in the controlled medium, it is called modulation. Also see *modulating controller.*

proposal a formal, written cost estimate or bid.

proposed design design of the living unit or building to be constructed. The design takes into account all qualities, details, and characteristics of the building that significantly affect the use of energy, such as construction, geometry, orientation, exposure, materials, equipment, and renewable energy sources.

proprietary sole ownership of property, a business, an item of labor, or an object that extends legal ownership rights.

protector, circuit an electrical device that will open an electrical circuit if excessive electrical conditions occur.

Protectorelay Honeywell trademark; see *primary control.*

protocol rules concerning the format and timing of messages transmitted between two communicating devices.

proton a particle in the center of an atom which has a positive electrical charge.

protractor an instrument used to measure degrees and angles of a circle.

prove to establish by measurement or test the existence of a specified condition, such as flame, level, flow, pressure, or position.

proved ignition ignition by an energy source which is supervised by a flame safeguard control that must detect the presence of energy for ignition prior to permitting the main fuel valve(s) to open.

proved pilot a pilot flame which is supervised by a flame safeguard control that must detect the presence of the flame prior to permitting the main fuel valve(s) to open.

proved spark ignition direct spark ignition which must be proved before the main fuel valve(s) can open. It is usually used with small oil burners. Also see *direct spark* and *proved ignitions.*

proven combustion air see *airflow switch.*

proven prepurge a system in which the programming control includes a provision for preventing burner operation until satisfactory airflow is established during prepurge.

pry bar a pry bar is a tool used for leverage, that is, to move heavy objects that would usually be hard to move unaided. Pry bars are used to lift, tilt, and pull objects.

psychrometer an instrument having both a dry and a wet bulb thermometer. It is used to determine the relative humidity in a space. Most instruments have an indexed scale to allow direct conversion from the temperature readings to the percentage of relative humidity.

psychrometric chart a chart that shows the relationship among the temperature, pressure, and moisture content of the air.

psychrometric measurement the measurement of temperature, pressure, and humidity using the psychrometric chart.

psychrometry the branch of physics relating to the measurement or determination of atmospheric conditions, particularly the amount of moisture mixed with the air.

P/T plugs pressure/temperature plugs that allow entrance into the system by the gauge stems of thermometers and pressure gauges without draining or removing the pressure of the system.

p-traps fittings named for the shape into which the tubing is bent.

P-type impurities impurities having less than four valence electrons that donate the holes to the semiconductor crystal.

pull box a metal box at a sharp corner in a conduit used to pull wires through the conduit.

pull down an expression indicating the action of removing refrigerant from all or part of the refrigeration system.

pull-in voltage the voltage value that causes the relay armature to seat on the pole face in an electric motor or generator.

pull-through describes an air-handling system that draws air over the heat exchanger before the air enters the fan itself.

pulley a flat wheel with a V-shaped groove. When it is attached to a drive and drive members, a pulley provides a means for driving a load.

pulsating DC a DC voltage that is not in "straight line" or "pure" DC form, such as DC voltage produced by a battery.

pulsation a panting of the flames in a boiler or furnace, indicating cyclic and rapid changes in the pressure in the combustion space.

pulse term referring to one cycle of ignition and combustion of a gas/air mixture in a pulse combustion furnace.

pulse combustion process repeated ignition of a gas/air mixture in a high-efficiency, gas-fired furnace.

pulse furnace furnace which has a tuned (resonant) combustion chamber. Part of the energy normally lost through the flue is returned to start the next pulse of combustion.

pulsing relay see *checking relay*.

pump any one of various machines which force gas or liquid into—or draw it out of—something by suction or pressure.

pump, centrifugal pump which produces fluid velocity and converts it to pressure head.

pump down the act of using the compressor or a pump to reduce the pressure in the low side of the system and put it in the high side.

pump-down control system a control system that closes a solenoid to allow the compressor to pump all the refrigerant from the low side of the refrigeration system into the high side. This system is used on large air-conditioning systems and some commercial refrigeration systems.

pump, fixed-displacement a pump in which the displacement per cycle cannot be varied.

pump head the difference in pressure on the supply and intake sides of a pump created by the operation of the pump.

pump, jet a pump system that uses high-pressure water from the pump through a jet venturi to pick up additional water from the supply system. The pump handles three to five times as much water as is supplied by the system.

pump, reciprocating single-piston a pump having a single reciprocating (moving up and down) piston.

pump, screw a pump having two interlocking screws rotating in a housing.

pump, short-cycling   a pump whose capacity is too large for the system, causing very short on and off cycles.

pump, submersible   a pump that is located below the level of water in the well. It uses multistage impellers to produce the pressure to lift water up the pipe. The motor is cooled by the flow of water through the pump.

pump, suction   a pump that depends on negative pressure in the inlet to lift water from the earth. More precisely, the pressure difference between the atmospheric pressure and pump inlet pressure forces water up the well casing. The maximum practical operating height is 15 feet.

pumping water level   the level to which the water in a well drops when the pump is removing the full-load water quantity.

punch   a tool with a flat surface used to forcefully drive a metal part, especially a pin.

purchase order   a business form that authorizes an employee to make a purchase on open account.

purge   the process of eliminating a substance from a pipe or furnace by flushing it out with another substance, as in purging a furnace of unburned gas by blowing air through it. Also see *postpurge* and *prepurge*.

purge extender   an auxiliary timer used with a programming control to lengthen the prepurge period at high fire in order to meet Factory Insurance Association (FIA) requirements. Some programming controls have optional plug-in purge extenders with field-selectable timing.

purge timer   an auxiliary timer used with a primary control to add prepurge capability. It may be an optional plug-in device with preset timing.

purger   device for removing noncondensable gas from refrigerant condensers or for removing low-concentration liquor from absorption system evaporators.

purging   the releasing of compressed gas to the atmosphere through some part for the purpose of removing contaminants from that part or parts.

purging hose   a hose through which gas, air, or water, or some other liquid is forced to cleanse away unwanted matter.

Purple peeper   Honeywell trademark; these detectors use a low-power sensing tube called an aquadag tube and require a rectification-type flame signal amplifier.

push-button switch   a switch that can be opened or closed by pressing buttons on the switch. Push-button switches come with a wide variety of purposes and labeling.

push rod   any metal rod that transmits force from one point to another.

pyrolysis   a chemical decomposition or breaking apart of the molecules of a substance produced by the action of heat.

pyrometer   an instrument for measuring high temperatures. A pyrometer measures higher temperatures than does a mercury thermometer. The typical range of temperature that these devices typically measure is from $-100°F$ to $1999°F$.

pyronometer   a device used to measure solar insulation in Btu per square foot per hour.

Q point   the quiescent operating point. The direct current bias values of amplifier voltages and currents.

quality   weight fraction of the vapor in a vapor/liquid mixture.

quality of wet vapor   fraction by weight of vapor in a mixture of liquid and vapor.

quenching   altering the characteristics of metal by heating, then quickly submerging it in a cooling agent.

quenching flame   a reduction in temperature whereby a combustion process is retarded or stopped.

quick-connect terminal   a common solderless type of electrical terminal with push-on connection.

quick-disconnect fittings   a mechanical fitting device used on refrigerant hoses that seals automatically when removed from an appliance.

R

R   symbol for refrigerant, electrical resistance, or thermal resistance.

RAM   random access memory.

rcr   relative climate ratio.

reg   regulator.

rel   recommended exposure limit.

resil   resilient.

RETA   Refrigerating Engineers and Technicians Association.

rev   reversible.

rf   radio frequency.

RH   relative humidity.

rheo   rheostat.

rms   root mean square.

ROM   read only memory.

RPA   Radiant Panel Association.

rpm   revolutions per minute.

RRF   Refrigeration Research Foundation.

rs   rotary scale.

RSES   Refrigeration Service Engineers Society.

rs232   a type of information transfer bus used to connect serial devices such as a printer or modem to a computer.

rtd   resistance temperature detector.

R-11, trichloromonofluoromethane   a low-pressure CFC synthetic chemical refrigerant which is suitable for either low- or high-temperature applications. R-11 is stable, nonflammable, and nontoxic. Leaks may be detected by using a torch, soap, or electronic leak detector. R-11 will absorb most of the moisture which may have entered the system when the system was open to the atmosphere. Also used as a cleaning fluid. Boiling point is 74.87°F. Chemical formula is CCl_3F. Refrigerant cylinder color code is orange.

R-12, dichlorodifluoromethane   a low-pressure CFC synthetic chemical refrigerant which was used in small air conditioners as well as domestic and commercial refrigeration systems. Has a boiling point of –21.62°F. Leaks may be detected by using a torch, soap, or electronic leak detector. Water is slightly soluble in R-12, and the resultant solution has a corrosive effect on most metals. Therefore, it is very important to make sure all the moisture is out of an R-12 system before charging it. Chemical formula is CCl_2F_2. Refrigerant cylinder color code is white.

R-13, chlorotrifluoromethane   is a high-pressure CFC refrigerant that has a boiling point of –114.6°F. Because of its high pressure and low critical temperature, it is unsuitable for ordinary applications. However, it is an excellent refrigerant in low-temperature systems at temperatures of –100°F or more below zero. It is nonpoisonous, nonirritating, nonflammable, and has no corrosive effect on metals. Chemical formula is $CClF_3$.

R-13b1, bromotrifluoromethane   is a low-temperature refrigerant with a boiling point of –71.95°F. Therefore, it is not suitable at such low temperatures as is R-13. An advantage of R-13b1 over R-13 is that its condensing pressure is not as high and it has a higher critical temperature. Its chemical formula is $CBrF_3$.

R-14, tetrafluoromethane   boiling point is –198.3°F. Chemical formula is CF_4.

R-21, dichlorofluoromethane   a HCFC refrigerant whose pressure and volume characteristics make it suitable for use only in centrifugal compressors. It is a slightly higher pressure refrigerant than R-11. Therefore, it does not require as high a suction vacuum and will produce more refrigeration than R-11 for the volume of refrigerant pumped. R-21 is nonpoisonous, nonirritating, and nonflammable. Boiling point is 47.8°F. Its chemical formula is $CHCl_2F$.

R-22, monochlorodifluoromethane   a low-pressure HCFC synthetic chemical refrigerant which was developed for refrigeration installations that need low evaporating temperatures. It is used only with reciprocating compressors. R-22 is stable, nontoxic, noncorrosive, nonirritating, and nonflammable. Water is soluble in R-22, so driers and desiccants should be used to remove moisture from systems using this refrigerant. Leaks may be detected with soap, torch, or electronic leak detector. Has a boiling point of –41.36°F. Chemical formula is $CHClF_2$. Refrigerant cylinder color code is green.

R-23, trifluoromethane   a HFC refrigerant that has a boiling point of –115.7°F. Chemical formula is CHF_3.

R-30, methylene chloride   boiling point is 104.4°F. Its chemical formula is CH_2Cl_2.

R-31   a HCFC refrigerant.

R-32, difluoromethane   a HFC refrigerant that has a boiling point of –61.1°F. Chemical formula is CH_2F_2.

R-32/125   an azeotrope refrigerant that has a boiling point of –62.5°F. Chemical formula is CH_2F_2/CHF_2CF_3.

R-40, methyl chloride   is an earlier refrigerant which was widely used in commercial systems and has a boiling point of –11.6°F. Chemical formula is CH_3Cl. In its pure state, R-40 has no effect on most metals. However, it should never be used with zinc or aluminum, for in contact with these metals, it breaks down to form a spontaneously combustible gas. If moisture gets into a R-40 system, an electrolytic action will take place which will dissolve natural rubber, which therefore cannot be used for gaskets or packing. R-40 is toxic and slightly asphyxiating. It can cause drowsiness, mental confusion, nausea, and even death.

R-50, methane   boiling point is –258.7°F. Chemical formula is CH_4.

R-111   a CFC refrigerant.

R-112   a CFC refrigerant.

R-113, trichlorotrifluoroethane   a CFC synthetic chemical refrigerant which is nontoxic and nonflammable. Used in low-capacity centrifugal chiller packaged units. Operates with very low system pressures, high gas volumes. Also used as an intermediate in the manufacture of specialty lubricants. Boiling point is 117.63°F. Chemical formula is $C_2Cl_3F_3$. Refrigerant cylinder color code is purple.

R-114, dichlorotetrafluoroethane   boiling point is 38.8°F. Chemical formula is $C_2Cl_2F_4$. Refrigerant cylinder color code is dark blue. A CFC refrigerant.

R-115, chloropentafluoroethane   boiling point is –38.4°F. Chemical formula is $CClF_2CF_3$. A CFC refrigerant.

R-121   a HCFC refrigerant.

R-122   a HCFC refrigerant.

R-123, dichlorotrifluoroethane   a HCFC refrigerant developed for low-pressure application. Boiling point is 82.17°F. Chemical formula is $CHCl_2CF_3$.

R-124, chlorotetrafluoroethane   a HCFC refrigerant that has a boiling point of 10.3°F. Chemical formula is $CHClFCF_3$.

R-125, pentafluoroethane   a HFC refrigerant that has a boiling point of –55.43°F. Chemical formula is CHF_2CF_3.

R-125/143a   an azeotrope refrigerant having a boiling point of –50.5°F. Chemical formula is CHF_2CF_3/CH_3CF_3.

R-131   a HCFC refrigerant.

R-132   a HCFC refrigerant.

R-133 a HCFC refrigerant.

R-134a, tetrafluoroethane a HFC refrigerant developed for refrigeration systems and as a possible replacement for R-12. Boiling point is –15.08°F. Chemical formula is CF_3CH_2F. Compatible lubricant is polyolester.

R-141b, dichlorofluoroethane boiling point is 89.6°F. The leading substitute for CFC-11 in rigid foam-blowing insulation applications such as construction (commercial, residential, and public), appliances, and transport vehicles. Chemical formula is CCl_2FCH_3. A HCFC refrigerant.

R-142b, chlorodifluoroethane boiling point is 14.4°F. Chemical formula is CH_3CClF_2. A HCFC refrigerant.

R-152a, difluoroethane boiling point is –13.0°F. Chemical formula is CHF_2CH_3.

R-160, ethyl chloride toxic refrigerant seldom used now. Boiling point is 54.32°F. Chemical formula is C_2H_5Cl.

R-170, ethane low-temperature application refrigerant. Boiling point is –127.85°F. Chemical formula is C_2H_6.

R-211 a CFC refrigerant.

R-212 a CFC refrigerant.

R-213 a CFC refrigerant.

R-214 a CFC refrigerant.

R-215 a CFC refrigerant.

R-216, dichlorohexafluoropropane boiling point is 96.24°F. Chemical formula is $C_3Cl_2F_6$. A CFC refrigerant.

R-217 a CFC refrigerant.

R-221 a HCFC refrigerant.

R-222 a HCFC refrigerant.

R-223 a HCFC refrigerant.

R-224 a HCFC refrigerant.

R-225 a HCFC refrigerant.

R-226 a HCFC refrigerant.

R-231 a HCFC refrigerant.

R-232 a HCFC refrigerant.

R-233 a HCFC refrigerant.

R-234 a HCFC refrigerant.

R-235 a CFC refrigerant.

R-241 a HCFC refrigerant.

R-242 a HCFC refrigerant.

R-243 a HCFC refrigerant.

R-244 a HCFC refrigerant.

R-251 a HCFC refrigerant.

R-252 a HCFC refrigerant.

R-253 a HCFC refrigerant.

R-261 a HCFC refrigerant.

R-262 a HCFC refrigerant.

R-271 a HCFC refrigerant.

R-290, propane low-temperature application refrigerant. Boiling point is –43.73°F. Chemical formula is C_3H_8.

R-318c, octafluorocyclobutane boiling point is 21.5°F. Chemical formula is C_4F_8.

R-401A, chlorodifluoromethane/difluoroethane/chlorotetrafluoroethane a blend of HFC-152a/HCFC-124 and HCFC-22. Boiling point is –26.5°F. Chemical formula is $CHClF_2/CH_3CHF_2/CHClFCF_3$. Compatible lubricant is polyolester or alkylbenzene.

R-401B, chlorodifluoromethane/difluoroethane/chlorotetrafluoroethane a blend of HFC-152a/HCFC-124 and HCFC-22. Boiling point is –29.5°F. Chemical formula is $CHClF_2/CH_3CHF_2/CHClFCF_3$. Compatible lubricant is polyolester or alkylbenzene.

R-402A, pentafluoroethane/propane/chlorodifluoromethane chemical formula is $CHClF_2/CHF_2CF_3/C_3H_8$. Boiling point is –56.6°F. Compatible lubricant is polyolester or alkylbenzene.

R-404A, pentafluoroethane/trifluoroethane/tetrafluoroethane a long-term, non-ozone-depleting replacement for

R-502 in low- and medium-temperature commercial refrigeration systems. Chemical formula is $CHF_2CF_3/CH_3CL_3/CF_3CH_2F$. Boiling point (bubble point temperature) is $-51.8°F$. Compatible lubricant is polyolester.

R-407C, difluoromethane/pentafluoroethane/tetrafluoroethane   a long-term, non-ozone-depleting replacement for HCFC-22 in various air-conditioning applications, as well as in positive displacement refrigeration systems. It is a ternary blend of HFC-32/HFC-125/HFC-134a. Boiling point at atmospheric pressure is -46.6 (bubble point temperature). Chemical formula is $CH_2F_2/CHF_2CF_3/CF_3CH_2F$. Compatible lubricant is polyolester.

R-409A, chlorodifluoromethane, chlorotetrafluoroethane, and chlorodifluoroethane   a blend of HCFC-22, HCFC-124, and HCFC-142b. Boiling point is $-32.4°F$. Compatible lubricant is alkylbenzene.

R-410A   an azeotropic mixture of 50% by weight HFC-32 and 50% by weight HFC-125. Chemical formula is $CH_2F_2CHF_2CF_3$. Boiling point is $-62.9°F$.

R-500   a low-pressure synthetic chemical refrigerant which is an azeotropic mixture of 73.8% by weight R-12 and 26.2% by weight R-152a. Refrigerant cylinder color code is yellow. Boiling point is $-28.3°F$. There is no chemical name or chemical formula for R-500. Water is highly soluble in R-500, and you must be extremely careful to keep water out of the system. Leaks may be detected with soap, torch, or electronic leak detector. Compatible lubricant is polyolester.

R-502   a low-pressure CFC synthetic chemical refrigerant for use in low-temperature refrigeration systems. An azeotropic mixture of 48.8% by weight R-22 and 51.2% by weight R-115. Boiling point is $-49.8°F$. It is usually used in systems which require temperatures between 0°F and $-60°F$. The pressure characteristics of R-502 are similar to those of R-22, but the lower condensing temperature permits better lubrication because of the increased viscosity of the oil at the lower temperature. Leaks may be detected with soap, torch, or electronic leak detector. R-502 is used only with reciprocating compressors and is often used for frozen-food storage cases, ice cream freezers, and in some frozen-food processing plants. Refrigerant cylinder color code is orchid. Chemical formula for the two refrigerants is $CHClF_2/CClF_2CH_3$.

R-502[5]   boiling point is $-49.8°F$. No chemical name.

R-503   a refrigerant which is an azeotropic mixture 40.1% by weight of R-23 and 59.9% by weight of R-13. Boiling point is $-126.1°F$.

R-504   a refrigerant which is an azeotropic mixture of R-32 and R-115. Boiling point is $-71.0°F$. No chemical formula.

R-507   a non-ozone-depleting azeotropic mixture of 50% by weight of HFC-125 and 50% by weight of HFC-143a. Chemical formula is CHF_2CF_3/CH_3CF_3. Boiling point is $-52.1°F$. Compatible lubricant is polyolester.

R-600, butane   a low-temperature application refrigerant that is sometimes used as a fuel. Boiling point is 31.1°F. Chemical formula is C_4H_{10}.

R-600a, isobutane   boiling point is 10.89°F. Chemical formula is CH_4H_{10}.

R-610, ethyl ether   boiling point is 94.3°F. Chemical formula is C_4H_{10}.

R-611, methyl formate   a low-temperature application refrigerant. Boiling point is 89.2°F. Chemical formula is $C_2H_4O_2$.

R-630, methyl amine   boiling point is 19.9°F. Chemical formula is CH_3NH_2.

R-631, ethyl amine   boiling point is 61.88°F. Chemical formula is $C_2H_5NH_2$.

R-702n, hydrogen (normal)   boiling point is $-423.0°F$. Chemical formula is H_2.

R-702p, hydrogen (para)   boiling point is –423.2°F. Chemical formula is H_2.

R-704, helium   boiling point is –452.1°F. Chemical formula is He.

R-717, ammonia   a popular refrigerant that is colorless in both the liquid and the vapor states but has a strong irritating odor. It is used for either industrial refrigeration or absorption systems. When ammonia combines with water, a caustic solution is formed which can burn the skin. This is especially true on any moist portion of the body, such as the eyes, nose, mouth, or any sweaty surface. It is flammable and can be explosive if mixed with air. As a liquid, it is lighter than water. As a vapor, it is lighter than air. Ammonia has no effect on metals if dry. However, it will attack copper and bronze in the presence of moisture. Ammonia will not corrode iron or steel. It has no effect on good lubricating oil but may sludge badly if there is moisture in the system. The odor will give you immediate warning of a leak and will form white smoke when brought in contact with a sulfur candle or burning sulfur stick. Ammonia is one of the cheapest refrigerants available. Boiling point is –28.0°F. Refrigerant cylinder color code is black. Chemical formula is NH_3.

R-718, water   boiling point is 212.0°F. Chemical formula is H_2O.

R-720, neon   boiling point is –410.9°F. Chemical formula is Ne.

R-728, nitrogen   boiling point is –320.4°F. Chemical formula is N_2.

R-729, air   boiling point is –317.8°F. No chemical formula.

R-732, oxygen   boiling point is –297.3°F. Chemical formula is O_2.

R-740, argon   boiling point is –302.6°F. Chemical formula is Ar.

R-744, carbon dioxide   sublimates at –109.2°F. Chemical formula is CO_2.

R-744a[2], nitrous oxide   boiling point is –129.1°F. Chemical formula is N_2O.

R-764, sulfur dioxide   gas once commonly used as a refrigerant. Chemical formula is SO_2. Cylinder color code is black. Boiling point is 14°F.

R-1120, trichloroethylene   boiling point is 189.00°F. Chemical formula is $CHCl=CCl_2$.

R-1150, ethylene   boiling point is –154.7°F. Chemical formula is C_2H_4.

R-1180, dichloroethylene   boiling point is 118.00°F. Chemical formula is $CHCl=CHCl$.

R-1270, propylene   boiling point is –53.86°F. Chemical formula is C_3H_6.

race   area on which bearings ride.

raceway (bearing)   the inner or outer ring that provides a contact surface for the balls or rollers in a bearing.

raceway (electrical)   a protected runway or enclosure for conductors. A continuous channel, conduit, or conduit body for holding conductors or cables.

radial commutator   the electrical contact surface on a rotor which is perpendicular to the shaft center line.

radial fan   describes a blower that has straight blades which are, to a large extent, self-cleaning, making them suitable for various kinds of material handling and grease-laden air. Wheels are of simple construction and have relatively narrow blades. They can withstand the high speeds required to operate at higher static pressures (up to 12″) but usually are noisier than forward-curved or backward-inclined blowers.

radial piping system   a perimeter heating system employing ducts or pipes that extend from the supply plenum to each register and radiate from a central heat source.

radiant-head burner   a raw gas burner with a head (or heads) constructed of refractory material. The raw gas is ejected from spuds into an opening in the head(s). Combustion heats the head(s) to incandescence, providing a large amount of radiant heat which tends to increase the speed of flame propagation and keep the flame shorter. Also see *raw gas burner.*

radiant heat   heat that passes through air-heating solid objects that, in turn, heat the surrounding area.

radiant heating   a heating system in which only the heat radiated from panels is effective in providing the heating requirements. The term radiant heating is frequently used to include both panel and radiant heating.

radiant losses   heat lost from a building through radiation from the walls.

radiant tube-type heater   an indirect-fired heating system in which heating is accomplished by radiation or convection from tubular elements. The tubes are gas-tight, heat-resistant, open at one or both ends, and capable of withstanding explosion pressure from ignition of fuel/air mixtures. Each tube has an inlet and/or burner arrangement where combustion is initiated, a suitable length where combustion occurs, and an outlet for the combustion products formed.

radiation   the process in which energy in the form of rays is emitted from atoms and molecules as they undergo internal change. Also see *infrared* (IR) and *ultraviolet* (UV) *radiation* and *visible light.*

radiation shield   a separate panel or panels interposed between heating surfaces and adjacent objects to reduce heat transmission by radiation. Also see *liner.*

radiation, thermal   the transmission of energy by means of electromagnetic waves of very long wavelength. Radiant energy of any wavelength may, when absorbed, become thermal energy and result in an increase in the temperature of the absorbing body.

radiator   a heating unit located within the room to be heated and exposed to view. A radiator transfers heat by radiation to objects it can "see" and by conduction to the surrounding air which in turn is circulated by natural convection. A radiator is also called a convector, but the term radiator has long been established.

radiator valve   a valve installed on a terminal unit to manually control the flow of water through the unit.

radionuclide   an unstable nucleus of an element that decays or disintegrates spontaneously, emitting radiation.

radius   the length of a line running from the center of a circle to the outside perimeter of the circle.

radius diffusion   the horizontal axial distance an airstream travels after leaving an air outlet before the maximum stream velocity is reduced to a specified terminal level.

radon (radon-222)   a chemically inert gas that undergoes radioactive decay by emitting an alpha particle.

ram air   air forced through an automotive air-conditioning condenser due to the rapid movement of the vehicle. This condenser is usually located behind the radiator.

random access memory   a particular type of memory-type building block that is commonly available in metal-oxide-semiconductor integrated circuit form and sometimes contains a given number of flip-flops. Bits of binary information can be written into, or taken away from, any of the flip-flops.

range   the difference between the minimum and maximum points of a control in which the control will function properly.

range (cooling range)   in a water-cooling device, the difference between the average temperature of the water entering the device and the average temperature of the water leaving it.

range hold in an autoranging meter, the ability to select a specific range instead of allowing the meter to select the range.

rangeability the ratio of the maximum controllable flow to the minimum controllable flow through a valve. For example, a valve with a rangeability of 50 to 1 and having a total flow capacity of 100 gallons per minute (gpm) fully open can accurately control a flow as low as 2 gpm.

Rankine scale temperature scale using Fahrenheit divisions, with absolute zero at $0°R$. The freezing point of water is $492°R$, and the boiling point of water is $672°R$.

rasp file the rasp file is used for cutting wood and for very soft metals.

ratchet flare nut box wrench a tool used where there is limited space in which a wrench handle may be moved.

ratchet handle used with socket wrench; enables user to apply a force in one direction for any fractional part of a revolution and return the handle to its original position without moving the socket.

rate input into an appliance.

rate action a condition where the controller senses the rate of change of temperature and provides an immediate change of output to minimize the eventual deviation.

rate time the time in minutes that rate action response precedes normal proportional action response.

rated input acceptable input to a furnace based on compliance with ANSI standards. The input is shown on the rating plate that is affixed to each furnace.

rated voltage that maximum voltage at which an electrical component can be operated for extended periods without undue degradation or safety hazard.

rating the designated limit of operating characteristics of a machine, apparatus, or device based on definite conditions. Load voltage, frequency, and other operating characteristics may be given in the rating.

raw gas burner a gas burner in which raw gas is ejected into the combustion chamber from multiple ports. Only secondary air is used for combustion; no mixing occurs before the gas is ejected. The ports are arranged to result in maximum mixing of gas and air. Examples are radiant-head, ring, and high-pressure gun burners.

raw water in ice making, any water used for ice making except distilled water.

reactance a measure of the combined effects of capacitance and inductance on an alternating current. The amount of such opposition varies with the frequency of the current. The reactance of a capacitor decreases with an increase in frequency: the opposite occurs with the inductance. Its symbol is "X" and it is expressed in units of ohms.

reactive circuit an AC circuit which has the property of inductance or capacitance.

reactive power (var) the "unused" power of an AC circuit that has inductance or capacitance and is absorbed by the magnetic or electrostatic field of a reactive circuit.

reactivity a description of the tendency of a substance to undergo chemical reaction either by itself or with other materials with the release of energy. Undesirable effects such as pressure buildup, temperature increase, or the formation of noxious, toxic, or corrosive by-products may occur because of the reactivity of a substance to heating, burning, direct contact with other materials, or any other condition in use or in storage.

read only memory (ROM) a semiconductor memory from which digital data can be repeatedly read out, but cannot be written into, as in the case for read/write memory.

read/write memory   a semiconductor memory into which logic 0 and logic 1 states can be written (stored) and read out again (retrieved).

readily accessible   describes a unit capable of being reached easily and quickly for operation, adjustment, and inspection.

real time   pertains to the actual time during which a physical process transpires. Also pertains to the performance of a computation during the actual time that the related process transpires, in order that results of the computation can be used in guiding that related process. Usually refers to a computer's ability to automatically interrupt lower priority tasks in process to immediately accomplish higher priority tasks.

ream   to scrape the inside edge of the end of tubing or a pipe in order to remove any loose bits of metal or any lip that formed during cutting.

reamed   description of tubing or pipe that has been scraped with a tool to remove burrs from a cut surface.

reamer   a cutting tool with a series of teeth or sharp cutting edges which is used to enlarge a hole.

recalibration   periodic adjustment of a gauge or meter to ensure accuracy.

receding dies   dies which are placed into slots of a threader that are backed by tapered posts. As the threader is rotated clockwise, the dies move deeper into sockets to create proper thread taper.

receiver   a storage chamber for liquid refrigerant in a mechanical refrigeration system. The bottom part of a condenser coil may also be used as a receiver.

receiver, auxiliary   an extra vessel used to supplement the capacity of the receiver when additional storage volume is required.

receiver-drier   a cylinder in a refrigeration system which is used for the storing of liquid refrigerant and which also has desiccant.

receiver heating element   an electrical resistance mounted in or around the liquid receiver used to maintain the high-side pressure when ambient temperatures fall below preset standards.

receptacle   a point along an electrical circuit to which a cord plug is attached for the purpose of using the current supplied by that circuit.

reciprocal   see *inverse*.

reciprocating   describes an action in which the motion is back and forth in a straight line.

reciprocating compressor   a compressor whose piston or pistons move back and forth in their cylinders.

recirculated air   return air passed through the conditioner before being supplied again to the conditioned space.

reclaim   to remove refrigerant in any condition from an air-conditioning or refrigeration system and then transport the recovered refrigerant to a dedicated refrigerant reclamation center to be reprocessed to new specifications (ARI 700), which may include distillation. Reclamation requires that the reprocessed refrigerant be certified through a chemical analysis.

reclamation   the process of restoring something to a useful condition.

recombination   the process in which a free electron fills an empty hole.

recommend   in many code compliance manuals, the word "recommend" refers to a procedure which should be done, but is not mandatory.

recording ammeter   an electrical instrument which uses a pen to record the amount of current flow on a moving paper circle or strip chart.

recording thermometer   an electrical instrument which uses a pen to record the amount of heat intensity on a moving paper circle or strip chart.

recording voltmeter an electrical instrument which uses a pen to record the intensity of the electromotive force (voltage) on a moving paper circle strip chart.

recovery the removal of refrigerant in any condition from a system and storage of it in an external refillable Department of Transportation (DOT) container. Recovery does not provide for any cleaning or filtration and is not concerned with testing or processing in any way.

rectangle a geometric figure with opposite sides equal in length and each corner forming a 90° angle.

rectification the conversion of alternating current to unidirectional or direct current. The process of changing AC into DC. Also see *flame rectification.*

rectification pilot see *pilot burner assembly.*

rectification system a flame proving system which operates on a DC flame signal provided by a rectification-type flame detector.

rectification-type flame detector one that uses the rectification principle to indicate the presence of a flame.

rectifier an electrical device that allows current to flow through it in only one direction. Used to convert alternating current into direct current.

rectifying flame rod a metal or ceramic rod used as a flame detector in a detection system using the flame rectification principle. Also see *flame rectification.*

rectifying photocell flame detector a detector that responds to the visible light (wavelength between 0.4 and 0.8 micron) emitted by a flame. It consists mainly of a high vacuum photocell that rectifies alternating current to direct current when exposed to visible light. The cathode of the photocell is coated with cesium oxide or another material that emits electrons when light strikes it.

recuperative coil secondary coil used to extract the latent heat from combustion gases.

recycle (controls) the process of going through another operating cycle. For a flame safeguard control, automatically going through another timer cycle after a shutdown in an attempt to restart the burner.

recycle (refrigerant) to remove refrigerant in any condition from an air-conditioning or refrigeration system and then reduce contaminants through oil separation, filtration, and other methods. This term usually applies to procedures implemented at the job site or at a local service shop. Recycled refrigerant may or may not be suitable for reuse.

recycle interlock a running interlock used with a primary or programming control which will shut down the burner if an improper condition occurs. The control will recycle and will restart the burner if the condition corrects itself. The interlock is usually a combustion air controller (airflow switch). See *running interlock.*

recycling cleaning refrigerant for reuse by oil separation or single or multiple passes through devices that reduce moisture, acidity, and particulate matter.

recycling control a flame safeguard control which recycles following a shutdown. It will restart the burner if conditions causing the shutdown have been corrected.

recycling unit machines used to remove most contaminants from refrigerant withdrawn from a system and to make the refrigerant suitable for reuse.

red iron oxide rust that forms on iron when oxygen from the air and moisture combine with it.

reducer a fitting that joins two tubes of unequal diameter.

reducing coupling a pipe fitting designed to change from one pipe size to another.

reducing flame   a rich flame or fire resulting from combustion of a mixture containing too much fuel and too little air. This kind of flame produces a reducing atmosphere.

redundancy   the duplication deliberately designed into a system to provide substitution in case of equipment or control failure.

reed switch   two or more highly conductive reeds encapsulated in a glass enclosure. Energy from a magnetic field will cause the reed contacts to open or close simultaneously.

reed valve   a thin, flat, tempered steel plate fastened at one end.

reefer   a refrigerated compartment.

re-expansion line   the curve on an indicator diagram which represents the pressure–total volume relationship of clearance fluid during the initial portion of the return stroke of the piston, prior to the opening of the suction valve.

reference lines   the solid lines on a blueprint or plot plan which show that an imaginary cut has been made at a point and that, in order to see that point in detail, you must look at another drawing. The arrow indicates the direction from which the section is viewed. The letters and numbers in the circle tell in what section and where the point will be found.

reference voltage   the constant voltage used as a reference point to which another voltage is compared.

reflected radiation   sunlight that is reflected from the surrounding trees, terrain, or buildings onto a surface exposed to the sky.

refractory   heat-resistant material used to line furnaces, kilns, ovens, and combustion chambers.

refractory block   a piece of refractory material molded with a conical or cylindrical hole through its center and mounted so

that the flame fires through this hole. The block helps to maintain continuous combustion, and reduces the probability of flashback and blowoff. Also called a burner block, refractory tile, or burner refractory.

refractory hold-in test   see *hot refractory hold-in test*.

refractory override test   see *hot refractory saturation test*.

refractory saturation test   see *hot refractory saturation test*.

refrigerant   a substance used in a refrigeration system to absorb heat in the evaporator by changing from a liquid to a gas and releasing this heat from the condenser when the substance returns to a liquid state.

refrigerant charge   the quantity of refrigerant that is required for proper operation of a closed-cycle refrigeration system.

refrigerant control   a device (either manual or automatic) which meters refrigerant and maintains a pressure differential between the high- and low-pressure sides of the mechanical refrigeration system while the unit is in operation.

refrigerant distributors   used to distribute the refrigerant simultaneously to several smaller tubes piped in parallel.

refrigerant dye   coloring agent that can be added to the refrigerant to help locate refrigerant leaks in a system. Not a highly recommended practice.

refrigerant, flammable   any refrigerant which will burn when mixed with air, such as ethyl chloride, methyl chloride, and the hydrocarbon refrigerants.

refrigerant migration   condensation of refrigerant vapor at the coldest point in the system during the off cycle.

refrigerant receiver   a refrigerant system component installed in the liquid line. It is designed to make space for liquid refrigerant flow due to the closing action of a self-regulating metering device.

refrigerant reclaim the reprocessing of refrigerant to new product specifications. This requires chemical analysis and usually requires processes available only at a reprocessing or manufacturing facility.

refrigerant recovery the removal of refrigerant from the system (or a section) to a cylinder. No testing is required.

refrigerant recycling the cleaning of refrigerant for reuse by reducing moisture, acidity, and foreign matter. Usually applies to procedures at job sites or local service shops.

refrigerant, secondary any volatile or nonvolatile substance in an indirect refrigerating system that absorbs heat from a substance or space to be refrigerated and rejects this heat to the evaporator of the refrigerating system.

refrigerant tables tables that show the properties of saturated refrigerants at various temperatures.

refrigerant velocity the speed of movement of gaseous refrigerant required to entrain oil mist and carry it back to the compressor.

refrigerating capacity the rate at which a system, compared with the cooling effect produced by the melting of ice, can remove heat. Usually stated in tons or Btu per hour.

refrigerating effect the amount of heat a given quantity of refrigerant will absorb in changing from a liquid to a gas at a given evaporating pressure.

refrigerating effect, condensing unit the rate of heat removal by the refrigerant assigned to the condensing unit in a refrigerating system; this is equal to the product of the mass rate of refrigerant flow produced by the condensing unit and the difference in the specific enthalpies of the refrigerant vapor entering the unit and the refrigerant liquid leaving the unit.

refrigerating medium any substance whose temperature is such that it is used, with or without a change of state, to lower the temperature of other bodies or substances below the ambient temperature.

refrigerating system, absorption a refrigerating system in which the refrigerated gas in the evaporator is taken up in an absorber and released in a generator upon the application of heat.

refrigerating system, central plant a system with two or more low sides connected to a single, central high side.

refrigerating system, chilled-water an indirect refrigerating system employing water as the circulating liquid.

refrigerating system, compression a refrigerating system in which the pressure-imposing element is mechanically operated.

refrigerating system, direct expansion a refrigerating system in which the evaporator is in direct contact with the refrigerated material or space or is located in air-circulating passages communicating with such spaces.

refrigerating system, mechanical a system where the evaporator coil produces cooling by absorbing heat from the surrounding air, raising the refrigerant to its boiling point and causing it to vaporize. The superheated vapor flows through the condenser, which condenses it into a liquid and gives off heat picked up in the evaporator coil. Then the liquid flows to the metering device, where it expands (lowering its temperature and pressure) to start the cooling cycle all over again.

refrigerating system, multiple a refrigerating system using the direct method in which the refrigerant is delivered to two or more evaporators in separate rooms or refrigerators.

refrigerating system, single-package a complete factory-made and factory-tested refrigerating system in a suitable frame or enclosure, which is fabricated and shipped in one or more sections and in which no refrigerant-containing parts are connected in the field.

refrigeration   in general, the process of transferring heat from a place where heat is not wanted to a place where it is unobjectionable. Removing heat from an enclosed space and maintaining that space at a temperature lower than its surroundings.

refrigeration cycle   a process during which a refrigerant absorbs heat at a relatively low temperature and rejects heat at a higher temperature.

refrigeration oil   a specially refined, chemically stable, dry, light oil that lubricates the compressor.

refrigeration system   combination of interconnected refrigerant-containing devices in which the refrigerant is circulated for the purpose of extracting heat to produce cooling.

refrigeration tables   tables that show the properties of saturated refrigerants at various temperatures.

refrigerator   a container and a means for cooling it, such as a domestic refrigerator; or a large container such as a storage refrigerator, service refrigerator, etc.

refrigerator, commercial   a general category referring to any of the many types of refrigerators used commercially. Included would be walk-ins, reach-ins, and refrigerated display cases (both service and self-service types), which are used by business establishments.

refrigerator, electric   a completely self-contained unit consisting of an insulated cabinet, evaporator, condenser, and an electric compressor.

refrigerator, gas   a refrigerator motivated by thermal energy of burning gas.

register (air)   the porting, grille work, or damper arrangement through which air is introduced into the combustion chamber around the burner ports or nozzles. It may also control the direction and velocity of the airstream for efficient mixing with the incoming fuel. A combination grille and damper arrangement covering on an air opening or end of an air duct. Also see *air register*.

register (electronic)   a short-term digital electronic storage circuit. The capacity of it is usually one computer word or byte.

regulation   a measure of the amount of voltage change that occurs in the output of a generator due to a change in the load.

regulator   a device that functions to keep a quantity or quantities at a certain value or between certain limits. Also see *atmospheric* (zero governor), *draft, gas pressure,* and *pressure regulators*.

regulator, suction pressure   an automatic valve or control device designed to maintain the pressure, and therefore the temperature, in an evaporator above a predetermined minimum.

regulator vent   the opening in the atmospheric side of the regulator housing permitting the in-and-out movement of air to compensate for the movement of the regulator diaphragm.

regulatory authority   the right, as of a government agency, to control an industrial process or mechanism in agreement with a rule.

reheat   to add heat to air to maintain the correct temperature after it has previously been cooled to some specified dew point to control humidity.

reheat system   a system that distributes cooled air to one or more zones and reheats the cooled air to meet the comfort requirements of other zones.

reinforced sheath   the outermost covering of a cable that has a cable sheath constructed in layers with a reinforcing material, usually a braided fiber, molded in place between layers.

relative humidity   the percentage of water vapor contained in a given amount of air at a specific temperature compared to the amount it could contain when 100% saturated. As air temperature changes, its ability to contain water vapor also changes. Ability to contain moisture increases with temperature. Therefore, as the temperature of a given amount of air containing a given amount of water vapor rises, the relative humidity is lowered.

relay   an electromechanical device with contacts that open and/or close when its coil is energized or de-energized in response to a change in the conditions of the electrical circuit. The operation of the contacts affects the operation of other devices in the same circuit or in other circuits. Also see *balancing, checking, flame, flame detector,* and *load relays.*

relay, changeover   a control used in some heat pumps to operate the reversing valve when changing from heating to cooling or vice versa.

relay chatter   noise due to the rapid opening and closing of relay contacts.

relay, impedance   a control that prevents compressor restart, after any safety control shutdown, until manual reset is established. Sometimes called a lockout relay.

relay, lockout   a relay used in conjunction with an automatic reset high-pressure control to cause manual reset interruption of the unit operation when high head pressure is encountered. Reset of the system is from a remote location by interruption of power to the circuit. Also called an impedance relay.

relay, magnetic   solenoid-operated relay or contactor; a switching relay that utilizes an electromagnet (solenoid) and an armature to provide the switching force.

relay, oil burner   dual-purpose control that monitors the operation of an oil burner and acts as a safety in the event of a flame failure.

relay, start   a magnetic switch that disconnects the start capacitor after the motor reaches rated speed. Terminals are 1 and 2 for the normally closed contacts and 2 and 5 for the relay coil. May also be called a potential relay.

relay, thermal   a switching relay in which a small heater warms a bimetal element that bends to provide the switching action.

relay, time-delay   a device for preventing short cycling of the compressor after safety shutdown by interrupting the circuit for several seconds before restoring the circuit. A resistive load.

reliable   possessing the degree of safety that indicates a reasonable freedom from hazards will be maintained during continuous or extended operation.

relief opening   the opening in a draft hood to permit ready escape to the atmosphere of flue products from the draft hood in event of no draft, back draft, or stoppage beyond the draft hood, and to permit inspiration of air into the draft hood in the event of a strong chimney updraft.

relief valve   a valve which opens at a designed pressure and bleeds a system in order to prevent a buildup of excessive pressure which might damage regulators and other instruments. Also see *vent valve.*

relight   immediate restoration of ignition, without preignition purging or interlock checks, after loss of the main burner flame. If the main burner flame is not reestablished, safety shutdown occurs. Also called ignition return.

reluctance   the force working against the passage of magnetic lines of force (flux) through a magnetic substance.

remote bulb a part of the expansion valve. The remote bulb assumes the temperature of the suction vapor at the point where the bulb is secured to the suction line. Any change in the suction vapor superheat at the point of bulb application tends to operate the valve in a compensating direction to restore the superheat to a predetermined valve setting.

remote bulb thermostat a control whose sensing element is located separately from the mechanism it controls.

remote control circuit an electric circuit that controls another circuit at a remote point.

remote power element control a device with its sensing element located apart from its operating mechanism.

remote system a refrigeration system which has its condensing unit located outside and separated from the evaporator. Sometimes referred to as a split system.

remote temperature set point ability to set a temperature control point for a space from outside the space. Often used in public areas.

renewable fuse a fuse in which the element, typically a zinc link, may be replaced after the fuse has opened, and which then may be reused. Renewable fuses are made to class H standards.

repeatability the ability of a controller or interlock to maintain a constant set point characteristic.

replacement package parts included in a single package intended for replacement of a device.

repulsion-start induction motor a motor which develops starting torque by the interaction of rotor currents and a single-phase stator field.

reset a process of automatically adjusting the control point of a given controller to compensate for changes in the outdoor tem-

perature. The hot deck control point is normally reset upward as the outdoor temperature drops. The cold deck control point is normally reset downward as the outdoor temperature increases. Also, to return a control or valve to its original position.

reset control a device for maintaining a pressure or temperature, usually in the heating or cooling medium, which is automatically changed as some other condition changes; that is, the controller is automatically reset to a different control point.

reset ratio the ratio of change in outdoor temperature to the change in control point temperature. For example, a 2:1 reset ratio means that the control point will increase 1° for every 2° change in outdoor temperature.

residual a remainder; a remaining force as in magnetism; leftover.

residual magnetism the magnetism that remains around a material after a magnetizing force has been applied.

residual oils oils which are too heavy to be evaporated in any normal evaporation and distillation process and so are left over from that process.

residual velocity the velocity of air that must be kept up in the occupied zone. It generally ranges from 20 to 70 fpm.

residue a substance left over at the end of a process.

resilient mount the mounting of a motor on flexible rubber feet or mounts to prevent the transmission of vibration to the base.

resistance, electrical the difficulty electrons encounter in moving through a conductor or substance. This causes heat in the carrier. The opposition to current flow. Measured in ohms, its symbol is R.

resistance heater a unit that uses electric conductors to supply heat. The amount of heat depends upon the conductor's electrical resistance.

resistance temperature detector   a temperature-varying resistor used for temperature measurements with a special resistance thermometer.

resistance, thermal   the reciprocal of thermal conductance.

resistive load   an electrical load which is characterized by not having any significant inrush current and which converts electrical energy directly into heat. When a resistive load is energized, the current rises instantly to its steady-state value, without first rising to a higher value. Power factor is one. Current and voltage are in phase with each other.

resistivity, thermal   the reciprocal of thermal conductivity.

resistor   a component of an electric circuit which acts to oppose current flow by virtue of its electrical resistance.

1. Composition resistor - a resistor made of carbon particles mixed with a doping material and provided with terminal leads to connect the resistor (usually cylindrical in shape) into a circuit. The resistance value is determined by the relative amounts of carbon and doping material used.
2. Fixed resistor - a resistor with one essentially constant resistance value (except for changes in temperature variations).
3. Wire-wound resistor - a resistor made by winding wire around a nonconducting cylinder. The resistance value is determined by the diameter and the number of turns of wire.
4. Variable resistor - a resistor constructed so that the value of resistance may be varied over a range, usually by mechanical means.

resolution   the magnitude of an input signal equal to a digit change in the least significant digit in the display. The smallest value an instrument can measure.

resonate   to maximize or minimize the amplitude or other characteristic of the response of a given system or device.

respiration   the heat generated by perishable food products while in storage.

respiratory system   the breathing system, including the lungs and air passages (trachea or windpipe, larynx, mouth, and nose), as well as the associated nervous and circulatory supply.

response   the reaction of a device or system to a control signal.

response time   see *flame failure response time*.

restore   to energize a load that has been shed.

restrictor   a device for producing a deliberate pressure drop or resistance in a line by reducing the cross-sectional flow area.

retentivity   the ability of a material to retain magnetism after a magnetizing force has been removed.

retrofit   term used in describing reworking an older installation to bring it up to date with modern equipment or to meet new code requirements.

return air   air that is drawn back into the ventilation system from the controlled space.

return branch   piping used to return water from a terminal to the circuit main pipe.

return, dry   a return pipe in a steam heating system which carries both water of condensation and air. The dry return is above the level of the water line in the boiler in a gravity system.

return ducts   ductwork that connects the conditioned space with the heating and cooling equipment so that return air may be reconditioned.

return intake   an opening through which air is removed from the conditioned space.

return line   the line that returns water (condensate) back to the boiler or return tank. Also see *return piping*.

return mains   the pipes that return the heating medium from the heating units to the source of heat supply.

return piping   the piping system that carries water from the terminal units back to the boiler.

return pump   a condensate or vacuum pump that returns condensate back to the boiler or storage tank.

return tapping   the opening in a boiler into which the pipe used for returning condensate or water to the boiler is connected.

return, wet   that part of a return main of a steam heating system which is filled with water of condensation. The wet return usually is below the level of the water line in the boiler, although not necessarily so.

returnable cylinder   refillable heavy-duty certified pressure vessel cylinder.

reverse-acting   with the output signal changing in the direction opposite to that in which the controller or measured variable changes. An example would be when an increase in the controlled or measured variable results in a decreased output signal.

reverse cycle   to direct the hot gas flow into the indoor or outdoor coil in a heat pump system to control the system for heating or cooling purposes.

reverse-cycle defrost   a method of heating the evaporator coil for defrosting purposes by using a valve to direct hot gas from the compressor to the evaporator.

reverse return   a two-pipe hot water heating system in which the first unit to receive water is the last to return it.

reversible motor   a motor which can be operated in either direction.

reversing relay   a relay that permits an SPDT thermostat to control heating and cooling equipment by forming an interlock that prevents mutual operation.

reversing valve   a device used to change the direction of refrigerant flow depending upon whether heating or cooling is desired.

revoke   to cancel or take back a permission or contract.

revolutions per minute   a measure of rotary speed; the number of rotations in a 60-second period; abbreviated as rpm.

Reynolds number   a numerical ratio of the dynamic forces of mass flow to the sheer stress due to viscosity.

rheostat   a type of variable resistor with one fixed terminal and a movable contact whereby the resistance through the rheostat can be adjusted to various levels.

ribbon cable   a cable consisting of two or more conductors laid parallel in one plane and held in place by some means.

rich mixture   an air/fuel mixture in which an excess of fuel is supplied in proportion to the amount of air available. Also see *fuel-rich*.

right angle   an angle that is formed by a line that is perpendicular to another line. A 90° angle.

right-hand motor rule   the rule applied to find the direction of motion of the rotor conductors of a motor.

ring burner   a gun-type, raw gas burner in which jets of gas are directed into whirling airstreams from orifices around the periphery of a ring at the mouth of the burner. Also see *gun-type* and *raw gas burners*.

ring valve   a flat, doughnut-shaped valve.

Ringelmann scale   unit measure of smoke opacity; one Ringelmann equals 20% smoke density, and 5 Ringelmanns equal 100% smoke density.

rise   the measured difference between the entering air temperature (return) and the leaving air temperature (supply).

riser   a vertical tube, pipe, or duct that carries fluid in any form from a lower to a higher level.

riser, electrical   the bundle of wires or cables which run vertically between floors of a building.

riser valve   a valve or device used to manually control the flow of a substance in vertical piping systems.

rising stem valve   a valve whose stem rises when the valve is opened.

rms value   the effective value of an alternating current sine wave which is calculated as the square root of the average of the squares of all the instantaneous values of the current throughout one cycle. Rms alternating current is that value of AC voltage that will produce as much power when connected across a resistor as the same amount of DC voltage.

rocker switch   a pivoted switch that is operated by pressing the protruding half, causing the flush half to protrude.

rod-and-tube   a method of opening and closing switches that uses the coefficient of expansion of two different metals. The rod has a low expansion rate, and the tube has a high expansion rate.

rollout switch   a heat-sensitive protective device that opens the circuit if flame migrates away from the burner box.

romex   type NM (nonmetallic) sheathed cable.

roof-mounted   describes an application where the unit is mounted on a platform designed to distribute the weight of the unit over as wide an area of the roof as possible.

rooftop unit   HVAC system placed on a roof and connected to ducts that supply conditioned air to the area below it.

root mean square   the effective value of an alternating periodic voltage or current.

rosin flux   a rosin-based flux containing an additive that increases wetting.

rotary   describes a circular, spinning, or turning motion.

rotary blade compressor   a mechanism for pumping fluid by revolving blades inside a cylindrical housing.

rotary compressor   a mechanism for pumping fluids by revolving vanes using rotating motion.

rotary oil burner   a burner in which atomization is accomplished by feeding oil to a rapidly rotating cup or to spinning plates. Centrifugal force throws off the oil in droplets at the periphery of the cup or plates. Also called a centrifugal atomizing oil burner. There are two basic types:

1. Horizontal rotary oil burner - oil is pumped through a horizontal, hollow drive shaft to a spinning cup. The axis of the cup is also horizontal.
2. Vertical rotary oil burner - the oil tank is mounted higher than the burner, and oil flows downward by gravity to the spinning plates.

rotary screw   a screw-shaped rotor, turning within a flexible stator, usually of rubber. Progressing cavities between screw and stator carry the fluid. They are used for pressures up to 75 psi and can handle abrasive mixtures or slurries, at slower speeds.

rotate   to turn or revolve around a common point.

rotating field   the magnetic field found in electric motors where the poles keep shifting to cause rotation.

rotating unit   alternately shedding and restoring loads assigned to a specific channel so that they will not be shed continuously. Also called alternating channels.

rotation   direction in which a motor shaft rotates; cw = clockwise; ccw = counterclockwise; rev = reversible (rotation can be changed). Motor manufacturer may specify rotation as viewed facing the shaft or facing the end of motor opposite the shaft. Always double-check the direction of shaft rotation.

rotor   the rotating part of an electrical generator or motor.

run   a length of duct carrying either warm or return air.

run capacitor   an electric device that is used to momentarily store electrons and create a second phase in the start winding circuits of single-phase motors. This type of capacitor is designed to stay in the circuit whenever the motor is running as a means of heat dissipation.

run factor   the percentage of the time the unit can be expected to operate to handle the heating load during the coldest month and the cooling load during the warmest month.

run out   length of duct between the main truck and the diffuser in a warm air system.

run period   the period of time after ignition trials and before the operating set point is reached during which the main burner is firing.

run winding   the electrical winding of a motor which has current flowing through it during normal operation. Draws the highest operating current.

running current   the steady-state current drawn from the line when the motor is running at its rated speed, or when the armature of a solenoid or coil is in its closed position.

running interlock   an interlock which proves a condition is proper for burner operation to continue through prepurge, ignition trials, and the run period. It is used with a primary or programming control which will shut down the burner if an improper condition occurs. The interlock may be a combustion air controller (airflow switch), a damper position indicator (low- or high-fire proving switch), or a fuel pressure switch. It can be a recycling type, or it may require manual reset. Also see *lockout* and *recycle interlocks*.

running time   the amount of time a machine is run per hour or per a 24-hour period.

rupture disc   a safety device which will automatically rupture at a predetermined pressure.

S

SAE   Society of Automotive Engineers.

SAVE   Society of American Valve Engineers.

SBCCI   Southern Building Code Congress International.

SBS   sick building syndrome.

sc   shading coefficient.

scfm   standard cubic feet per minute.

SCR   silicon-controlled rectifier.

SDMA   Spiral Duct Manufacturers Association.

SEER   seasonal energy efficiency ratio.

SEIA   Solar Energy Industries Association.

SES   Standards Engineering Society.

SFPE   Society of Fire Protection Engineers.

shpg   shipping.

slv   sleeve.

SMACNA   Sheet Metal and Air Conditioning Contractors National Association.

SME   Society of Manufacturing Engineers.

SNM   special cable designed for use in hazardous locations.

spd   speed.

SPE   Society of Petroleum Engineers or Society of Plastics Engineers.

SPED   Society of Piping Engineers and Designers.

SPI   Society of the Plastics Industry.

SRCC   Solar Rating and Certification Corporation.

ssov   safety shutoff valve.

SSU   Saybolt seconds universal.

ssv   suction service valve.

STEL   short-term exposure limit.

STI   Steel Tank Institute or Steel Tube Institute.

STLE   Society of Tribologists and Lubrication Engineers.

SWE   Society of Woman Engineers.

syn   synchronous.

saddle valve   a valve body shaped so that it may be clamped around a pipe or tubing to gain access without having to void or drain the water distribution system.

SAE flare fitting   tube flared to Society of Automotive Engineer (SAE) standards.

safe start check   a feature of a flame safeguard control to prevent a burner start if a flame is detected, or if a condition simulating a flame exists in the flame detection circuit.

safety can   approved container of not more than five-gallon capacity. It has a spring-closed lid and spout cover. It is designed to relieve internal pressure safety when exposed to fire.

safety cap   a cap of a cylinder that protects the valves and regulator.

safety control circuit   a circuit involving one or more safety controls or controllers.

safety control/controller   an automatic control or interlock (including relays, switches, and other auxiliary equipment used to form a safety control system) which is intended to prevent unsafe operation of the controlled equipment.

safety device   a control that is added to detect a dangerous condition and stop an action or take a new action to remedy the problem.

safety factor   the ratio of extra strength or capacity to the calculated requirements to ensure freedom from breakdown and ample capacity.

safety ground   the wire (usually green or bare) that connects the equipment grounding conductor to the earth ground.

safety head   a type of spring-loaded compressor cylinder head that allows for lifting and expansion in case liquid enters the cylinder and the piston attempts to compress it.

safety limit controller   see *limit*.

safety motor control   an electrical device used to open a circuit if the temperature, pressure, and/or the current flow exceeds safe conditions.

safety plug   a device which will release the contents of its container above normal pressure conditions and before rupture pressures are reached.

safety shutdown (lockout)   the action of shutting off all fuel and ignition energy to the burner by means of a safety control or controls such that restart cannot be accomplished without manual reset. Also see *lockout switch*.

safety shutdown test   a series of tests for a given flame safeguard control to make certain that the control will cause safety shutdown for all the conditions that it should. For all flame safeguard controls, safety shutdown should occur if a flame is not established or if it goes out. Some flame safeguard controls should cause safety shutdown for other conditions as well, such as opening of a preignition interlock during prepurge, opening of a lockout interlock anytime after a few seconds, or detection of a flame (or a condition simulating a flame) during prepurge.

safety shutoff valve (ssov)   a valve that is automatically closed by the safety control system or by an emergency device to completely shut off the fuel supply to the burner. The valve may be opened automatically, or it may have to be manually opened. Also see *fluid power;* and *first stage oil, main fuel, manual reset, pilot, second stage oil,* and *solenoid valves.*

safety switch   see *lockout switch*.

safety thermostat   a thermostat that limits the temperature of an appliance.

safety valve   a safety device for a steam boiler that opens at a preset pressure to allow excessive steam to escape.

sail switch   an airflow switch with a metal or plastic sail which is inserted into the airstream. The switch is actuated when the velocity of the air striking the sail reaches a specified value.

salt brine   a solution of water and some type of salt with a freezing point below 32°F.

sampling assembly   a hand-held rubber squeeze pump used to force samples of flue products through various testing devices.

sandblast   to blow sand at high velocity with compressed air against objects to clean them.

sash crack   sum of all perimeters of all ventilators, sashes, or doors based on the overall dimensions of such parts expressed in feet (counting two adjacent lengths of the perimeter as one).

saturated air   air that contains the maximum water vapor it can hold at a given temperature. Air at 100% relative humidity.

saturated conditions   term used to indicate the boiling or condensing point of a substance, which is dictated by a specific combination of temperature and pressure.

saturated pressure   the force in a pressure vessel that matches the temperature of a certain contained gas at a condition where any removed heat would cause condensation, and added heat would cause evaporation.

saturated steam   steam that contains no moisture. It is saturated with heat, since additional heat will raise the temperature above the boiling point, and the removal of heat will result in the formation of water.

saturated temperature   the temperature at which a liquid turns to a vapor or a vapor turns to a liquid.

saturated vapor   vapor at the same pressure and temperature as the liquid it contacts.

saturation   the state of being completely filled, charged, or treated with something so that no more can be taken in.

saturation pressure   boiling point of a liquid.

saturation temperature   the temperature at which boiling or condensation can take place.

Saybolt seconds universal (SSU)   a measurement of oil viscosity. The number of seconds it takes oil at a standard temperature (130°F for lighter oils and 210°F for heavier oils) to flow through a hole of a standard size and fill a 60-milliliter flask.

scale   a measurement band on a test instrument. Any film or oxidation deposit formed on a metal surface immersed in water.

scale trap   a pipe fitting that separates scale from water.

scaling   the formation of lime and other deposits on the water-side surfaces of heat exchangers.

scanner   a collective term applied to all flame radiation detectors.

scavenger pump   a mechanism used to remove fluid from a sump or container.

schematic diagram   a pictorial representation of an electrical circuit showing components, lines, and connections in symbolic form and in relationship to each other.

Schrader valve   a valve that uses a valve core, like a tire-valve stem, to gain access to a sealed system.

scientific notation   the use of powers of 10 to simplify large and small numbers.

score   to make a scratch mark or line to show a starting point or cutting line.

scotch boiler   a horizontal, fire-tube boiler consisting of a cylindrical steel shell with one or more cylindrical, internal combustion chambers located (generally) in the lower portion, and with a bank or banks (passes) of tubes attached to both end closures. The combustion chamber(s) and tubes are completely surrounded by water. A scotch boiler is described by a number of passes, and by whether it is a dryback boiler (for stationary service) or a wetback boiler (for marine or stationary service). Also see *dryback, firetube, multipass,* and *wetback boilers.*

scotch yoke   a mechanism used to change reciprocating motion into rotary motion or vice versa. Used to connect the crankshaft to the piston in a refrigeration compressor.

screw compressor   a rotary compressor that employs two intermeshed, counterrotating screws for positive displacement.

screw extractor   a tool used to remove broken bolts, screws, etc. from holes.

screw pump   see *screw compressor.*

screw threads   a helical ridge of uniform section formed inside of a hole (as in a nut) or on the outside of a fastener (as in a screw or bolt).

screwdriver   a hand tool used for turning screws. The length of a screwdriver is measured from the tip of the blade to the beginning of the handle. Screwdrivers come in eight basic designs: standard, Phillips, clutch head, Allen, stubby, offset, torque, and starting.

screws   threaded fasteners used to obtain a good hold and provide a means for repeatedly removing fastened parts.

scroll-type compressor   one that involves the mating of two spiral coils (scrolls) to form a series of crescent-shaped pockets.

SE-type cord   a 600-maximum-volt cord that has a temperature range of –58°F to +221°F. It is a heavy-duty, all-temperature cord used for construction equipment motors and outdoor lighting.

seal air   the air supplied to any device at a significantly higher pressure than the surrounding air for the specific purpose of excluding contaminants from the surrounding atmosphere.

seal, bellows   metal bellows used in a shaft seal, or in place of packing for valves. Also used in long pipelines instead of gaskets to compensate for expansion of the line with temperature changes.

seal, compressor   a device to prevent the leakage of refrigerant gas at the point where the crankshaft must pass through the crankcase. Usually takes the form of two finely finished surfaces separated only by a thin film of oil and maintained under pressure by means of a spring.

seal leak   the escape of oil/or refrigerant at the junction where the shaft exits the housing.

seal, shaft   see *shaft seal.*

sealed   tightly closed; not open to the atmosphere. Having a nonleaking union between two elements.

sealed unit   a hermetic motor compressor assembly that has the motor and compressor inside a sealed dome or housing.

sealed VA   the VA after the controlled device has been operated or energized. The sealed VA of an electromagnetic device will be different for all devices depending upon the design of the particular device. The sealed VA can be supplied by the manufacturer.

seasonal efficiency   the consummate efficiency of a heating system over a 12-month period considering flue losses, electrical consumption, warm-up and cool-down cycles, pilot losses, and fuel consumption, when compared to the design loss of the building and the annual degree day value for the geographical area of the building.

seasonal energy efficiency ratio (SEER) total cooling output of an air conditioner during its normal annual usage period for cooling (in Btu) divided by the total electric energy input during the same period as determined by conditions.

seasonal peak   the maximum demand placed on the utility's capacity resulting from seasonal factors. Some utilities have summer peaks, some have winter peaks, some both.

seat   that portion of a valve mechanism against which the valve presses to effect shutoff.

seat, front   the part of a refrigeration valve that forms a seal with the valve button when the valve is in the closed position.

second law of thermodynamics   heat will flow only from a material at a higher temperature to a material at a lower temperature.

second stage oil valve   in oil burners with two firing rate levels (stages), the automatic safety shutoff valve which opens to admit more fuel when the higher combustion rate is required. The second stage may be optional.

secondary air   air which is introduced at the point of combustion or air which is not mixed with the fuel before it enters the combustion chamber.

secondary cell   a cell that can be charged by applying DC voltage from a battery charger.

secondary control   safety device used to shut off the system if certain unsafe conditions exist.

secondary refrigerating system   a refrigerating system in which the condenser is cooled by the evaporator of another or primary refrigerating system.

secondary surface   a coil surface, such as a fin, that is not in direct contact with the refrigerant.

secondary voltage   the output, or load supply voltage of a transformer or substation. Can be higher or lower than the applied (primary) voltage.

secondary winding   the coil of a transformer into which voltage is induced. Energy is delivered to the load circuit by the secondary winding.

sectional boiler   see *cast iron sectional boiler.*

sectional header boiler   see *water-tube boiler.*

Seebeck effect   the phenomenon in which an electric current is generated when two different adjacent metals are heated.

Seebeck EMF   the open-circuit voltage caused by the difference in temperature between the hot and cold junctions of a thermocouple circuit.

seize   when two parts rub together so that they get hot and force the lubricant out of the area they gall and finally freeze or stick together.

selective absorber surface   surface used to increase the temperature of a solar collector.

self-checking circuit   see *dynamic amplicheck* and *dynamic self-check.*

self-contained   describes a refrigerating system having all working or major parts in one unit that can be moved without disconnecting any refrigerant lines.

self-inductance   the phenomenon where a magnetic field is induced in a conductor carrying the current.

semiautomatic burner   see *semiautomatic system.*

semiautomatic system   a system which requires some manual operation; the burner is started and ignited manually; purged, sequenced, and modulated automatically; and stopped manually, with certain steps and conditions supervised by safety interlocks.

semiconductor   a material that has electrical properties of current flow between those of a conductor and an insulator, and is used to manufacture solid-state devices such as diodes and transistors.

semiconductor fuses   fuses used to protect solid-state devices.

semihermetic compressor   a motor compressor design that combines the benefits of the hermetic and open-type compressors. This type of compressor is kept hermetic by the use of gasketed openings and fittings and is field serviceable.

sensible heat   the heat energy which changes the temperature of a substance without changing its state. This heat is measured with a thermometer.

sensible heat factor   the ratio of the sensible heat cooling load to the total heat load.

sensible heat ratio   the ratio of the sensible (heating or cooling) load to the total heat load.

sensing bulb   a sensing element placed and located on the suction line at the outlet of the evaporator coil to control the operation of the TXV located at the inlet of the evaporator coil.

sensing element   the first system element or group of elements. The sensing element performs the initial measurement operation.

sensing tube   an electron tube which is sensitive to ultraviolet flame detectors. Also see *aquadag tube* and *ultraviolet power tube*.

sensitivity   the ratio of the rate of response of a controller to each unit of change of the controlled device.

sensor   an element used in a detector which perceives the presence of radiant energy and converts it into electrical energy.

separator, oil   a device used to separate refrigerant oil from refrigerant gas and return that oil to the crankcase of the compressor.

sequence   see *timer sequence*.

sequence controls   group of devices which act in series or in a time order.

sequencer   a time-delay-type relay that uses a heater wire or element as the method to activate the contacts.

sequential lightoff   in a multiburner system, the ignition of the pilots one at a time, one following the other in a predetermined order. Each pilot is in a separate valve zone (see *valve zone*). Each pilot must be proved before the next one can be ignited. After all pilots have been proved, all main burners are ignited in unison. (The main burners are all in a single valve zone.)

serial number   a unique identifying number assigned to a machine or part.

Series 90   Honeywell nomenclature designating a group of controllers and motors which are characterized by low-voltage, three-wire, modulating operation.

series circuit   a circuit in which the components are arranged end to end with only one continuous path, and so the same current flows through all components in the circuit. Considered to be a voltage divider circuit.

series loop   a forced hot water heating system with the terminal units connected so that all the water flowing through the circuit passes through each series-connected unit in the circuit.

series/parallel circuit   a combination of series (single-path) and parallel (multiple-path) circuits.

series resistance   any sum of resistances installed in sequential order within one circuit.

serpentining   the arrangement of tubes in a coil to provide circuits of the desired length. Intended to keep pressure drop and velocity of the substance passing through the tubes within the desired limits.

serrated   having sawlike teeth or notches along the cutting edge.

Servel system   one type of continuous operation absorption refrigerating system.

service   all the conductors and equipment for supplying electrical energy to the dwelling.

service compartment   a normally enclosed compartment of an assembly to which ready access must be gained by the operator for occasional operations such as lighting the pilot; or the adjustment, cleaning, and servicing of such parts of the equipment as air filters, blowers, motors, and controllers.

service conductors   a portion of the electrical service system consisting of the conductors that carry electrical energy from the utility transformers to the entrance pipe or conduit on the building.

service connection   a point at which the fuel, atomizing medium, or power is connected to the boiler, firing equipment, or controlled devices.

service drop   connecting wires from the power lines to the point of entry to the building.

service entrance   the associated cables, conduit, boxes, and meters used to bring electric power from the main power line to the building.

service factor   a measurement which states the percent beyond the rated load or horsepower which a motor can carry without overheating. A 1.15 service factor means the motor can deliver 15% more than the rated horsepower without injurious over-heating. A 1.0 service factor motor should not be overloaded beyond its rated horsepower. The ambient temperature of the environment must be within the defined limits.

service lateral   underground service conductors extending from the street main to the service entrance conductors.

service manifold   an instrument equipped with suction and discharge/liquid pressure gauges and with hoses for connection to the suction and discharge/liquid service valves and to a refrigerant cylinder, recovery machine, or vacuum pump.

service valve   a device to be attached to the system which provides an opening for the gauges and/or charging lines. Also provides means of shutting off or opening gauges and charging ports, and controlling refrigerant flow in the system.

serviceability   an installation is classified as serviceable when sufficient area is provided for access to control panels, electrical connections, and refrigerant lines. The better the access, the higher the serviceability of the system.

serviceable hermetic   a hermetic unit housing the compressor and the motor that can be disassembled by use of bolts and threads.

servo   a servo motor supplies power to a servo mechanism. A servo mechanism is a lower power device (electrical, hydraulic, or pneumatic) used to put in operation and control a more complex or powerful mechanism.

servo mechanism   a closed-loop system which initiates an input signal with deviation from a desired condition; the signal is fed back into the control system until a continued response eliminates the signal.

set point   a predetermined value to which a controller or interlock is adjusted and at which it performs its intended function.

set screws   fasteners used primarily to hold pulleys and fan wheels to shafting material.

severe-duty   describes a totally enclosed motor with extra protection (shaft slinger, gasketed terminal box) to resist entry of contaminants. Used in extra-duty, damp, or other nonhazardous contaminated environments.

SEW-A type cord   a 600-maximum-volt cord that has a temperature range of −58°F to +221°F. It is a heavy-duty, all-temperature cord that is UL listed for outdoor use and used for construction equipment motors and outdoor lighting.

shaded-pole motor   a small special type of single-phase alternating current induction motor that utilizes a copper shading coil to provide the necessary displacement for starting. This motor has low starting torque and is used for light starting loads. It has no brushes or commutator.

shading coil   a large copper wire, loop, or band connected around part of a magnetic pole piece to oppose a change of magnetic flux. The loop produces a tiny magnetic field that is out of phase with the main poles, which aids in starting the motor.

shaft a long, thin, usually cylindrically shaped part.

shaft end end of the motor where the rotor shaft exists.

shaft seal a device used to prevent leakage between the crankshaft and the housing.

shall term used to indicate provisions that are mandatory if compliance with the standard is claimed. In reference to the National Electric Code (NFPA 70), it indicates a mandatory requirement.

shank the shaft of a tool, such as a screwdriver, drill bit, or nut driver.

sharp freezing refrigeration at a temperature slightly below freezing, with moderate air movement.

shear strength the ability of a joint to withstand a parallel or right angle force.

sheath the material, usually an extruded plastic or elastomer, applied outermost to a wire or cable. Very often referred to as a jacket.

sheave a wheel or pulley with a grooved rim, used with a belt to transfer rotary motion.

shed to de-energize a load in order to maintain a kW demand set point.

sheet metal a term that refers to metal that is formed in sheets one-eighth of an inch thick or less.

shell-and-coil a designation for heat exchangers, condensers, and chillers consisting of a tube bundle within a shell of casing.

shell-and-tube flooded evaporator a device which flows water through tubes built into a cylindrical evaporator or vice versa.

shell-type condenser a cylinder or receiver which contains condensing water coils or tubes.

shielded cable a special cable used with equipment that generates a low-voltage output. Used to minimize the effects of frequency noise on the output signal.

shim a thin piece of metal used for filling space, leveling, etc. Materials used for shims.

shipping bolts packaging bolts that stabilize heavy equipment in transit. They should be removed before operation of the equipment.

short a short circuit. Also, to intentionally bypass part of a circuit with a jumper.

short circuit an abnormal connection of relatively low resistance between two points of a circuit, resulting in a flow of excess (often damaging) current between these two points.

short-circuit rating the maximum short-circuit current an electrical component can sustain without the occurrence of excessive damage when protected by an overcurrent protective device.

short-cycling describes a system that starts and stops more frequently than it should.

short-term exposure limit the concentration of a substance to which workers can be exposed continuously for a short period of time without suffering adverse effects.

shorted capacitor a situation where the two aluminum plates of a capacitor are touching each other.

shorted to ground describes a situation where the windings of a motor are touching the case. Ohmic value is zero.

should a word used to indicate provisions that are not mandatory but are desirable as good practice.

shroud a housing over the condenser or evaporator.

shunt any parallel connection in a circuit.

shunt (meter) a resistor connected in parallel with a meter movement to extend the range of current the meter will measure.

shutdown   the total process of terminating the operation of a combustion system; also see *safety* and *unison shutdown*.

shutoff valve   see *manual shutoff* and *safety shutoff valves*.

shutter   a movable screen or cover that opens and closes an aperture. Also see *air shutter*.

shutter control   a damper assembly and pressure-operated actuator used on systems with nonunloading-type hermetic compressors in an air-cooled condensing unit to maintain minimum required condensing pressure during low ambient operation.

SI unit   (Le Systeme International d'Unites) a unit in the metric system of measurement adopted by most technical industries throughout the world.

sick building syndrome (SBS)   term that refers to a set of symptoms that affect a number of building occupants during the time they spend in the building and diminish or go away during periods when they leave the building. Cannot be traced to specific pollutants or sources within the building.

side cutters   a pliers-like, sharp-edged wire cutter.

sight glass, liquid   a glass tube or window in a refrigerating system which shows the amount of refrigerant or presence of gas bubbles in the liquid line.

sight glass, oil   a glass "bull's-eye" located in the compressor crankcase permitting visual inspection of the compressor oil level.

sight glass, steam boiler   a glass tube located on a steam boiler application to show the level of the water line externally that corresponds to the water level internal to the steam boiler.

sighting pipe   a pipe, mounted to the front plate of a combustion chamber, through which an optical flame detector sights the burner flame.

signal   an electrical current used to convey digital, analog, audio, or video information.

silica gel   a chemical compound used as a drier, which has the ability to absorb moisture. When it is heated, the moisture is released and the compound may be reused.

silicon-controlled rectifier (SCR)   an electronic semiconductor which contains silicon. The gate of the SCR must be triggered before the device will conduct current.

silicosis   a condition of massive fibrosis of the lungs, causing shortness of breath. It is caused by prolonged inhalation of silica dusts.

silver brazing   a brazing process in which the brazing alloy contains some silver for joining the alloy. The process is considered to be above 800°F.

silver solder   a solder that has silver added for strength.

sine wave AC current   a waveform of a single-frequency alternating current. The graphical representation of all points traced by the sine of an angle as the angle is rotated through 360 degrees.

single-circuit system   a hydronic system composed of only one circuit.

single-cut file   a single-cut file that has one set of parallel lines or cuts running across the face. The single-cut file is used for finish surfaces.

single-family house   a building containing one or two living units or a townhouse, including a manufactured house (modular) but not a manufactured house (mobile home).

single-phase   describes a device by which only one alternating voltage or current is produced or used.

single-phase motor   an electric motor which operates on single-phase alternating current.

single-phasing   that condition which occurs when one phase of a three-phase system opens, either in a low-voltage (secondary) or high-voltage (primary) distribution system.

Primary or secondary single-phasing can be caused by any number of events. This condition results in unbalanced loads in polyphase motors and, unless protective measures are taken, causes overheating and failure.

single-pole breaker circuit breaker used to disconnect the black (hot) wire on a 120-volt single-phase branch circuit.

single-pole, double-throw switch (SPDT) an electric switch with one pole blade and operated by two contact points, the first being normally open and the second being normally closed.

single-pole, single-throw switch (SPST) an electric switch with one pole blade and one contact point that opens and closes.

single-port burner a burner in which the entire air/gas mixture flows from a single port.

single-seated valve a valve with only one seat and one disc; generally suitable for tight shutoff; requires more force to close than a double-seated valve of the same size. Also see *cage valve*.

single-stage air compressor a system where air is compressed once and forced into the hose or tank; can be a single or multicylinder unit. Normally used for air pressures below 150 psi.

single-stage compressor compressor having only one compressive step between inlet and outlet.

single-stage oil pump pump used on a one-pipe gravity feed system, where the supply of oil is located higher than the oil pump burner assembly.

single-thickness flare when the part of the tubing that forms the flare is the thickness of the tubing.

sintered oil bearing a porous bearing metal, usually bronze, which has oil in its pores.

sinusoidal describes current that varies in proportion to the sine of an angle or time function; e.g., ordinary alternating current.

siphoning the flow of liquid, through a closed tube, from a higher to a lower level.

site plan a layout of the building to be conditioned and its location on the ground, as well as all buried utility lines, cables, pipes, and/or conduits.

SJ-type cord a 300-maximum-volt cord that has a temperature range of –40°F to +140°F. It is a medium-duty, general-purpose cord, used for power tools, floor polishers, sanders, and portable lighting.

SJE-type cord a 300-maximum-volt cord that has a temperature range of –58°F to +221°F. It is a medium-duty, all-temperature cord, used for blowers, motors, dryers, and outdoor lighting.

SJEW-A type cord a 300-maximum-volt cord that has a temperature range of –58°F to +221°F. It is a medium-duty, all-temperature cord that is UL listed for outdoor use and used for blowers, motors, dryers, and outdoor lighting.

SJO-type cord a 300-maximum-volt cord that has a temperature range of –40°F to +194°F. It is a medium-duty cord having a jacket that resists swelling and decomposing when exposed to oil and grease. Used for motors, power tools, and portable lighting.

SJOOW-A type cord a 300-maximum-volt cord that has a temperature range of –58°F to +221°F. It is a medium-duty cord having a jacket that resists swelling and decomposing when exposed to oils, acids, and chemicals. It is also abrasion- and flame-resistant. Used for motors, power tools, lighting, blowers, and industrial equipment.

SJOW-A type cord a 300-maximum-volt cord that has a temperature range of –40°F to +194°F. It is the same as SJO cord but it is UL listed for outdoor use and used for motors, power tools, and portable lighting.

SJT-type cord a 300-maximum-volt cord that has a temperature range of 0°F to +140°F. It is a medium-duty, general-purpose cord used for motors, power tools, lawn and garden equipment, and appliances.

SJTO-type cord a 300-maximum-volt cord that has a temperature range of 0°F to +140°F. It is a medium-duty cord having a jacket that resists swelling and decomposing when exposed to oil and grease. Used for motors, power tools, and lighting.

SJTW-A type cord a 300-maximum-volt cord that has a temperature range of 0°F to +140°F. It is a medium-duty, general-purpose cord that is UL listed for outdoor use and used for motors, power tools, and lawn and garden equipment.

skin condenser condenser using the outer surfaces of the cabinet as the heat radiating medium.

skirted guide see *characterized guide* and *valve skirt.*

slab-mounted describes an installation where the unit sets on a level flat slab located high enough above the surface of the earth (grade level) to eliminate moisture problems.

sledge hammer a hammer used for breaking and pounding. A sledge hammer usually has a long handle.

sleeve a tube or tube-like part that fits around another part.

sleeve bearing a bearing made of a sleeve bushing, not a ball or a roller bearing. Preferred where low noise level is important, as on fan and blower motors. Unless otherwise stated, sleeve-bearing motors can be mounted in any position, including shaft-up or shaft-down (all-position mounting).

slide-type damper a damper consisting of a single blade which moves normal (at right angle) or near normal to the flow.

sliding armature an armature that mounts between two slots in a contactor frame and moves up and down the slots when the contactor is energized.

sling psychrometer a humidity-measuring device with wet and dry bulb thermometers. It is rapidly moved through the air when measuring humidity.

slinger ring a ring fastened around the circumference of an axial fan. The slinger ring picks up cool condensate and flings it against the face of the condenser, increasing subcooling.

slip the difference between the speed of the rotating magnetic field of an induction motor and the speed of the rotor under full load.

slip joint pliers slip joint pliers can be locked into two different positions for different applications. There are many types of slip joint pliers. Each kind has a different grip size and handle size.

slip rings metal rings connected to the rotating armature windings in a generator. Brushes sliding on these rings provide connections for the external circuit.

slope coil an evaporator that sits diagonally in a plenum.

slot insulation also called slot liner. The insulation lining the slot containing the motor windings.

slow blow fuse a fuse with a built-in trip delay commonly used in HVAC installations due to the power surge on start-up.

sludge oil or mineral waste deposit in a crankcase or boiler.

slug detached mass of liquid or oil which causes an impact or hammer in a circulating system.

slugging condition in which a mass of liquid enters a compressor, causing hammering. Low or no superheat measurement.

smoke an air suspension (aerosol) of particles, usually but not necessarily solid, often originating in a solid nucleus, formed from combustion or sublimation. Also defined as carbon or soot particles less than 0.1 micron in size which result from the incomplete combustion of carbonaceous materials such as coal, oil, tar, and tobacco.

smoke detector a detective device which monitors smoke density and actuates an alarm system if the opacity exceeds a preset level. Also see *stack smoke detector*.

smoke pipe see *chimney connector*.

smoke test a test made to determine the completeness of combustion.

snake a flexible wire used to push or pull wires through a conduit, a partition, or other inaccessible place. Also see *fish tape*.

snap ring pliers pliers used to either take off or install snap rings by either expanding or decreasing the size of the ring.

snap switch a switch with contacts that make and break quickly through mechanical linkage.

SO-type cord a 600-maximum-volt cord that has a temperature range of –40°F to +194°F. It is a heavy-duty cord having a jacket that resists swelling and decomposing when exposed to oil and grease. Used for tools, cranes, hoists, and industrial equipment.

soap bubble test a method of detecting leaks by coating them with a soap solution. Any major leak will cause bubbles to form.

soapstone a type of rock cut into narrow strips and used as a marking device. It will not break up as easily as chalk.

socket a device for electrical connection of a plug, bulb, etc.

socket wrench a wrench used to remove nuts which do not have any obstructions over them.

sodium a silver-white, alkaline, metallic element, found in nature only in combined form. Its symbol is Na.

soft flame a flame partially deprived of primary air such that the combustion zone is extended and the inner cone is ill-defined.

soft hammer a soft-headed hammer made of different sorts of material, such as rawhide, rubber, wood, plastic, or lead. It is used to drive parts into place or to separate them without damage to the surface.

soft soldering see *soldering*.

soft start kit a kit consisting of a PTC thermistor used to provide added torque for the motor on start-up. Wired in parallel with the run capacitor.

software a term used to describe all computer programs, whether in machine, assembly, or high-level language.

soil swing curve the effect of air and solar changes on soil temperatures from the surface to a depth of 12 feet.

soil temperature variation an assumed figure that is a balance between the allowable earth temperature and the depth of the pipe loop location.

solar cell also known as a photovoltaic cell. A device that converts solar radiation directly into electricity.

solar collector a device used to trap solar radiation, usually having an insulated black surface.

solar constant the solar intensity incident on a normal surface located outside the earth's atmosphere at a distance from the sun equal to the mean distance between the earth and the sun. At sea level in July the solar intensity value is about 300 Btu per (sq ft) (hr) since about 28% is absorbed in the earth's atmosphere.

solar energy the energy received by the earth from the sun.

solar energy systems systems used to collect, convert, and distribute solar energy in forms useful within a business or residence. A passive system uses no additional energy from other sources for the distribution of the solar generated heat. An active system may use blowers, supplementary coils, etc.

solar heat   heat from visible and invisible energy waves from the sun.

solar payback   the point at which the investment for a solar system has saved enough money in fuel bills to pay for itself.

solder   a metal alloy of tin and lead used to join two metal surfaces together, or to patch metal parts or surfaces.

solder pot   a device using a low-melting solder and an overload heater sized for the amperage of the motor it is protecting. The solder will melt and open the circuit when there is an excessive overload.

soldering   the process of joining two metals by adhesion of a low-melting-temperature metal (less than 800°F).

soldering gun   a soldering gun is used to solder electrical connections. It comes in fixed and adjustable wattages.

solenoid   a coil of wire which, when current flows through it, will act as a magnet and will pull a movable iron core, or armature, to a central position.

solenoid valve   an automatic safety shutoff valve which is opened or closed by the action of a solenoid upon an armature attached to the valve disc, resulting in fast opening and closing times (less than one second). It is widely used for low-volume duty, such as a pilot valve, or a main fuel valve in a small- to medium-size on/off system. Also called a magnetic valve. Also see *armature* and *solenoid*.

solid   the form of a substance in which the motion of the molecules is restricted, giving it a definite shape and volume. The form that is neither gas nor liquid.

solid absorbent refrigeration   a refrigeration system which uses a solid substance as an absorber of the refrigerant during the cooling part of the cycle and releases this refrigerant when heated during the generating part of the cycle.

solid fuel heating   a system that uses solid natural resources such as wood or coal to provide heat.

solid-state   utilizing the electronic properties of solid crystalline materials (usually semiconductor in type). The interaction of light, heat, magnetic fields, and electric currents in these crystalline materials is involved in solid-state devices. Less power is required to operate solid-state devices, and a greater variety of effects can be obtained.

solid-state device   a group of electronic components that perform jobs similar to vacuum tubes, but unlike tubes they are not electrodes enclosed in glass, but rather are specifically prepared solid matter.

solidify   to make or become firm, hard, or solid; to crystallize.

solidus   melting point of a solder or filler material.

solubility   the ability of a substance to be dissolved by, or in, another substance.

soluble   a substance that can be dissolved in a given liquid.

solute   a component (originally solid, liquid, or gas) of a solution, usually present in a smaller amount than the solvent.

solution   a liquid which has another liquid or solid completely dissolved in it. A lithium bromide water solution, commonly used in absorption systems, is water with a quantity of lithium bromide dissolved in it. Strong and weak solutions are those with high and low concentrations, respectively, of another liquid or solid.

solvent   (1) a substance capable of dissolving another substance, especially grease or oil. (2) A liquid component of a solution usually present in greater amount than the solute.

solvent cement   chemical used to soften and join plastic pipe and fittings.

sone   a calculated sound loudness rating.

soot   a black substance, consisting mostly of small particles of carbon, which can result from incomplete combustion and appears as smoke. Soot gives smoke its color.

SOOW-A type cord   a 600-maximum-volt cord that has a temperature range of –58°F to +221°F. It is a medium-duty cord the same as SJOOW-A cord used for motors, machine and power tools, lighting, blowers, construction and industrial equipment, cranes, and hoists.

sound power level   the acoustic power radiating from a sound source, expressed in decibels.

sound tracer   an instrument which helps to locate sources of sound.

source   the part of an electrical system that supplies energy to other parts of the system, such as a battery which supplies energy for a flashlight.

sources of ignition   devices or equipment that, because of their intended modes of use or operation, are capable of providing sufficient thermal energy to ignite flammable gas-air mixtures.

south pole, magnetic   that part of the magnet into which the magnetic lines of flux flow.

SOW-A type cord   a 600-maximum-volt cord that has a temperature range of –40°F to +194°F. It is the same as SO cord but is UL listed for outdoor use and used for tools, cranes, hoists, and industrial equipment.

space, confined   for the purpose of the National Fuel Gas Code (NFPA 54), a space whose volume is less than 50 cubic feet per 1,000 Btu per hour of the aggregate input rating of all appliances installed in that space. Rooms communicating directly with the space in which the appliances are installed, through openings not furnished with doors, are considered a part of the unconfined space.

space heater   a heater used to raise the temperature of the space within a building to the desired comfort level for human occupancy.

space thermostat   a thermostat whose sensor is located in the controlled space.

span   the algebraic difference between the upper and lower values of the range.

spanner wrench   used to make adjustments on packing and other notched nuts.

spark gap   a gap between two electrodes. When a high potential difference is imposed across the electrodes, current will jump across the gap, creating an electrical spark for the purpose of igniting the pilot.

spark generator   a high-voltage transformer which produces a spark, used to ignite gas pilots or oil burners (direct spark ignition).

special-purpose motors   motors designed for a particular application. Developed when an OEM has refined the operating characteristics or construction features of the motor. Does not have standard operating characteristics or standard mechanical features.

special tools   tools that are not available on the open retail market.

specific density   a statement of mass per unit of volume measurement.

specific gravity   the ratio of the weight or mass of a given volume of a substance to that of the same volume of a standard (water for liquids and solid; air or hydrogen for gases) at the same temperature.

specific heat   in the foot-pound-second system, the amount of heat (Btu) required to raise 1 pound of a substance 1°F. In the centimeter-gram-second system, the amount of heat (cal) required to raise 1 pound of a substance 1°C. For example, the specific heat of water is 1 and the specific heat of air is .24.

specific humidity   is the actual weight of water vapor mixed in the air. This weight is expressed in pounds of water vapor per pound of dry air.

specific volume   the volume of a substance per unit of mass. The cubic feet of air and water vapor per pound of dry air.

specifications   the detailed description of a component or system.

speed (rpm)   the running speed of an AC motor is dependent upon the number of poles and the frequency of the power source.

$$rpm = \frac{120 \times frequency}{number\ of\ poles}$$

Number of poles	Synchronous speed	Normal speed
2	3600	3450
4	1800	1725
6	1200	1075
8	900	825

speed handle   the speed handle is used with a socket wrench when the nut or bolt is easy to get to and when loosening or tightening can be done.

speed ratio   the ratio or relationship of input speed divided by output speed. Speed ratio is normally expressed as X:1.

speed regulation   the ability of a motor to maintain a steady speed with changes in load.

spillage   combustion products flowing from the appliance air openings or draft hood relief openings due to a malfunction of the venting system.

spiral   curved flutes with a sharp cutting edge.

splash method   a method for more efficient evaporation in which water, dropping from a higher level in a cooling tower, splashes on slots with air passing through them.

splash system, oiling   a method of lubricating moving parts by agitating or splashing.

splashproof motor   a motor protected from falling droplets from any angle up to 100 degrees from vertical.

splice   connection of two or more conductors.

spline   one of a series of grooves, cut lengthwise, around a shaft or hole.

split   the difference between the temperature of the air or liquid entering a coil and the coil operating temperature.

split-phase motor   a motor with two stator windings. The most common type of single-phase induction motor. Equipped with a starting winding displaced in magnetic position from, and connected in parallel with, the main winding. Generally, this motor has low to moderate locked-rotor torque with high locked-rotor amps and high breakdown torques, and it is used on belt-drive blowers, fans, pumps, etc. The start winding in this motor is disconnected by a centrifugal switch or potential relay after the motor attains speed, then operates on the main or run winding.

split rings   a group of copper bars mounted on the end of a rotor shaft of a DC motor and connected to the brushes and the rotor windings.

split system   a refrigeration or air-conditioning installation which places the condensing unit outside or at a remote location from the evaporator. Also applies to heat pump installations.

spoiler screw   a screw or bolt moved in or out of the gas jet stream in a burner to control the primary air injection.

spot smoke tester   an instrument used to measure the free carbon content of the flue products from a fossil-fuel-fired unit. The result is obtained by comparison to a standard using spots of carbon or black color of varying density.

spray angle   a specific coverage that a fuel oil nozzle must conform to. It must match up with the size and shape requirements of the combustion chamber and burner.

spray cooling   a method of refrigerating by spraying refrigerant inside of an evaporator or by spraying refrigerated water.

spray pond   a means of cooling condenser water by spraying it into the cooler ambient air. The falling water is then collected in a pond surrounding the spray.

spread   this is the maximum width of the air pattern at terminal velocity. It is measured in feet.

spreader burner   a low-pressure gas burner which uses venturi action to introduce part of the air required for combustion. The venturi delivers the air/fuel mixture to a large vertical port, where a spreader plate spreads the flame toward the outside wall of the combustion chamber. Also called a large port burner. Also see *inspirating* and *partial premix burners*.

spring benders   springs that are designed to be slipped over tubing to completely cover the area of the bend and to prevent kinking.

spring-loaded relief valve   a class of pressure valves employing a preloaded spring. The valve opens when the spring tension is exceeded and automatically closes when the pressure falls below a preset value.

spring range   the range through which the signal applied must change to produce total movement of the controlled device from one extreme position to the other.

spring return actuator   an actuator which is automatically driven to the closed position by a spring mechanism when power is removed. Also see *actuator*.

SPT-1 type cord   a 300-maximum-volt cord that has a temperature range of +32°F to +140°F. It is a light-duty or general-duty cord used for lamps, speakers, and appliances.

SPT-2 type cord   a 300-maximum-volt cord that has a temperature range of +32°F to +140°F. It is a light-duty cord but with heavier construction than SPT-1 cord and used for lamps, speakers, and appliances.

SPT-3 type cord   a 300-maximum-volt cord that has a temperature range of +32°F to +140°F. It is a medium-duty cord but with heavier construction than SPT-2 cord and used for tools, major appliances, fans, and motors.

spud   see *orifice spud*.

square   to machine, cut, or make at a right angle. A geometric figure with four equal length sides and four 90° angles.

square (units)   refers to a measurement of two dimensions, length and width.

square feet of steam   refers to the rating of the radiators to be used in a steam heating system.

square foot of heating surface or radiation   equivalent direct radiation (EDR). The amount of heating surface that will emit 240 Btu per hour when supplied with 215°F steam and surrounded by air at 70°F. The equivalent square foot of heating surface may have no direct relation to the actual surface area.

square head cock   a type of valve often used as a balancing valve. In place of the valve handle, the stem is made square. A wrench is used to adjust the valve setting.

square mil   the area of a square one mil by one mil.

squirrel cage blower   a fan which has blades parallel to the fan axis and moves air at right angles or perpendicular to fan axis.

squirrel cage rotor   a solid rotor, used in AC induction motors, which has round metal conductors joined together at the ends and placed inside the laminated metal motor core.

squirrel cage winding   a permanently short-circuited winding, usually uninsulated and chiefly used in induction motors, having its conductors uniformly distributed around the periphery and joined by continuous end rings. This secondary circuit is usually called the rotor.

ST-type cord   a 600-maximum-volt cord that has a temperature range of 0°F to +140°F. It is a heavy-duty, general-purpose cord, used for motors, power tools, construction equipment, and portable lighting.

stability   the quality of a burner that enables it to remain lit over a wide range of fuel/air mixture ratios when its surroundings are at room temperature.

stable unchanging or not subject to change.

stable atom an atom that will not release electrons under normal conditions.

stable flame a flame envelope that retains its form and continuity over the entire range of firing rates (low fire, high fire, and modulating) for a burner.

stack one or several flues or pipes arranged to let the products of combustion escape to the outside; a single smoke pipe or chimney. The thickness of the stator.

stack control see *stack switch*.

stack effect the difference in pressure in a building due to the difference between the building temperature and the outside ambient temperature.

stack height the height of a gravity convector between the bottom of the heating unit and the top of the outlet opening.

stack loss see *flue gas loss*.

stack smoke detector a smoke detector mounted on a stack to monitor the smoke produced by a boiler, oven, or furnace. The sensor consists of a photocell mounted on the stack opposite a light source. An alarm relay pulls in whenever smoke opacity exceeds a preset level or if the light source burns out.

stack switch a combustion-monitoring device used with oil burners. If the temperature in the vent does not attain the required temperature, ignition failure is assumed and the switch interrupts the circuit to the burner.

stack thermometer a high-temperature thermometer used to measure the heat of the furnace exhaust gases.

stage a level of operating capacity for a component or system.

stage differential the change in temperature at the thermostat needed to turn heating or cooling equipment off once it is turned on.

staged system a system that has more than one mode of heating or cooling operation.

staging interval the minimum time period for shedding or restoring two sequential loads.

staging thermostat a thermostat that is designed to open and close more than one set of contacts to control several modes of heating or cooling operation.

stand-alone system any control system that performs all control functions without direction from any other unit.

stand by an additional machine which is used as a substitute in times of emergency.

standard air see *standard conditions*.

standard air density .075 pounds per cubic foot. Equivalent to dry air at 70°F and at sea level. 1/13.33 cubic foot.

standard atmosphere a condition where air is at 14.7 psia pressure at 59°F, a pressure of 29.92 inches of Hg, and a relative humidity of 30%.

standard conditions used as a basis for air-conditioning calculations. These are a temperature of 68°F, a pressure of 29.92 inches of Hg, a specific volume of 13.33 cubic foot, a specific density of .075 pounds per cubic foot, and a relative humidity of 30%.

standard cubic feet per minute the volume of air delivered by a compressor or required by a pneumatic tool.

standard marks marks on either side of a threader indicating the exact position for the change plate. If deeper threads are required, the change plate is positioned above the standard marks. If shallower threads are required, the change plate is positioned below the standard marks.

standby the state or condition of equipment which will permit complete resumption of stable operation within a short period of time. The state of a flame safeguard control while awaiting a call for heat; power is available at the control, but the operating sequence has not yet begun.

standing pilot gas burner ignition system in which a pilot flame remains lit between cycles of on/off burner operation.

standing pressure test method of leak detection that involves pressurizing the system and testing the following day to determine if pressure loss has occurred.

star transformer a three-phase transformer that has the ends of the windings connected to a common point. The star transformer produces a balance of all hot legs to ground.

star winding a winding layout of some three-phase motors in which the ends of the windings are connected together.

start capacitor an electric device that is used to store electrons momentarily, creating a second phase in starting windings of single-phase motors. This type of capacitor is designed to stay in the circuit only a short period of time.

start interlock an interlock which proves a condition is proper for burner start-up. If it is open, the burner cannot be started. It may be a valve-closed interlock, damper position indicator (low- or high-fire proving switch), fuel pressure switch, electrical start switch, or oil preheater controller.

start relay a normally closed potential relay used to disconnect either the start capacitor or the start winding once the motor comes up to speed and generates sufficient back emf.

start/stop station a control panel at which the operator can manually turn on or turn off remote electric equipment.

start winding a winding in an electric motor used only during a brief period when the motor is starting.

starter a motor energizing switch with an overload cutout that can be reset.

starting holding coil circuit the circuit in a magnetic starter that is energized when the start button is pressed to close the main contacts and which remains energized as long as the main current flows through the starter to the motor.

starting screwdriver a tool used to help put in or take out screws. Some have twisting centers or magnetized ends. Once the screw has been started, a common screwdriver should be used.

starting switch, centrifugal a centrifugally operating switch usually used in connection with split-phase and capacitor-start motors to open or disconnect the starting winding circuit after the rotor has attained a predetermined speed, and to close or reconnect it prior to the time the rotor comes to rest.

starting torque the amount of turning force produced by a motor as it begins to turn from a stopped position.

starved coil an evaporator that is receiving insufficient refrigerant and developing excessive superheat.

state, gaseous one of three states or phases of matter; characterized by greatest freedom of molecules and a lack of any inherent fixed shape or volume.

state, liquid one of three states or phases of matter; characterized by limited freedom of molecules and by substantial incompressibility.

state, solid one of the three states or phases of matter; characterized by stability of dimensions, relative incompressibility, and molecular motion held to limited oscillation.

static balancing balancing without rotation or knife-edge balancing.

static charge an electrical charge that is bound to an object. An unmoving electrical charge.

static checkout tests tests performed on a flame safeguard system before mounting the flame safeguard control and without operating the burner to ensure correct wiring and proper operation of external controllers, limits, interlocks, valves, transformers, and motors.

static discharge head   vertical distance (in feet) from pump to point of discharge.

static electricity   electricity that results from electrons being displaced and not returning to the original atoms; usually results from friction.

static head   the pressure due to the weight of a fluid in a vertical column or, more generally, the resistance due to lift.

static pressure   the pressure which tends to burst a pipe. It is used to overcome the frictional resistance to flow through the pipe. Expressed as a unit of pressure, it may be given in either absolute or gauge pressure. It is frequently expressed in feet of water column or (in the case of pipe friction) in mil-inch of water column per foot of pipe.

stationary blade compressor   a rotary pump which uses a blade inside the pump to separate the intake chamber from the exhaust chamber.

stator   that portion of the motor on which the coils are wound.

status indicator   a PC card, which is optional, whose function it is to give a visual readout of the operating or failure modes of a cuber at a glance.

steam   water in the vapor phase or state. The vapor formed when water has been heated to its boiling point, corresponding to the pressure it is under.

steam-atomizing oil burner   see *atomizing oil burner.*

steam, dry saturated   steam at the saturation temperature corresponding to the pressure, and containing no water in suspension.

steam generator   see *packaged boiler.*

steam heating system   a heating system in which the heating units give up their heat to the room by condensing the steam furnished to them by a boiler or other source.

steam jet refrigeration   a refrigeration system which uses a steam venturi to create a high vacuum (low pressure) on a water container causing water to evaporate at low temperature.

steam, superheated   steam at a temperature higher than the saturation temperature corresponding to the pressure.

steam trap   an automatic valve which traps air but allows condensate to pass while preventing passage of steam.

steam, wet saturated   steam at the saturation temperature corresponding to the pressure, and containing water particles in suspension.

Stellite   trade name for a very hard metal alloy.

stem   that part of a service or globe valve that is turned to open or close the valve.

stem travel   the movement of a valve stem along the axis of its stroke.

step-down transformer   a transformer that has a secondary voltage lower than its primary voltage.

step-up transformer   a transformer that has a secondary voltage higher than its primary voltage.

stepped-down voltage   a voltage decrease produced by a transformer with more windings in its primary than in its secondary.

stepped-up voltage   a voltage increase produced by a transformer with more windings in its secondary than its primary.

stepper motor   a motor which provides precise control by operating in a series of steps, as dictated by an external temperature sensor.

stethoscope   an instrument used to detect sounds.

stick-tight nozzle   a nozzle designed to hold the flame on the nozzle rather than floating in front of it. This is necessary in premix burners since the rate of flame propagation is high due to the lean mixture used. Also see *flame retention nozzle.*

stinger leg   a high-voltage wire from a three-phase delta transformer.

stoichiometric air/fuel ratio   the air/fuel ratio which results in complete burning without excess air. Also see *perfect combustion.*

stoker   a machine used to supply a furnace with coal.

stoker combustion rate   this rate is expressed in terms of the number of pounds of fuel or the Btu developed per square foot of stoker grate area per hour.

storage battery   another term used for lead acid secondary cells.

storage capacity   the volume of fluid which may be safely stored in a vessel such as a receiver.

straight-blade   the straight blade (or standard) screwdriver is the most popular screwdriver. There are two types of standard screwdrivers, the keystone and the cabinet bit. The main difference between them is the way the tips are ground.

straight drill   this drill is the most popular and useful. It is generally lightweight and can be used in almost any location. Has a drill angle of 118°.

straight-through valve   a valve with one inlet and one outlet. A fluid entering the inlet port flows straight through to the outlet port. It can be a two-position valve or a modulating valve. Also called a two-way valve.

straight-tube boiler   see *water-tube boiler.*

strain relief   a device which firmly attaches the power cord to the appliance.

strainer   a device such as a screen or filter used to retain solid particles while liquid passes through. Does not contain a desiccant material.

strand   a single uninsulated conductor.

stranded conductor   a conductor of several strands of solid wire twisted together. Standard cables have 7, 19, and 37 strands.

strap-type pipe wrench   a wrench that has a nylon strap attached so that it allows the strap to be tightened around the pipe and tightened without marring the pipe.

stratification of air   a condition in which there is little or no air movement in a room. Air lies in different temperature layers.

stratosphere   the atmosphere between 7 and 30 miles above the earth where a layer of ozone filters out harmful ultraviolet light.

street elbow   an elbow fitting that is threaded internally at one end and externally at the other.

stress   the resultant internal force that resists change in the size or shape of a body acted on by external forces.

strike   door part of a door latch.

striker   this is a device such as a friction lighter that is used to light a torch.

stroboscope   a light-emitting device that can be adjusted to the speed of a rotating shaft to make it appear to stand still. The dial reads in rpm so the speed can be instantly noted.

stroke   a single movement of a piston, stem, or crank arm from one end of its range to the other. For a reciprocating engine, a stroke constitutes a half revolution of the engine and equals twice its crank radius.

stubby   describes a short screwdriver used to work in small or hard-to-fit places.

stubs   short copper or copper coated steel pipes welded or brazed into openings in the housing of a hermetic compressor for attaching tubing or valves.

stud   bolt extending from the front or rear of a device, such as a motor, by which it is mounted. Often used on small, direct-drive fans and blowers.

stuffing box a packing gland surrounding a shaft, stem, or rod to prevent leakage.

STW-A type cord a 600-maximum-volt cord that has a temperature range of 0°F to +140°F. It is a heavy-duty, general-purpose cord that is UL listed for outdoor use and used for motors, power tools, construction equipment, and portable lighting.

S-type cord a 600-maximum-volt cord that has a temperature range of –40°F to +140°F. It is a heavy-duty, general-purpose cord used for machine tools, motors, drills, and power tools.

subbase see *wiring subbase*.

subcooled term that describes a substance at a temperature that is below its saturation point.

subcooling cooling a liquid below its saturation temperature corresponding to the pressure. Subcooling is measured by comparing the temperature of the liquid line to what the liquid temperature would ordinarily be at the measured discharge pressure.

subcooling coil a supplementary coil in an evaporative condenser, usually a coil or loop immersed in the spray water tank, that reduces the temperature of the liquid leaving the condenser.

sublimation a condition where a substance changes from a solid to a gas without becoming a liquid, thus skipping a change of state.

submaster controller a controller whose set point is reset by a master controller.

submerged vertical boiler see *fire-tube boiler*.

submersible motor a motor whose housing is designed so that the motor can run completely submerged under water.

substance any form of matter or material.

substation a station in a power transmission system in which electrical power is transformed into a conveniently used form. The station may consist of transformers, switches, circuit breakers, and other auxiliary equipment.

subsystem a number of systems which operate independently but are commonly linked to a higher level controller.

suction gas the refrigerant vapor in an operating refrigeration system found in the tubing from the evaporator to the compressor and in the compressor shell.

suction lift a situation where the liquid source is lower than the pump. Pumping action creates a partial vacuum and atmospheric pressure forces liquid up to the pump. Theoretical limit of suction lift is 34 feet; practical limit is 25 feet or less, depending on pump type and elevation above sea level.

suction line tube or pipe used to carry refrigerant gas from the evaporator outlet to the compressor inlet.

suction line accumulator a device (sometimes an accessory) used to prevent liquid floodback from entering the compressor.

suction manifold a device to distribute suction gas equally from a common suction line to multiple compressors connected in parallel.

suction pressure refrigerant pressure on the low side of the refrigeration system. Generally speaking, it is the pressure between the metering device and the compressor inlet. Also called back pressure, low-side pressure, or crankcase pressure.

suction pressure control valve a device located in the suction line which maintains constant pressure in the evaporator during the running portion of the cycle.

suction riser a vertical tube or pipe that carries suction gas from an evaporator on a lower level to a compressor on a higher level.

suction service valve a two-way manually operated valve, located at the inlet to the compressor, which controls suction gas flow and is used to service the unit.

suction side   low-pressure side of the system extending from the refrigerant metering device through the evaporator to the inlet of the compressor.

suction temperature   the boiling temperature of the refrigerant corresponding to the suction pressure of the refrigerant.

suction-type mixer   see *aspirator mixer*.

suction valve   a valve which controls the flow of refrigerant from the suction line into the compressor cylinder head.

sulfur content   manufacturers of fuel oil keep the sulfur content of fuel oils as low as possible. Sulfur in fuel oil becomes a pollutant when it is burned. For a fuel oil to receive a Grade 1 rating, it can have no more than 0.5% sulfur. Grade 2 fuels can have no more than 1.0% sulfur.

sulfur dioxide   see *R-764*.

sump   a storage or collecting tank for liquids.

sun effect   solar energy transmitted into space through windows and building materials.

superheat   the temperature of vapor above its boiling point, or the difference between the temperature at the evaporator outlet and the converted temperature of the refrigerant evaporating in the evaporator. For example, with a refrigerant gas temperature of 50°F and an evaporating temperature of 40°F, the superheat would be 10°F.

superheat switch   this is a normally closed safety switch. It stops the compressor if the system is low on refrigerant.

superheated vapor   a gas that has been heated to a temperature that is above its boiling point as a liquid at the existing pressure.

superheater   a heat exchanger arranged to cool liquid going to the evaporator; this heat is used to superheat the vapor leaving the evaporator.

supervise   to monitor a condition requiring attention and initiate corrective action if necessary.

supervisory control   a higher level manual or automatic control (central or network) of a normally stand-alone control system.

supervisory fuel cock   a manually operated plug cock, used for shutting off fuel, which has an electric interlock. Its primary purpose is to minimize the hazard of lighting off manually ignited multiburner equipment.

supply   a fuel or water line flowing into a component. A water line or air duct carrying heated or cooled fluid to the conditioned space for heat transfer.

supply air   the conditioned air being supplied to the occupied space.

supply air ducts   ducts that carry the conditioned air to the conditioned space. May be square, rectangular, round, or oval, and made of metal or fiberglass.

supply branch   the piping used to supply heated water or air from a main, circuit main, or trunk to the terminal unit or diffuser.

supply main   the pipe used to distribute water from a boiler, or conditioned air to the supply branches.

supply piping   that portion of the piping system that carries water from the boiler to the terminal units or to the point of use.

supply tank   a tank connected directly to oil burning equipment.

supply tapping   the opening in a boiler into which the supply main is connected.

supply voltage   the energy source supplied to the controller and/or auxiliary device.

surface plate   a tool with a very accurate, flat surface that is used for measuring purposes and for lapping flat surfaces.

surge   the modulating action of temperature or pressure before it reaches its final value or setting.

surge, electrical   a transient variation in the current or voltage at a point in the circuit. Surges are generally unwanted and temporary.

surge tank   a container connected to a refrigerating system which increases gas volume and reduces rate of pressure change.

SVT-type cord   a 300-maximum-volt cord that has a temperature range of 0°F to +140°F. It is a heavy-duty, general-purpose flexible cord, used for vacuum cleaners and office equipment.

swage   the process of enlarging one tube end so that the end of another tube of the same size will fit within.

swaged joint   the joining of two pieces of copper tubing by expanding or stretching the end of one piece of tubing to fit over the other piece.

swaging tool   a tool used to enlarge a piece of tubing for solder or braze connection.

swamp cooler   evaporative-type cooler in which air is drawn through porous mats soaked with water. The efficiency of this machine is dependent upon the wet bulb temperature.

swash plate (wobble plate)   device used to change rotary motion to reciprocating motion, used in some refrigeration compressors.

sweat fitting   a metal fitting with close tolerances that is joined by sweating.

sweat fittings   a tinning process where the tubing is coated with a thin layer of solder, joined, then heated until both layers of solder fuse.

sweating   (1) condensation of moisture from air on cold surfaces. (2) Method of soldering in which the parts to be joined are first coated with a thin layer of solder.

sweet water   a term sometimes used to describe tap water.

sweet water brine   water with a freezing point of 32°F.

swing space   room needed to turn a nut or bolt.

swinging armature   an armature used in a contactor that is mounted on a line and moves up and down in a swinging motion.

switch   a mechanical or electrical device that makes or breaks contacts to either complete or open an electrical circuit; may be automatic or manual. Also see *interlock;* and *airflow, lockout, low oil temperature, master, pressure, sail,* and *valve-closed indication switches.* Typical switches are: normally open (N/O) - a contact pair which is open when the device is in the de-energized position; normally closed (N/C) - a contact pair which is closed when the device is in the de-energized position.

switch, auxiliary   an accessory switch available for most damper motors and control operators that can be arranged to open or close an electric circuit whenever the control motor reaches a certain position.

switch configuration   the terms pole and throw in combination with the terms single and double are used to describe the action of electric switches. A single-pole switch has functionally one movable contact. A double-pole switch has two. A single-throw switch can connect to only one circuit or one fixed contact. A double-throw switch can connect a common lead to either of two circuits or two different fixed contacts. These features are usually abbreviated SPST—single-pole, single-throw; SPDT—single-pole, double-throw, etc.

switch, disconnect   a switch usually provided for a motor that completely disconnects the piece of equipment from the power source.

switch, flow   control installed in the liquid circuit. Used to prevent operation of the unit when the liquid flow is not up to the required rate.

switch, mode   the position selector switch on the zone thermostat that selects the type of operation of the system. These positions are cooling, off, heating, auto, and emergency heat.

switching relay   device that operates by a variation in the conditions of one electrical circuit to affect the operation of devices in the same (or another) circuit. Used to increase switching capability and isolate electrical circuits. Also provides for electrical interlocks within a system.

symbol   letter or picture representing some part of an electric circuit, an electrical device, or component.

symptom   a characteristic of a machine's performance that indicates a malfunction.

synchronous motor   an AC motor that operates at a constant speed regardless of the load applied.

synchronous speed   the speed of the rotating magnetic field set up by the stator of an induction motor. In a synchronous motor the rotor locks into step with the rotating magnetic field. To determine synchronous speed the formula cycles (Hz) × 120/the number of poles is used.

synthetic dust weight arrestance   a measurement of a filter's ability to remove synthetic dust from test air.

synthetic rubber, neoprene   a soft, resilient material made of a synthetic chemical compound.

syphon seal   a corrugated metal tubing used to hold a seal ring and provide a leakproof connection between the seal ring and compressor body or shaft.

system   a set or arrangement of components so related or connected as to form a unity or organized whole; a collection of consecutive operations and procedures required to accomplish a specific objective. Also see *automatic, closed-circuit oil, conductivity flame rod, dead end/line, flame detection,* *flame safeguard, manual, multiburner, rectification,* and *semiautomatic system.*

system analysis   method to evaluate trade-offs among envelope components and heating, ventilating, and air-conditioning equipment such that the building's annual energy cost does not exceed a value specified by a building that meets the prescriptive requirements of the standard.

system-dependent recovery equipment   equipment that makes use of an appliance's own components to remove refrigerant from the appliance.

system, forced circulation   a heating, air-conditioning, or refrigerating system in which the heating or cooling fluid circulation is caused by a fan or pump.

system, gravity circulation   a heating or refrigerating system in which the heating or cooling fluid circulation is caused by the motive head due to difference in densities of cooler and warmer fluids in the two sides of the system.

system lag   the difference in temperature between the point at which the thermostat closes and the point at which the thermostat starts to rise or fall.

system temperature   the average of the temperatures of the water leaving the boiler and the water returning to the boiler.

T

td   temperature difference.

teao   totally enclosed, air-over.

tefc   totally enclosed, fan-cooled.

TEMA   Tubular Exchanger Manufacturers Association.

tenv   totally enclosed, non-ventilated.

THHN   a 90°C 600-volt wire.

THWN   a 75°C 600-volt wire.

TIEQ   Total Indoor Environmental Quality Coalition.

tlc   total load change.

tlv   threshold limit value.

TSARC   Thermal Storage Applications Research Center.

TXV   thermostatic expansion valve.

tachometer   a device which measures or records the speed or velocity of a motor in revolutions per minute.

tagout   the practice of placing tags on all operational switches to inform others that repairs are in process.

tail pipe   outlet pipe from the evaporator.

tang   a prong on a chisel or file that fits into a shaft or handle.

tank, supply   separate tank connected directly or by a pump to an oil-burning appliance.

tankless water heater   a heat exchanger that heats service hot water as used and therefore does not employ a storage tank. Also called an instantaneous heater.

tap-a-line   a device used to puncture or tap a line where there is no service access. Sometimes referred to as a saddle valve or piecing valve.

tap drill   a drill used to form a hole prior to placing threads in the hole. The drill is the size of the root diameter of the tap threads.

tap, electrical   a method of obtaining or drawing current from a circuit.

tap, mechanical   a device to thread the inside of a pipe or fitting.

tapered   a piece of material that increases or decreases in size at a consistent rate.

taps   on a multispeed motor, wires or terminals that make it possible to select the number of poles being used.

tare weight   the weight of a container or cylinder before being filled.

technician (as defined under Section 608 of EPA)   anyone who performs mainte-nance, service, or repair operations that could reasonably be expected to release Class I or Class II substances from appli-ances into the atmosphere. Technicians may be installers, contractor employees, in-house service personnel, or owners.

tee   a T-shaped fitting that connects three lengths of pipe or tubing at right angles to each other.

teflon   a synthetic rubber material used for O-rings, pipe thread compound, and slide valve mechanisms.

temperature   the degree or intensity of hot-ness or coldness of anything as measured by a thermometer. The measurement of the intensity or speed of molecular motion. Also see *ambient* and *ignition temperature*.

temperature, absolute   temperature expressed in degrees above absolute zero.

temperature, absolute zero   the zero point on the absolute temperature scale, 459.69° below the zero of the Fahrenheit scale, 273.16° below the zero of the Centi-grade scale.

temperature, ambient   the temperature of the air around the object under consideration.

temperature coefficient of resistivity   the amount of resistance change of a mater-ial per degree of temperature rise.

temperature, condensing   the tempera-ture of the fluid in the condenser at the time of condensation.

temperature, critical   the saturation tem-perature corresponding to the critical state of the substance at which the properties of the liquid and vapor are identical.

temperature, dew point   the temperature at which the condensation of water vapor in a space begins for the given state of humidity and pressure as the temperature of the vapor is reduced. The temperature corresponding to saturation (100% humidity) for a given absolute humidity at constant pressure.

temperature difference   the number of degrees between two temperatures; determines the speed of heat transfer from the hotter to the colder substance.

temperature, discharge   the temperature of the gas leaving the compressor.

temperature drop   a measurement of the difference in heat between two points of a system, such as at the furnace plenum and the outlet grille.

temperature, dry bulb   the temperature of the air measured with an ordinary thermometer. It indicates only sensible heat changes.

temperature, effective   an arbitrary index which combines into a single value the effect of temperature, humidity, and air movement on the sensation of warmth or cold felt by the human body. The numerical value is that of the temperature of still, saturated air which would induce an identical sensation.

temperature, entering   the temperature of a substance as it enters a piece of equipment.

temperature, evaporating   the temperature at which a fluid boils under the existing pressure.

temperature, final   the temperature of a substance as it leaves a piece of equipment.

temperature glide   a range of condensing or evaporating temperatures for one pressure. Found in blended or ternary refrigerants.

temperature-humidity index   an index that combines dry bulb and wet bulb temperatures to estimate human response to the environment.

temperature, mean radiant   the temperature of a uniform black enclosure in which a solid body or occupant would exchange the same amount of radiant heat as in the existing nonuniform environment.

temperature range   the specific span of temperatures within which safety or operating controls are designed to operate.

temperature-regulated valve   a valve that is open or closed, depending upon the temperature of the fluid it controls.

temperature rise   the amount of heat a motor generates above ambient, or the temperature difference between the supply and return air temperatures.

temperature, room   temperature of any room, as for example (1) a room in which a refrigerator is being operated or tested; (2) a room being conditioned for the comfort of occupants. Used colloquially to mean ordinary temperature one is accustomed to find in dwellings.

temperature, saturation   the boiling point of a refrigerant at a given pressure. It is considered to be the evaporator temperature in refrigeration.

temperature-sensing bulb   bulb containing a fluid and bellows or diaphragm. Temperature increase on the bulb causes the bellows or diaphragm to expand.

temperature, suction   the temperature of the gas as it enters the compressor.

temperature, wet bulb   the temperature of the air measured with a thermometer having a bulb covered with a wetted wick.

temperature, wet bulb depression   the difference between the wet bulb and the dry bulb temperatures.

tensile strength   a term denoting the greatest longitudinal tensile stress a substance can bear without tearing apart or rupturing.

terminal   a point on an electrical device where connections may be made.

terminal connectors   small metal ends of varying size and shape that crimp onto the wires to make connections simpler and faster.

terminal reheat system   centralized blower and cooling system that supplies cool air to multiple zones. Each zone contains a hot water coil or electric heater that reheats the cooled supply air as determined by the zone thermostat.

terminal unit   a radiator, conveyor, or the like that heats the conditioned space by transferring heat carried by hot water or steam.

terminal velocity   the velocity of an airstream, in feet per minute, at the end of its throw.

terminate   to end an action or sequence of events such as a defrost cycle or employment.

ternary   having three elements, parts, or divisions.

test charge   an amount of refrigerant vapor forced into a refrigeration system to test for leaks.

test cord   an electrical cord that supplies current directly to the compressor terminals for testing and service purposes.

test dial, gas supply meter   one of the recording dials that indicate a quantity of gas per revolution of the dial.

test light   a light provided with test leads used to test or probe electrical circuits to determine their condition.

tests   procedures for determining the manner in which equipment is functioning, or for determining the existence, type, and location of any trouble. See *hot refractory hold-in, hot refractory saturation, ignition interference, ignition spark response, pilot turndown, safety shutdown,* and *static checkout tests.*

theoretical combustion   see *perfect combustion.*

therm   a quantity of heat equivalent to 100,000 Btu (25,200 kcal).

thermal   having to do with heat.

thermal aging   exposure to a given thermal condition or a programmed series of conditions for prescribed periods of time.

thermal alloying   the act of uniting two different metals to make one common metal by the use of heat.

thermal balance point   the lowest outdoor temperature at which the heat pump can supply 100% of the heating required for the space.

thermal bulb   a sealed probe charged with a fluid that expands or contracts when heated or cooled; used to sense remote temperatures.

thermal capacity   the capacity of a substance for storing heat. It is expressed in the amount of heat required to raise the temperature of a substance a given amount or to change its state—such as from liquid to vapor.

thermal conductivity   the ability of a given substance to conduct heat. The thermal conductivity is the reciprocal of the thermal resistance.

thermal cutout   an overcurrent device which protects the circuit during excessive heating conditions.

thermal delay relay   a relay that prevents short cycling of compressor by delaying the thermostat's call for cooling for several seconds.

thermal efficiency   the output of a machine (expressed in Btu) divided by the input (expressed in Btu).

thermal energy   heat. Measured in calories or Btu.

thermal expansion   the expansion of a material when subjected to heat.

thermal head   the head produced by the difference in the weight of the heated water in the supply side of the system and the cooler water in the return side. This is the only head available to cause circulation of water in a gravity system.

thermal internal   the tendency of a substance to resist temperature changes.

thermal mass   material with significant heat capacity and surface area that affects building loads by absorbing or releasing heat, or both, due to the fluctuation of any of the following: (1) interior temperature; (2) interior radiant conditions; (3) exterior temperature; (4) exterior radiant conditions.

thermal mass wall insulation position   (1) exterior insulation position - describes a wall having mass thermally coupled directly to the room air and having the entire effective mass layer on the interior of an insulation layer. (2) Integral insulation position - wall having mass thermally coupled to room air and having either insulation and mass materials well mixed, as in wood (logs), or substantially equal amounts of mass material on the interior and exterior of insulation, as in concrete blocks with insulated cores. (3) Interior insulation position - wall having mass located on the exterior of the insulating material(s) or otherwise not meeting either of the above definitions for exterior or integral positions.

thermal overload   an overload device that senses the current draw of a load by the heat produced, which is proportional to the current draw.

thermal overload element   the alloy piece used for holding an overload relay closed. It melts when the current draw is too great.

thermal protector   a protective device built into motors which protects them from overheating due to overload or failure to start. Basic types are automatic reset and manual reset. With the automatic reset type, when the motor cools, the protector automatically restores power. Automatic reset protective devices should not be used where unexpected restarting would be hazardous. The manual-reset type is equipped with an external button that must be pushed to restore power to the motor. Recommended where unexpected restarting could be hazardous, such as saws, conveyors, etc.

thermal radiation   the transmission of heat from a hot surface to a cooler one in the form of invisible electromagnetic waves, which, on being absorbed by the cooler surface, raise the temperature of that surface.

thermal rating   the maximum and/or minimum temperature at which a material will perform its function without undue degradation.

thermal relay (hot-wire relay)   an electrical control used to activate a refrigeration system. This system uses a wire to convert electrical energy into heat energy.

thermal resistance   the change in the electrical resistance of a material when subjected to heat. Resistance to heat flow from conductors to outer surface of insulation or sheath in a wire or cable.

thermal resistivity   thermal resistance of a unit cube of material.

thermal timer   a device which will actuate one or more switches when heated bimetal warps sufficiently.

thermistor   a solid-state device whose electrical resistance varies with temperature. Its temperature coefficient of resistance is high, nonlinear, and negative. Also see *posistor*.

thermocouple   a device for measuring temperature consisting of two electrical conductors of dissimilar metals joined at a point, called the hot junction, and where a voltage proportional to the temperature is developed across the output. This volt's open circuit (VOC) voltage is usually 18-30 millivolts. One type of thermocouple is used in pilot safety systems to prove the existence of a pilot flame.

thermocouple lead wire   similar to thermocouple wire except that the degree of accuracy in temperature measurements is not as high and it is used to transmit thermocouple information to remote indicators.

thermocouple thermometer   an electrical instrument which uses a thermocouple as a source of electrical flow that is connected to a milliammeter calibrated in temperature degrees.

thermocouple wire   a two-conductor cable, each conductor employing a dissimilar metal, made specifically for temperature measurements.

thermodisk defrost control   an electrical switch with a bimetal disk which is controlled by electrical energy.

thermodynamics   the science which deals with mechanical action or relations of heat.

thermodynamics, laws of   two laws on which rest the classical theory of thermodynamics. These laws have been stated in many different, but equivalent ways. The first law: (1) when work is expended in generating heat, the quantity of heat produced is proportional to the work expended; and conversely, when heat is employed in the performance of work, the quantity of heat which disappears is proportional to the work done (Joule); (2) if a system is caused to change from an initial state to a final state by adiabatic means only, the work done is the same for all adiabatic paths connecting the two states (Zemansky); (3) in any power cycle or refrigeration cycle the net heat absorbed by the working substance is exactly equal to the net work done. The second law: (1) it is impossible for a self-acting machine, unaided by any external agency, to convey heat from a body of lower temperature to one of higher temperature (Clausius); (2) it is impossible to derive mechanical work from heat taken from a body unless there is available a body of lower temperature into which the residue not so used may be discharged (Kelvin); (3)

it is impossible to construct an engine that, operating in a cycle, will produce no effect other than the extraction of heat from a reservoir and the performance of an equivalent amount of work (Zemansky).

thermoelectric refrigeration   a refrigeration mechanism which depends on the Peltier effect. Direct current flowing through an electrical junction between dissimilar metals provides a heating or cooling effect, depending on the direction of current flow.

thermomastic   a type of material that has a high heat-absorbing ability. Used to prevent overheating of a device when making solder or brazed-type connections.

thermometer   a device for measuring the intensity of heat. May be dial, spirit, or electronic type.

thermometer bulb   the rounded lower end of a thermometer.

thermometer, digital   a thermometer that uses solid-state circuitry and direct reading digital numbers for temperature readouts. These thermometers are easier to read and are more accurate than ordinary spirit or column-type thermometers.

thermometer, stack temperature   a thermometer with a range of 200°F to 1000°F used to measure the temperature of the flue products from fossil-fuel-type heating units.

thermometer well   a pocket or recess in a system, designed to hold a thermometer bulb; a temperature test point.

thermometry   the measurement of heat.

thermomodule   a number of thermocouples used in a parallel circuit to achieve low temperatures.

thermopile   a number of thermocouples connected in series in a single unit (all the hot junctions are heated together), producing a much higher voltage than the individual thermocouples, usually in the range of

500–750 millivolts. Some types may be used as sources of electrical energy.

thermoplastic   insulation that will resoften and distort from its formed shape by being heated above a critical temperature peculiar to the material.

thermostat   an automatic controller that responds to temperature changes to maintain the temperature within predetermined limits.

thermostat, defrost   a thermostat mounted on the outdoor coil that initiates or terminates the defrost cycle when the temperature of the coil reaches the preset cut-in/cutout set points of the control.

thermostat, direct-acting   an instrument for activating a control circuit upon sensing a predetermined low temperature.

thermostat, modulating   a temperature controller that employs a potentiometer winding instead of switch contacts.

thermostat, on-and-off   a thermostat designed to open or close an electric circuit in response to a temperature change.

thermostat, operating   a thermostat that controls the operating temperature of a device.

thermostat, outdoor   a control used to limit the amount of auxiliary electric heat according to the outdoor ambient temperature to reduce electrical surges and cost.

thermostat, reverse-acting   an instrument for activating a control circuit upon sensing a predetermined high temperature.

thermostat, room   a thermostat properly located in a room so as to respond to representative room temperature and thereby control heating or cooling devices.

thermostat, safety   a thermostat that automatically limits the temperature of an appliance.

thermostat, subbase   when installed with a thermostat, it permits selection of function

of heating, cooling, automatic changeover, emergency heat, continuous fan operation, or off position.

thermostatic control   a device which operates a system or part of a system based on temperature changes.

thermostatic expansion valve   a control valve operated by temperature and pressure within the evaporator coil which controls the flow of refrigerant. The power element feeler bulb is attached to the outlet of the evaporator coil. May be internally or externally equalized.

thermostatic motor control   a device used to control the cycling of the unit through the use of a control bulb attached to the evaporator.

thermostatic valve   a valve controlled by thermostatic elements.

thermostatic water valve   a valve used to control the flow of water through the system that is actuated by a temperature difference. Used on units such as water-cooled compressors or condensers.

thread   a spiral groove cut into the outside of a pipe or the inside of a pipe fitting with a similar taper. When inside and outside threads of the same size are joined together properly, they form a leakproof connection.

thread angle   the V-angle of the threads. The sides of the threads normally form a 60° angle.

thread-cutting oil   a lubricating oil used to keep the dies lubricated and cool and to prevent the teeth of dies from breaking. Thread-cutting oil contains a sulfur, lard, or mineral base.

thread joint compound   nonhardening material used on pipe to ensure a tight seal.

threaded rod   metal rod with its entire length threaded. It can easily be cut to any length with a hacksaw.

threader   a device or tool used to cut thread on a piece of pipe.

threads per inch   measurement determined by counting the number of crests (or roots) per inch of threaded section.

three-phase current   operating by means of a combination of three alternating current circuits which differ in phase by one-third of a cycle (120 mechanical degrees). This type of motor can yield high starting and breakdown torques. They are more efficient than single-phase motors, and larger horsepower ratings can be furnished. May be Delta or Wye.

three-phase delta connection system   in wiring, this arrangement employs three wires. Assuming 100 amps and 1000 volts in each phase winding, the pressure between any two conductors is the same as the pressure in the winding, and the current in any conductor is equal to the current in the winding multiplied by the square root of 3, that is $100 \times 1.7321 = 173.21$ amps, or 173 amps.

three-phase, four-wire system   a three-phase, three-wire system having a fourth wire connected to the neutral point of the source, which may be grounded.

three-phase motor   an induction type of motor that has a very high starting torque and requires no special starting apparatus. The motor must be operated on three-phase current. Rotation can be changed by reversing any two leads.

three-way switch   a three-terminal switch in which a circuit may be switched to either of two paths.

three-way valve   see *diverting* and *mixing valves*.

three-wheel cutter   a cutter with three cutter wheels, two of which have replaced the rollers. It is used to cut pipe when complete rotation is impossible.

threshold current   the symmetrical rms-available current at the threshold of the current-limiting range, where the fuse becomes current-limiting when tested to the industry standard. This value can be read off a peak let-through chart. A threshold ratio is the relationship of the threshold current to the fuse's continuous current rating.

threshold limit value (TLV)   a term used by the ACGIH to express the airborne concentration of a material to which nearly all workers can be exposed day after day without adverse effects. "Workers" means healthy individuals. The young, old, ill, or naturally susceptible have lower tolerances and need to take additional precautions. ACGIH expresses TLVs in three ways: (1) TLA-TWA, the allowable time-weighted average concentration for a normal eight-hour workday or forty-hour workweek; (2) TLV-STEL, the short-term exposure limit or maximum concentration for a continuous exposure period of fifteen minutes (with a maximum of four such periods per day, with at least sixty minutes between exposure periods, and provided that the daily TLV/TWA is not exceeded); (3) TLV-C, the ceiling exposure limit or the concentration that should not be exceeded even instantaneously.

throttle   to reduce or cut off fluid flow.

throttling   the expansion of gas through an orifice or controlled opening without the gas performing any work in the expansion process.

throttling range   in proportional controllers the change in a controlled variable required to move the controlled device or devices from one extreme limit of travel to the other.

throttling valve   see *firing rate valve*.

through-the-wall   describes a type of air-conditioning installation in which the unit's chassis is mounted through the outer wall of the building, with the evaporator inside, the condenser outside, and the other components in between.

throw, air   the length of an airstream from the discharge register to the point where its velocity drops below 50 feet per minute.

throw, electrical   movement of the pole (switch) in an electrical device.

throw, mechanical   the distance between the center lines of the crankshaft and the connecting rod journal; the offset in a crankshaft which is equal to half the stroke of the piston.

thrust   the force acting lengthwise along the axis of a shaft either towards or away from it.

thyristor   an electronic component that has only two states of operation: on or off.

tie rods   rods that hold the sections of cast iron sectional boilers in tight contact. They pass entirely through the sections.

tight shutoff   virtually no flow or leakage when the valve is in its closed position. Generally speaking, only single-seated valves have tight shutoff. Double-seated valves can be expected to have 2 to 5% leakage in the closed position.

time-delay fuse   a circuit-interrupting device that permits momentary overcurrent for circuits normally drawing heavy current for a short time. Used for inductive- and capacitive-load circuits.

time-delay relay   a relay in which there is a delay between the time the coil is energized or de-energized and the time when the contacts open or close. Often used to control fans for greater heating or cooling efficiency.

timed trial for ignition   refers to burners (usually oil) using direct spark ignition of the main burner. See *main burner flame-establishing period.*

timed trial for main flame   see *main burner flame-establishing period.*

timed trial for pilot   see *pilot flame-establishing period.*

timed two-position action   a variation of the two-position action in which the on periods are prematurely shortened. Although this may be accomplished by many means, it is usually accomplished in electric room thermostats by means of a heating element which is energized during the on cycle (for heating) and off periods (for cooling).

timeout   on a status indicator, this is a condition caused by a timing circuit that will cut the cuber off, if the ice harvest is not triggered in the amount of time determined by the preset timer adjustment.

timer   a timing device used in a flame safeguard programming control to sequence the operation of a burner system. It consists of an AC synchronous motor driving a series of cams which open or close several sets of switch contacts at predetermined times.

timer clock   a mechanical or electric device used to monitor the actual time of day.

timer cycle   the time required for a complete rotation of the timer in a flame safeguard programming control, excluding the time the timer stops for high-fire or low-fire proving and the run period.

timer, defrost   a timer that operates at the same time as the refrigeration system. After a set period of operating time, the timer trips to initiate a defrost operation if the termination switch is closed.

timer dial   a rotating disk on the end of the timer which shows what sequence period the programming control is in. It enables the operator to determine if the system is operating properly and, in some cases, to move the timer to the proper positions for checkout or troubleshooting.

timer motor   an electric motor which drives a cam that actuates the defrost switch at specific time intervals to begin defrosting of the outdoor coil when a heat pump is in the heating cycle.

timer sequence   the order in which timer functions are performed in a programming control.

timer thermostat   a thermostat control which includes a clock mechanism. Unit automatically controls the room temperature and changes the temperature according to the time of day.

timers   mechanisms used to control on and off times of an electrical circuit.

tin snips   heavy-duty shears for cutting sheet metal.

tinning   the practice of coating a clean soldering iron with molten solder to facilitate further soldering.

tip jack   a single conductor socket which connects to the F terminal of a flame signal amplifier, used for troubleshooting the amplifier and flame relay.

tip speed   the speed of the outer edge of a fan blade or blower.

toggle switch   an electrical circuit control that is opened or closed by flipping a projecting lever.

tolerance   amount of variation or change allowed from a standard accuracy, especially the difference between the allowable maximum and minimum sizes of some mechanical or electrical part. For example, a 50 mfd run capacitor with a tolerance of plus or minus 10% may be from 45 to 55 mfd.

ton of refrigeration   the refrigeration effect equal to the melting of one ton of ice in 24 hours. It may be expressed as 288,000 Btu per 24 hours (2,000 pounds of ice × 144

(latent heat of fusion) or 12,000 Btu per hour or 200 Btu per minute.

ton refrigeration unit   a unit which removes the same amount of heat in 24 hours as the melting of one ton of ice.

torch ignition   manual ignition of a pilot in a semiautomatic system, or manual ignition of the main burner in a manual system.

torque   the force produced by twisting or rotating equipment. Can be measured in foot-pounds (ft/lbs), inch-pounds (in/lbs), ounce-feet (oz/ft), or ounce-inches (oz/in). In motors, the torque values are locked-rotor torque or starting torque, breakdown torque, and pull-up torque. They are defined as follows:

1. Breakdown torque - the maximum torque which a motor will develop with rated voltage applied at rated frequency without an abrupt drop in speed.
2. Locked-rotor torque - the minimum torque which a motor will develop at standstill, with rated voltage applied at rated frequency. Also called starting torque or breakaway.
3. Pull-up torque - the minimum torque developed by an alternating current motor during the period of acceleration from standstill to the speed at which breakdown torque occurs with rated voltage applied at rated frequency.

torque, full-load   maximum torque delivered without overheating.

torque, stall   torque developed when starting.

torque, starting   amount of torque available, when at 0 rpm, to start and accelerate the load.

torque wrench   a special wrench which may be used to measure the torque or pressure applied to a nut or bolt head.

torr   a unit of pressure equal to $1/760$ atmosphere or approximately 1 mm of mercury.

total air   the total amount of air supplied to a burner. It is the sum of primary, secondary, and excess air.

total charge   the amount of refrigerant needed for a system's operation, plus the refrigerant needed to fill the lines.

total cooling capacity   the combined latent and sensible heat removal abilities of a cooling unit. It is expressed in Btu/h at standard rating conditions as specified by the American Society of Refrigerating Engineers.

total cooling effect   the difference between the total enthalpy of the dry air and water vapor mixture entering a unit per hour and the total enthalpy of the dry air and water vapor (and water) mixture leaving the unit per hour, expressed in Btu per hour.

total current   the current that flows from the voltage source of a circuit.

total energy management   conservation concept where a building is looked at in terms of its total energy usage, rather than the requirements of its separate systems.

total equivalent warning impact (TEWI)   a unit of measurement that assesses the total effect CFCs, HCFCs, and HFCs have on global warming.

total head   the sum of discharge head, suction lift, and friction losses.

total heat   the sum of sensible and latent heat. It is also referred to as enthalpy.

total heat load   all the sources of heat for a conditioned space including infiltration, conduction, radiation, and internally generated heat.

total pressure   the sum of both the static pressure and the velocity pressure of a moving stream of air at the point where the measurement is taken.

total resistance   the total opposition to current flow in a circuit which may be found by removing the voltage source and connecting an ohmmeter across the points where the source was connected.

total suspended particles   the weight of particulate matter suspended in a unit volume of air.

total voltage   the voltage supplied by a source.

tower, water   an enclosed device for evaporatively cooling water by contact of air.

tower, water, atmospheric   one in which the air movement through the tower is dependent only upon atmospheric conditions. Also known as natural-draft cooling tower.

tower, water, forced-draft   a mechanical-draft water-cooling tower having one or more fans located in the air entering the tower.

tower, water, induced-draft   a mechanical-draft water-cooling tower having one or more fans located in the air leaving the tower.

townhouse   a living unit in which one or more walls are partition, lot line, or common walls, but not containing common floor and ceiling combinations.

toxic   poisonous, hazardous to life.

tracks   moves over or along; traverses.

trade names   manufacturers' marketing names. Because of pioneering development, or merely common usage, some control devices are referred to by their manufacturer's marketing names. Control technicians should not let this become confusing.

transducer   a device that is actuated by power from one system and supplies power in another form to a second system.

transformer   an electromagnetic device, with two or more coils linked by magnetic lines of force, used to increase or decrease

AC voltage. With a voltage increase, current decreases, and vice versa. In HVAC controls the transformer usually converts line voltage (115 V) to a low voltage (24 V).

transformer rectifier   a combination transformer and rectifier in which the input is AC. May be varied and then rectified to DC.

transient   an instantaneous voltage surge through a circuit that may be caused by lightning, static electricity, or the activation of inductive loads.

transistor   a small, solid-state electronic component employing a semiconductor such as germanium or silicon to perform the functions of amplifying, switching, or controlling electrical signals. The transistor has replaced the older vacuum tube in a variety of applications because of its many advantages: mechanical rigidity, long life, freedom from heater current, and ability to operate at low voltages with relatively high currents. Complex circuits utilize many transistors and other circuit components which may be integrated into a single chip.

transmission   heat loss or gain from a building through exterior components such as windows, walls, floors, etc.

transmission, heat, coefficient of   one of a number of coefficients used in the calculation of heat transmission by conduction, convection, and radiation through various materials and structures.

transmission line   a system of conductors suitable for conducting electric power or signals efficiently between two or more terminals. Also known as line.

transmission power loss   the amount of energy lost during transmission due to electrical resistance. Transmission power loss is determined using the equation: power loss $= I^2R$.

transmissivity   the capacity of a material to transmit radiant energy. Transmittance is the ratio of the radiant flux transmitted through a body to that incident to it.

transmittance, thermal (U factor)   the time rate of heat flow per unit area under steady conditions from the fluid on the warm side of a barrier to the fluid on the cold side per unit temperature difference between the two fluids.

transmitter   a sensor (not a controller) that transmits a directly functional signal in proportion to the variable measured. This proportion is factory set and cannot be adjusted. With this control there is no ability for sensitivity adjustment.

transom   a window directly above a door, often used to mount a window air conditioner.

trap   a vertical U-shaped offset filled with water and located beneath plumbing fixtures to form a seal against the passage of foul odors or gases.

travel coefficient   the ratio between the flow at a given valve stem position and the flow through the valve at its wide open position; expressed as a decimal fraction.

triac   three-lead semiconductor that allows current flow in two directions when a preset voltage is applied at one of the leads.

trial for ignition   refers to burners (usually oil) using direct spark ignition of the main burner. See *main burner flame-establishing period.*

trial for main flame   see *main burner flame-establishing period.*

trial for pilot   see *pilot flame-establishing period.*

triangle   a three-sided geometric figure.

trichlorotrifluoroethane   complete name for R-113. A Group 1 refrigerant. Chemical components that make up this refrigerant are chlorine, fluorine, and ethane.

triode   a three-element electronic device, usually a vacuum tube.

triple point   the pressure-temperature condition in which a substance is in equilibrium in solid, liquid, and vapor states.

troposphere   part of the atmosphere immediately above the earth's surface in which most weather disturbances occur.

troubleshooting   the process of observing a malfunctioning system's operation and diagnosing the cause of the malfunction.

truck, refrigerated   a commercial vehicle equipped to maintain a temperature below atmospheric conditions.

true power   the average power consumed by a circuit (or component) during one full cycle of alternating current. Measured directly with a wattmeter.

trunk   the largest or main circuit that carries the combined capacity of two or more subcircuits. The main duct of an air system.

try cocks   usually three in number. Located on water column or on boiler itself. Under pressure the top try cock should show steam and the lower two, water. Under a vacuum air will enter through openings. Try cocks are used to check water in glass and may be used to maintain proper water level if glass is broken.

tube   a small-diameter, flexible pipe, usually made of copper, aluminum, or plastic.

tube, capillary   in refrigeration practice, a tube of small internal diameter used as a liquid refrigerant flow control or expansion device between the high and the low sides; also used to transmit pressures from the sensing bulb of some temperature controls to the operating element.

tube, constricted   a tube that is restricted in diameter.

tube, finned   heat transfer tube or pipe with extended surfaces in the form of fins, discs, or ribs.

tube, soft copper   deoxidized and dehydrated seamless soft copper tube, thoroughly annealed to assure quality for bending and flaring.

tube-within-a-tube   describes a water-cooled condensing unit in which a small tube is placed inside a larger tube. Refrigerant passes through one tube while water flows through the other.

tubeaxial fan   an air-moving device in which the airflow is parallel or axial to the shaft on which the propeller is mounted. The propeller is housed in a cylindrical tube or duct. This design enables duct fans to operate at higher static pressures than propeller fans. Commonly used in spray booth and other ducted exhaust systems. As static pressure is increased, horsepower increases and cfm decreases.

tubing   a fluid-carrying pipe.

tubing cutter   a tool used to make an accurate 90-degree cut on either hard or soft cutter.

tubing, precharged   a refrigeration line set that is fitted with quick-connect type fittings on each end. The line has been factory evacuated and filled with refrigerant. The line may also be evacuated and sealed or pressurized with nitrogen.

tuned circuit   an electronic circuit, containing both inductance and capacitance, which is adjusted to resonate or operate at a specified frequency.

tungsten load   incandescent lamps are tungsten loads. The cold resistance of a tungsten load is extremely low. This can result in inrush currents of as much as 6 times the steady-state current, causing contact erosion or welding. Tungsten contact ratings are specified as amp-t or amp tungsten.

tunnel burner   a gas burner in which the actual combustion begins in a refractory tunnel or tuyere block. It is a relatively high-capacity partial premix type of gun burner, which uses the kinetic energy of the gas stream issuing from the orifice to bring in at least part of the air required for combustion. A wide range of control of flame characteristics is obtained by adjustment of the primary air, thus causing combustion to be delayed until secondary air can reach the air/fuel mixture. Also see *gun-type* and *partial premix burners*.

turbine   an engine driven by the pressure of steam, water, or air against the curved vanes of a wheel.

turbulence   fluid flow which is not parallel to the wall of the pipe or duct through which the fluid is flowing.

turndown range   the range of firing rates over which satisfactory combustion may be obtained. For example, the firing rate of a burner with a 4 to 1 turndown range can be varied from about 25% to 100%.

turndown ratio   the ratio of the maximum usable flow to the minimum controllable flow through a valve; usually somewhat less than the rangeability, as the maximum usable or required flow is usually less than the total flow capacity of a valve.

turns   the number of wire loops in a coil, especially in a transformer.

turns ratio   the ratio of the number of turns of the primary winding (N_p) of a transformer to the number of turns of the secondary winding (N_s).

tuyere   a nozzle or opening through which combustion air is introduced into a combustion chamber.

two-mode switching   two-stage switching operations such as start/stop, on/off, and open/closed.

two-pipe system (fuel oil)   a piping system where one pipe (suction) is used for the supply, while the other is used for the return of any unused oil from the burner. This system is considered to be self-priming.

two-pipe system (hot water)   a heating system using two separate pipes to supply and return water from the terminal units.

two-position action   the type of action in which the output signal is changed to either a maximum or minimum value with no intermediate steps (contrast to proportional).

two-position actuator   an actuator which moves a damper or valve to either of only two positions — on or off (open or closed) or high or low. Also see *actuator*.

two-position valve   a valve which is either fully open or fully closed, with no positions in between. Also called an on-off valve.

two-stage air compressor   a system where air is compressed in the first stage (larger diameter cylinder), cooled in the intercooler, then compressed again in the second stage (smaller diameter cylinder). Used where air pressure is above 150 psi.

two-stage firing   describes a system in which the combustion rate of the burner can be set at either of two fixed levels.

two-temperature valve   a pressure-opened valve used in the suction line on multiple refrigeration systems which maintains evaporators in the system at different temperatures.

two-way valve   see *straight-through valve*.

type "B" vent   a gas-only vent pipe that is composed of two pieces of pipe. The inner pipe is made of aluminum and the outer is made of galvanized steel. It is round in shape.

type "BW" vent   a gas-only vent pipe that is composed of two pieces of pipe. The inner pipe is made of aluminum and the outer is made of galvanized steel. It is oval in shape and used with wall furnaces.

type "L" vent   a gas/oil vent pipe that is composed of two pieces of pipe. The inner pipe is made of stainless steel and the outer is made of galvanized steel.

types of motors   electric motors are classified by operating characteristics and type of power required.

1. Capacitor-start (CS) motor - a type of single-phase induction motor that has a capacitor in series with the starting winding only during the starting operation. This type of motor has high locked-rotor torque with low amp draw, and high breakdown torques used on hard-starting applications such as compressors, positive displacement pumps, conveyors, etc.

2. Capacitor-start, capacitor-run (CSR) motor - performance and applications are similar to those of capacitor-start, induction-run motors; the capacitor enables operation at lower current demand and improved efficiency. Used on larger single-phase hp ratings.

3. Permanent split-capacitor (psc) motor - single-phase induction motor which has a capacitor continuously in the start (auxiliary) winding. Unlike the split-phase or capacitor-start type motors, there is no centrifugal switch to disconnect the start windings. This type motor has low starting torque and is best suited for direct-drive applications such as fans, blowers, etc. Psc motors are much more efficient than shaded-pole motors.

4. Shaded-pole (SP) motor - a special type of single-phase induction motor that utilizes a copper shading coil to provide the necessary displacement for starting. Low starting torque; typically used in direct-drive fans, blowers, etc.

5. Split-phase (SP) motor - the most common type of single-phase induction motor. Equipped with a start winding displaced in magnetic position from,

and connected in parallel with, the run winding. The start winding is disconnected from the circuit by either a potential (or start) relay or a centrifugal switch. Generally, this motor has low to moderate locked-rotor torque with high locked-rotor amps and high breakdown torques. Used on belt-drive blowers, fans, pumps, etc.

6. Three-phase motor - operates on three-phase power (three power lines) dependent upon designs; can yield high starting and breakdown torques. They are more efficient than single-phase motors, and larger hp ratings can be furnished. Found in all larger size motors.

7. Direct current motor - requires direct current supply and is primarily used for adjustable-speed-drive applications or motor vehicles.

8. Universal motor - one that can be operated on either AC or DC; brush type. Used primarily in high-speed applications such as drills, saws, etc.

U

U   thermal transmittance.

U$_o$ overall thermal transmittance.

UAJAPPFI   United Association of Journeymen and Apprentices - Plumbing/Pipe Fitting Industry.

UEL   upper explosive limit.

UL   Underwriters Laboratories.

USCEA   United States Council for Energy Awareness.

USDA   United States Department of Agriculture.

USECRE   United States Export Council for Renewable Energy.

USMA   United States Metric Association.

UV   ultraviolet.

U factor   the factor representing resistance to heat flow of various building materials.

UL approved   Underwriters Laboratory approved.

UL labeled   see *labeled*.

UL listed   a product certification, indicating that the product meets certain safety standards set for it by Underwriters Laboratories. Not a product endorsement.

ultimate CO_2   the percentage of carbon dioxide in dry combustion products when a fuel (gas) is completely burned with exactly the amount of air needed for complete combustion. This is the theoretical maximum CO_2 which can be obtained for a given gas in burning the gas in air.

ultralow   refers to temperatures ranging from –50°F to –250°F.

ultraviolet   invisible radiation waves with frequencies shorter than wavelengths of visible light and longer than x-ray.

ultraviolet degradation   the degradation caused by long-term exposure of a material to sunlight or other rays containing ultraviolet radiation.

ultraviolet flame detector   a detector that responds to the ultraviolet radiation (wavelength between 0.02 and 0.4 micron) emitted by a flame. Also see *Minipeeper* and *Purple peeper*.

ultraviolet power tube   a high-power electron tube sensitive to ultraviolet radiation. When saturated with ultraviolet radiation, this tube delivers about 1/10 watt to the flame signal amplifier. The flame relay requires about 3/4 watt to pull in, so little power amplification is required.

ultraviolet (UV) radiation   invisible, electromagnetic waves of high frequency (short wavelength—between 0.02 and 0.4 micron). Ultraviolet radiation comprises a little less than one percent of the light spectrum.

unconditioned space   space within a building that is not conditioned space.

undercharged   a refrigeration system which is short of, or lacking in, refrigerant.

underground cable   cable specially designed for below-grade installations. Type UF is an approved underground cable.

undersized   describes the capacity of a machine or system that cannot keep up with the load applied. An air-conditioning system that runs continuously and doesn't cool the conditioned space to the required setting is said to be undersized.

Underwriters Laboratories   an independent organization that sets safety standards for motors and other electrical equipment. A laboratory which tests devices and materials for compliance with the standards of construction and performance established by the laboratory and with regards to their suitability for installation in accordance with the appropriate standards of the National Board of Fire Underwriters.

unheated space   space within a building that is not heated space.

union   a fitting used to connect two straight lengths of pipe or tubing, neither of which can be turned.

unison lightoff   in a multiburner system, ignition of all pilots at the same time. All pilots are in the same valve zone (see *valve zone*). When all pilots have been proved, all main burners are ignited at the same time.

unison shutdown   a characteristic of a multiburner system; if the flame goes out or the flame signal is lost for any one burner in the valve zone, all burners in that zone are shut down automatically.

unit   a factory-made, encased assembly of the functional elements indicated by its name, such as air-conditioning unit, room-cooling unit, humidifying unit, etc.

unit bearing   an all-position mounting bearing, constructed with a long, single-sleeve bearing. For fan duty only.

unit cooler   a direct-cooling, factory-made, encased assembly including a cooling element, fan and motor, and directional outlet.

unit heater   a self-contained, automatically controlled, vented fuel-burning device having an integral means for circulation of air. It is not intended for attaching pipes or ducts for the distribution of the heated air. A unit heater may be floor mounted or suspended.

unit heater cooler   a self-contained, packaged air conditioner for localized temperature control.

unit ventilator   a terminal unit in which a fan is used to mechanically circulate air over the heating coil. These units are constructed so that both outdoor and room air may be circulated to provide ventilation as well as heat. These units may contain a cooling coil for summer operation.

unitary cooling and heating equipment   one or more factory-made units that normally include an evaporator or cooling coil, or a compressor and condenser combination, and may include a heating function as well. Where such equipment is provided in more than one assembly, the separate assemblies shall be designed to be used together.

unitary heat pump   one or more factory-made units that normally include an indoor conditioning coil, compressor(s), and outdoor coil or refrigerant-to-water heat exchanger, including means to provide both heating and cooling functions. When such equipment is provided in more than one assembly, the separate assemblies shall be designed to be used together.

universal joint   a type of swivel for a socket wrench handle that permits reaching around objects.

universal motor   a brush-type motor that is designed to operate on either AC or DC. Used primarily in high-speed applications such as drills, saws, etc.

universal orifice   a combination fixed and adjustable orifice designed for the use of two different gases, such as LPG and natural gas.

universal replacement part   a part which can be used as a replacement part for many different models of equipment, including that of different manufacturers.

unloader   a device on or in a compressor for equalizing the high- and low-side pressures for a brief period during start-up, in order to decrease the starting load on the motor or to disengage certain cylinders of a multicylinder compressor to modulate the unit's cooling capacity.

unproved ignition   ignition by an energy source assumed to be energized during the main burner flame-establishing period.

unvented   an appliance which is not provided with a flue pipe or flue collar, and from which the combustion products are freely emitted into the space in which the appliance is located.

updraft   excessively low air pressure existing at the outlet of a chimney or stack which tends to increase the velocity and volume of gases passing up the stack.

upfeed system   a hydronic system in which the supply main is located below the level of the terminal units.

upflow furnace   a central furnace which has an essentially vertical airflow which discharges air at or near the top of the furnace; as distinguished from a downflow furnace.

upper explosive limit   the maximum concentration of a combustible gas or mixture of gases in air or oxygen that will ignite and burn (propagate a flame).

upshot burner   a gas burner in which the gas is delivered vertically from below the combustion chamber, resulting in a vertical flame.

upstream   the area that is closer to the source of fluid flow.

urethane foam   a type of insulation which is used in between inner and outer walls of an appliance, display case, or container.

useful oil pressure   the difference in pressure between the discharge and suction sides of the compressor oil pump.

utility gases   natural gas, manufactured gas, liquefied petroleum gas/air mixtures, or mixtures of any of these gases.

utility rate structure   a utility's approved schedules of charges to be made in billing for utility service rendered to various classes of customers.

utility service   the utility company. Also, the amount and configuration of voltage supplied by a utility company. There are four main types of commercial utility services: 208 volts AC Wye, 480 volts AC Wye, 240 volts AC Delta, and 480 volts AC Delta.

utility transformer   primary and secondary coils of wire that reduce (step down) the utility supply voltage for use within a facility.

U-tube manometer   a low-pressure measuring instrument having the measuring liquid in a U-shaped tube where the pressure pushes down on the fluid-measuring material and supports it on the other side.

UV power tube   see *ultraviolet power tube*.

V

V   volt.

va   volt-ampere.

VAC   volts alternating current.

vav   variable air volume.

VDC   volts direct current.

VI   Vibration Institute.

VMA   Valve Manufacturers of America.

VOM   volt-ohm-milliammeter.

VRC   Valve Remanufacturers Council.

VTVM   vacuum tube voltmeter.

V belt   endless belt having a cross section resembling a truncated triangle or V. Usually of reinforced rubber, V belts transfer rotary motion. Can be either smooth or notched.

V block   a V-shaped groove in a metal block to hold round objects.

V_{max} maximum (peak) voltage in an alternating current cycle.

V pulley   a pulley that is used with a V belt.

V_{rms} root mean square voltage; it is the average voltage and is equal to the maximum (peak) voltage multiplied by 0.707.

VA   volt-ampere. A designation of power in terms of voltage and current.

vacuum   an enclosed space from which practically all air has been removed; a reduction of pressure below atmospheric pressure; a space with nothing at all in it.

vacuum control system   in many automobile air-conditioning systems, the intake manifold vacuum is used to operate dampers and controls in the system.

vacuum controller   a controller which can be set to operate at pressures less than atmospheric pressure.

vacuum pump   a special high-efficiency compressor used to create high vacuums for testing or drying purposes.

Vacuumstat   a Honeywell trademark; see *vacuum controller*.

valence electrons   electrons in the outer orbit of an atom. The number of atoms in this orbit dictates whether the material is a conductor or an insulator.

valve   a device used to isolate a part of a piping system by stopping flow; for controlling or regulating pressure or flow of a fluid or liquid. Capable of regulating the flow (cut-off, diversion, or modulation) of the medium moving through the pipe. Also see *cock;* and *automatic control, butterfly, diaphragm, diverting, double-seated, firing rate, manual shutoff, mixing, safety shutoff, single-seated, solenoid, straight-through, two-position,* and *vent valves.*

valve, automatic control   a valve that combines a valve body and a valve actuator or motor. A signal from some remote point can energize the actuator either to open or close the valve, or to proportion the rate of flow through the valve.

valve, back-pressure   an automatic valve located between the evaporator outlet and the compressor inlet that is responsive to its own inlet pressure, or to the vapor flow when necessary, to prevent the evaporator pressure from falling below a selected value.

valve body   the portion of the valve body through which the medium flows.

valve body rating   the maximum pressure which a valve body can withstand. The actual body rating is the maximum safe permissible fluid pressure at a given temperature. The nominal body rating is a specified rating (often cast on the valve body) based on the specified body material and universally accepted construction characteristics determined by specifications issued by authorities having jurisdiction. It provides a convenient method of classifying the valve by pressure for identification purposes. The nominal body rating is not the same as the actual body rating. Also, the maximum rating of the valve may be limited to the value below the body rating by the packing and disc material.

valve bonnet   the removable cover or top of the valve body (attached by screws). The bonnet assembly may include the valve trim.

valve, cap seal   a manual valve whose seal is protected by a tightly fitting cap.

valve, charging   a valve located on the liquid line, usually near the receiver, through which refrigerant may be charged into the system.

valve, check   valve that allows fluid to flow in one direction only.

valve-closed indication switch   a single-pole, double-throw switch in a valve actuator, which can be wired to either make or break a circuit when the valve is in the closed position. When used with a valve with a second seat (not to be confused with a double-seated valve), it constitutes a valve-closed interlock. The second seat closes the valve before it reaches the end of its stem travel. The valve-closed indication switch in the actuator operates only after the valve stem continues past the point at which the second seat has closed the valve. Also see *valve-closed interlock.*

valve-closed interlock   an interlock which ensures that the automatic main fuel valve(s) is closed before allowing burner operation to start or to proceed through pre-purge; usually used as a preignition interlock. Also see *valve-closed indication switch.*

valve closing time   the time it takes an automatic valve to close completely after it is de-energized by a flame safeguard control.

valve, condenser shutoff   a valve located in the hot gas discharge line at the inlet of the condenser.

valve, constant pressure   a controlling device for regulating the flow of volatile refrigerant into the cooling unit, actuated by changes in pressure of the low side.

valve, cylinder discharge   the valve in a compressor through which the gas leaves the cylinder.

valve, cylinder suction   the valve in a compressor through which the gas enters the cylinder.

valve, diaphragm   a form of packless valve, manually or mechanically actuated. Also a valve actuated by the pressure of a motivating fluid on one side of the diaphragm which seals the motivating fluid from the flowing fluid controlled by the valve. Flowing and motivating fluids can be, but need not be, the same.

valve, direct-acting   a valve which closes with the admission of fluid pressure to a diaphragm and opens when pressure is released.

valve disc   the movable portion of a valve which comes into contact with the seat as the valve closes, and which controls the flow of the medium through the valve. A contoured disc controls the flow by a shaped end, sometimes called a valve plug, and is usually end-guided at the top or at the bottom (or both) of the valve body. A V-port disc has a cylinder (called a skirt or guide) which rides up and down in the seat ring. The skirt guides the disc, and the shaped openings in the skirt vary the flow area. A quick-opening disc is machined so that maximum flow is quickly achieved when the disc lifts from the seat. It is either end-guided or guided by wings riding in the seat ring.

valve, discharge   on a compressor, the valve which allows compressed refrigerant to flow from the cylinder to the discharge port.

valve, emergency relief   a manually operated valve for the discharge of refrigerant in case of fire or other emergency.

valve, equipment shutoff   a valve, located in the piping system, used to shut off individual pieces of equipment.

valve, expansion   a type of refrigerating metering control which maintains a pressure difference between the high and low sides in the refrigeration system. The valve is caused to operate by pressure in the low or suction side to redirect the opening of the valve on the high side.

valve, float   a regulating valve controlled by liquid level or a valve actuated by a float in a liquid container.

valve flow characteristic   the relationship between the stem travel, or lift, expressed in percentage, and the flow of fluid through the valve, expressed in percentage of full flow. Also see *equal percentage* and *linear characteristics*.

valve guide   the part of the valve disc that keeps the disc aligned with the valve seat. Also see *characterized guide* and *valve skirt*.

valve, king   a manual stop valve located between the outlet of the receiver and the inlet of the metering device.

valve, low-side float   a float valve that operates by change in level of low-pressure liquid, opens at low level, and closes at high pressure.

valve, modulating   a valve that can be positioned anywhere between fully on and fully off to proportion the rate of flow in response to a modulating controller.

valve, packless   a valve which does not use packing to prevent leaks around the valve stem. Flexible material is generally used to seal against leaks and still permit valve movement.

valve, pilot   a small-capacity pressure control valve used to control the action of a larger capacity control valve.

valve plate   that part of a compressor located between the top of the compressor body and the head. Usually contains the compressor suction and discharge valves.

valve plug   a term used to describe a disc that has a solid, shaped end (instead of a skirted guide) to characterize flow through a valve. In some valves, the plug may serve as a guide.

valve port   the flow-controlling opening between the seat and the disc of a valve. It does not refer to the body size nor to the end connection size of the valve. Regardless of the pipe size, the valve port size determines the flow.

valve, pressure relief a safety valve design used to prevent the development of a dangerous condition by relieving pressure, temperature, or vacuum in a hot water supply system.

valve, purge a shutoff valve that, when opened, vents noncondensable gases.

valve ratings maximum fluid pressure and temperature ratings are limitations placed upon a valve by the maximum pressure and temperature to which the valve may be subjected. Determining factors may be packing, body material, disc material, or actuator limitations. Also see *capacity index, close-off rating, pressure drop, rangeability, tight shutoff, travel coefficient, turndown ratio, valve body rating,* and *valve flow characteristic.*

valve, reducing a valve that reduces high inlet pressure to the required lower outlet pressure.

valve, reverse-acting a valve that opens with the admission of fluid pressure to a diaphragm and closes when pressure is released.

valve, reversing the control used to regulate the flow of the hot high-pressure vapor from the compressor and the cool low-pressure vapor to the compressor from the coils, depending upon the direction of heat flow desired.

valve-seal-over-travel interlock see *valve-closed interlock.*

valve seat the stationary portion of a valve with which the movable portion (disc) comes into contact to stop flow completely.

valve, service a device used by service technicians to check the operating pressures, or to charge or evacuate a refrigeration system.

valve, service shutoff a valve, installed by the serving gas supplier between the service meter, or source of supply, and the customer piping system, to shut off the entire piping system.

valve skirt a valve guide which has notches or Vs cut into it to characterize the flow through the valve; also known as a skirted guide or a characterized guide.

valve, slide the slide valve portion of the reversing valve that shifts the refrigerant flow.

valve, solenoid a valve actuated by magnetic action by means of an electrically energized solenoid.

valve stem a cylindrical shaft which is moved manually or by an actuator, and to which the disc is attached.

valve, stop a valve that is a shutoff valve but is not a valve for controlling the flow of refrigerant.

valve, suction a valve in a refrigeration compressor which allows vaporized gas to enter the cylinder from the suction line and prevents its return.

valve, thermostatic radiator a device that combines a temperature-sensitive power unit with a valve. Mounts in the hot water or steam supply pipe adjacent to a radiator. May also be applied to baseboard and similar types of heaters. Requires no electricity.

valve trim all parts of a valve that are in contact with the flowing medium, but are not a part of the valve shell or casting. Seats, discs, stems, and packing rings are all trim items.

valve, two-position a valve that is either fully on or fully off with no intermediate position. Also referred to as an on-off valve.

valve, TXV, biflow a thermostatic expansion valve that is designed to provide pressure reduction and refrigerant flow control in either direction.

valve, water-regulating a valve that regulates the flow of water through the condenser while it is running. Most water-regulating valves are controlled by the head pressure of the refrigeration system.

valve zone   a section of a multiburner system which is controlled by one valve (or one set of valves, e.g., double-block-and-bleed). For example, "five burners per zone" means one valve controls the gas to five burners.

vane ratio   in air distributing devices, the ratio of depth of vane to shortest opening width between two adjacent grille bars.

vanes   the blades mounted on a rotor inside a compressor or other rotating machine.

vapor   the gaseous form of any substance which is usually a liquid or a solid; a gas, near equilibrium with the liquid phase of the substance, which does not follow the gas laws.

vapor barrier   a thin plastic or metal foil sheet used in air-conditioned structures to prevent water vapor from entering the insulating material. Vapor barriers are always installed on the warm side of the insulation layer.

vapor-charged   describes lines and component parts of a system which are charged at the factory. It also describes a type of refrigerant charging where only vapor or gas is introduced into the refrigeration system.

vapor density   the weight of a vapor or gas compared to the weight of an equal volume of air; an expression of the density of the vapor or gas calculated as the ratio of the molecular weight of the gas to the average molecular weight of air, 29. Mw of gas/29 = vapor density. Materials lighter than air have vapor densities of less than 1.0. Materials heavier than air have vapor densities greater than 1.0. All vapors and gases will mix with air, but the lighter materials will tend to rise and dissipate (unless confined). Heavier vapors and gases are likely to concentrate in low places (along or under floors; in sumps, sewers, and manholes; in trenches and ditches) where they may create a fire, explosion, or health hazards.

vapor line   found only in dual-action heat pumps, it is the suction line in the cooling mode and the hot gas discharge line in the heating mode.

vapor lock   a condition where liquid is trapped in a line because of a bend or improper installation which prevents the vapor from flowing.

vapor pressure   the pressure exerted by a saturated vapor above its own liquid in a closed container.

vapor pressure curve   a graphic presentation of various pressures produced by refrigerant under various temperatures.

vapor, saturated   a vapor condition which will result in condensation into droplets of liquid as vapor temperature is reduced.

vapor, superheated   vapor at a temperature which is higher than the saturation temperature (i.e., boiling point of water) at the existing pressure.

vapor, water   used commonly in air-conditioning terminology to refer to steam in the atmosphere.

vaporization   the change of liquid into a gaseous state.

variable   a factor or condition which can be measured or altered by a control system, such as temperature, pressure, flow, liquid level, humidity, weight, or chemical composition.

variable air volume controller   a device having electronic or pneumatic components used to regulate the volume of air in a distribution system.

variable air volume system   centralized HVAC system that supplies conditioned air to zones where a regulator and a thermostat determine the volume of air delivered to the space.

variable pitch pulley   a pulley which can be adjusted to provide different pulley ratios.

variable resistor   a resistor whose resistance value can be varied between its minimum and maximum values.

varistor   a resistor that changes its resistance value with a change in voltage. Varistors are used to protect electronic circuits from transient voltage spikes.

vars   unit for the measurement of reactive power.

vector   a line that represents the direction and magnitude of a quantity.

velocimeter   an instrument used to measure air velocities using a direct-reading air-speed-indicating dial.

velocity   the rate of motion in a particular direction in relation to time speed.

velocity meter   a meter used to detect the velocity of fluids, air, or water.

velocity, outlet   the average discharge velocity of primary air being discharged from the outlet, normally measured in the plane of the opening.

velocity pressure   in a moving fluid, the pressure capable of causing an equivalent velocity as applied to move the same fluid through an orifice such that all pressure energy expended is converted into kinetic energy.

velocity, terminal   the highest sustained airstream velocity existing in the mixed air path at the end of the throw.

vent   a small hole or opening to permit passage or escape, as of a gas. Also, to allow to escape through a hole. Also see *gas vent.*

vent connector   the pipe which connects a gas-fired device to a gas vent or chimney. Also called breeching or flue pipe.

vent damper   a device intended for installation in the venting system (in the outlet of or downstream of the appliance draft hood) of an individual, automatically operated fuel-gas burning unit and which is designed to open the venting system automatically when the appliance is in operation and to close off the venting system automatically when the appliance is in a standby or shutdown condition. Can be electrically, mechanically, or thermally actuated.

vent gases   products of combustion from gas appliances plus excess air and dilution air in the venting system above a draft hood.

vent pipe   a vertical pipe used to ventilate plumbing systems and to remove odors and sewer gases from the building to the outside and to provide circulation of air to and from any part of the drainage system.

vent stack   the upper portion of a waste or soil stack extending through the roof of a building, installed primarily for the purpose of providing circulation of air.

vent valve   an electrically operated, normally open valve which allows any gas which leaks through any upstream valve(s) to escape to the outside atmosphere. Also called a relief valve. Also see *bleeding* and *double-block-and-bleed.*

vented gas categories   these consist of the following:

1. Category 1. An appliance which operates with a nonpositive vent static pressure and with a vent gas temperature that avoids excessive condensate production (over 275°F) in the vent. Usually 76% efficient or less with a draft hood or a 78 to 82% efficient furnace with an induced draft blower.
2. Category 2. An appliance which operates with a nonpositive vent static pressure and with a vent gas temperature that may cause excessive condensate production (less than 275°F) in the vent. No furnace is made today in this category.
3. Category 3. An appliance that operates with a positive vent static pressure and

with a vent gas temperature that avoids excessive condensate production (275–360°F) in the vent.

4. Category 4. An appliance that operates with a positive vent static pressure and with a vent gas temperature that may cause excessive condensate production (100–275°F) in the vent.

vented wall furnace   a self-contained, vented, fuel-gas burning appliance complete with grilles or equivalent, designed for incorporation in, or permanent attachment to, the structure of a building and furnishing heated air, circulated by gravity or by a fan, directly into the space to be heated through openings in the casing. Such appliances should not be provided with duct extensions beyond the vertical and horizontal limits of the casing proper, except that boots not to exceed 10 inches beyond the horizontal limits of the casing for extension through the walls of nominal thickness are permitted. When such boots are provided, they shall be supplied by the manufacturer as an integral part of the appliance. This definition excludes floor furnaces, unit heaters, direct vent wall furnaces, and central furnaces.

ventilation   the process of supplying or removing air, by natural or mechanical means, to or from any space. Such air may or may not be conditioned.

ventilation air   the air required for the removal of excessive external heat surrounding an appliance, or for the removal of such heat within the enclosure in which the appliance is located.

ventilator   see *exhaust fan.*

venting   the removal of combustion products as well as process fumes to the outer air.

venting system   a continuous open passageway from the collar or draft hood of a gas-burning appliance to the outside atmosphere for the purpose of removing flue or vent gases.

venturi   a short tube with a constricted, throat-like passage that increases the velocity and lowers the pressure of a fluid passed through it.

venturi mixing burner   see *inspirating burner.*

vertical boiler   see *fire-tube boiler.*

vertical riser   a vertical portion of the suction line, usually used with an oil trap, in a refrigeration system.

vertical rotary oil burner   see *rotary oil burner.*

very-high-pressure appliance   an appliance that uses a refrigerant with a low boiling point below 58°F at atmospheric pressure.

vibration   a periodic motion of the particles of an elastic body or medium in alternately opposite directions from the position of equilibrium when that equilibrium has been disturbed. A quivering or trembling motion.

vibration absorber   a flexible, shock absorbing fitting installed next to or below a vibrating component to prevent the transfer of vibration through the line or base.

vibration eliminator   soft or flexible substance or device which will reduce the transmission of a vibration.

vibration isolators   mounting pads for vibrating machinery that prevent the transmission of the vibration to other parts of the building.

vibration switch   a circuit control that shuts down machinery in case of excessive vibration.

virgin refrigerant   new, original, nonrecycled refrigerant.

viscosity   the property of a liquid that results in a resistance to flow. Viscosity decreases as the temperature increases. The unit of the coefficient of viscosity is called the poise.

viscosity, absolute   the force per unit area required to produce unit relative velocity between two parallel areas of fluid a unit distance apart.

viscous   thick, resistant to flow. Applied to a liquid.

vise grips   adjustable pliers that can be locked at a desired opening.

vise jaws   serrated jaws which are part of a clamping device (part of the pipe vise). The lower jaw is stationary while the upper jaw is adjustable to allow for holding different size pipes.

visible light   light that can be perceived by the naked eye. Electromagnetic waves with frequencies between those of infrared and ultraviolet, with wavelengths between 0.4 and 0.8 micron.

vital heat   heat generated by the ripening of fruits and vegetables in storage.

vitreous   refers to a composition of materials that resemble glass, such as lavatories, electrode holders, or drainpipes.

volatile liquid   a liquid which evaporates easily and rapidly at a low temperature and pressure.

volt   a unit of electromotive force. One volt will produce a current flow of one ampere through a one-ohm resistance.

volt-ampere   the unit of measurement of apparent power. Also the unit of electrical power. Abbreviated va.

volt-ohm-milliammeter (VOM)   a multi-function, multirange meter which usually is designed to measure voltage, current, and resistance.

voltage   a term used to indicate the electrical potential difference or electromotive force in an electrical circuit. It is voltage or electrical pressure which causes current to flow.

voltage control   a device used to provide some electrical circuits with uniform or constant voltage.

voltage drop   a term expressing the amount of voltage loss from the original input in a conductor or load.

voltage rating   a rating that indicates the amount of voltage that can be safely connected to a device.

voltage regulator   a device or circuit that maintains a constant value of voltage.

voltage relay   a normally closed relay wired into a motor's start winding circuit. The relay remains closed upon start-up due to a voltage drop in the circuit. As the motor attains rated speed, the back electromotive voltage rises and operates a magnetic relay that opens the N/C start winding contacts that are in series with the start windings. Also referred to as a start relay or a potential relay.

voltaic cell   a cell produced by suspending two dissimilar elements in an acid solution. A potential difference is developed by chemical action.

voltmeter   an instrument used to measure the voltage values.

volume   the three-dimensional capacity of a given space.

volume, specific   the volume of a substance per unit mass; the reciprocal of density. Its units are cubic feet per pound, cubic centimeters per gram, etc.

volumetric efficiency   term used to express the relationship between the actual performance of a compressor or vacuum pump and the calculated performance of the pump based on its displacement versus its actual pumping ability.

volumetric efficiency, apparent   the ratio of length of suction line, on indicator card, to stroke.

volumetric efficiency, due to cylinder heating   the ratio of the total to the apparent volumetric efficiency. Also called real or no-clearance volumetric efficiency.

volumetric efficiency, total   the ratio of the actual volume of gas removed by a compressor or pump to the actual displacement of the compressor or pump.

volute   the case containing the spinning rotor in a centrifugal compressor or pump.

VOM (volt-ohm-milliammeter)   a common test instrument which combines a voltmeter, ohmmeter, and milliammeter in one case.

vortex tube   a mechanism for cooling or refrigerating which accomplishes cooling effect by releasing compressed air through specially designed openings. Air expands in rapidly spiraling columns which separate slower moving molecules (cool) from the faster moving molecules (hot).

vortex tube refrigeration   refrigerating or cooling devices using the principle of vortex tubes.

vortexing   a whirlpool action in the sump of a cooling tower or receiver.

W

W   symbol for watt, wattage, or width.

WDA   Wholesale Distributors Association.

WOHMA   Waste Oil Heating Manufacturers Association.

WQR   Water Quality Research.

WSC   Water Systems Council.

WSFO   weather service forecast office.

WSO ap   weather service office (airport)

walk-in cooler   a large commercial refrigerated space kept below room temperature.

wall heat capacity   effective wall heat capacity (Btu/ft^2 × °F) for purposes of calculating thermal mass performances for exterior walls. It is the sum of the products of the mass of each individual material in the wall per unit area of wall surface times its individual specific heat.

wall thickness   a term expressing the thickness of a layer of applied insulation or jacket.

walls   those portions of the building envelope that are vertical or tilted at an angle of 30° or less from the vertical plane. These include above-grade, where all of the exterior wall of any given story (if 50% or more of the gross exterior wall area of the story) is exposed to outside air, and below-grade, where all of the exterior wall of any given story (if more than 50% of the gross exterior wall area of the story) is below grade.

warm side   the side of any partition which is at the higher temperature.

warm-up burner   a burner usually smaller than the main burner, which is ignited by another ignition source, and is used to warm up the boiler.

warp switch   an electrical control with a bimetal heat-sensing element that changes shape when heated, causing the contacts to open or close.

warranty   an assurance of a product's proper performance.

washer   a flat, metal ring used to lock a nut in place, or fill a space. Can be lock, flat, star, or fender.

waste pipe   any pipe that receives the discharge of any fixture except the water closet.

waste water   condenser water that is discharged to a sewer rather than being recycled.

water box   a container or reservoir at the end of a chiller where water is introduced and contained.

water chiller   a refrigeration system that cools water that is pumped into other parts of the system to maintain the desired condition in a specific area.

water, circulating in a water-cooled or water-cooling device, the quantity of water entering the device per unit of time.

water column abbreviated as WC. A unit used for expressing pressure. One inch water column equals a pressure of 0.578 oz/in^2.

water column, boiler a column of piping located on the upper outside of the boiler shell to maintain a water level. Consists of try cocks, water glass gauge, low-water cut-off, pressure gauge, and pressuretrols.

water-cooled condenser a condensing unit that is cooled by water.

water, cooling water used for condensation of refrigerant; condenser water.

water defrosting the use of water to melt ice and frost from the evaporator during the off cycle.

water, domestic pure water intended for human consumption.

water hammer a violent fluctuation in pressure within a pipeline caused by the sudden stopping or slowing down of flow velocity by rapidly opening or closing a faucet or valve. This usually causes a loud noise.

water heater an appliance for supplying hot water for domestic or commercial purposes.

water jacket in a compressor, the water used for cooling the cylinder head and/or walls.

water-leg boiler a firebox boiler in which the water vessel extends to the base on both sides of the combustion chamber. Also see *firebox boiler.*

water level surface or height of still water.

water main the principal water supply line.

water, make-up water that is supplied to replenish lost water, as, for example, water used to replace that lost by evaporation.

water manometer instrument used to measure pressure in inches of water column. There are 27.93 inches of water column in one psig.

water, raw in ice making, any water used for ice making except distilled water.

water regulating valve an operating control valve that regulates the opening of the valve in relation to the high-side refrigerant pressure.

water, return water off the liquid source heat pump that is returned to the source of supply.

water, service line the water supply line that runs from the street main to the building.

water source, buried closed-loop when water is circulated through a closed-loop pipe system to use heat transfer between the loop and the earth as a heat energy source or sink.

water source, reservoir a body of water, such as a large lake or stream, used as a heat energy source or sink.

water table the top surface of the water in a water-bearing unconsolidated formation. The top surface of an aquifer.

water treatment the treatment of water with chemicals to reduce its scale-forming properties or to change other undesirable characteristics.

water-tube boiler a boiler in which the water and steam pass through tubes surrounded by the products of combustion. Water-tube boilers have capabilities for higher pressures and much greater outputs than fire-tube boilers. There are two general types— straight-tube and bent-tube.

1. Straight-tube boiler (also called horizontal) - the main bank of tubes is straight and on a slope of 5 to 15° from the horizontal. This type has further classifications: sectional header boiler - the tube bank is comprised of multiple parallel sections, each section having a front and rear header connected by vertical rows of tubes, all within a common drum.

   a. Box header boiler - the tubes in the bank are connected by two inclined, rectangular headers (a front and a rear).

b. Cross-drum boiler - a sectional header or box header boiler in which the axis of the horizontal drum is at right angles to the center lines of the tubes in the main bank.

c. Longitudinal drum boiler - a sectional header or box header boiler in which the axis of the horizontal drum is parallel to the center lines of the tubes in the main bank (in a horizontal plane).

2. Bent-tube boiler - consists of two or more drums, requiring the tubes to be bent outward radially near their ends in order to interconnect the drums. The multiple drums result in very high outputs (over one million pounds of steam per hour, or 1250 million Btu/h), so this type of boiler is usually found in power plant installations. One version, called a low head boiler, has three drums with relatively short tubes in a vertical plane.

water vapor   water contained in atmospheric air; actually, it is low-temperature superheated steam.

water vapor retarder   material or construction that adequately impedes the transmission of water vapor under specified conditions. Water vapor retarders have a water vapor permeance of less than 1.0 perm when tested in accordance with ASTM E 96-92.

waterside explosion   see *explosion*.

watertight   describes equipment that is constructed so that water or moisture is excluded from an enclosure.

watt   the unit of electrical power. In a purely resistive alternating current circuit or a direct current circuit, one watt of power is consumed by a load when one volt causes a flow of one ampere through the load. Watts equal volts times amps. Also equal to one joule per second and to $1/746$ of one horsepower.

watt-hour   a unit of electrical energy expenditure. It is the equivalent of one watt of power operating for one hour of time.

watt-hour meter   a meter which indicates the instantaneous rate of power consumption of a device or circuit. It is used by electrical power companies to monitor consumers' electrical consumption.

watt meter   an instrument used to measure electrical power.

watt-second   the energy related to one watt acting for one second; one joule.

Watt's law   the mathematical relationship of power to voltage and current. In a DC circuit or a purely resistive AC circuit, power equals voltage times current.

watts output   torque (ounce-inches) × speed (rpm) divided by 1352.

waveform   a graphic representation of the different voltage values of an electrical current over a period of time.

wavelength   the distance between corresponding points on two successive waves of a periodic waveform. The quotient of the velocity of propagation divided by the frequency.

wax   an ingredient in many lubricating oils which may separate out if cooled sufficiently.

weather stripping   pliable material that seals cracks around windows, doors, and openings to prevent infiltration.

weatherproof   describes electrical devices designed to be protected from the weather.

weight switch   an electrical control used in an ice maker. It is actuated by a water-filled canister and reset when the canister empties.

weight valve   a valve used with a high-side-float refrigerant metering system to prevent evaporation in the line between the float and the evaporator when the system is in the off cycle.

welding   the connection of metal objects by partially melting and fusing them together.

well casing   a perforated, noncorrosive pipe (PVC or steel) inserted into a well to keep the walls from collapsing. Allows both the insertion of a submersible pump and free flow of water into the well.

well casing screen   a section of well casing made of stainless steel screen located below the pumping level of the well to allow water entry into the casing.

well water source, closed-loop   a system that removes water from the earth by means of a drilled or bored well and returns it to the earth by means of a separate drilled or bored well.

well water source, open-loop   a system that removes water from the earth by means of a drilled or bored well and returns the water to the earth through a separate disposal system.

western union splice   a standard splice made by twisting two wires together.

wet bulb   device used in the measurement of the relative humidity. Evaporation of moisture lowers the temperature of the wet bulb compared to that of the dry bulb in the same atmosphere.

wet bulb depression   the difference between the wet and dry bulb temperatures. Indicates the percentage of relative humidity.

wet bulb hygrometer   see *psychrometer.*

wet bulb temperature   the lowest temperature which will register on a standard thermometer having its bulb enclosed in a wet wick over which air is circulated. This reading can be plotted with the dry temperature on a psychrometric chart to determine the relative humidity. The wet bulb reading is always lower than the dry bulb temperature unless the relative humidity is 100%. Then they are the same. The instrument used to obtain the wet and dry bulb reading is a sling psychrometer.

wet bulb thermometer   a thermometer whose bulb is covered with a piece of water-soaked cloth. The lowering of temperature that results from the evaporation of water around the bulb indicates the air's relative humidity.

wet cell battery   a cell or connected group of cells that converts chemical energy into electrical energy by reversible chemical reactions.

wet compression   the mixing of liquid refrigerant with the suction vapor entering the compressor; this causes the compressor's discharge to be saturated instead of superheated.

wet filter   an air filter saturated with water or oil to increase its filtering ability.

wet heat   describes a heating system using either hot water (hydronic) heat or steam heat.

wet steam   when steam contains particles of water that have not been evaporated, it is said to be wet.

wetback boiler   a scotch, fire-tube boiler with a steel baffle at the back of the furnace to direct the products of combustion from the combustion chamber to the second pass. The baffle covers the rear end of the furnace and tubes and is completely water cooled. The boiler gets its name from the wall of water between the baffle and the rear end of the boiler. Also see *fire-tube* and *scotch boilers.*

wetted hole   the portion of the well below the static water level in the well.

wetted-surface cooling tower   an application where water in a cooling tower is spread over a wetted surface while air is passed over it to enhance evaporation.

Wheatstone bridge   a resistor-testing device consisting of a bridge with four main arms containing a resistor in each arm. With known values for three resistors, the value for the unknown resistor can be computed.

wholesaler   the middleman between the manufacturer and retailer. One who sells to the retailer in whole quantities for resale to the customer.

wild leg the 208-volt (1.732×120 volts) source produced by one line in a closed Delta connection.

wind chill factor the still air temperature that would have the same chilling effect on human skin as the combination of the recorded wind speed and ambient temperature.

wind effect the increase in evaporation rate due to air travel over a water surface.

winding one or more wire turns which form a continuous coil or conductive path.

window unit a common term used when referring to air conditioners which are placed in a window.

wiper the moving contact which makes contact with a terminal in a stepping relay or switch. In a potentiometer, the contact that moves along the element, dividing the resistance according to its mechanical position.

wire a conductor, bare or insulated.

wire, drawing restriction of area for a flowing fluid, causing a loss in pressure by (internal and external) friction without loss of heat or performance of work; also called throttling.

wire gauge refers to the system of sizing wire by its diameter; starting with 0000 or 000 as the largest diameter and going up to size 40 or above for the smallest diameter.

wire nut a connector for wires, tightened like a screw or nut.

wire stripper a tool that removes the insulation from wire.

wiring diagram a diagram representing electrical devices by symbols and their interconnections. Types are schematic, pictorial (or line), and installation.

wiring subbase a panel, providing terminals for connecting external devices (controllers, interlocks, etc.), on which the thermostat or flame safeguard control is mounted.

wobble plate-swash plate type of compressor designed by General Motors to compress gas and having pistons with piston motion parallel to the crankshaft.

Woodruff key a device used to align and hold a flywheel, pulley, or other rotating mechanism on a shaft. Often half-moon shaped.

work the result of energy expended. The transfer of energy from one object to another, measured in force multiplied by distance, or foot-pounds.

work, effective net mechanical energy required by, or load imparted to, the piston of a compressor.

work hardening the tendency of metal to become stiff and brittle when hammered or bent.

work, indicated work equivalent of indicator card area for a reciprocating compressor or engine.

work order the written authorization to service or install equipment.

working level one working level of radon-222 daughters will give out alpha particle energy of 1.3×10^5 meV in one liter of air upon decay to lead-210.

working level month exposure to 1 working level for a working month of 173 hours.

working range the desired controlled or measured variable values over which a system operates.

working voltage the maximum continuous voltage a capacitor will withstand. Also referred to as the voltage rating.

wrist pin a retaining peg that joins a connecting rod to a piston.

wrought iron iron of low carbon content useful because of its toughness, ductility, and malleability.

wye connection also referred to as a star connection. A wye system is a four-wire connection made by joining one end of each of three windings. Wye systems provide three single-phase 120-volt circuits for light residential loads and can also be used to provide a 208-volt three-phase source when three of the four conductors are used.

X

X   symbol for reactance.

x-axis   the horizontal axis on a graph or chart.

Y

y-axis   the vertical axis on a graph or chart.

yellow flame burner   see *long-flame burner.*

yellow tips   the appearance of yellow tips in an otherwise blue flame, indicating the need for additional primary air.

yield strength   the minimum stress at which a material will start to physically deform without further increase in load.

yoke   that part of the flaring tool that fits over the block.

yoke vise   a vise used for holding pipe while it is being worked on. The yoke vise has an upper and lower serrated jaw and operates on a hinge, allowing it to be opened and closed to hold pipe. A chain vise, however, has a bottom jaw and a chain which loops around the pipe and holds the pipe securely while allowing it to be tightened.

Z

Z   symbol for impedance.

Zener diode   a diode that has a constant voltage drop when operated in the reverse direction. Zener diodes are commonly used as voltage regulators in electronic circuits.

zeotrope   a refrigerant blend that changes volumetric composition and saturation temperatures as it evaporates or condenses at constant pressures. Zeotropes have a temperature glide as they evaporate and condense. Zeotrope and nonazeotrope mean the same thing.

zerk fitting   a fitting outfitted with a one-way check valve that is used to inject grease for lubricating a bearing.

zero (absolute pressure and temperature)   in absolute measuring systems, the absence of a condition, e.g., heat or pressure. In nonabsolute systems, an arbitrary starting point for measurement.

zero adjustment   a mechanical means (by a dial, screw, or button, for example) for setting a meter pointer on the zero mark of the meter scale.

zero gas   gas at atmospheric pressure (zero gauge pressure), usually supplied by a zero governor.

zero governor   a regulating device which is normally adjusted to deliver gas at atmospheric pressure (zero gas) within its flow rating. Also called an atmospheric regulator.

zero governor burner   a power burner in which gas is supplied at atmospheric pressure (zero gas) maintained by a zero governor. A fan, or blower, blows the air through a venturi, where venturi action pulls the gas into the airstream. The quantity of gas drawn into the airstream is a direct function of the air velocity, so the air/fuel ratio will remain constant regardless of the air volume. The firing rate is controlled by air adjustment alone. Also see *aspirating, forced-draft,* and *premix burners.*

zero ice   trade name for dry ice.

zero potential   having zero or no voltage.

zone   specific area to be heated or cooled at a specified temperature and controlled by one thermostat. Zones within a building may require different indoor design temperatures based on their ultimate use. Also see *valve zone.*

zone, comfort (average)   the range of effective temperature over which the majority (80% or more) of adults feel comfortable.

zone, comfort (extreme)   the range of effective temperatures over which one or more adults feel comfortable.

zone controls   controls used to maintain each specific area or zone within a building at a desired condition. Can be hydronic or forced air.

zone system   a hydronic system in which more than one thermostat is used. This permits independent control of room air temperature at more than one location.

zone valves   controls used to maintain each specific area or zone within a building at a desired temperature or condition.

zoning   the practice of dividing a building into small sections for heating and cooling control. Each section is selected so that one thermostat can be used to determine its requirements.

zoning, mixed-air   hot and cold air are mixed in just the right proportions to maintain the desired zone temperature. The air is channeled into a heating section (hot deck) and cooling section (cold deck) and then mixed.

zoning, multiple-unit   zoning where a separate heating/cooling unit is used for each zone.

zoning, volume   zoning in which there is just one central heating and cooling unit with ducts leading to each zone.

Appendix
Useful Data

Multiply	by	to obtain
Acres	0.405	Hectares
Acres	43.560	Square feet
Acres	4047	Square meters
Acres	1.562×10^{-3}	Square miles
Acres	5645.38	Square varas
Acres	4840	Square yards
Amperes	0.10	Abamperes
Amperes	3×10^9	Statamperes
Atmospheres	76.0	Centimeters of mercury
Atmospheres	29.92	Inches of mercury
Atmospheres	33.90	Feet of water
Atmospheres	10.333	Kilograms per square meter
Atmospheres	14.70	Pounds per square inch
Atmospheres	1.058	Tons per square foot
British thermal units	0.2520	Kilogram-calories
British thermal units	777.5	Foot-pounds
British thermal units	3.927×10^{-4}	Horsepower-hours
British thermal units	1054	Joules
British thermal units	107.5	Kilogram-meters
British thermal units	2.928×10^{-4}	Kilowatt-hours
Btu per minute	12.96	Foot-pounds per second
Btu per minute	0.02356	Horsepower
Btu per minute	0.01757	Kilowatts
Btu per minute	17.57	Watts
Btu per cubic foot per minute	0.1220	Watts per square inch
Bushels	1.244	Cubic feet
Bushels	2150	Cubic inches
Bushels	0.03524	Cubic meters
Bushels	4	Pecks
Bushels	64	Pints (dry)
Bushels	32	Quarts (dry)
Centimeters	0.3397	Inches
Centimeters	0.01	Meters
Centimeters	393.7	Mils
Centimeters	10	Millimeters
Centimeter-grams	980.7	Centimeter-dynes

Multiply	by	to obtain
Centimeter-grams	10^{-5}	Meter-kilograms
Centimeter-grams	7.233×10^{-5}	Pound-feet
Centimeters of mercury	0.01316	Atmospheres
Centimeters of mercury	0.4461	Feet of water
Centimeters of mercury	136.0	Kilograms per square meter
Centimeters of mercury	27.85	Pounds per square meter
Centimeters of mercury	0.1934	Pounds per square inch
Centimeters per second	1.969	Feet per minute
Centimeters per second	0.03281	Feet per second
Centimeters per second	0.036	Kilometers per hour
Centimeters per second	0.6	Meters per minute
Centimeters per second	0.02237	Miles per hour
Centimeters per second	3.728×10^{-4}	Miles per minute
Cubic centimeters	3.531×10^{-5}	Cubic feet
Cubic centimeters	6.102×10^{-2}	Cubic inches
Cubic centimeters	10	Cubic meters
Cubic centimeters	1.308×10^{-6}	Cubic yards
Cubic centimeters	2.642×10^{-4}	Gallons
Cubic centimeters	10	Liters
Cubic centimeters	2.113×10^{-3}	Pints (liquid)
Cubic centimeters	1.057×10^{-3}	Quarts (liquid)
Cubic feet	62.43	Pounds of water
Cubic feet	2.832×10^{-4}	Cubic centimeters
Cubic feet	1728	Cubic inches
Cubic feet	0.02832	Cubic meters
Cubic feet	0.03704	Cubic yards
Cubic feet	7.481	Gallons
Cubic feet	28.32	Liters
Cubic feet	59.84	Pints (liquid)
Cubic feet	29.92	Quarts (liquid)
Cubic feet per minute	472.0	Cubic centimeters per second
Cubic feet per minute	0.1247	Gallons per second
Cubic feet per minute	0.4720	Liters per second
Cubic feet per minute	62.4	Pounds of water per minute
Cubic inches	16.39	Cubic centimeters
Cubic inches	5.787×10^{-4}	Cubic feet
Cubic inches	1.639×10^{-5}	Cubic meters
Cubic inches	2.143×10^{-5}	Cubic yards
Cubic inches	4.329×10^{-3}	Gallons
Cubic inches	1.639×10^{-2}	Liters
Cubic inches	0.03463	Pints (liquid)
Cubic inches	0.01732	Quarts (liquid)
Cubic meters	10^{6}	Cubic centimeters
Cubic meters	10^{3}	Liters
Cubic yards	7.646×10^{5}	Cubic centimeters
Cubic yards	27	Cubic feet
Cubic yards	46.656	Cubic inches
Cubic yards	0.7646	Cubic meters
Cubic yards	202.0	Gallons

Multiply	by	to obtain
Cubic yards	764.6	Liters
Cubic yards	1616	Pints (liquid)
Cubic yards	807.9	Quarts (liquid)
Cubic yards per minute	0.45	Cubic yards per second
Cubic yards per minute	3.367	Gallons per second
Cubic yards per minute	12.74	Liters per second
Degrees (angle)	60	Minutes
Degrees (angle)	0.01745	Radians
Degrees (angle)	3600	Seconds
Dynes	1.020×10^{-3}	Grams
Dynes	7.233×10^{-5}	Poundals
Dynes	2.248×10^{-6}	Pounds
Ergs	9.486×10^{-11}	Kilograms
Ergs	1	Dyne-centimeters
Ergs	7.376×10^{-8}	Foot-pounds
Ergs	1.020×10^{-3}	Gram-centimeters
Ergs	10^{-7}	Joules
Ergs	2.390×10^{-11}	Kilogram-calories
Ergs	1.020×10^{-8}	Kilogram-meters
Feet	12	Inches
Feet	0.3048	Meters
Feet	0.36	Varas
Feet	⅓	Yards
Feet of water	0.02950	Atmospheres
Feet of water	0.8826	Inches of mercury
Feet of water	304.8	Kilograms per square meter
Feet of water	62.43	Pounds per square foot
Feet of water	0.4335	Pounds per square inch
Foot-pounds	1.286×10^{-3}	British thermal units
Foot-pounds	1.356×10^{7}	Ergs
Foot-pounds	5.050×10^{-7}	Horsepower hours
Foot-pounds	1.356	Joules
Foot-pounds	3.241×10^{-4}	Kilogram-calories
Foot-pounds	0.1383	Kilogram-meters
Foot-pounds	3.766×10^{-7}	Kilowatt-hours
Foot-pounds per minute	1.286×10^{-3}	Btu per minute
Foot-pounds per minute	0.01667	Foot-pounds per second
Foot-pounds per minute	3.030×10^{-5}	Horsepower
Foot-pounds per minute	3.241×10^{-4}	Kilogram-calories per minute
Foot-pounds per minute	2.260×10^{-5}	Kilowatts
Foot-pounds per minute	7.717×10^{-2}	Btu per minute
Foot-pounds per minute	1.818×10^{-3}	Horsepower
Foot-pounds per minute	1.945×10^{-2}	Kilogram-calories per minute
Foot-pounds per minute	1.356×10^{-3}	Kilowatts
Gallons	8.345	Pounds of water
Gallons	3785	Cubic centimeters
Gallons	0.1337	Cubic feet
Gallons	231	Cubic inches
Gallons	3.785×10^{-3}	Cubic meters

Multiply	by	to obtain
Gallons	4.951×10^{-3}	Cubic yards
Gallons	3.785	Liters
Gallons	8	Pints (liquid)
Gallons	4	Quarts (liquid)
Gallons per minute	2.228×10^{-3}	Cubic feet per second
Gallons per minute	0.06308	Liters per second
Grains (troy)	1	Grains (av)
Grains (troy)	0.06480	Grams
Grains (troy)	0.04167	Pennyweights (troy)
Grams	980.7	Dynes
Grams	15.43	Grains (troy)
Grams	10^{-3}	Kilograms
Grams	10^3	Milligrams
Grams	0.03527	Ounces
Grams	0.03215	Ounces (troy)
Grams	0.07093	Poundals
Grams	2.205×10^{-3}	Pounds
Hectares	10^4	Square meters
Horsepower	42.44	Btu per minute
Horsepower	33,000	Foot-pounds per minute
Horsepower	550	Foot-pounds per second
Horsepower	1.014	Horsepower (metric)
Horsepower	10.70	Kilogram-calories per minute
Horsepower	0.7457	Kilowatts
Horsepower	7.457	Watts
Horsepower (boiler)	33,520	Btu per hour
Horsepower (boiler)	9,804	Kilowatts
Horsepower-hours	2547	British thermal units
Horsepower-hours	1.98×10^6	Foot-pounds
Horsepower-hours	2.684×10^6	Joules
Horsepower-hours	641.7	Kilogram-calories
Horsepower-hours	2.737×10^5	Kilogram-meters
Horsepower-hours	0.7457	Kilowatt-hours
Inches	2.540	Centimeters
Inches	10^3	Mils
Inches	0.03	Varas
Inches of mercury	0.03342	Atmospheres
Inches of mercury	1.133	Feet of water
Inches of mercury	345.3	Kilograms per square meter
Inches of mercury	70.73	Pounds per square foot
Inches of mercury	0.4912	Pounds per square inch
Inches of water	0.07355	Inches of mercury
Inches of water	25.40	Kilograms per square meter
Inches of water	0.5781	Ounces per square inch
Inches of water	5.204	Pounds per square foot
Inches of water	0.03613	Pounds per square inch
Kilograms	980,665	Dynes
Kilograms	10^3	Grams
Kilograms		Poundals

Multiply	by	to obtain
Kilograms	2.2046	Pounds
Kilograms	1.102×10^{-3}	Tons (short)
Kilogram-calories	3.968	British thermal units
Kilogram-calories	3086	Foot-pounds
Kilogram-calories	1.558×10^{-3}	Horsepower-hours
Kilogram-calories	4183	Joules
Kilogram-calories	426.6	Kilogram-meters
Kilogram-calories	1.62×10^{-3}	Kilowatt-hours
Kilogram-calories/minute	51.43	Foot-pounds per second
Kilogram-calories/minute	0.09351	Horsepower
Kilogram-calories/minute	0.06972	Kilowatts
Kilometers	10^5	Centimeters
Kilometers	3281	Feet
Kilometers	10^3	Meters
Kilometers	0.6214	Miles
Kilometers	1093.6	Yards
Kilowatts	56.92	Btu per minute
Kilowatts	4.425×10^4	Foot-pounds per minute
Kilowatts	737.6	Foot-pounds per second
Kilowatts	1.341	Horsepower
Kilowatts	14.34	Kilogram-calories per minute
Kilowatts	10^3	Watts
Kilowatt-hours	3415	British thermal units
Kilowatt-hours	2.655×10^6	Joules
Kilowatt-hours	1.341	Horsepower-hours
Kilowatt-hours	3.6×10^6	Joules
Kilowatt-hours	860.5	Kilogram-calories
Kilowatt-hours	3.671×10^5	Kilogram-meters
Log 10 N	2.303	Log EN or in N
Log EN or in N	0.4343	Log 10 N
Meters	100	Centimeters
Meters	3.2808	Feet
Meters	39.37	Inches
Meters	10^{-3}	Kilometers
Meters	10^3	Millimeters
Meters	1.0936	Yards
Miles	1.609×10^5	Centimeters
Miles	5280	Feet
Miles	1.6093	Kilometers
Miles	1760	Yards
Miles	1900.8	Varas
Miles per hour	44.70	Centimeters per second
Miles per hour	88	Feet per minute
Miles per hour	1.467	Feet per second
Miles per hour	1.6093	Kilometers per hour
Miles per hour	0.8684	Knots per hour
Months	30.42	Days
Months	730	Hours
Months	43,800	Minutes

Multiply	by	to obtain
Months	2.628×10^6	Seconds
Ounces	8	Drams
Ounces	437.5	Grains
Ounces	28.35	Grams
Ounces	0.0625	Pounds
Ounces per square inch	0.0625	Pounds per square inch
Pints (dry)	33.60	Cubic inches
Pints (liquid)	28.87	Cubic inches
Pounds	444,823	Dynes
Pounds	7000	Grains
Pounds	453.6	Grams
Pounds	0.454	Kilograms
Pounds	16	Ounces
Pounds	32.17	Poundals
Pounds of water	0.01602	Cubic feet of water
Pounds of water	27.68	Cubic inches of water
Pounds of water	0.1198	Gallons of water
Pounds of water/minute	2.669×10^{-4}	Cubic feet of water per second
Pounds per cubic foot	0.01602	Grams per cubic centimeter
Pounds per cubic foot	16.02	Kilograms per cubic meter
Pounds per cubic foot	5.786×10^{-4}	Pounds per cubic inch
Pounds per cubic foot	5.456×10^{-9}	Pounds per mil foot
Pounds per cubic yard	0.593	Kilograms per cubic meter
Pounds per square foot	0.01602	Feet of water
Pounds per square foot	4.887	Kilograms per square meter
Pounds per square foot	6.944×10^{-3}	Pounds per square inch
Pounds per square inch	0.06804	Atmospheres
Pounds per square inch	2.307	Feet of water
Pounds per square inch	2.036	Inches of mercury
Pounds per square inch	703.1	Kilograms per square meter
Pounds per square inch	144	Pounds per square foot
Pounds per square inch	0.0703	Kilograms per square centimeter
Quarts	32	Fluid ounces
Quarts (dry)	67.20	Cubic inches
Quarts (liquid)	57.75	Cubic inches
Quintals	100	Kilograms
Rods	16.5	Feet
Square centimeters	1.973×10^5	Circular mils
Square centimeters	1.076×10^{-3}	Square feet
Square centimeters	0.1550	Square inches
Square centimeters	10^{-6}	Square meters
Square centimeters	100	Square millimeters
Square feet	2.296×10^{-5}	Acres
Square feet	929.0	Square centimeters
Square feet	144	Square inches
Square feet	0.09290	Square meters
Square feet	3.587×10^{-8}	Square miles
Square feet	0.1296	Square varas
Square feet	1/9	Square yards

Multiply	by	to obtain
Square inches	1.273×10^6	Circular mils
Square inches	6.452	Square centimeters
Square inches	6.944×10^{-3}	Square feet
Square inches	10^6	Square mils
Square inches	645.2	Square millimeters
Square kilometers	10^6	Square meters
Square meters	10^5	Square centimeters
Square miles	640	Acres
Square miles	27.88×10^6	Square feet
Square miles	2.590	Square kilometers
Square miles	3,613,040.45	Square varas
Square miles	3.098×10^6	Square yards
Square yards	2.066×10^{-4}	Acres
Square yards	9	Square feet
Square yards	0.8361	Square meters
Square yards	3.228×10^{-7}	Square miles
Square yards	1.1664	Square varas
Tons, long	2240	Pounds
Tons, long	1.016	Tons, metric
Tons, metric	10^3	Kilograms
Tons, short	2000	Pounds
Tons, short	0.907	Tons, metric
Yards	0.9144	Meters

Prior to charging a system with refrigerant, good practice calls for evacuation to deep vacuum levels to remove noncondensable gases and also to evaporate and remove any trapped moisture from within the system. The chart below shows the equivalence of low pressure readings in microns with other familiar pressure/vacuum units. It also lists the temperature at which water will vaporize at each pressure.

Pressure/Vacuum Equivalents

Absolute pressure above zero base		Vacuum below one atmosphere		Approximate fraction of one atmosphere	Vaporization temperature of H_2O in °F @ each pressure
Microns	psia	mm Hg	Inches of mercury		
0	00.0	760.00	29.921	——	——
50	0.001	759.95	29.92	1/15000	−50
100	0.002	759.90	29.92	1/7600	−40
150	0.003	759.85	29.92	1/5100	−33
200	0.004	759.80	29.91	1/3800	−28
300	0.006	759.70	29.91	1/2500	−21
500	0.010	759.50	29.90	1/1500	−12
1000	0.019	759.00	29.88	1/760	1
2000	0.039	758.00	29.84	1/380	15
4000	0.077	756.00	29.76	1/190	29
6000	0.116	754.00	29.69	1/127	39
10000	0.193	750.00	29.53	1/76	52
15000	0.290	745.00	29.33	1/50	63
20000	0.387	740.00	29.13	1/38	72
30000	0.580	730.00	28.74	1/25	84
50000	0.967	710.00	27.95	1/15	101
100000	1.930	660.00	25.98	2/15	125
200000	3.870	560.00	22.05	1/4	152
500000	9.670	260.00	10.24	2/3	192
760000	14.696	0.00	0.00	1 atmosphere	212

Low Voltage Wiring Diagram Codes*

Color/terminal		Function (mode of operation)
R (red)	V	Hot switched leg of 24-volt AC power used on heating-only thermostats and heat/cool thermostats with a common power supply.
W (white)	H	Heating—single stage.
Y (yellow)	C	Cooling—single stage.
G (green)	F	Fan circuit.
B	Z	Heating circuit—constantly energized through a manual switch.
O	D	Cooling circuit—constantly energized through a manual switch.
R_h	M	Isolated power terminal for a heating circuit used on heat/cool thermostats with isolated circuits—jumper supplied.
R_c	V	Isolated power terminal for a cooling circuit used on heat/cool thermostats with isolated circuits—jumper supplied.
W_1	H1	Heating—first stage of two-stage units.
W_2	H2	Heating—second stage of two-stage units.
Y_1	C1	Cooling—first stage of two-stage units.
Y_2	C2	Cooling—second stage of two-stage units.
X	L	Warning light (dirty filter, electric heat, service light, etc.)
4	R	Same as R.

*As with any wiring situation, always consult appropriate wiring diagrams first.

Linear Measure

1 centimeter	= 0.3937 inch		1 square inch	= 6.452 square centimeters
1 decimeter	= 3.937 inches		1 square foot	= 144 square inches
1 dekameter	= 1.9884 rods			= 9.2903 square decimeters
1 inch (in.)	= 2.54 centimeters			= 0.0929 square meter
	= 25.4 millimeters		1 square meter	= 1.196 square yards
1 foot (ft)	= 12 inches			= 1550 square inch
	= 3.048 decimeters			= 10.76 square feet
	= 30.48 centimeters		1 square yard	= 9 square feet
1 yard (yd)	= 3 feet			= 0.8361 square meter
	= 0.9144 meter		1 square mile	= 640 acres
1 mile	= 5,280 feet			= 2.59 square kilometers
	= 1760 yards		1 acre	= 43,560 square feet
	= 1.6093 kilometers			= 4840 square yards
1 meter	= 100 centimeters			= 160 square rods
	= 1000 millimeters			= 0.4047 hectare
	= 1.094 yards		1 square kilometer	= 0.386 square mile
	= 3.28 feet		1 square rod	= 0.00625 acre
	= 39.37 inches		1 square meter	= 10,000 square centimeters
1 kilometer	= 1000 meters			= 11.196 square yards
	= 0.62137 mile			= 10.76 square feet
1 millimeter	= 1000 microns (or micrometers)		1 square centimeter	= 100 square millimeters
1 rod	= 0.5029 dekameter			= 0.155 square inches
1 square centimeter	= 0.155 square inch		1 nautical mile	= 6080 feet
	= 0.001076 square foot		1 hectare	= 2.47 acres
1 square decimeter	= 0.1076 square foot			= 1.853 kilometers

Volume

1 cubic centimeter	=	0.061 cubic inch
1 cubic decimeter	=	0.0353 cubic foot
1 cubic inch	=	16.39 cubic centimeters
1 cubic foot	=	28.347 cubic decimeters
	=	1728 cubic inches
	=	28.32 liters
1 cubic yard	=	27 cubic feet
	=	0.7646 cubic meter
1 cubic meter	=	1000 liters
	=	1.308 cubic yards
	=	35.31 cubic feet
1 imperial gallon	=	277.4 cubic inches
	=	4.55 liters
1 U.S. gallon	=	0.833 imperial gallon
	=	3.785 liters
	=	.3785 dekaliter
	=	231 cubic inches
1 U.S. barrel (petroleum)	=	42 U.S. gallons
	=	35 imperial gallons
1 liter	=	1000 cubic centimeters
	=	0.22 imperial gallon
	=	0.2642 U.S. gallon
	=	61 cubic inches
	=	0.908 quart (dry)
	=	1.0567 quarts (liquid)
1 quart (dry)	=	1.101 liters
1 quart (liquid)	=	0.9463 liter
1 dekaliter	=	2.6417 gallons

Weight

1 English ton	=	0.9027 metric ton
1 pound (lb)	=	16 ounces (oz)
	=	7000 grains (gr)
	=	454 grams (g)
	=	0.454 kilogram (kg)
1 grain	=	64.8 milligrams (mg)
	=	0.0648 gram
	=	0.0023 ounce
1 gram	=	1000 milligrams
	=	0.03527 ounce
	=	15.43 grains
1 kilogram	=	1000 grams
	=	2.2046 pounds
1 metric ton	=	1.1023 English tons
1 ounce	=	28.35 grams
1 pound	=	0.4536 kilogram
1 U.S. short ton	=	2000 pounds
	=	907 kilograms
1 U.S. long ton	=	2240 pounds
	=	1016 kilograms
1 metric ton	=	1000 kilograms
	=	0.984 U.S. long ton
	=	1.102 U.S short tons
	=	2205 pounds

Temperature Conversions

$$°F = (1.8 \times °C) + 32$$
$$°F_{absolute} = °F + 460$$
$$°C = 1.8 (°F - 32)$$
$$°C_{absolute} = °C + 273$$

Pressure

1 atmosphere	=	14.696 pounds per square inch (lb/in.^{2}; psi)
1 inch of H^{2}O (gauge) at 62°F	=	0.0361 psi
	=	5.20 pounds per square foot (lb/ft^2)
1 foot head of water at 62°F	=	0.433 psi
1 inch of mercury	=	0.491 psi

Density of Water (at 62°F)

1 cubic foot	=	62.5 pounds
1 pound	=	0.01604 cubic foot
1 gallon	=	8.33 pounds

Power and Heat

1 British thermal unit (Btu)	=	778 foot-pounds (ft•lb)
	=	0.252 calorie (cal)
1 calorie	=	3088 foot-pounds
	=	3.968 Btu
1 kilowatt (kW)	=	1000 watts (W)
	=	738 foot-pounds per second (ft•lb/s)
	=	1.341 horsepower (hp)
1 horsepower	=	33,000 foot-pounds per minute (ft•lb/min)
	=	0.746 kilowatts
1 kilowatt-hour (kWh)	=	3413 Btu
	=	860 calories
1 horsepower-hour (hp•h)	=	2544 Btu
1 boiler horsepower (bhp)	=	10 square feet of boiler heating surface (water-tube boiler)
	=	12 square feet of boiler heating surface (fire-tube boiler)
	=	34.5 pounds per hour of evaporation from and at 212°F.

Fractional Equivalents

Fraction		Decimal		Millimeters
1/64	=	0.015625	=	0.397
1/32	=	0.03125	=	0.794
3/64	=	0.046875	=	1.191
1/16	=	0.0625	=	1.588
5/64	=	0.078125	=	1.984
3/32	=	0.09375	=	2.381
7/64	=	0.109375	=	2.778
1/8	=	0.1250	=	3.175
9/64	=	0.140625	=	3.572
5/32	=	0.15625	=	3.969
11/64	=	0.171875	=	4.366
3/16	=	0.1875	=	4.763
13/64	=	0.203125	=	5.159
7/32	=	0.21875	=	5.556
15/64	=	0.234375	=	5.953
1/4	=	0.2500	=	6.350
17/64	=	0.265625	=	6.747
9/32	=	0.28125	=	7.144
19/64	=	0.296875	=	7.541
5/16	=	0.3125	=	7.938
21/64	=	0.328125	=	8.334
11/32	=	0.34375	=	8.731
23/64	=	0.359375	=	9.128
3/8	=	0.3750	=	9.525
25/64	=	0.390625	=	9.922
13/32	=	0.40625	=	10.319
27/64	=	0.421875	=	10.716
7/16	=	0.4375	=	11.113
29/64	=	0.453125	=	11.509
15/32	=	0.46875	=	11.906
31/64	=	0.484375	=	12.303
1/2	=	0.5000	=	12.700
33/64	=	0.515625	=	13.097
17/32	=	0.53125	=	13.494
35/64	=	0.546875	=	13.891
9/16	=	0.5625	=	14.288
37/64	=	0.578125	=	14.684
19/32	=	0.59375	=	15.081
39/64	=	0.609375	=	15.478
5/8	=	0.6250	=	15.875
41/64	=	0.640625	=	16.272
21/32	=	0.65625	=	16.669
43/64	=	0.671875	=	17.066
11/16	=	0.6875	=	17.463
45/64	=	0.703125	=	17.859
23/32	=	0.71875	=	18.256
47/64	=	0.734375	=	18.653

Fraction		Decimal		Millimeters
3/4	=	0.7500	=	19.050
49/64	=	0.765625	=	19.447
25/32	=	0.78125	=	19.844
51/64	=	0.796875	=	20.241
13/16	=	0.8125	=	20.638
53/64	=	0.828125	=	21.034
27/32	=	0.84375	=	21.431
55/64	=	0.859375	=	21.828
7/8	=	0.8750	=	22.225
57/64	=	0.890625	=	22.622
29/32	=	0.90625	=	23.019
59/64	=	0.921875	=	23.416
15/16	=	0.9375	=	23.813
61/64	=	0.953125	=	24.209
31/32	=	0.96875	=	24.606
63/64	=	0.984375	=	25.003
64/64	=	1.0000	=	25.400

mm	inches	mm	inches	mm	inches	mm	inches
0.1 = 0.0039		0.2 = 0.0079		0.3 = 0.0118		0.4 = 0.0157	
0.5 = 0.0197		0.6 = 0.0236		0.7 = 0.0276		0.8 = 0.0315	
0.9 = 0.0354		1 = 0.0394		2 = 0.0787		3 = 0.1181	
4 = 0.1575		5 = 0.1969		6 = 0.2362		7 = 0.2756	
8 = 0.3150		9 = 0.3543		10 = 0.3937		11 = 0.4331	
12 = 0.4724		13 = 0.5118		14 = 0.5512		15 = 0.5906	
16 = 0.6299		17 = 0.6693		18 = 0.7087		19 = 0.7480	
20 = 0.7874		21 = 0.8268		22 = 0.8661		23 = 0.9055	
24 = 0.9449		25 = 0.9843		26 = 1.0236		27 = 1.0630	
28 = 1.1024		29 = 1.1417		30 = 1.1811		31 = 1.2205	
32 = 1.2598		33 = 1.2992		34 = 1.3386		35 = 1.3780	
36 = 1.4173		37 = 1.4567		38 = 1.4961		39 = 1.5354	
40 = 1.5748		41 = 1.6142		42 = 1.6535		43 = 1.6929	
44 = 1.7323		45 = 1.7717		46 = 1.8110		47 = 1.8504	
48 = 1.8898		49 = 1.9291		50 = 1.9685		51 = 2.0079	
52 = 2.0472		53 = 2.0866		54 = 2.1260		55 = 2.1654	
56 = 2.2047		57 = 2.2441		58 = 2.2835		59 = 2.3228	
60 = 2.3622		61 = 2.4016		62 = 2.4409		63 = 2.4803	
64 = 2.5197		65 = 2.5591		66 = 2.5984		67 = 2.6378	
68 = 2.6772		69 = 2.7165		70 = 2.7559		71 = 2.7559	
72 = 2.8346		73 = 2.8740		74 = 2.9134		75 = 2.9528	
76 = 2.9921		77 = 3.0315		78 = 3.0709		79 = 3.1102	
80 = 3.1496		81 = 3.1890		82 = 3.2283		83 = 3.2677	
84 = 3.3071		85 = 3.3465		86 = 3.3858		87 = 3.4252	
88 = 3.4646		89 = 3.5039		90 = 3.5433		91 = 3.5827	
92 = 3.6220		93 = 3.6614		94 = 3.7008		95 = 3.7402	
96 = 3.7795		97 = 3.8189		98 = 3.8583		99 = 3.8976	
100 = 3.9370							

Volume

Volume of a rectangular solid: Volume = A × B × C
where   A = height
          B = width
          C = depth

Circumference of a circle: C = 3.1416 × diameter

Surface of a cylinder: $S = 3.1416D \times H + \dfrac{2 \times 3.1416D^2}{4}$

Volume of a cylinder: $V = \dfrac{3.1416D^2}{4} \times H$

where   D = diameter
          H = height

Area of a ring: $\text{Area} = \dfrac{3.1416D^2}{4} - \dfrac{3.1416d^2}{4}$ or $\dfrac{3.1416\,(D^2 - d^2)}{4}$

where   D = diameter of outer ring
          d = diameter of inner ring

Area

Area of a rectangle: Area = A × B
where   A = height
          B = width

Area of a triangle: Base × ½ perpendicular height

Area of a trapezoid: ½ sum of parallel sides × perpendicular height

Area of a regular polygon: ½ sum of sides × inside radius

Area of a parallelogram: Base × perpendicular height

Area of a circle: $A = \dfrac{3.1416 \times D^2}{4}$

or 3.1416 r^2
or 0.78540 × D^2
or 0.07958 × C^2
where   C = circumference
          D = diameter
          r = radius

Pipe Thread Data—Fitting Allowance

Size of pipe	Thread make-up	# of threads per inch
1/8″	1/4″	27
1/4″	3/8″	18
3/8″	3/8″	18
1/2″	1/2″	14
3/4″	9/16″	14
1″	5/8″	11½
1¼″	11/16″	11½
1½″	11/16″	11½
2″	3/4″	11½
2½″	15/16″	8
3″	1″	8
3½″	11/16″	8
4″	1⅛″	8
5″	1¼″	8
6″	15/16″	8
8″	17/16″	8
10″	1⅝″	8
12″	1¾″	8